# THE MAHDI WEARS ARMANI

An Analysis of the
Harun Yahya Enterprise

Södertörns högskola 2013

Södertörns högskola
SE-141 89 Huddinge

www.sh.se/publications

© Anne Ross Solberg

Cover Image: Scanpix
Cover Design: Jonathan Robson
Layout: Jonathan Robson & Per Lindblom

Printed by Elanders Sweden, Stockholm 2013

Södertörn Doctoral Dissertations 80
ISSN 1652-7399
ISBN 978-91-86069-68-1 (print)
ISBN 978-91-86069-69-8 (digital)

Department of Literature, History of Ideas, and Religion
University of Gothenburg 32
ISSN 1102-9773
ISBN 978-91-628-8723-0

CONTENTS

ACKNOWLEDGEMENTS..................................................................................i
CHAPTER 1: Introduction..................................................................................1
   1. Introduction ..................................................................................................1
   2. Statement of purpose....................................................................................2
   3. The curious case of Harun Yahya................................................................3
      3.1. 1979–1989: The emergence of the *Adnancılar* group ........................3
      3.2. 1990–1999: Creationism and legal troubles...........................................5
      3.3. 1999–2007: The Harun Yahya enterprise: Going global .......................7
      3.4. 2007–2012: Adnan Oktar steps into the limelight.................................8
      3.5. From reclusive *cemaat* leader to flamboyant talk show host ...............8
   4. Defining the Harun Yahya enterprise..........................................................11
   5. The water for the mill: the finances of the enterprise..................................13
   6. Method and material ...................................................................................17
      6.1. Method...................................................................................................17
      6.2. Primary material: The works of the Harun Yahya enterprise..............18
      6.3. Previous research...................................................................................22
   7. Analytical framework..................................................................................23
      7.1. Fragmentation of authority and new media..........................................23
      7.2. Harun Yahya as a *da'wa* enterprise......................................................25
      7.3. Islam as a discursive tradition ...............................................................28
      7.4. The discourse of the Harun Yahya enterprise as rhetoric.....................30
      7.5. Social movement theory and framing ...................................................31
   8. Outline of chapters .....................................................................................35
   9. Notes on transliteration and translation .....................................................36

CHAPTER 2: The Turkish Context....................................................................37
   1. Introduction ................................................................................................37
   2. General background: Modern Turkey.........................................................38
      2.1. Late Ottoman Empire and the birth of the Turkish republic ..............38
      2.2. The modern Turkish republic ...............................................................39
      2.3. 1970s and 1980s: The rise of political Islam .........................................40
      2.4. Approaches to Turkish modernity and Islam .......................................42
   3. The discursive field: Islamic thought in Turkey..........................................43
      3.1 Said Nursi and the Nur movement........................................................44
         3.1.1. Islamic modernism in Turkey.....................................................44
         3.1.2. The life of Said Nursi ..................................................................45

    3.1.3. The Risale-i Nur ................................................................................................46
        3.1.4. The "Third Said" and the expansion of the Nur movement...............................48
   3.2. Islamic thought in Turkey between the state and civil society ...................................50
        3.2.1. Nationalism, ethnicity and minorities in Turkey..................................................51
        3.2.2. The alliance between Islam and rightist nationalism ..........................................53
        3.2.3. Neo-Sufism and political Islam.............................................................................55
        3.2.4. The ideology of the Milli Görüş............................................................................55
        3.2.5. The Turkish-Islamic synthesis and the Turkification of Islam ........................56
  4. Opportunity spaces: The Islamic revival post-1980s.............................................................58
   4.1 Theoretical perspectives on the Islamic revival ............................................................59
   4.2 The scene in the 1980s ........................................................................................................60
   4.3. Identity politics and the construction of difference .....................................................61
   4.4. The failure of political Islam and the rise of the JDP ..................................................63
   4.5. The Gülen movement .........................................................................................................65
        4.5.1. Fethullah Gülen's vision.........................................................................................66
        4.5.2. From political Islam to faith activism: Gülen vs. Milli Görüş ...........................68
  5. Concluding remarks....................................................................................................................70

CHAPTER 3: Nationalism and Conspiracism...............................................................................75
  1. Introduction ................................................................................................................................75
  2. Conspiracism...............................................................................................................................75
  3. Harun Yahya's Jewish-Masonic conspiracy theories ...........................................................77
   3.1. Judaism and Freemasonry..................................................................................................77
   3.2. The *Holocaust Deception* controversy ...........................................................................79
   3.3. Anti-Semitism and Harun Yahya .....................................................................................81
   3.4. The Islamist movement of the 1990s and the Harun Yahya enterprise....................82
  4. Yahya's shift towards ecumenism ............................................................................................84
   4.1. The evolution of Yahya's conspiracism...........................................................................84
   4.2. The turn to ecumenism ......................................................................................................86
   4.3. Yahya's ecumenical discourse and the Gülen movement ............................................87
   4.4. Yahya's conspiracism and nationalist discourses in the 1990s...................................89
   4.5. Conspiracism and ecumenism in the English works ...................................................92
  6. Atatürkism, nationalism and neo-Ottomanism.....................................................................93
  7. Appropriating Atatürk...............................................................................................................93
   7.1. The cult of Atatürk and politics of identity ....................................................................93
   7.2. Harun Yahya's turn towards Atatürkism........................................................................94
   7.3. Harun Yahya's Atatürk.......................................................................................................96
  8. The nationalist discourse of Harun Yahya..............................................................................98
  9. Turkish-Muslim moral superiority and Neo-Ottomanism..................................................99
  11. Concluding remarks................................................................................................................ 102

CHAPTER 4: The Islamic creationism of Harun Yahya............................................................. 107
  1. Introduction .............................................................................................................................. 107
  2. The evolution of creationism in local and global contexts ................................................ 108

- 2.1. What is creationism? Taxonomy and definitions ............................................. 108
- 2.2. The source of the trouble: Darwin's theory of evolution ................................ 109
- 2.3. The emergence and evolution of creationism in the US ................................. 110
  - 2.3.1. The response to Darwin: From accommodation to confrontation .............. 110
  - 2.3.2. Creationism and fundamentalism ............................................................. 110
  - 2.3.3. Scientific creationism .............................................................................. 111
  - 2.3.4. Intelligent Design .................................................................................... 113
  - 2.3.5. Creationism goes global .......................................................................... 114
- 2.4. Islam and science ........................................................................................ 114
  - 2.4.1. Searching for harmony between Islam and science ................................. 115
  - 2.4.2. Said Nursi ............................................................................................... 115
  - 2.4.3. Science in the Qur'an ............................................................................. 117
- 2.5. The emergence of Islamic creationism in Turkey ......................................... 118
  - 2.5.1. Early Muslim responses to Darwin's theory of evolution ......................... 118
  - 2.5.2. Antievolutionism in Turkey ..................................................................... 118
- 3. The Islamic Creationism of Harun Yahya ........................................................... 120
  - 3.1. *The Evolution Deceit*: Yahya's attack on Darwinian evolution ..................... 120
  - 3.2. A brief synopsis of *The Evolution Deceit* ..................................................... 121
  - 3.3. The targets of critique .................................................................................. 122
  - 3.4. Methods of critique ...................................................................................... 124
    - 3.4.1. The moral case against evolution ........................................................... 124
    - 3.4.2. The scientific case against evolution ...................................................... 125
      - 3.4.2.1. Rejection of evolution itself: Paleontological arguments ................... 127
      - 3.4.2.2. Rejection of the neo-Darwinian synthesis ......................................... 128
      - 3.4.2.3. Arguments regarding the origin of life .............................................. 129
      - 3.4.2.4. The argument from design ............................................................... 129
      - 3.4.2.5. The secret behind matter: Yahya's anti-materialism and idealism ..... 131
    - 3.4.3. The religious case against evolution ....................................................... 133
    - 3.4.4. Conspiratorial and cosmological framework .......................................... 135
    - 3.4.5. The narrative and visual rhetoric of scientificity .................................... 137
    - 3.4.6. The creationist campaign of Harun Yahya ............................................. 138
- 4. Why antievolutionism? ....................................................................................... 140
- 5. Concluding remarks .......................................................................................... 141

CHAPTER 5: The Mahdi, the End Times and the Turkish-Islamic union ................... 145
1. Introduction ......................................................................................................... 145
2. Eschatology, apocalypticism, millennialism and messianism ............................... 146
  - 2.1. Islamic eschatology ...................................................................................... 147
  - 2.2. Contemporary Islamic apocalypticism ......................................................... 149
  - 2.3. Said Nursi's ideas about a coming Golden Age for the Mahdi ..................... 150
3. Harun Yahya's apocalyptic works ........................................................................ 152
4. The Mahdi and the Golden Age ........................................................................... 153
  - 4.1. The Mahdi .................................................................................................... 154

- 4.2. The End Times in the Qur'an .................................................................. 158
- 4.3. The Mahdi in *Risale-i Nur* ..................................................................... 159
- 4.4. Jesus, Dabbat al-Ardh and ad-Dukhan ................................................. 161
- 5. Themes in Harun Yahya's apocalypticism and their development ............ 163
  - 5.1. Targeting a global audience: Jesus Will Return ................................... 163
  - 5.2. Temporalizing the apocalypse ............................................................. 163
  - 5.3. The Golden Age and the redemption of a Turkish-Islamic union ........ 164
  - 5.4. Forces of evil: Materialism, Darwinism and atheist Freemasonry ...... 168
  - 5.5. Yahya's apocalypticism and contemporary Arab apocalyptic literature ............... 168
  - 5.6. Harun Yahya and the use of Nursi's teachings as a template ............. 170
- 6. The rhetoric of apocalypticism .................................................................. 171
  - 6.1. Apocalypticism as a framework for the *da'wa* of Harun Yahya ......... 171
  - 6.2. Yahya's apocalypticism and the question of interpretive authority ...... 174
    - 6.2.1. Sources and strategies: Yahya's apocalypticism as a form of exegesis ......... 174
    - 6.2.2. Charismatic authority: The Harun Yahya as the center of a cosmic drama ....... 176
  - 6.3. Framing the hardships and successes of Adnan Oktar ....................... 179
- 7. Concluding remarks ................................................................................. 182

## CHAPTER 6: Concluding Analysis .................................................................. 185
- 1. Summarizing discussion ............................................................................ 185
  - 1.1. The Turkish context, Islamic revival and opportunity spaces .............. 186
  - 1.2. Nationalism and conspiracism .............................................................. 187
  - 1.3. Creationism ........................................................................................... 188
  - 1.4. Ecumenism ............................................................................................ 190
  - 1.5. Apocalypticism, Mahdism and a Turkish-Islamic union ..................... 191
- 2. General discussion ..................................................................................... 194
  - 2.1. Rhetoric and framing ............................................................................ 194
  - 2.2. Argumentative strategies and authority ............................................... 194
  - 2.3. Contemporary Islamic discourses, *da'wa* and "market Islam" ......... 195
  - 2.4. Adnan Oktar's televangelism revisited ................................................. 196
  - 2.5. The global impact of the Harun Yahya enterprise today .................... 199

## IMAGE APPENDIX ........................................................................................... 201

## REFERENCES .................................................................................................. 213

ACKNOWLEDGEMENTS

The writing and completion of this dissertation would not have been possible without the help and support of a number of people. While the views expressed herein and any errors or omissions remain my sole responsibility, I wish to acknowledge mentors, colleagues, friends and institutions whose advice, support and contributions have proved invaluable along the way.

First of all, I am deeply indebted to my supervisors, Susanne Olsson and Göran Larsson for their unwavering support and guidance. Göran provided crucial direction during the early stages, and has continued to offer generous support and insightful comments throughout. I am immensely grateful to Susanne who has been my primary advisor during the major part of this dissertation. She has been solid as a rock during the final and most intense phase, and her constant encouragement as well as her frequent, thorough and perceptive feedback has been crucial to the finalization of this dissertation. I could not have wished for better supervisors and consider myself very fortunate for having had the opportunity to benefit from the expertise of both.

I also want to express my sincere gratitude to Catharina Raudvere for her careful reading of my 80 percent manuscript. Her insightful comments and suggestions have been a great help in the final stages of revision.

The research seminar for the Study of Religions at Södertörn University has been a great source of inspiration and support over the last four years. In this regard, I would especially like to thank Jenny Berglund, Staffan Nilsson, Jessica Moberg, Hans Geir Aasmundsen, Willy Pfändtner, Göran Ståhle, Gunilla Gunner, David Westerlund, Jörgen Straarup, Anna Tessman, Elisabete Suzana, Ingela Visuri and Feyzullah Yilmaz. I am especially grateful to Simon Sorgenfrei and David Thurfjell for taking the time to read and offer valuable input on specific chapters. David has been a great source of inspiration throughout this project, and has shared many valuable insights that have helped me rethink my ideas.

A very special thanks goes to my friend, colleague and office-mate Ann af Burén. It was a serendipitous meeting with her at the Swedish Research Institute in Istanbul that led me to Södertörn in the first place. I have benefited greatly from her encouragement, good advice and intellectually invigorating company, and found motivation in our many interesting discussions over the last four years.

My gratitude goes to the Committee for Educational Sciences at the Swedish Research Council who has financed the research project Negotiating Knowledge: European Muslims Between Competing Worldviews, which this study is a part of.

I am also grateful to Teacher Education at Södertörn University for funding the final year of my doctoral dissertation.

I am fortunate to have had the opportunity to present my research at the Center for Middle Eastern Studies (CMES) in Lund on two occasions. In this regard I would like to thank the head of the center, Leif Stenberg, and scholars of Islamology at the Center for Theology and History of Religion at Lund University, Anders Ackfeldt, Simon Stjernholm, Jonas Otterbeck and Philip Halldén, for offering valuable comments and advice. I am particularly thankful to the organizers of the Modern Turkey Seminar Series, Umut Özkırımlı and Andrea Karlsson, for their support and for sharing their insights and expertise on Turkey, and a special thanks to Andrea for her continued encouragement and friendship throughout this work process. I would also like to extend my gratitude to Martin Riexinger and Stefano Bigliardi who have generously let me read their as of yet unpublished manuscripts.

My thanks also go to the research seminar at Gothenburg University for critiquing an early outline of this dissertation, and to the participants of the Nordic workshop for PhD students in Islamology and Middle East Studies in Gothenburg, especially to Bjørn Olav Utvik who took the time to read and offer valuable feedback on a chapter draft. I would also like to express my appreciation to Jonathan Robson for his reliable assistance with typesetting, layout and cover design, and to Calle Aaro and Lisa Stålnacke for help with other practicalities.

I am grateful to The Swedish Research Institute in Istanbul for granting me a scholarship that enabled me to spend a month at the Institute during my research. Thanks also to Sedat Altan at the Science and Research Foundation in Istanbul for generously providing me with material. Additionally, I am grateful to a number of other individuals in Turkey who have provided their time and assistance but who wish to remain anonymous. I extend a special note of thanks to Adrian Marsh for his mentorship during one of my several stays in Turkey during the last four years.

On a personal note, I owe a great deal to family and numerous friends who have offered support and encouragement during this work process. In this regard I would like to mention in particular Cecilie Endresen (who lured me back into academia some years ago), Barbro Bredesen Opset and Kristin Aasmundsen. I am especially thankful for the continuous support and help from my parents Bjørg Ross Solberg and Ottar Solberg, and last, but not least, a big thank you to Gudveig Storhaug for providing constant reassurance and encouragement during the most intense phases of this dissertation.

Anne Ross Solberg
Stockholm, May 2013

CHAPTER 1
# Introduction

## 1. Introduction

During the summer of 2007, thousands of copies of a 6-kilo heavy and lavishly illustrated book titled the *Atlas of Creation* were sent unsolicited and free of charge to schoolteachers, university departments and state leaders all around the world from Istanbul, Turkey.[1] Published under the name of Harun Yahya, the basic premise of the book was to refute the theory of evolution through an examination of the fossil records. This mass distribution of the *Atlas of Creation* attracted international attention to Islamic creationism as a phenomenon on the rise, and to the Turkish author and religious leader Harun Yahya as its leading proponent globally. A report commissioned by the Council of Europe in 2007 warns against a rising current of Islamic creationism, and identifies the work of Harun Yahya as the main contribution to this current (Brasseur 2007, pp. 5–7). Based on this report, the Council of Europe Parliamentary Assembly passed a resolution urging its members to defend and promote scientific knowledge, firmly oppose the teaching of creationism and promote the teaching of evolution (PACE 2007). Harun Yahya's Islamic creationism has received ample attention from science educators and various media outlets internationally. Relatively little has been written about Harun Yahya from the perspective of the study of religions, however. This dissertation aims to make a contribution to this field.

Behind the brand name "Harun Yahya" a tremendously well-funded religious enterprise is in operation, devoted not merely to the debunking of Darwinism, but also to promoting Islam and calling people to faith. Harun Yahya is allegedly the pen name of Adnan Oktar, a Turkish author and religious leader.[2] Backed by his supporters, Oktar channels massive financial recourses into producing and distributing material and spreading his message in a variety of different ways. More than 300 books have been published under the name of Harun Yahya, covering a wide range of faith-related and political topics. In addition to publishing books and DVDs and organizing numerous conferences and

---

[1] See image appendix, p. 2.
[2] The connection between Adnan Oktar the individual and Harun Yahya as an alleged pen name will be further discussed below.

exhibitions, the "Harun Yahya enterprise"[3] also operates hundreds of Internet websites where video, audio and textual material based on the works of Harun Yahya is made freely available in a variety of different languages. As such, Adnan Oktar can be seen to represent a new generation of preachers who utilize the viral communication opportunities of the Internet and other contemporary means of advertising to promote their message. Oktar is an interior designer by education, and has no formal training in either Islamic studies or science. Nevertheless, many seem to perceive him as a significant Muslim figure, chiefly due to his propagation of Islamic creationism. "Harun Yahya" was for example included among the top 50 most influential Muslims in the world in the 2010 edition of the *500 Most Influential Muslims* (Lumbard & Nayed 2010).

In so far as Adnan Oktar and his associates are engaged in the propagation of Islam, their efforts may be described as *da'wa*: The act of inviting or calling people to Islam.[4] However, in recent years, Oktar and his associates have drawn attention not merely as an enterprise that publishes books and websites on Islamic topics, but also as an enterprise that promotes Adnan Oktar himself as a particularly significant and influential person. Since 2011, Oktar hosts a glitzy talk show on his own TV channel A9 TV, which has become an Internet phenomenon. Although Oktar's televangelism is not a primary focus in the following chapters, I will briefly present and describe Yahya's TV shows below and use them as a departure point from which to introduce the Harun Yahya enterprise as well as themes and issues that will be discussed in the course of this dissertation.

The objective of this introductory chapter is to introduce the topic of this thesis and its purpose, and to outline my approach, method, material and analytical framework.

## 2. Statement of purpose

The focus of this study is the complex phenomenon that is the Harun Yahya enterprise, and the aim is to shed light on it by describing, analyzing and contextualizing key themes in the discourse of the enterprise. Part of the purpose is thus empirical and descriptive, and draws on material produced by Harun Yahya. I identify and describe four key themes in his works, namely conspiracy theories, nationalism/neo-Ottomanism, creationism and apocalypticism/Mahdism. I will also examine how these themes have developed over time and analyze the relationship between them.

However, as argued by Russell McCutcheon, the task of scholars of religion is not merely "to study *how* it is that [the religious] believe and behave" but

---

[3] This phrase will be further discussed in section 4.
[4] I will further discuss the meaning of the term *da'wa* in section 7.2.

also, having gathered this descriptive information, "to theorize as to *why* it is that they believe and behave as they do" (McCutcheon 2003, p. 148). This study's point of departure is the notion that the Harun Yahya enterprise can be understood as a phenomenon that has emerged out of and developed in a particular historical and social context. Hence, part of purpose of this study is to contextualize and historicize the selected key themes in relation to both Turkish and global contexts.

The main research question of the study may therefore be stated as: *What* is Harun Yahya saying, *how* is he saying it and *why*? More specifically, the study seeks to address the following questions: What themes is Harun Yahya focusing on and why? What is the relationship between these themes and what purpose do they serve? Why did these themes come to acquire such a prominent role within the Harun Yahya's enterprise? How does Yahya argue and what strategies does he employ in order to legitimize his teachings as Islamic? How has Yahya's discourse changed over time and why?

The teachings and ideas of Harun Yahya as they appear in the many works published in the framework of the Harun Yahya enterprise are closely entangled with the history of Adnan Oktar and his associates. As we shall see, the experiences of Oktar and the community around him are incorporated into the *da'wa* discourse of Harun Yahya. In the following section, I will therefore introduce the Harun Yahya enterprise by outlining Oktar's life story and the history of the group's emergence and development. The Harun Yahya enterprise is now active globally, but it emerged in a local context, and I will here concentrate on early developments. In the empirical chapters, additional comments on the development will be presented when deemed necessary for the contextual analysis.

## 3. The curious case of Harun Yahya

### 3.1. 1979–1989: The emergence of the *Adnancılar* group

Adnan Oktar was born Adnan Arslanoğulları in 1956 into a secular middleclass family in Ankara, Turkey. In 1979, Oktar moved to Istanbul to study fine arts at the Academy of Fine Arts (now Mimar Sinan University). Making impassioned speeches on topics such as Darwinism, Freemasonry and the coming Mahdi to his fellow students, he gathered a small group of sympathizers, and this circle widened over the next few years. In 1985, journalist Ruşen Çakır wrote a story about this emerging new urban *cemaat* (religious community) in Istanbul in the news magazine *Nokta* under the title "Adnan Hoca'nın kolejli müritleri" (The college disciples of Adnan Hoca), drawing media attention to the group (Çakır

1985).⁵ In 1986, Oktar transferred to the Department of Philosophy and Literature at Istanbul University, and the group continued to recruit affluent university students, especially on the Boğaziçi University campus. The group began to be referred to in the media as *Adnan hocacılar* (adherents of Adnan Hoca) or *Adnancılar* (adherents of Adnan) ("Yargıtay: Adnan Hocacılar Örgüt" 2007), and became known for the *sosyetik* (high society) lifestyle enjoyed by Oktar and his wealthy, urban and private college-educated followers ("Islama Sosyetik Yorum" 1990).

In June 1986, Oktar gave an interview to Nazlı Ilıcak, a well-known conservative journalist, in the daily *Bulvar* ("Adnan Hoca Paranoyak" 1987). In the wake of this interview, Oktar was charged with "making propaganda with the aim of weakening or destroying national sentiments" by the Istanbul State Security Court. He was subsequently arrested and imprisoned for a total of 19 months, first in a regular prison and then later transferred to the criminal ward in Bakirköy Hospital, where he was diagnosed with paranoid schizophrenia (Güner 1986). This marked the beginning of a series of legal troubles and negative press for Adnan Oktar and his associates in Turkey.

Throughout the 1980s, the *Adnancılar* group was perceived as a relatively conservative group influenced by the Turkish Muslim scholar and activist Said Nursi (1878–1960), practicing and promoting "mainstream" Sunni Islam, albeit with an urban and modern image attracting young "born-again Muslims" from wealthy families.⁶ In the late 80s, however, Oktar met Edip Yüksel, a Kurdish-Turkish Islamist who had abandoned Islamism in 1986 and adopted the "Qur'an-alone" theology of Rashad Khalifa, the Egyptian-American sheikh who inspired the United Submitters International (Haddad & Smith 1993, pp. 137–168).⁷ The contact between Oktar and Yüksel is recounted in a chapter on the Adnan Oktar community in *Ayet ve Slogan*, a much-referenced survey of contemporary Islamic movements in Turkey (Çakır 1990). Çakır views both Yüksel and Oktar as representatives of a "modernist" method of preaching Islam. According to Çakır, Oktar got acquainted with Yüksel in the late 1980s and became convinced by his Qur'anist ideas. However, with time, Yüksel allegedly grew irritated over Oktar's unwillingness to express these views

---

⁵ *Hoca* is used here in the meaning of "religious teacher".
⁶ Said Nursi founded the Nur movement, one of the most influential Islamic movements in modern Turkey. I will deal with Said Nursi and the Nur movement in Chapter 2.
⁷ Belonging within a school of thought often referred to as Qur'anism, Rashad Khalifa rejected the hadiths and held that the Qur'an is the only canonical text in Islam. Khalifa produced works claiming that the miraculousness of the Qur'an is confirmed by science, emphasizing especially the importance of the number 19 (Haddad & Smith 1993). The website of United Submitters International is available at www.masjidtucson.org [Accessed 19.03.2013]. Edip Yüksel migrated to the US in 1989 and settled in Tuscon, Arizona, to work with Khalifa. Khalifa was assassinated in 1990, but Yüksel continues to promote his own version of Qur'an-only radical reformist theology. He runs his own website <www.19.org> [Accessed 19.03.2013].

publicly. In one meeting, Yüksel secretly recorded a conversation between Oktar and himself, where Oktar apparently expresses his agreement with Yüksel's ideas. These recordings were later leaked to the pro-Islamic press, who relished in the revelation that Oktar, like Yüksel himself, had deviated from Islam as they saw it.[8] This episode led to an embittered break between Yüksel and Oktar, who have been archenemies ever since.[9]

Despite the break with Yüksel, Oktar apparently continued to express and teach Qur'anist views and reformist theology within the group (Çakır 1990, p. 259). Unhappy with this theological shift, many conservative members left the group, some to join the Gülen movement, the followers of the Turkish preacher Fethullah Gülen (b. 1941) (Çakır 1990, p. 269).[10] Oktar's alleged turn towards Qur'anism and a skeptical stance towards the hadith literature did not transpire in the publications of Harun Yahya, however. As we shall see, Yahya refers to hadiths as legitimate sources of religious guidance, and hadiths also figure prominently in the works of Harun Yahya dealing with apocalyptic themes.

## 3.2. 1990–1999: Creationism and legal troubles

From 1990 onwards, Oktar began structuring the activities of the group into a more organized form. The group members were allocated tasks and functions according to their capacities and expertise. One group was for instance given the task of generating funds for the organization, while others were set to do research, collect material and write texts.[11] Founded in 1990, the group's activities became professionalized through *Bilim Araştırma Vakfı* (BAV) (The Science Research Foundation), of which Oktar was the honorary president. BAV became the main platform for the group's activities and the public face of the community around Oktar, organizing conferences, advertising campaigns and distributing many of the books published in the name of Harun Yahya for free.

---

[8] An alleged transcript of the conversation between Oktar and Yüksel was published in the Islamic journal *Girişim* in 1989 (Çakır 1990, p. 255).
[9] Yüksel's main website, 19.org, was blocked in Turkey in 2007 by court decision due to Oktar and his lawyers complaints that Yüksel's article titled "Harun Yahya: The Promised Mahdi?" was slanderous. As a consequence, all blogs hosted by the open source tool WordPress were blocked in Turkey. The founder of WordPress, Matt Mullenweg, published the letter he received from Oktar's lawyers (Mullenweg 2007). After being arrested by Turkish police in 2008, Yüksel contacted various media and human rights organizations asking them to publish a letter where Yüksel claims that the arrest was a consequence of the complaints of "cult leader" Oktar and his lawyers. The letter was among other places published on the official English website of the Muslim Brotherhood (Yüksel 2008).
[10] This split is also confirmed by "Mehmet", a former prominent member of the group who prefers to remain anonymous (personal interview, 04.02.2012). The Gülen movement is a broadly based social and religious movement inspired and headed by the Turkish preacher Fethullah Gülen. Often described as a neo-Nur movement, it is the most influential Islamic movement in Turkey today. I will describe this movement further in Chapter 2, section 4.5.
[11] Personal interview with "Mehmet", 04.02.2012.

Within the framework of BAV, the group launched a series of advertising campaigns in the early 1990s to profile itself as an Atatürkist organization. Oktar gave interviews where he criticized *gericiler ve yobazlar* (reactionaries and fanatics) and distanced himself from Islamism ("Adnan Hoca Artık Atatürkçü ve Vakıf Başkanı" 1990). Shedding the Islamic attire that he had worn in the 80s, Oktar began donning his trademark designer T-shirts and pastel suits. In 1995, the community around Oktar founded *Milli Değerler Koruma Vakfı* (MDKV) (The Foundation for Protection of National Values), with Oktar as honorary president, and continued to profile itself as a group working for Atatürkist and national values.[12]

Until the mid-90s, Oktar had published only a handful of books, some under the name Harun Yahya, some using other pseudonyms such as Cavit Yalçin. From 1996 onwards, a great number of books were published under the name of Harun Yahya. Already in 1986, Oktar had published booklets attacking Darwinism and materialism, but in the mid-90s, the campaign against the theory of evolution was stepped up. In the framework of BAV, the Harun Yahya enterprise also organized a number of international conferences on the topic of the theory of evolution, inviting prominent creationists from the US (see Chapter 4). BAV also organized conferences with a neo-Ottoman perspective on Turkey's foreign policy and regional issues (see Chapter 3). While the activities of Oktar and the BAV organization were flourishing in some respects, they were also on the radar of the authorities and were involved in several legal and criminal cases, which were followed closely by the Turkish media. In 1991, for example, Oktar was arrested for possession of cocaine, but later acquitted ("Nihayet" 1999). Members of BAV distributed flyers of nine professors defending the theory of evolution against Yahya's anti-evolution campaign, accusing them of being Maoists.[13] The professors won a civil court case against BAV for defamation in 1999, and were awarded 4000 USD each (Ortega 2005).

The boost in BAV's activities in the mid-90s indicates increased economic power. The Turkish journalist Fatih Altaylı claimed that companies under the influence of Oktar had made big business deals with municipalities where the Islamist Welfare (*Refah*) Party had come to power in the local elections in 1994 (Arda 2009). These claims resulted in Oktar and his associates initiating libel cases against Altaylı, with varying results. In November 1999, Oktar and 75 other members of BAV were arrested in a large-scale police operation, where the police seized photos, videotapes and documents allegedly intended to be used for blackmailing purposes ("Nihayet" 1999; Grove 2008). Oktar and 17 BAV members were charged with using threats for personal benefit and for

---
[12] Website of *Milli Değerler Koruma Vakfı* available at <www.mdkv.org> [Accessed 19.03.2013].
[13] One of the professors, Aykut Kence, showed me one of the flyers in question (personal interview with Aykut Kence, 17.07.2009).

establishing an organization with criminal intent. Then Minister of Interior Saadettin Tantan commented on the arrests saying that "Adnan Oktar is as dangerous as Apo" ("Adnan Hoca, Apo Kadar Tehlikeli" 1999).[14] Oktar was imprisoned without trial for 9 months, and claimed that himself and the other members were subjected to torture by the hands of the police, and accused "masons and communists" of being behind the operation ("Komünistlerle Mason Locaları Komplo Kurdu" 2000).

### 3.3. 1999–2007: The Harun Yahya enterprise: Going global

The scandals that erupted in 1999 seriously damaged Oktar's and BAV's already tarnished image in Turkey. Many members left the community, and one might have anticipated the community's decline. On the contrary, however, the 2000s was when Oktar and his associates developed a global publishing enterprise, and Oktar became known as the world's most prominent Islamic creationist under the name of Harun Yahya. Around the turn of the millennium, the Harun Yahya enterprise began publishing their first books in English and with time also other languages. Available in Islamic bookstores worldwide, the books were cheap, with an attractive and lavish layout, presenting Islamic topics in a simple and straightforward manner. It also produced videos based on the books, often using unaccredited BBC or Discovery Channel footage (Riexinger 2008).

In this period, the Harun Yahya enterprise also discovered the vast opportunities offered by the Internet in terms of mass communication. Great resources were put into designing inviting and attractive websites, and making a vast amount of books and videos available online in a variety of formats and languages.[15] The enterprise's effective use of the opportunities offered by new technologies was a significant factor in the transforming of Adnan Oktar, by now a despised figure within the multitude of Islamic groups in Turkey, into Harun Yahya, internationally known Islamic scholar and expert on creationism (Lumbard & Nayed 2010). During the 2000s, Harun Yahya virtually exploded into the cybersphere. Today, searching the Internet for information about Islam related to various topics is quite likely to send you to a page set up by the Harun Yahya enterprise. The global campaign of the Harun Yahya enterprise culminated in the mass distribution of the *Atlas of Creation* in 2007, and brought international attention to the Harun Yahya enterprise.

---

[14] Apo is a nickname for Abdullah Öcalan, the leader of the Kurdish nationalist movement PKK engaged in armed struggle against the Turkish state, who is now serving a life sentence for terrorist activities.

[15] See image appendix, pp. 6–12.

## 3.4. 2007–2012: Adnan Oktar steps into the limelight

After the mass distribution of the *Atlas of Creation*, international media outlets referred to its author as a "mysterious" character (Heneghan 2008a). Although the person behind the pen name Harun Yahya was well known to the Turkish public as the controversial "Adnan hoca" through the Turkish media's reporting on Oktar and his and his associates' many run-ins with the law over the years, Oktar himself had rarely appeared in public. However, after 2007, he began assuming an increasingly more visible and public role. He began doing frequent interviews with international media outlets, and held an international press conference in Çırağan Palace, one of the most exclusive hotels in Istanbul, in September 2008 (Yahya 2008a). Shortly after, Oktar also began appearing on Turkish local TV channels in the Black Sea region, giving interviews but also hosting his own TV shows. In 2011, the Harun Yahya enterprise founded a satellite TV station, A9 TV, which broadcasts on various cable network in Turkey and streams live over the Internet.[16]

A9 TV broadcasts documentaries based on the works of Harun Yahya, but also features talk shows with Adnan Oktar as the host. These talk shows have in recent years become the main platform through which Oktar seeks to reach his audience both in Turkey and abroad, and have brought on a new phase of both fame and notoriety for Oktar and the Harun Yahya enterprise. The shows are streamed live and are simultaneously translated to English, and "highlights" of the shows are available for streaming or downloading. Parallel to television becoming an important medium for promoting Oktar and his message, the printed works began to be published as written by "Harun Yahya (Adnan Oktar)". Thus, a notable development in the Harun Yahya enterprise in later years is the increased promotion of Adnan Oktar the individual, both in Turkey and globally.

## 3.5. From reclusive *cemaat* leader to flamboyant talk show host

Broadcast in the framework of the Harun Yahya enterprise, Adnan Oktar's unusual form of televangelism has elicited attention especially in Turkey, but also from international news media (Bierman 2013). The topics discussed on the talk show largely reflect the content of the books of Harun Yahya: The mostly female participants on the show read texts from a teleprompter taken from the works of Harun Yahya on Darwinism, the miracle of creation and other topics, and various news which Oktar comments upon in the light of these works as well as hadiths and verses from the Qur'an. In terms of their content, these shows preach Islam as promoted by the Harun Yahya enterprise. Adnan Oktar is by no means the only Muslim preacher using television as a platform for

---

[16] <www.a9.com.tr> [Accessed 19.03.2013].

reaching his audience. Famous Muslim televangelists include the Egyptian preacher Amr Khaled (Olsson 2013) and the Indian preacher Zakir Naik (Haqqani 2011).

What is unusual about these talk shows, however, is the setting in which these topics are discussed. The studio is glitzy and ostentatiously decorated. Oktar is usually flanked by a handful of sexy, blonde, big-breasted and surgically enhanced women, with heavy make-up and tight-fitting designer tops.[17] Oktar himself sports expensive-looking designer suits, and frequently compliments the female participants for their beauty, often comparing them to cats.[18] Oktar is addressed as "my Master" and appears to elicit immense respect and adoration from his female entourage.[19] In between discussing religious matters and current affairs, they listen and dance to the latest and most popular club hits in flashing disco lights.[20] Oktar responds to what is presented as letters from the viewers, and comments on American celebrities such as Britney Spears and Kim Kardashian (HarunYahyaEnglish 2011a).

Thousands of clips from Oktar's shows have been made available on YouTube and other social video sharing sites, many by the Harun Yahya enterprise itself. Some of these clips have had millions of views.[21] Adnan Oktar has become an Internet phenomenon, or what is known as an Internet *meme*.[22] Several parodies of Oktar's show have also been broadcast on Turkish TV.[23]

---

[17] These women are often referred to in the media as "Adnan's angels" (most probably a reference to the film *Charlie's Angels*, which features three sexy and glamorous detectives). See image appendix, p. 5.

[18] For this reason, the women are also nicknamed "Adnan's kittens" in Turkish media. In a clip that has been much shared on various social media, Oktar compliments a non-Turkish female guest on the show in broken English and compares her to a big cat (voithandwabco 2011). While some of these women are guests who have been invited to the show, others have been part of the Harun Yahya enterprise for years and play an active part in the shows. Occasionally Oktar's shows feature attractive males, which Oktar also compliments for their handsomeness (Yaratilistr 2012a).

[19] The participants on the show address Oktar as "hocam", which in the English translations of the show is rendered as "my Master". In one clip, Oktar asks his female followers "Let me make enemies and hypocrites burst with envy: Do you love me?" The women reply, "I love you more than anything else in the world", and "I love you more than my life, for the sake of Allah, I love you like crazy" (Yaratilistr 2011).

[20] In one especially popular clip on YouTube, Oktar and his associates listen to the track "Gangnam Style" by the Korean group PSY, which was a massive Internet sensation in 2012. Oktar performs dance moves with his hands, and the female participants follow Oktar's seemingly improvised choreography (AdnanOktarMuzik 2012).

[21] The Harun Yahya enterprise has posted a large amount of clips from Oktar's TV shows on their own YouTube channel. Since 2010, "Yaratilistr", one of the YouTube channels run by the Harun Yahya enterprise, has uploaded a total of 16.368 video clips and received a total of 72.043.970 views, and has 87.485 subscribers (per 22.04.2013). The currently most viewed clip from Oktar's show, where a beautiful female guest on the show calls Oktar an "amazing man", has nearly 4 millions views on YouTube per 04.04.2013 (Yaratilistr 2012c).

[22] Deriving from Richard Dawkins' notion of memes as a cultural equivalent to genes in order to explain how rumors, catch-phrases, melodies, or fashion trends replicate through a popu-

Although Harun Yahya's TV evangelism is not the topic of this thesis, I have briefly described these shows in order to illustrate the fact that the Harun Yahya enterprise entails more than the publication of books and websites. Furthermore, these shows may serve as a tool to highlight key aspects of the Harun Yahya enterprise. First of all, the shows demonstrate the media-savvy and market-oriented approach of the Harun Yahya enterprise. Oktar's televangelism is a bewildering spectacle that challenges normative expectations of what Islamic proselytism is or should be, and it has sparked both ridicule and indignation. Commenting on the TV shows, anthropologist Daniel Martin Varisco calls the Harun Yahya enterprise "a sexed-up Disney version of Islam" (Varisco 2013). An old truism of marketing is that "sex sells". Using sex as a marketing tool is rather less common in the propagation of Islam, however. In a study of the commercialization of broadcast television in Turkey, sociologist Ayşe Öncü describes how Islamic TV channels failed to lure viewers away from the seductions of "infotainment broadcasting", and therefore largely abandoned religiously edifying programs in favor of more mainstream broadcasting (Öncü 2012, p. 132). Nevertheless, these "alternative-Muslim" channels, such as Samanyolu TV, retained a "code of Islamic modesty" that set them apart from "regular" commercial TV broadcasting in Turkey. Oktar's shows, however, contravene most notions of Islamic modesty, and instead resemble popular daytime variety-TV shows on Turkish commercial channels. Yet, these shows are presented as religious programs that aim to preach the message of Islam. Featuring popular elements such as sexy women and hit music in a religious program is as an unusual method by which to market Islam. Nevertheless, the Harun Yahya enterprise seeks to justify these aspects with reference to Islamic tradition. For example, Oktar claims in one program that there are many hadiths to the effect that the prophet also likes blonde hair (Yahya 2012a).

In the course of this dissertation, I will examine the way in which the Harun Yahya enterprise employs popular themes and discourses and places them into an Islamic discursive framework. I will also seek to shed light on how Yahya's understanding of Islam is presented in the works of Harun Yahya, and how this interpretation may be understood in relation to the context in which it emerged and developed. As we shall see, the way in which Adnan Oktar is construed as a charismatic and significant figure in these TV shows is paralleled in the works of Harun Yahya. In a sense, these shows can be understood as a culmination of developments that I will describe and analyze in the course of this dissertation, and I will return to this in the final chapter.

---

lation, Internet memes are phenomena that rapidly gain popularity or notoriety on the Internet, often in the form of inside jokes (Bauckhage 2011).

[23] Ismail Baki, a comedian on the Turkish TV channel Fox TV, has made a series of parodies of Oktar's show (Ismailbakiofficial 2012). Oktar has laughingly commented on these parodies in his own shows, remarking that Baki is "a very talented guy" (Yaratilistr 2012b).

## 4. Defining the Harun Yahya enterprise

The focus of this dissertation is the collective effort that I choose to denominate as "the Harun Yahya enterprise". Harun Yahya is, as stated above, officially the pen name of Adnan Oktar. According to the authorized biography of Oktar, it is "formed from the names "Harun" (Aaron) and "Yahya" (John) in the esteemed memory of the two Prophets who struggled against infidelity" (Yahya 2002g, "About the Author"). I take the printed publications published in the name of Harun Yahya as primary material for this study. However, approaching these works as the works of Adnan Oktar is problematic. It is highly doubtful that Adnan Oktar has written over 300 books alone. The magnitude of the production suggests that the books have been penned by ghostwriters, or that they are the outcome of collaboration between Oktar and his associates. Although Oktar insists that he is in fact the author when confronted with this in interviews, he explains that he has a team of researchers that presents him with material, which he then "compiles and organizes" into books.[24] Thus, when I refer to Harun Yahya in the following, it is implied that I am referring to a constructed persona created by a collective of individuals, rather than merely to the individual Adnan Oktar. When I use Adnan Oktar, however, I refer to Adnan Oktar the individual. Oktar appears as the leader of this community, and it is reasonable to assume that Oktar has approved the material published under the name Harun Yahya, and that the books thus reflect his views. At the same time, however, it is likely that the various individuals that have participated in the community at various times have left their mark and contributed to and shaped the discourse.

What, then, is this collective that I refer to as the Harun Yahya enterprise? As the historical account above indicates, Oktar has surrounded himself with an Istanbul-based group of supporters since the late 80s. Oktar himself reports that he has a core group of researchers consisting of around 30 people.[25] Additionally, he claims to have around 200–300 supporters who are more or less involved in the group's activities.[26] Biographies of Adnan Oktar note that that a group of 20-30 young people was formed from 1982 to 1984, suggesting that the size of the core circle around Oktar has remained relatively stable, although some individuals have left the group while new members have joined.[27] The identities

---

[24] Personal interview with Adnan Oktar, 07.01.2009.
[25] Excerpt from an interview with Oktar rendered in the Frequently Asked Questions-section on the main Harun Yahya website, available at <http://harunyahya.com/bilgi/faq> [Accessed 19.03.3013].
[26] Personal interview with Adnan Oktar, 07.01.2009.
[27] From an article titled "The Story of Adnan Oktar's Life (Harun Yahya)" which is available on several websites claiming harunyahya.com as source. This article is currently not available from harunyahya.com, however. See for instance <www.muslimummah.org/articles/articles.php?itemno=257&&category=Famous%20Person> [Accessed 19.03.2013].

of some of these people are known through their involvement in the two main foundations of which Adnan Oktar is the honorary president, BAV and MDKV. Oktar's closest associates include Tarkan Yavaş, the CEO of BAV, and Altuğ Berker, the CEO of MDKV, both of which appear to have been part of the group since the early 1990s. Other key figures are Dr. Oktar Babuna, who came into the public eye in 1999 in Turkey due to a controversial blood donation campaign (Aslaneli 1999), and his four sisters.[28] In a much-publicized court case in 2006, Babuna and his sisters made scandalous accusations against their parents after their parents criticized Oktar publicly for having brainwashed their children.[29] Twelve members of BAV are named in the documents of the court case against Oktar and BAV in 1999 ("Adnan'in GSM Ajani" 1999). Several of these are part of the group of women appearing on Oktar's recent talk shows.[30] Thus, there appears to be a certain degree of continuity in the group.

In the Turkish media, Oktar and his followers are referred to as a *cemaat*, a religious community, led by Adnan Oktar. Aside from rumors and the accounts of ex-members circulating in Turkish media, little is known about the religious practices of this community, however.[31] Little is also known regarding the power relations within the group. Anthropologist Jenny B. White is one of many who refer to Oktar as a "cult leader" (White 2012). Although I have met both Adnan Oktar and other members of the Harun Yahya enterprise, I have not conducted extensive fieldwork among the group.[32] I am therefore not in a position to evaluate the relationship between Oktar and the members of the group, the question of leadership, or the members' motivation. In the following, I therefore

---

[28] Dr. Babuna started a charity campaign in Turkey to find a compatible bone marrow donor after being diagnosed with leukemia in the United States. The campaign initially received massive support from the media, NGOs and authorities in Turkey, but the mood changed after the Turkish Minister of Health declared the campaign illegal and began an investigation on suspicions that the campaign was a fraud. *Hürriyet Daily News* dubbed Babuna "the presently most controversial figure in Turkey" ("The Babuna Chaos" 1999).

[29] Oktar Babuna and his sisters Fatma Ceyda Ertüzün, Ayşegül Hüma Babuna, Ferhunde Eda Babuna ve Tuba Babuna accused their parents among other things of being "*Sabetayists*" (Sabatteans) (see Chapter 3), sexually immoral behavior and of having abused them sexually as kids (Sarıkaya 2006).

[30] E.g. Didem Ürer, Beyza Bayraktar and Ebru Yılmaz Atilla. See image appendix, p. 5.

[31] Ex-members of the group have claimed that the group engage in practices that depart from what is custom according to Sunni Islam, e.g. ritual prayer 3 times a day instead of 5, allowing for the performance of prayer without doing *abdest* (ritual washing) or without covering the head for women ("3 Rekat Namaz" 1999). In a recent TV show, Oktar appears to confirm that it is acceptable to read the Qur'an without performing *abdest*, and for women to pray without covering the head, and argues that "by introducing a whole series of requirements, people are kept away from the Qur'an" (13kahraman 2012a). In an interview with Al Jazeera from 2007, Oktar declares that he follows the Hanafi school of *ahl al-Sunna*, and claims that both he and his associates pray five times a day, and observe all obligatory (*farz*) religious duties (Bilim Araştırma Vakfi 2007).

[32] I had my first encounter with members of the Harun Yahya enterprise in 2005, and I conducted an interview with Adnan Oktar in 2009.

refer to the members as associates rather than followers of Oktar. Although this community may well be approached and understood as a form of "cult" or New Religious Movement, that is not the focus of this study.[33] I approach this community as a collective that seeks market shares both in the Turkish and global religious market through the production, marketing and dissemination of religious products. I therefore conceptualize it as an enterprise.

The term enterprise refers either to a project or undertaking, or a company or business. Both definitions are arguably relevant to Oktar and his associates. Many contemporary Islamic movements are grass-root movements in the sense that they rely on broadly based and spontaneous support within a local community. Although the group around Oktar also relies on the ability to mobilize people for a cause, its structure and manner of recruiting bear closer resemblance to professional recruitment than to a broadly based social movement. From the very outset, Oktar sought to recruit supporters from a particular segment of society: Wealthy, presentable, well-educated young people with skills within business, languages or the academia, which Oktar believed would be of benefit for his undertaking.[34]

## 5. The water for the mill: the finances of the enterprise

The seemingly unlimited financial resources of the Harun Yahya enterprise generate both curiosity and speculations.[35] Producing and sending thousands of copies of the *Atlas of Creation* to addresses all over the world, purchasing advertising space in newspapers and even on London buses,[36] organizing free conferences,[37] purchasing a large amount of domain names on the Internet,[38] and setting up a TV station require a massive amount of capital. What is the source of these funds, or as the question is asked in Turkish: Where does the water for this mill come from? ("Bu Değirmenin Suyu Nereden" 1999). Adnan Oktar

---

[33] The term "cult" has largely been abandoned as an analytical term in the study of religions due to its negative connotations and its associations with stereotypes regarding "brainwashing" or "mind control" (Lewis 2004, pp. 5–7).

[34] In an interview in 2011, Oktar explains that he deliberately sought to recruit people for his *tebliğ* effort who were "attractive, wealthy, educated and sophisticated, in a position of influence" because "I had limited resources and little time. In order to have an impact in society, I wanted to use the most effective power possible" (Zeki Ademoğlu 2011).

[35] The question I am most frequently met with when presenting papers on the Harun Yahya enterprise is "where do they get their money from?"

[36] In 2009, the British Humanist Association and Richard Dawkins gave support to the Atheist Bus Campaign, which placed ads with the slogan "There's probably no God. Now stop worrying and enjoy your life" on London buses. The Harun Yahya enterprise responded with its own ad campaign, with the slogan "Modern Science Demonstrates That God Exists" (See image appendix, p. 3).

[37] See image appendix, p. 3.

[38] A list of some of the domain names owned by Yahya is available at <http://harunyahya.com/list/type/5> [Accessed 19.03.2013].

claims that the money is generated by those who are involved in the group and sympathize with the cause, and denies that the group receives any external funding.[39] Not everyone is convinced by this, and there are various speculations concerning possible external funders. Tuncay Özkan, an alleged spy and key informant and suspect in the ongoing Ergenekon investigation in Turkey, claims that Adnan Oktar is funded by Israel (Vahiterek 2010).[40] The Harun Yahya enterprise has had close contact with various relatively marginal religious groups from Israel such as a group calling themselves the "re-established Sanhedrin", and has invited the latter to Istanbul (Bartholomew 2005). However, the claim that the state of Israel financially supports the Harun Yahya enterprise must be considered in the light of how such allegations of support from Israel are a common way of attempting to discredit someone in the Turkish context.[41] In Chapter 3, I suggest that the increased contact between the Harun Yahya enterprise and Jewish groups do not necessarily indicate financial support from Israel, but may in fact have other explanations.

The Harun Yahya enterprise has been in contact with American creationists since the 1990s, and some suspect that Harun Yahya receives funding from them. Cited by Reuters journalist Tom Heneghan, physicist Taner Edis doubts the rumors of support from American creationists, noting that "American creationists I talk to basically envy Harun Yahya's financial resources. If there were any funds flowing, it would be from Adnan Oktar to the creationists" (Heneghan 2008b). The same article also raises doubts about another rumor, that the Harun Yahya enterprise receives Saudi support. Heneghan cites an unnamed Islam expert who alleges that Saudi support is unlikely, considering that Yahya's teachings clash with several aspects of Wahhabi theology. Although external financial backing cannot be ruled out, the significance of such support should not be overestimated. It seems unlikely that any external funder dictates the discourse of the Harun Yahya enterprise.

What appears to be the most likely source of the finances of the Harun Yahya enterprise is the enterprise itself and its supporters. A former member describes how one segment of Adnan's associates was given the task of generating funds for the enterprise. Additionally, all members of the group were expected to contribute financially.[42] This type of fundraising is common in many religious groups in Turkey, including the Gülen movement. Through the contributions of members –

---

[39] Personal interview with Adnan Oktar, 07.01.2009.
[40] The Ergenekon investigation is the judicial investigation into a shadowy secularist ultra-nationalist network with alleged links to the military, which is accused of plotting to overthrow the government in Turkey. See for instance Jenkins (2011).
[41] An example are a series of popular books written by Ergün Poyraz, which claim to document that Recep Tayyıp Erdoğan and Abdullah Gül are in fact minions for Israel (Poyraz 2007). See a further discussion of this in Chapter 3.
[42] Personal interview with "Mehmet", 04.02.2012.

many of whom are successful businesspeople – as well as various business ventures run by the movement such as Bank Asya, the Gülen movement has developed into one of the richest religious communities in Turkey.[43] Compared to the Gülen movement, the Harun Yahya enterprise is a small outfit. However, the Harun Yahya enterprise has been recruiting among the wealthiest social stratum in Turkey from the outset, and many of the members are wealthy and successful in business.[44] It is therefore not entirely unlikely that the enterprise is in fact self-funding, as Adnan Oktar himself claims.

The question whether the substantial assets of the Harun Yahya enterprise have been acquired legally is a different matter. The wealth of the Harun Yahya enterprise has been a source of speculation for decades, and has also attracted the suspicion of the Turkish authorities. In 1999, Oktar and several members of BAV were charged with using threats for personal benefit and creating an organization with the intent to commit a crime. An article in Milliyet lists companies that according to the Turkish prosecutor are tied to the Harun Yahya enterprise (Bilgin 2000). The Harun Yahya enterprise was accused of using blackmailing and sex traps as a way in which to generate money (Özkan 2000). The legal process against Oktar and BAV lasted two years, during which most of the complainants retracted their claims. The case therefore lapsed in 2005, but was taken up again in 2008 by another prosecutor, and in May 2008, Oktar was sentenced to 3 years of prison for creating an illegal organization for personal gain ("Adnan Oktar'a 3 Yıl Hapis" 2008; Grove 2008). Oktar and BAV appealed the sentence, and on December 28th 2009 the Supreme Court of Appeal overturned the conviction (Erdal 2010; Atik 2012). The *çete* (criminal organization) case against Oktar and six other BAV members continues, however.[45] Oktar and BAV have responded to these charges by claiming that they are the victims of a conspiracy by the Ergenekon network in collaboration with Freemasons.[46]

None of the above theories regarding the finances of the Harun Yahya enterprise can be ruled out entirely, and so the question of the source of the money remains somewhat of a mystery. The main significance of the considerable finances of the Harun Yahya enterprise is arguably the fact that it is this

---

[43] Helen Rose Ebaugh discussed the financing of the Gülen movement at length in her sociological analysis of the Gülen movement (Ebaugh 2009).
[44] In an extensive interview with Turkish journalist Nagehan Alçı in the news program MedCezir on the TV channel Beyaz TV, Oktar explains that "all my friends are very rich" and claims they have become even more successful through the sound advice he has been giving them (Zeki Ademoğlu 2011).
[45] Several Turkish newspapers reported in February 2013 that the next court hearing in Istanbul 2nd Heavy Penal Court was set to April 26th 2013. However, I have been unable to obtain any information regarding this court hearing after April 26th 2013, which may indicate that the court hearing has been further delayed.
[46] Available at <www.bilimarastirmavakfi.org> [Accessed 19.03.2013].

wealth that enables the enterprise to market Harun Yahya and his ideas on the global scale that it does.

Harun Yahya is one of many contemporary popular Muslim authors who – to borrow Peter Mandaville's expression – is seeking to capture "market shares" in the contemporary marketplace for Islamic *tabligh* and *da'wa* (Mandaville 2007, p. 4).[47] The Harun Yahya enterprise can be viewed as an example of what is referred to in the sociology of religion as *religious commodification*, a process by which religion adopts the logic of the market, where faith is repackaged and tailor-made to meet market demands (Kitiarsa 2010). The intersection between religious traditions and market economy is nothing new, but the Harun Yahya enterprise is, I will argue, a particularly salient example of a religious enterprise that exists in the intersection between religion, popular culture, consumer capitalism and modern marketing technologies, and therefore invites an analysis on how religion is marketized.[48]

The Harun Yahya enterprise can be understood within the framework of global religious trends, such as the emergence of evangelizer-entrepreneurs who

> market a reformed version of their faith, purified of its superstitious cultural accretions, and substitute an ideal, universal, enlightened creed in tune with progress and the betterment of humanity and the environment (Levitt et al. 2010).

I hope to show in this dissertation that Yahya introduces, presents and alters discourses in response to changing demands of "the market".

In conceptualizing the way in which the Harun Yahya enterprise operates, it is certainly tempting to borrow terms from the field of marketing communications. Harun Yahya is the *brand name* of the outfit. The sheer ubiquity and availability of the material provides Yahya with what marketers term *reach*, defined as the number of people exposed to the message.[49] Much effort is also put into *packaging*; the books are colorful and lavishly illustrated, and the websites are well designed. The organization employs a recognizable *brand language*: Easily understandable with a characteristically confident tone of voice. The question of finance discussed above, has great bearing upon the Harun Yahya enterprise's marketing methods, but seemingly less so upon the *content*. What, then, is the exact *product* Harun Yahya is marketing? Describing and analyzing this product, is the focus of this dissertation.

---

[47] The Arabic word *tabligh* means to "deliver (the message)", and refers to the act of making the message of Islam known to people.
[48] This will be further discussed below in section 7.1., where I discuss the fragmentation of authority in contemporary Islam, the effect of new media and globalization on religious discourses and the emergence of "market Islam".
[49] <http://marketing.about.com/od/marketingglossary/g/reachdef.htm> [Accessed 19.03.2013].

# 6. Method and material

## 6.1. Method

This dissertation seeks to examine the Harun Yahya enterprise by analyzing and contextualizing a selected material, which I will demarcate below. I identify key themes in the texts of Harun Yahya, and examine how these themes have developed over time. I analyze the texts by examining the arguments and argumentative strategies employed by Yahya and placing them into a social and historical context.

One way in which to understand the ideas of Harun Yahya is as addressing specific concerns that are linked with a particular interpretation of Islam; that is, as *theological* doctrines that have emerged in a particular context and that are influenced by other Islamic thinkers. Although I will attempt to trace the Islamic discursive field that Yahya's ideas have emerged out of, I approach the texts of Harun Yahya primarily as texts written with the intention to *persuade* the readers, and therefore as texts that can be analyzed as *rhetoric*. I therefore focus on the argumentative strategies Yahya uses, and how Yahya engages with and employs various ideas and discourses in order to persuade his audience and gain credibility. I also seek to explain why it makes sense for Yahya to use those methods. Below I will explain further what I mean by *rhetorical analysis*.

I also aim to shed light on *why* Yahya presents these ideas, by providing an analytical context. The method that will be employed in the effort to make sense of these texts is *historicization* and *contextualization*. The themes I concentrate on have been a part of the discourse of the Harun Yahya enterprise from the beginning of the late 80s, namely anti-Darwinism, Judeo-Masonic conspiracy theories, nationalism/neo-Ottomanism and ideas about a coming Mahdi and a Golden Age for Islam. I examine how these themes have evolved in the works of Harun Yahya, both over time and in relation to changing local and global contexts. I historicize the teachings of Harun Yahya by tracing the currents, movements and ideas that have given shape to Harun Yahya's Islamic discourse, focusing in particular on the Islamic modernism of Said Nursi and the Nurcu movement. Additionally, I seek to provide relevant background to the Harun Yahya enterprise by comparing the ideas espoused by Yahya with other local and global currents and developments.

The purpose of contextualizing the teachings of Harun Yahya is not just to trace how ideas have emerged historically and show how they can be understood as part of broader local and global trends. I also approach Harun Yahya as a religious entrepreneur that avails not merely of emerging marketing techniques and technologies, but also of changing social and political conditions as market opportunities. The Harun Yahya enterprise can be understood as a product of the local and global context in which it emerged, but also as en entrepreneurial setup that adapts its religious products to various markets, employing both mass marketing and niche marketing as strategies. I will therefore seek to explain developments and changes in Yahya's discourse with reference to the Harun Yahya enterprise's attempt to appeal to various segments, both in Turkey and globally.

## 6.2. Primary material: The works of the Harun Yahya enterprise

The abovementioned ambiguity of authorship presents a methodological problem: How to identify which works to include as material? What constitute the works of Harun Yahya? In compliance with the understanding that "Harun Yahya" is a construct and that the Harun Yahya enterprise is a collective effort, I apply the following criteria: Firstly, I define as the works of Harun Yahya those works that have been published in the name of Harun Yahya and/or that are referred to, cited or listed as the works of Harun Yahya in other works published by Harun Yahya.[50] Secondly, I also define as the works of Harun Yahya articles, videos and other material that appear on the main web domains operated by the Harun Yahya enterprise, namely harunyahya.com, harunyahya.org and harunyahya.net, as well as websites that are listed and linked to on these main websites. In these cases, then, I identify the author as "Harun Yahya". Although recognizing that there is a collective behind the pen name "Harun Yahya", I refer to Yahya with the pronouns "he" and "his" in the interest of readability. In a broader sense, however, I also consider statements made by Adnan Oktar in interviews and in TV shows, material published by Bilim Araştırma Vakfı and the broadcasts of A9 TV as sources for the discourse of the Harun Yahya enterprise. In practical terms then, there is no difference between "the discourse of Harun Yahya" and "the discourse of the Harun Yahya enterprise".

The stated purpose of this dissertation is to examine the Harun Yahya enterprise by analyzing the discourse of Harun Yahya. The source material therefore consists of texts in a broad sense: The total production of material published in the framework of the Harun Yahya enterprise.[51] This includes printed publications (books, booklets, articles, leaflets, posters); documentaries (available on published DVDs and in various video formats online);[52] audio

---

[50] This may seem like a rather cumbersome definition, but, as will be discussed in Chapter 3, there are some books published in the name of Harun Yahya that Adnan Oktar later has denied responsibility for.

[51] Norman Fairclough argues that "texts" are "social events" and include more than just the printed word (see below) (Fairclough 2005). The Harun Yahya enterprise has also organized numerous conferences, advertising campaigns and creation museums, but these are more difficult to document.

[52] See image appendix, p. 4.

podcasts, hundreds of websites; TV shows and interviews featuring Adnan Oktar/Harun Yahya.

I take as my primary source material the printed publications published in the name of Harun Yahya. I concentrate in particular on the earliest works, because part of my aim is to examine the emergence of the Harun Yahya enterprise and document changes in the discourse over time. Only a handful of works were published in the name of Harun Yahya before the late 1990s. These books were sold in regular Turkish bookstores, and some were distributed for free. They thus reached a fairly wide audience in Turkey, and constituted the main platform for the transmission of ideas for the Harun Yahya enterprise at the time. The end of the 1990s marked the beginning of a new phase for the Harun Yahya enterprise, as it turned its eyes on a global market. A vast amount of books were published in the name of Harun Yahya, not only in Turkish but also in several other languages. The enterprise established its own publishing companies, and also established cooperation with distributors in other countries.[53]

Although the printed publications are still distributed in bookstores worldwide, over the course of the 2000s, the Internet has become an increasingly important tool for disseminating the ideas of Harun Yahya. Most of the books of Harun Yahya have been made available online as free downloadable document files. Much of the online material is reproduced or reworked versions of texts appearing in the printed publications. The main hub of Harun Yahya online is www.harunyahya.com (English) and www.harunyahya.org (Turkish).[54] Most of the Harun Yahya material currently available on the web can be accessed through these pages: Books can be downloaded or read online in different formats; documentaries can be streamed or downloaded; A9 TV is streamed around the clock. There are links to other Harun Yahya websites, the websites are constantly updated with news and new material, and the sites can be viewed in a variety of languages.

The Harun Yahya enterprise appears to have a large degree of control over the production, since it both controls the publishing companies as well as the content available at any given time on the many web domains it operates. Only the most recent editions of books are available from the websites, and some older publications are no longer listed. As noted by German scholar of religion Martin Riexinger, Harun Yahya blocked his websites for Internet Archive in 2004, and it is therefore difficult to document the history of the online development (Riexinger 2008).[55] Hence, the material presently available at the

---

[53] A list of these publishing houses is available at <www.harunyahya.com/bilgi/yayinevleri#nor> [Accessed 19.03.2013].
[54] See image appendix, p. 12.
[55] Getting a full overview over the bibliography of Harun Yahya has proven to be difficult. Many books have been published in several editions, and it is mostly only the newest editions that are now available for purchase or download. The Harun Yahya enterprise has not

Harun Yahya websites must be understood as the result of an editorial process that reflects how the Harun Yahya enterprise wishes to be perceived currently. As earlier printed works were distributed more widely as physical print copies, many of them can be obtained from second hand bookstores. These physical copies, then, both constitute the most reliable source for documenting changes in the discourse of the Harun Yahya enterprise over time, as well as offering a valuable insight into the earliest formulations of Yahya's ideas.

Over 300 books have been published in the name of Harun Yahya to date, covering a wide range of faith-related and political topics. Thematically, the works may be broadly divided into three categories: Books devoted to creationism and antievolutionism; books about Islam and faith-related issues; and books on history and politics. These themes overlap, however. The Harun Yahya website currently categorizes the works according to the following topics: For Children; Mahdi, Jesus and End Times; The Secret Beyond Matter; Atheist Freemasons and Their Errors; People of the Book and Prophets; History, Politics and Strategy; Collapse of the Theory of Evolution; Signs Leading to Faith and Miracle of Creation; Morality of Qur'an and Deep Thinking; Outlook to other Faiths and Philosophies; Harun Yahya and Influences; Turkish Islamic Union.

I have identified four key themes that have been part of the discourse of the Harun Yahya enterprise since the late 80s and early 90s: Judeo-Masonic conspiracy theories, nationalism/neo-Ottomanism, creationism and apocalypticism.[56] In the three empirical chapters, I will therefore focus on these themes and examine how they develop over time. I have chosen not to deal with conspiracy theories in a separate chapter, as this theme is interwoven with the other themes. I deal with both conspiracy theories and nationalism/neo-Ottomanism in Chapter 3, as these are both political themes linked with the Turkish context. I will also return to conspiracy theories in Chapter 5.

In order to be able to show both continuity and change in the production of Harun Yahya, I am not limiting my choice of material to a particular period, but rather including the whole time period from 1987 until the end of my research in 2012.

According to his authorized biography, Adnan Oktar began publishing booklets on Darwinism in the early 1980s.[57] The first book to be published in the

---

responded to my requests of a full list of publications. Two of his publishers abroad did however provide me with a list of works. Nevertheless, I have been able to obtain physical editions of early works that are relevant for my analysis, which are no longer available on the websites.

[56] Ecumenism may be identified as a fifth theme, but this is a theme that develops later in Yahya's works, as we shall see.

[57] A book titled *Canlılar ve Evrim* (Living Creatures and Evolution) was published by Bilim Araştırma Grubu in 1986 (Bilim Araştırma Grubu 1986). According to the main Harun Yahya website, Adnan Oktar himself prepared this book: "In 1986 [Adnan Oktar] collected all his research on Darwinism's true face in the book *Living Things and Evolution*, which for many

name of Harun Yahya, however, was *Yahudilik ve Masonluk* (Judaism and Masonry) (Yahya 1987b).[58] In this book, Yahya promotes the popular conspiracy theory that Jews and Freemasons are working in cohort, and that they erode the religious and material values of Turkey by promoting materialism, Darwinism and immoral lifestyles. Conspiracy theories regarding Freemasons continue to be prominent in Yahya's works, but anti-Jewish themes have been toned down, as we shall see. In 1990, the Harun Yahya enterprise begins publishing political works with Atatürkist, Turkish nationalist and neo-Ottoman themes. In Chapter 3, I argue that the development of both the conspiratorial and nationalist themes in Yahya's works must be understood against the background of the Turkish context in which Yahya was operating.

The theme that earned Harun Yahya a wide audience both in Turkey and globally, however, is what Yahya terms "the intellectual struggle against Darwinism" (Yahya 2008c), and this is the topic of Chapter 4. A majority of the works of Harun Yahya is centered on refuting the theory of evolution and asserting the truth of divine creation. The analysis of Harun Yahya's Islamic creationism will take as its starting point the first English edition of *The Evolution Deceit: The Scientific Collapse of Darwinism and its Ideological Background* (Yahya 1999a), as this may be considered the bedrock of his campaign of evolution, and contains most of the elements that he has later expanded upon in other works.[59] It was after the publication of *The Evolution Deceit* in 1999, translated from the Turkish edition published in 1997, that Oktar's publication activities and campaign against evolution gained momentum.

The analysis of Harun Yahya's Mahdism and apocalypticism, the topic of Chapter 5, is primarily based on the first edition of *Mehdi ve Altın Çag: Islam'in Dünya Hakimiyeti* (Mahdi and the Golden Age: The World Supremacy of Islam) (Yahya 1989), but also includes later works in order to show the development of this topic over time.[60] The analysis of printed publications will be supplemented with material from websites published in the name of Harun Yahya, including his TV appearances. An additional primary source is interviews given by Adnan Oktar to newspapers, magazines and TV stations both in Turkey and internationally.

The works of Yahya have been translated to a vast number of different languages.[61] The translations are mostly direct or reworked translations of books already published in Turkish. One of the most translated publications, *The*

---

years was used as the sole reference showing the scientific invalidity of the theory of evolution" (Yahya 2007f).
[58] See image appendix, p. 4.
[59] See image appendix, p. 2.
[60] See image appendix, p. 2.
[61] There are books in 46 different languages available on harunyahya.com, but most of the books are only available in a few languages.

*Evolution Deceit*, is currently available in 19 different languages. In this dissertation, I am concentrating mainly on works in Turkish and English, as these are the two major languages that Yahya's works are available in, and since English was the first language aside from Turkish that Yahya's books were made available in. Concentrating on these two languages allows me to compare and identify changes in emphasis from the Turkish context to the global context. Although it would be interesting to examine which works are made available in e.g. Arabic, such an examination lies beyond the scope of this dissertation.

As argued above, the history of Oktar and his associates constitute an important context for understanding the discourse of the Harun Yahya enterprise. Yahya's trouble with the law, and Turkish authorities, play an important part in the public perception of the Harun Yahya enterprise. This is not a reception study, and it does not purport to assess the extent and nature of Harun Yahya's influence as an author and religious figure. However, since much of Harun Yahya's discourse is formulated in response to various detractors and critics, the reception of Harun Yahya is relevant in so far as it bears upon how Yahya frames his ideas. As secondary literature on the development of the movement itself is scarce, my historical account relies on newspaper articles and other secondary sources. This account will also be supplemented with interviews with Adnan Oktar himself and other stakeholders.

In each empirical chapter, I present and motivate the selection of the material more thoroughly.

## 6.3. Previous research

Although Harun Yahya has received much attention from the media both in Turkey and internationally, scholarly literature on the Harun Yahya enterprise is scarce. The first lengthy account of Adnan Oktar and the community around him is a chapter in Ruşen Çakır's *Ayet ve Slogan* titled "Mucizevi Atatürkçüler: Adnan Oktar ve Edip Yüksel" (Miraculous Atatürkists: Adnan Oktar and Edip Yüksel) (Çakır 1990). German scholar Hannelore Schönig published an article titled "Aids als das Tier (dabba) der islamischen Eschatologie: Zur Argumentation einer türkischen Schrift" in *Die Welt des Islams* (Schönig 1990), where she analyzes Harun Yahya's booklet *Aids Kur'an'da bahsi gecen Dabbet-ul-arz* (Is AIDS the Beast mentioned in the Qur'an?) (Yahya 1987a).

Most scholarly accounts of Harun Yahya focus on Yahya's creationism in the framework of the study of Islam and science or religion and science. American physicist Taner Edis has been writing on Islamic creationism in Turkey since the early 90s, and wrote a report on Harun Yahya's creationism as presented in *The Evolution Deceit* in 1999 for the US-based National Center for Science Education (Edis 1999). He also wrote a chapter on Yahya's creationism in his book *An Illusion of Harmony: Science and religion in Islam* (Edis 2007). Martin Riexinger has also written several articles on Yahya's Islamic creationism that I have benefited from. The first appeared in the ISIM newsletter as "The Islamic Creationism of Harun Yahya" (Riexinger 2002). "Propagating Islamic Creationism on the Internet" (Riexinger 2008) focuses on Yahya's use of the Internet as a method of propagation. *The Handbook of Religion and the Authority of Science* (Lewis & Hammer 2011) features a chapter by Riexinger on Muslim responses to evolution, which also features Harun Yahya. Additionally, Riexinger deals with Harun Yahya in the context of the Nurcu movement in his professorial thesis (*Habilitationsschrift*) (Riexinger 2009). One of the foremost experts on creationism, Ronald L. Numbers, included a section on the activities of Oktar and BAV in the expanded edition of *The Creationists* (Numbers 2006). While drawing on these studies that approach Yahya's creationism from the perspective of religion and science, in this study I also examine creationism in a broader framework as one of several themes in the discourse of the Harun Yahya enterprise.

## 7. Analytical framework

In my effort to describe and analyze the discourse of the Harun Yahya enterprise, I will not employ a strict theoretical framework or methodology, but rather draw on several analytical perspectives. In this section, I will first introduce a discussion on relevant global developments in Islam as a context to the Harun Yahya enterprise, such as the fragmentation of authority prevalent in contemporary Islam and the influence of globalization on Islamic missionary efforts. Moreover, I discuss theoretical and analytical perspectives and concepts that will be employed when analyzing the Harun Yahya enterprise. Related to religion as a social construction, a definition of Islam as a discursive tradition is presented. I explain what I mean by analyzing the discourse of Harun Yahya as rhetoric, and present analytical concepts from social movement theories that I use in my analysis of the material.

### 7.1. Fragmentation of authority and new media

An aspect of religion in late modernity is arguably the fact that an increasing portion of the production and dissemination of religious knowledge is taking place outside traditional sites of authority. No person or institution has monopoly on sacred authority, if they ever did. Dale Eickelman and James Piscatori argue that a salient feature of contemporary Islam is a "fragmentation of authority" (Eickelman & Piscatori 2004, p. 131). Various new actors that are not sanctioned by or emerging from traditional centers of Islamic learning, now compete to "speak for Islam". The struggle for authority is not peculiar to Islam, nor is it unique to contemporary Islam (Zaman 2006, p. 206). However, the context in which authority is articulated and defended is radically different now than before the 20th century. What has brought about this new challenge to authority is the spread of mass education, literacy and mass communication. As argued by Bryan Turner, "modern information technology change the social conditions by which political and religious authority are produced" (Turner 2007, p. 117).

The burgeoning of new media, in particular the Internet, offers expanded opportunities for various actors striving to establish themselves as religious authorities. This has led to an expansion of interpretations and interpreters of Islam, who often do not emerge from the traditional sites of Islamic learning, but from secular institutions of education. In principle, anyone can set up a website and begin to interpret, present or promote Islam. As American Muslim scholar Muqtedar Khan puts it, "the Internet has made everyone a mufti" (cited in Sisler 2007, p. 209). Global information technologies such as the Internet "undermine traditional forms of religious authority because they expand conventional modes of communication, open up new opportunities for debate and create alternative visions of the global community" (Turner, 2007, p. 120).

Eickelman and Piscatori have also coined the phrase the "objectification of Muslim consciousness" to capture the way in which Muslim religiosity in a globalized world has become more self-conscious and reflexive (Eickelman & Piscatori 2004, p. 37). The preoccupation with questions such as "what is Islam?" and "what does it mean to be a good Muslim?" has engendered a growing market for religious literature that systematizes Islamic thought.

As noted by Turner, the competition for authority is taking place in a variety of vernacular languages, not merely Arabic (Turner 2007, p. 133). Migration has created Muslim diasporic communities in many countries, and English, for instance, is increasingly becoming a language through which Islamic knowledge is being transmitted within and between these diasporic communities (Turner 2007, p. 127). Many young Muslims bypass *ulama* and imams in order to learn about Islam from pamphlets and sources in English, and especially from the Internet: "In the absence of sanctioned information from recognized institutions, Muslims are increasingly taking religion into their own hands" (Mandaville 2001, p. 168)

New media and the globalization of Islam have also led to a diversification of Islamic discourses. A myriad of different voices are competing for sacred authority and putting forward their own particular interpretation of Islam. Most of these are not trained experts, *ulama,* and their interpretations therefore constitute challenges to the trained religious experts, which we with some caution may refer to as "establishment Islam".[62] "Class and mass Islam" have

---

[62] Thomas Gerholm uses the term "Establishment Islam" to refer to *ulama* (sing. *'alim*), i.e. religious and juridical specialists and experts who have been considered the most qualified in understanding divine law (Gerholm 1997).

often been treated as analytically separable categories, where the first has often been the subject of textual analysis while the latter has been the subject of behavioral analysis. However, argues Jon Anderson, the emergence of a new public space challenges this distinction (Anderson 2003, p. 2)

A common contemporary scholarly approach to understanding the multitude of different interpretations emerging as a result of globalization and modern communication technologies is to analyze how these different interpretations and discourses legitimize their teachings as authentic Islam. "The struggle for authority" has become a paradigm within which various interpreters of Islam are being considered. Since the competition is high, the interpreters try to legitimize their interpretations as authentic and Islamic. As I will discuss in the next chapter, in order to appreciate the factors that have shaped Islamic discourse in Turkey, it is important to keep in mind the way in which the Turkish state has sought to domesticate and nationalize Islam for the purpose of control and national unity. The legitimacy of this normative discourse is contested, and has led to the emergence of a multitude of alternative discourses. One such discourse is *Nurculuk*, the school of thought established by Said Nursi. As the following chapters will show, this is an important point of reference for Harun Yahya.

Harun Yahya can be regarded as one of the new Islamic "micro-intellectuals", in Eickelman's terminology (Eickelman & Anderson 2003, p. 12), who challenge traditional Islamic authority. He is not a traditionally trained Islamic scholar, he uses the Internet and he writes in vernacular language rather than Arabic. He is not concerned with interpreting Islamic law in a contemporary context.

In a sense, Harun Yahya is bypassing the scramble for authority, as he seemingly addresses an audience that does not primarily ask about his credentials, but take his ideas about Islam at face value. In the course of this dissertation, therefore, I will not approach Harun Yahya primarily as someone participating in the struggle for interpretive authority. This, however, does not mean that he does not try to legitimize himself as an authoritative voice. As we shall see, Yahya arguably appeals to both rational and charismatic authority in his effort to convince his audience, but his claims to authority, if they may be considered as such, are not predicated upon traditional scholarly authority. Rather than considering Yahya in the scholarly framework of an internal Islamic struggle for authenticity and authority, it may therefore be more useful to see him as part of a broader trend of Islamic *da'wa*, global evangelism and "market Islam".

## 7.2. Harun Yahya as a *da'wa* enterprise

The expressed goal of the Harun Yahya enterprise is to "convey the Qur'an's message, encourage readers to consider basic faith-related issues such as Allah's existence and unity and the Hereafter; and to expose irreligious systems' feeble foundations and perverted ideologies" (Yahya 2001c). On the main Harun Yahya website, Adnan Oktar is presented as a man who has

> dedicated his life to telling of the existence and oneness of Almighty Allah, to disseminating the moral values of the Qur'an, to the intellectual defeat of materialist and atheist ideologies, to propagating the real Atatürk way and to defending the permanence of the state and the unity of the nation.[63]

The Harun Yahya enterprise presents itself as an enterprise with a missionary purpose, and is thus a part of the above-mentioned fragmentation of authority within contemporary Islam. Yahya's works are presented as texts meant to edify the readers by providing moral and intellectual instruction. The focus on the calling to the Islamic faith is also reflected in the motto of the Harun Yahya enterprise: "An Invitation to the Truth". The Harun Yahya enterprise thus presents itself as a form of *da'wa* enterprise. The Oxford Dictionary of Islam defines *da'wa* as "the invitation or call to Islam" (Esposito 2003, p. 61). By this definition, various activities by Muslim individuals or groups (or states) aimed towards calling people to faith may be termed *da'wa*, and Islamic books that explicitly aim to propagate a message with the aim of calling or inviting people to faith may be termed *da'wa* literature.

The Turkish transliteration of *da'wa* is *dava*, but its lexical meaning differs from the Arabic. In common Turkish usage it does not carry the meaning of religious mission, but rather denotes "cause" or "ideal".[64] The Harun Yahya enterprise refers to Oktar as a "*dava adamı*", which translates as "a man with a cause" or an "idealist" (Yahya 2008e). In the Turkish context, this term has connotations with striving for nationalist and Islamic ideals. It is an honorific term that is often applied to Said Nursi, Fethullah Gülen and Necip Fazil Kisakurek (1904–1983) by their sympathizers, to signal that these are people who have struggled and made sacrifices for the sake of Islamic and nationalist ideals.[65] The Harun Yahya enterprise thus presents Oktar/Yahya as someone who is not just communicating the message of Islam, but is involved in an intellectual struggle for the sake of Islamic ideals. Instead of the Arabic *da'wa*, the Harun Yahya enterprise employs the related Turkish term *tebliğ*, which translates as "communicating or conveying a message" (Yahya 2012d). *Tebliğ* is the Turkish transliteration of the Arabic *tabligh*, which in modern usage is interchangeable with *da'wa* in the meaning of propagation of faith (Esposito 2003, p. 309).

---

[63] Available at <www.harunyahya.com/bilgi/yazarHakkinda> [Accessed 19.03.2013].
[64] Another meaning of *dava* in Turkish is lawsuit, case or legal action.
[65] Necip Fazıl Kısakürek was a Turkish poet, Islamic intellectual and activist who founded the influential journal *Büyük Doğu* ("Great Orient").

The concept of Islamic *da'wa* has had different meanings throughout the history of Islam, and was in the early period of Islam linked with *jihad* as well as struggles for political legitimacy. Since the late 19th century, *da'wa* has re-emerged as an important concept among Muslims largely due to the development of Islamist ideas and practices (Janson 2002, p. 5). Like Christian mission, Islamic *da'wa* has been transformed and developed in response to processes associated with modernity, such as secularism and globalization.

Harun Yahya is targeting both a Turkish and global audience, and so his concept and practice of Islamic mission and activism must be understood within both a local and global context. In Chapter 2, I will deal with the Turkish context in more detail, and examine the conditions that shaped Islamic modernist discourses in Turkey. The attempt to counter irreligion by synthesizing religion and science and presenting an evidence-based faith is represented most comprehensively in Turkey by Said Nursi and the Nur movement. Secondly, both on state level and in the Islamic movement there has been a strong tendency towards the nationalization and Turkification of Islam. As we shall see, Yahya's method of *da'wa* draws inspiration from the Turkish Nur movement in many respects, including its emphasis on providing evidence for faith. In distinction to the various Nurcu groups, however, Yahya is in particular seeking to reach and persuade secular segments of Turkish society, and this approach is reflected in his Islamic discourse (13kahraman 2012b).

With time, however, Harun Yahya has also become a global actor. While some forms of *da'wa* focus on converting non-Muslims to Islam, other interpret *da'wa* as calling Muslims back to what they regard to be a purer form of religion practiced by the Prophet Muhammad and the early Muslim community (Esposito 2003, p. 64). Some contemporary movements on the other hand, focus on "universal invitation within faith rather than conversion of non-Muslims" (Esposito 2003). As we shall see, Yahya's form of *da'wa* in the global context arguably belongs to the latter category.

Current *da'wa* activities are influenced by globalization. As noted by sociologist Olivier Roy and others, the growth of Islamic "evangelism" can be understood as a product of globalization where influences from for instance American evangelism, has affected *da'wa* methods among Muslims living in the Western world. Roy notes that many contemporary *da'wa* movements share with American evangelism the propensity to "reject culture, philosophy, and even theology to favor a literalist reading of sacred texts and an immediate understanding of truth through individual faith" (Roy 2006).

Sociologist Patrick Haenni also draws parallels between American evangelism and a new generation of Islamic preachers and televangelists that call on followers to reconsider Islam's role in their personal lives rather than focus on political demands (Haenni 2005). He notes how these Islamic preachers resemble American evangelists not only in terms of their talk show-like form of religious broadcasting, but also in the way they construct publishing empires around their personality. Haenni views these new religious preachers as part of a globalized culture he calls "market Islam" (Haenni 2005). Market Islam, in Haenni's analysis, is anti-state, socially conservative and economically liberal. It promotes a market-friendly religiosity that is *bourgeois* and cosmopolitan, and encourages Islamic consumer lifestyles. There is little talk of social justice, instead prosperity is praised and encouraged (Haenni 2005).

These perspectives on contemporary forms of Islamic proselytism challenge the narrow view of Islamic activism as a response to social deprivation or Middle Eastern politics, considering instead Islamic activism in broader terms as a form of faith activism that owes as much to a global religious revival, processes of globalization, the development of new media and an emerging Muslim public sphere (Eickelman & Anderson 2003, p. 1).

## 7.3. Islam as a discursive tradition

In the framework of this dissertation, I am approaching Harun Yahya as someone who claims to be engaged in a struggle for Islam, and the enterprise can therefore be regarded as an Islamic effort. What presuppositions underlie the use of the adjective "Islamic" and the noun "Islam"? In what way is it meaningful to regard the Harun Yahya enterprise as an Islamic effort? In the view of many believers, there is only one true interpretation of Islam.[66] Others – both believers and non-believers – allow for multiple interpretations, but would still hold that there are interpretations – and interpreters – that are disqualified on various grounds. They may hold, for instance, that only those with sufficient scholarly knowledge of Islam and/or formal authority should interpret Islam. From the perspective of the academic study of religion, however, normative statements regarding what Islam is or is not, what it should or should not be, or who is entitled to interpret or represent it, reflect an "insider's" perspective.

The picture painted of the Harun Yahya community by former members, his critics, the Turkish media and the Turkish court, is that of a criminal mafia organization engaging in blackmail and other illegal activities, and as a cult led by a megalomaniac leader. Scholars and non-scholars both in Turkey and elsewhere have warned me that Adnan Oktar is merely "a charlatan", "a criminal" or "a crackpot", and is therefore not worthy of academic study, especially not as a representative of Islam. Daniel M. Varisco, for instance, takes a highly negative view of Yahya and accuses him of "abusing Islam" (Varisco

---

[66] In a recent survey conducted by the Pew Research Center, Muslims were asked whether they believe there is only one true way to understand Islam's teachings or if multiple interpretations are possible. In 32 of the 39 countries surveyed, half or more Muslims say there is only one correct way to understand the teachings of Islam (Bell 2012).

2012). From an analytical point of view however, I believe it is neither prudent nor possible to try to discern between "sincere" and "instrumental" religiosity.

Does this mean that anyone who claims to be a Muslim is a Muslim, or that any statement regarding Islam should be counted as part of Islam? Such an approach would render the notions of Islam and Muslim void as analytical categories. Talal Asad has addressed this paradox in his essay "The Idea of an Anthropology of Islam" and argues that Islam must be understood and approached as "a discursive tradition" (Asad 1986). What makes something Islamic is not some essential characteristic, argues Asad, but rather discursive practices; that is, practices that relate to the founding texts of Islam:

> If one wants to write an anthropology of Islam one should begin, as Muslims do, from the concept of a discursive tradition that includes and relates itself to the founding texts of the Qur'an and the Hadith. Islam is neither a distinctive social structure nor a heterogeneous collection of beliefs, artifacts, customs, and morals. It is a tradition (Asad 1986, p. 14).

Islam is a constantly evolving tradition, and individuals within this tradition construct new interpretations as a response to changing conditions around them. However, the interpretations must also to some extent meet certain demands set by that tradition in order to appear convincing to those who identify themselves as part of that tradition.

Adnan Oktar does not claim to be an Islamic scholar. Instead he often refers to himself as "a humble soldier", or "an ordinary servant of Allah", thus portraying himself as someone serving Islam, rather than as a scholar interpreting Islam.[67] However, any attempt to convey the message of Islam is necessarily an act of interpretation. In works published by the Harun Yahya enterprise, Harun Yahya cites, comments on and interprets the Qur'an, the hadiths and Islamic scholars such as Said Nursi. Islam constitutes the discursive framework and cultural repertoire within which Harun Yahya constructs and formulates his ideas. Thus, regardless of what opinions one may have regarding Adnan Oktar's and his associates' morality, methods, motives or the potential undesirable ramifications of their work, the Harun Yahya enterprise arguably aspires to partaking in the "ongoing conversation" that is the discursive tradition of Islam, and may therefore be analyzed as one among a multitude of voices laying claim to representing Islam in late modernity. Due to their ubiquity and accessibility, the works of Harun Yahya serve as a source of knowledge about

---

[67] "Ben de ne hocayım, ne alimim. Allah'ın aciz bir kuluyum sadece" (I am neither a *hoca* (religious leader) nor an *alim* (religious scholar), I am merely a humble servant of God) (Akkaya 2013). Presenting oneself as "an average guy" is a strategy also used by other popular Islamic preachers, such as Amr Khaled, and may be a way to "circumvent critique when talking about Islam without having the "right" position or education" (Olsson 2013).

Islam for a substantial number of people.[68] The discourse of the Harun Yahya enterprise therefore forms part of a diversity of Islamic discourses that constitute the fragmented bricolage of contemporary Islam.

Asad concludes his essay by arguing that the anthropology of Islam "will therefore seek to understand the historical conditions that enable the production and maintenance of specific discursive traditions, or their transformation – and the efforts of practitioners to achieve coherence" (Asad 1986, p. 23). Islam as a discursive tradition can be seen as a repertoire that both offers opportunities and sets limitations. Islamic discourses are formulated in response to changing environments, challenges and opportunities. In line with this, in this dissertation I seek to understand the historical conditions that enabled the production and maintenance of the discourse of the Harun Yahya enterprise.

This view of Islam as a discursive tradition builds on the theoretical approach of this dissertation that springs from a view of religion as a social construct. Social constructionism is an epistemological paradigm that underpins many contemporary theoretical approaches within the humanities and social sciences. It is not a singular theory, but rather a term used to describe a variety of approaches whose shared characteristics include a critical stance towards taken-for-granted knowledge, emphasis on the historical and cultural specificity of concepts and categories, and the idea that knowledge is sustained by social processes (Burr 2003). In a social constructionist view, the social world is understood as the product of social processes, and from this follows anti-essentialism: The claim that there is no given, determined nature to the world or people (Burr 2003, p. 5). Another implication of a social constructionist view is that meaning is produced collectively, and that it is through language that social reality is constructed.

For our purposes, viewing religion as a social construct has two important theoretical and methodological implications. Firstly, it means that religious ideas, concepts and practices must be understood within a social and cultural context. Secondly, since social reality and meaning is constructed through language, religious ideas must be analyzed as *discourse* that is socially embedded.

## 7.4. The discourse of the Harun Yahya enterprise as rhetoric

I have stated that the main focus of this dissertation is the discourse of the Harun Yahya enterprise. "Discourse" is a complex and much-used term within the academia with a number of different meanings. In a broad sense, "discourse"

---

[68] In a study by Attiya Ahmad on emerging Islamic piety among female migrant workers in Kuwait, one of her informers report reading the books of Harun Yahya, describing them as "scientific" and "practical" Muslim books (Ahmad 2010, p. 300). The Young Bangladeshi informants of Samuel and Rozario also often mentioned the books of Harun Yahya (Samuel & Rozario 2010, p. 432).

is often employed within the humanities and social sciences to express the notion that language, speech, ideas, concepts and practices are socially situated. Discourse in this sense is linked with the notion that ideas are socially constructed, and implies that texts must be understood as products of social contexts rather than as merely the product of the will or intention of an individual agent. The term discourse is especially associated with the works of Michel Foucault, where it is intimately linked with power and ideology. In this study, I do not purport to conduct discourse analysis in the Foucauldian sense. While recognizing that the discourse of Harun Yahya must be understood as a product of a social context, I employ the term discourse in a less specialized manner, to refer to a set of propositions that Yahya puts forward regarding various themes.

In this dissertation, I approach the works of Harun Yahya as religious discourse that incorporates various strategies in order to persuade its readers to accept its various propositions, for instance that the theory of evolution is wrong. The discourse of the Harun Yahya enterprise can therefore be analyzed as *rhetoric*. Jim Kuypers defines rhetoric as "the strategic use of communication, oral or written, to achieve specifiable goals" (Kuypers 2010, p. 288). Rhetorical analysis is concerned with studying and theorizing different techniques and devices of persuasion. While classic rhetoric is associated with the art of persuasion particularly in the political arena, contemporary studies of rhetoric address a broader scope of human discourse, including religious discourse. In this study, I will not conduct rhetorical analysis in the strict sense, but rather borrow concepts and perspectives from the field of rhetorical analysis. I will for instance avail of Stephen O'Leary's analysis of apocalyptic discourse as a form of rhetoric in Chapter 5 (O'Leary 1994).

I will also borrow concepts form the field of rhetorical analysis known as *framing*, defined as "the process by which communicators act – consciously or not – to construct a particular point of view that encourages the facts of a given situation to be viewed in a particular manner" (Kuypers 2009, p. 182). As we shall see, Yahya constructs both past and current events in ways that appear to confirm his religious teachings. Framing is also a concept used in social movement theory, which I will discuss next as a possible perspective from which to view the rhetoric of the Harun Yahya enterprise.

## 7.5. Social movement theory and framing

Much contemporary theorizing around Islamic movements draws from social movement theory. Social movement theory is not one coherent theory, but rather an umbrella term for various theories that seek to explain how social mobilization occurs. In *Islamic Activism: A Social Movement Approach*, Quintan Wiktorowicz seeks to adapt the theoretical framework of contemporary social movement theory to Islamic activism (Wiktorowicz 2004). Wiktorowicz notes that early attempts to understand Islamic movements were rooted in functionalism and regarded Islamic mobilization as fueled by discontent caused by various structural strains, such as the experience of relative deprivation, the growing influence of Western culture, or political grievances (Wiktorowicz 2004). Such strain-based theories have been criticized for being overly simplistic (Wiktorowicz 2004, p. 9). Resource mobilization theory (RMT) was formulated in response to these socio-psychological approaches, and emphasized instead the rational, strategic and organized aspects of collective action. According to RMT, movements rely on the successful mobilization of organizational resources and *movement entrepreneurs* who offer incentives to entice actors to join (Wiktorowicz 2004, p. 10).

However, in addition to grievances, resource availability and movement entrepreneurs, there are also external and contextual factors of opportunity and constraint that affect the success and failure of social movements. The importance of these structures are emphasized within a branch of social movement theory known as the Political Process Model (PPM), where they are referred to as *political opportunity structures*, which I will discuss further in Chapter 2.

Since the 1980s, social movement theorists have also focused on the construction, articulation and dissemination of meaning in social movements, referred to as *framing processes* (Wiktorowicz 2004, p. 15, Snow and Benford 1988), which I deem to be analytically useful for my purposes. The process of framing produces what David Snow and Robert Benford term *collective action frames*, defined as:

> interpretive schemata that simplifies and condenses the world out there by selectively punctuating and encoding objects, situations, events, experiences and sequences of actions within one's present or past experiences (Snow and Benford 1992, p. 137).[69]

According to Snow and Benford, collective action frames are constructed as the participants in a movement negotiate an understanding of what the problem is and who is to blame (diagnostic framing), articulate solutions (prognostic framing) and urge others to act (motivational framing). These are identified as the three *core framing tasks* of a movement. [70] Contemporary social movement theories (SMT), then, emphasize three dimensions as the central dynamics behind social movements: *Mobilizing structures* (e.g. movement entrepreneurs), *political*

---

[69] The concept of frames is generally attributed to Ervin Goffman (Goffman 1974).
[70] Frame salience is related to the extent to which the ideas and beliefs are perceived as central to the targets lives and have "cultural resonance".

*opportunity structures*, and *framing processes*. In the following, I will discuss how these concepts may be beneficial as analytical tools in this dissertation.

Firstly, can the Harun Yahya enterprise be conceived of as Islamic activism? Wiktorowicz defines Islamic activism as "the mobilization of contention to support Muslim causes" (Wiktorowicz 2004, p.2). This is a purposefully broad definition, covering a variety of forms of collective action rooted in Islamic symbols and identities, including propagation movements (Wiktorowicz 2004, p. 2). The Harun Yahya enterprise engages in the propagation of various ideas, including Islamic creationism, and may thus be conceived of as a form of Islamic activism.

Social movement theory has in particular been concerned with contentious politics, i.e. movements that engage in one or more forms of social protest. However, social movement theory has also been employed as theoretical framework to explain the success of movements that are non-contentious. For example, Muhammed Çetin approaches the Gülen movement from a social movement theory perspective, arguing that in distinction to many other social movements, this movement does not seek to alter or overthrow the system, but to effect change from within the system (Cetin 2010).

The Gülen movement is a broadly based transnational civic movement estimated to have several million followers worldwide (Ebaugh 2009). The Harun Yahya enterprise, in comparison, is based on neither grass-root support nor mass mobilization. It is rather a small community numbering at most a few hundred people based in Istanbul, albeit with a potentially massive reach through their books and websites. The Harun Yahya enterprise is thus not a movement in the conventional sense, but it can be understood as a form of collective action. The emergence and continued existence of the Harun Yahya enterprise relies on mobilization of material, human and organizational resources. Hence, key concepts from social movement theory such as *framing*, *opportunity spaces* and *movement entrepreneur* may therefore be useful for understanding the Harun Yahya enterprise.

In this dissertation, I do not intend to employ social movement theory as a fully-fledged methodology, but rather borrow concepts that I argue may be valuable as analytical and descriptive tools in the analysis of the relationship between the rhetoric of the Harun Yahya enterprise and the market in which it operates. One of the main advantages of SMT lies in its potential for linking the Harun Yahya enterprise, its discourse and the context in which it emerged, through the concepts of *movement entrepreneur*, *framing* and *political opportunity*. SMT highlights the dynamic interaction between *agency* (the movement entrepreneur) and *structure* (the socio-political context), through the concept of *framing* as tool for mobilization.

Social theories are often classified in terms of the extent to which they appear to emphasize *structure* or *agency*, that is, the extent to which they understand events, ideas and practices as socially determined, or as produced by the intentions and will of agents. Focusing on the importance of the social and political context runs the risk of social determinism, that is, overemphasizing the causal role of the social context to the extent that the initiative, will and personal choice of individual agents disappears from sight. Many contemporary social theories attempt to strike a balance between structure and agency, and to underscore the dynamic interplay between the two (Ritzer & Goodman 2004, p. 378). I concur with linguist Norman Fairclough that "social agents are not 'free' agents, they are socially constrained, but nor are their actions totally socially determined" (Fairclough 2003, p. 22). In my approach to the Harun Yahya enterprise, I therefore seek to combine theoretical approaches and methods in such a way as to be able to highlight the dynamic interplay between structure and agency. Following SMT, Islamic activism is neither understood merely as a product of structural factors, nor as a "solo performance in which the doctrine or biography of one actor at a time causes that actor's behavior" (Wiktorowicz 2004, p. x).

The emergence and continued existence of the Harun Yahya enterprise depend on the one hand on the presence of a *movement entrepreneur*, Adnan Oktar, and the mobilization of various resources: Financial resources, organizational resources and human resources who are involved in business, research, writing, translation, managing a large number of websites, organizing conferences, and so on.

The notion of *opportunity structures* may be a valuable contribution with regards to addressing the question of why the Harun Yahya enterprise emerged *when* and *where* it did, and why it focuses on the themes it does. Part of the purpose of the context that will be provided is to locate the ideas of Harun Yahya both within the history of Islamic thought in Turkey as well as within global currents. However, I wish to underline that I do not understand the Harun Yahya enterprise as merely idea-driven. As I will argue, it must also be understood in context of a broader mobilization of political Islam, and here SMT offers tools for considering structural factors. Social movement theory models have already been employed by political scientists in order to explain the mobilization of political Islam in Turkey (Eligür 2010; Yavuz 2003). Eligür employs the term *political opportunity structures* while Hakan Yavuz employs the term *opportunity spaces* to describe various factors that contributed to the Islamic revival and the mobilization of political Islam in Turkey. In Chapter 2, I will draw on both these scholars in my account of the Turkish context.

I will also employ the concept of *framing*. While frame analysis is a specific methodology within social movement theory, the concept of framing in a more general sense has gained currency within the social sciences, and is used in a meaning akin to that of discourse. The aim of the Harun Yahya enterprise is, as I understand it, to reach and convince as many people as possible. In order for the enterprise to be successful it has to be able to mobilize resources for the cause. I therefore suggest that the discourse of Harun Yahya may be conceived of in terms of diagnostic, prognostic and motivational *frames* that mobilize action and construct meaning for the participants in the Harun Yahya enterprise, and as *rhetoric* that aims to convince a larger audience of readers and sympathizers.

This perspective is also in line with the above discussion of Islam as a discursive tradition and religion as a social construction. Rather than regarding Yahya's ideas as "pre-given" or emanating from some objectified notion of Islam, the concept of framing allows me to view those involved in the Harun Yahya enterprise as "signifying agents actively engaged in the production and maintenance of meaning for constituents, antagonists, and bystanders or observers" (Benford & Snow 2000, p. 613). *Essentialism*, the reducing of Islamic activism to a product of an Islamic "mentality", is thus avoided.

## 8. Outline of chapters

Although the Harun Yahya enterprise is now a global enterprise, it emerged in the Turkish context, and sought to establish itself within the multitude of other Islamic movements and communities that gave shape to the Islamic revival Turkey in the 1980s and 1990s. Chapter 2 therefore introduces the Turkish context in which Harun Yahya emerged, focusing in particular on the dynamic interplay between modernity, Islam and nationalism as the driving forces of modern Turkish history, the development of various Islamic discourses and the immediate context of the post-coup environment of the 1980s in which the Harun Yahya enterprise emerged.

Chapter 3 focuses on how Harun Yahya has adapted and employed various popular discourses in Turkey. I seek to offer explanations both for why Yahya have focused on these particular themes in his works, as well as explaining changes in his discourse over time. The chapter examines conspiracy theories as a theme in Yahya's works, and analyzes these themes in relation to the Turkish context. It examines anti-Semitic rhetoric in the works of Harun Yahya, and seeks to explain why this rhetoric is gradually shed in favor of a more ecumenical discourse. It also traces the employment and development of nationalist themes in the works of Harun Yahya, from Atatürkist nationalism to neo-Ottomanism.

Chapter 4 contextualizes, describes and analyzes Harun Yahya's creationist discourse. It traces the emergence of Islamic creationism in Turkey, and examines how Yahya has developed his particular brand of creationism by drawing on both Turkish and Protestant creationist material. It analyzes Yahya's arguments against evolution and for creation, and addresses the question of why creationism has come to take such a prominent place in the discourse of Harun Yahya. Chapter 5 examines Harun Yahya's works dealing with apocalypticism. The chapter describes *what* Harun Yahya teaches regarding the Mahdi and the End Times, *how* he argues and what sources and strategies he employs to support his interpretations. The chapter also analyzes *why* the messianic figure of the Mahdi and the notion of an imminent End Times occupy such a pivotal position in the discourse of the Harun Yahya enterprise. Chapter 7 draws together the conclusions of the preceding chapters into a final analysis.

## 9. Notes on transliteration and translation

I have used modern Turkish orthography not only for words of Turkish origin, but also for words of Arabic or Persian origin when they appear in a Turkish context (textually or culturally). For example, I use the term *cemaat* (Ar. *jama'a*) to denote a religious community, as this is a much-used term in the Turkish context. For Arabic terms that have entered English vocabulary such as *hadith*, I use the English transliteration of the Arabic *hadith* and not *hadis*, the modern Turkish orthography.

Pronunciation of Turkish modern letters that have not been transliterated:

c j as in John
ç ch as in *church*
ş sh as in *ship*
ı io as in *motion*, or e as in *women*
ö French eu as in *deux*
ü French u as in *durée*
ğ unvocalized, lengthens preceding vowel

Unless otherwise indicated in the notes, the translations from foreign language sources are by the author. Hence, when citing Yahya's early works in Turkish I will not specify that the citations are translations, as this will be apparent from the fact that I refer to Turkish titles. I use the Sahih International translation of the Qur'an available from Quran.com, apart from when citing Harun Yahya's translations of the Qur'an. Yahya indicates in his Turkish works that he is using a translation of Ali Bulaç (Bulaç 1983), while referring to a translation by Abdalhaqq & Bewley in his English works (Bewley & Bewley 1999).

CHAPTER 2
# The Turkish Context

## 1. Introduction

The purpose of this chapter is to examine the Turkish context in which Harun Yahya emerged. My point of departure is the proposal that the emergence of the Harun Yahya enterprise and the particular Islamic discourse it promotes must be understood within the context of the Islamic revival and the development of nationalist and Islamic discourses in Turkey. While Islamic revivalism is a global phenomenon, the way in which it has unfolded in Turkey has been shaped by sociopolitical and historical conditions particular to Turkey. The history of modern Turkey has been shaped through the dynamic interaction between three forces or reference points: Islam, nationalism and modernity (Findley 2010).

As someone involved in *tabligh*, preaching (about) Islam, Harun Yahya is a stakeholder in the articulation of Islam in the contemporary setting, and his ideas and teachings must be traced to and grasped within the intellectual context in which he emerged. The Harun Yahya enterprise is a religious community united around a charismatic leader, representing a distinct in-group identity within the multitude of pro-Islamic communities and movements in contemporary Turkey. Its emergence and continued existence as a community must therefore be located within this diversity. In this chapter I will thus attempt to map out both the discursive field and the sociopolitical conditions out of which the Harun Yahya enterprise emerged. The chapter is divided into three main parts. The first part gives a brief chronological introduction to modern Turkish history, from the late Ottoman Empire and the transition to a Turkish national state, to the present. The second part analyzes the discursive field out of which Harun Yahya has emerged, tracing historically the currents, movements and ideas that have given shape to Harun Yahya's Islamic discourse, and focusing in particular on Said Nursi and the Nur movement. The third part focuses on the more immediate sociopolitical context that the Harun Yahya enterprise emerged out of, namely the post-coup environment of the 1980s and the Islamic revival that followed in its wake. The distinction between these three parts should not be understood as clear-cut, but rather reflects interconnected perspectives.

## 2. General background: Modern Turkey

### 2.1. Late Ottoman Empire and the birth of the Turkish republic

The history of modern Turkey is quite unique in the Muslim world.[1] Although other Muslim countries have also undergone secularizing reforms in the 20th century, the reforms pushed through under the leadership of Mustafa Kemal Atatürk in the 1920s and 1930s was arguably the most radical secularization program ever attempted in a country with a Muslim majority (Göle 2001, p. 19). Turkish modernity was not born with the foundation of the republic, however. Westernization began in the 19th century, during the Tanzimat era (1839–1876), when a number of modernizing reforms where implemented in order to combat the decline of the Ottoman Empire and curb nationalist tendencies throughout the territories of the empire. Rising nationalist consciousness also influenced Ottoman intellectuals. Some of the bureaucrats from the Tanzimat period founded *Yeni Osmanlılar* (The Young Ottomans) in 1865, a secret Turkish nationalist organization calling for further reforms and the establishment of a constitutional government. The Young Ottomans were followed by the Young Turks movement and its political organization the Committee of Union and Progress, who staged a revolution against Sultan Abdülhamid and established a constitutional government in 1908.[2]

In the late Ottoman period, a number of competing and converging ideas and currents were circulating among Ottoman intellectuals: Nationalism, Ottomanism, pan-Islamism and Turkism, as well as Western ideas of secularization. Namık Kemal, the most prominent member of the Young Ottomans, sought to synthesize Western ideas of modernization with Islam (Helvaci 2010). Ziya Gökalp (1876–1924), the main ideologue of CUP, was an ardent nationalist and tried to combine nationalism with Islam. He thought Islam should be taken as a purely ethical religion, free from all legal and social rules, and saw no contradiction in adopting European civilization alongside Islamic values (Poulton 1997, p. 77). Other leading members of the Young Turk movement were influenced by materialist and positivist ideas that began circulating among the Ottoman intelligentsia in the later part of the 19th century. Abdullah Cevdet (1869–1932), one of the founding members of the CUP, was not only an ardent defender of Western values, but also an atheist and materialist (Özdalga 1998). Influenced by the ideas of the German materialist philosopher Ludwig Büchner (1824–1899) and the French positivist Auguste Comte (1798–1857), the radical

---

[1] I use the term Muslim world here in the geo-political sense, as referring to Muslim-majority countries or regions.
[2] The Committee of Union and Progress was the official name of the party of the Young Turks, who ruled the former Ottoman Empire between 1908 and 1918.

fraction of the Young Turks promoted a crude kind of materialism dominated by positivism, empiricism, realism and evolutionism, and saw Islam as an obstacle on the way to progress (Güzel 2007; Riexinger 2009; Mardin 2005).

This radical materialist and positivist current became influential in the Young Turk movement in the early 20th century and influenced the founders of the republic and Kemalist ideology (Hanioğlu 2012). Mustafa Kemal (1881-1938) and his collaborators initially sought to appeal to Islam in the struggle against the Greeks during the Turkish War of Independence (1919-1923), but were ultimately convinced that Islam and Turkish nationalism were incompatible (Poulton 1997). In the end, Ottomanism gave way to Turkish nationalism, and attempts to synthesize Islam and modernization gave way to radical secularizing ideas. Turkishness replaced Islam as the basis for governing legitimacy, and secularist nationalism inspired by materialist ideas was pitted against Islamic identity, which was associated with the Ottoman era and with backwardness. This in turn shaped the formulation of Islamic discourses in Turkey, and as we shall see, the Islamic modernist movement founded by Said Nursi in particular.

## 2.2. The modern Turkish republic

The modern Turkish republic was established in 1923 as the successor state to the Ottoman Empire, one of the largest and longest lasting empires in history. Through the institution of the caliphate – the succession to the Prophet Muhammed (570-632) – the Ottoman sultans were also the symbolic leaders of the Islamic world, until Mustafa Kemal Atatürk formally abolished the caliphate in 1924.[3] Under the banner of modernization, Atatürk initiated a series of secularizing reforms. He abandoned sharia law, ordered the closure of religious schools and Sufi lodges and banned the *tarikats* (Sufi orders). These orders were not eradicated, however, and especially the Nakşibendi orders continued to be influential and would provide the structure for the social, political and cultural Islamic movements that would later emerge.

Atatürk's modernization program was eventually consolidated into the six "arrows" of official Kemalist ideology: Republicanism, populism, secularism, revolutionism, nationalism and statism. Secularism or *laïcité* was undoubtedly the core element of this ideology, and would also prove to be the most contested one. The clause that declared Islam as state religion was removed from the constitution in 1928, and the state was officially declared secular in 1937. Turkish *laiklik* differs significantly from both French *laïcité* and other forms of secularism. The French concept of *laïcité* is normally understood to refer to the absence of religious involvement in government affairs and the absence of state involvement in religious affairs, the aim being separation of church and state and the privatization

---

[3] At that time he was only Mustafa Kemal. He was given the surname Atatürk, father of the Turks, in 1935 when surnames were introduced in Turkey.

of religion. However, Kemalist *laiklik* is not merely concerned with limiting the influence of religion and separating religion from the state, but also with placing it under strict state control. The Kemalist state sought to monopolize religion and become the only supplier of its own version of religion, destroying and marginalizing "unofficial" religious forces (Webb 2007). Replacing the *Şeyhülislam* of Ottoman times, the Grand Assembly established the Turkish Presidency of Religious Affairs (the Diyanet) in 1924, and this institution has since been the highest religious authority in the country, and a key instrument in an effort to create an "enlightened" and nationalized Islam in the service of the nation state building project. In the early Republican period, however, the *Diyanet* was largely a purely administrative body with minimal functions.

Atatürk's radical secularization policies mostly affected the urban centers, widening the gap between an urban elite espousing Kemalism as a form of civic religion, and the largely Muslim population. A multi-party system was introduced in 1946, and in 1950, *Demokrat Partisi* (the Democrat Party – DP) won a landslide victory, partly due to its appeal to the religious sensibilities of the masses. The strict secularist policies were softened somewhat, leading to a gradual re-emergence of Islam. A theological faculty was set up at Ankara University, and religious high schools known as *Imam-Hatip* were set up for the training of imams and preachers. The Diyanet's status expanded from a purely administrative body to a national religious institution mentioned in the 1961 Constitution, which was implemented after a military coup in 1960. The unpopular obligation for the *ezan* (the call to prayer) to be read in Turkish was lifted. Despite these liberalizing measures, the Democrat Party was still firmly opposed to any form of politicization of Islam. The 1961 constitution reaffirmed the secular character of the state, but in practice there was little difference from the 1950s. Islamic and conservative currents were pitted against growing left-wing radicalism, and the Nur movement (see below) grew stronger. Islamic thought at the time emphasized the essential importance of Islam as part of "Turkishness" and national identity (Yildiz 2006, p. 43).

## 2.3. 1970s and 1980s: The rise of political Islam

The 1970s saw the growth of political Islam and the *Milli Görüş* (National Outlook) movement; the formation of which the Nakşibendi İskenderpaşa Sufi lodge led by *şeyh* Mehmed Zahid Kotku (1897–1980) played a crucial role.[4] Named so after a manifesto written by Necmettin Erbakan, the Milli Görüş movement equated nation and religion in a form of "Islamist nationalism".

---

[4] *Şeyh* (Arabic: Sheik) is used here in the sense of Sufi leader or teacher. This is the sense in which the term is usually used in Turkey. The meaning of the word "sheik" in Arabic is "elder" or "leader", and in Arab contexts it is often used as an honorific term to refer to an Islamic scholar or tribal leader.

Invoking Turkey's heroic Ottoman past, it argued that "a Turkey great once again" required a return to Islamic values and a strengthening of its Islamic identity. The Milli Görüş movement founded a succession of Islamist political parties under the leadership of Erbakan. First appearing as *Milli Nizam Partisi* (MNP – The National Order Party) in 1970, its heyday was under the name *Refah Party* (RP – The Welfare Party) (1983–1998). Throughout the 1970s, Turkish society was polarized by intense sectarian and ideological conflict. The military decided to step in to end the cycle of left-right violence, and carried out a military coup on 12 September 1980. The coup leaders perceived militant leftism as the greatest threat to the country's stability, and therefore utilized Islamic institutions and symbols in an attempt to bridle the ideological conflicts riddling the country. The state attempted to fuse religious and national identity, and an ideology referred to as *Türk-İslam Sentezi* (the Turkish-Islamic synthesis) achieved a semi-official status for a time. These changes paved the way for a greater role for Islam both in public space and in politics. The center-right government led by Turgut Özal – an ethnic Kurd with strong connections to the Nakşibendi *tarikat* – led to religious ideology entering into important state bodies such as the Ministry of Education. It was Özal's minister of education Vehbi Dinçerler who took the initiative to introduce creationism in schools, which I will return to in Chapter 4. Religious education was made compulsory, and there was a marked increase in the budget of the Diyanet and an increase in religious personnel.

This greater emphasis on Islam as an important part of Turkish identity and as a basis for morality contributed to a resurgence in religious activity and consciousness in the 1980s (Tapper 1994, p. 3). Özal's liberalization policies and privatization of the media enabled Islamic activists to propagate their message to a broader audience. There was a proliferation of new Islamic radio and TV channels, as well as a host of Islamic publications, magazines and newspapers. A new class of Islamic intellectuals emerged, who often challenged both the secular order and the official Islam of the Diyanet (Yildiz 2006; Meeker 1994). The old Sufi *tarikats* transformed into *cemaats*, well-organized civil society organizations which functioned as strong social and business networks, aiding the emergence of a new Muslim *bourgeoisie*.[5]

The rise of political Islam culminated in a coalition government between the Islamist *Refah Partisi* (Welfare Party) and the rightist *Doğru Yol Partisi* (True

---

[5] Meaning path or method, a *tarikat* is a Sufi order or brotherhood. *Cemaat* is a broader term denoting religious community. Bekim Agai explains the difference between *tarikat* and *cemaat* thus: "Cemaat can be defined as the combination of a specific discourse with certain forms of social relations. Unlike a Sufi brotherhood, the cemaat has no formal act to bestow membership. Indeed affiliation can only be gained through a transactional process of mutual acknowledgment of the personal commitment to the cemaat, its aims and hierarchies" (Agai 2007, p. 157).

Path Party), in which Necmettin Erbakan was made prime minister in 1996. This lead to what has been called "the soft coup", where the Kemalist military-bureaucratic establishment forced the prime minister to resign, and set up a number of measures to restrict the increasing influence of political Islam. The proliferation of Islamic activism and the liberalizing policies of the state also led to a greater diversity in the Islamic discourse throughout the 80s and 90s. The idioms of democracy and human rights were incorporated, and many Muslim intellectuals adopted a more universal discourse of basic rights and liberties, departing from the nationalist conservatism dominating the discourse in previous decades (Yildiz 2006). These transformations eventually led to a split in the Islamic political movement into a traditional and reformist camp. The reformist camp founded AKP, the post-Islamist party that won a landslide election in 2002, and is still currently in power in Turkey (2013).

## 2.4. Approaches to Turkish modernity and Islam

In recent decades, many scholars have criticized the presentation of the birth of the Turkish republic as an "epistemological break", emphasizing instead continuity with the late Ottoman Empire (Mardin 2005; Findley 2010). Early accounts of the emergence of Turkish modernity were much influenced by modernization theory (Lewis 1961). Findley writes that the greatest flaw of these earlier histories was the "teleological vision of an upward march from Islamic empire to secular republic" (Findley 2010, p. 1). I concur with this critique. More recent accounts challenge this view, regarding the driving force of change as "reformist dynamism" rather than a radical break with the Ottoman past. This recent scholarship is closely linked with a more general critique of modernization theory within academia. Modern Turkey was viewed by modernization theorists as a shining example of how modernization leads to secularization. However, the Islamic resurgence gaining momentum from the 1970s onwards indicates the complexity of Turkish modernism and the shortcomings of the secularization thesis.[6]

Carter Vaughn Findley proposes instead the thesis that the emergence of modernity in Turkey should not be understood in terms of the "development of secularism", but rather in terms of the dialectical interaction between two approaches to modernity; a secular current and a conservative Islamic current (Findley 2010).[7] Although these currents interacted, in certain moments they

---

[6] For a more general discussion on the secularization thesis and the revitalization of Islam, see Bruinessen (2007, p. 283)

[7] Findley does not define what he means by "conservative" in this context, I therefore assume that it refers to the general understanding of conservatism as denoting the political and social viewpoint that emphasizes the value of traditional institutions and practices and supports only gradual or minimal changes in society (Britannica Online). This is also the sense in which I will use the term.

met in antagonistic clashes. The state-led secularizing policies led to a polarization of society and contributed to the emergence of Islamic movements that challenged the secularist hegemonic discourse. According to political scientist Hakan Yavuz, the efforts on the part of Islamic social movements to try to revitalize Ottoman-Islamic culture have led to the "vernacularization of modernity" – the redefining of the discourses of modernity in Islamic terms – and a form of internal secularization of Islam in terms of rationalization, nationalization, and the accommodation of faith to the overriding exigencies of reason and evidence (Yavuz 2003, p. 5).[8] I will return to this notion below in my analysis of the Harun Yahya enterprise.

Two recurring themes in the discourse of Islamic movements in Turkey are particularly significant for our purpose of contextualizing the Harun Yahya enterprise: Firstly, the attempt to counter irreligion by synthesizing religion and science and presenting an evidence-based faith. This current is represented most comprehensively by Said Nursi and the Nur movement. Secondly, both on state level and in the Islamic movement there has been a strong tendency towards the nationalization and Turkification of Islam. Rather than a blank rejection of modernity then, Islamism in Turkey may rather, as Yavuz suggests, be understood in terms of its engagement with various elements of modernity and attempts to accommodate these within an Islamic framework. The remainder of this chapter will deal with Islamic discourses in Turkey in a broad sense, both the various discourses it encompasses and the socio-political conditions that facilitated it.

## 3. The discursive field: Islamic thought in Turkey

The development of Islamism and Islamic discourses in modern Turkey must be grasped in the context of the global Islamic revival of the 20th century, and the emergence of political Islam as a global phenomenon. At the same time, due to its unique history, the manner in which these discourses and movements have evolved is specific to Turkey. In the following, I will reserve the term Islamism to denote the overt politicization of Islam in terms of advocating the reordering of government and society in accordance with laws prescribed by Islam. I will use the term pro-Islamic to denote Islamism in a looser and broader sense, encompassing the goals of Islamic movements as defined by Hakan Yavuz: "Islamic movements seek to reconstitute identities, institutional structures, ways of life, and the moral code of society through participating, influencing, or controlling cultural, educational and economic spheres" (Yavuz 2003, p. 23). In terms of the vision and strategies of Islamic movements in Turkey, a distinction

---

[8] Hakan Yavuz, assistant professor in political science at Utah University, is the author of several influential works on the development of political Islam in Turkey.

may be made between faith-based Islamic movements which emphasize religion as a basis for morality and identity and seek to transform individuals and society, and political Islamic movements which seek to attain political power, although this distinction is far from clear-cut. The Nur movement falls most comfortably into the first category, and since the Harun Yahya enterprise may also be regarded as affiliated with the Nur movement, it is the most relevant category for our purposes.

The most prominent *Leitmotif* in the history of modern Turkey is an alleged cultural and political struggle between secularists and Islamists. However, there is no simple binary opposition between pro-Islamic and republican nationalist ideologies. Rather, in Turkish intellectual circles there has been a multitude of different currents and ideologies converging, intersecting, competing and clashing at various times. These various currents, debates and configurations of ideas can be conceptualized as a discursive field, which can be defined as "the discursive terrain(s) in which meaning contests occur" (Snow et al. 2004). The purpose of this section is to map out the discursive context that the Harun Yahya enterprise emerged out of. The section is divided into two main parts. The first part focuses on Said Nursi and the Nur movement. As we shall see, Said Nursi is a major point of reference in the works of Harun Yahya, and his life and works are therefore outlined in some detail. The second part focuses on identifying and outlining a number of other themes that are relevant for understanding the intellectual and political context out of which that Harun Yahya emerged.

## 3.1 Said Nursi and the Nur movement

### 3.1.1. Islamic modernism in Turkey

The emergence of Islamic modernism is understood partly as a response to political events in the aftermath of the disintegration of Muslim empires and the subsequent domination in the region by Western powers, and denotes the efforts by Muslim scholars to bridge the gap between Islam and European Enlightenment (Moaddel 2005). In the late Ottoman period, conservative *ulama* in Turkey and also the Nakşibendi orders generally defended a view of the Qur'an and Islamic law as the sole source of wisdom (Özdalga 1998). However, some more reform-minded Ottoman Islamists influenced by the ideas of al-Afghani (1838–1897) and Muhammad Abduh (1849–1905) contended that Islam needed to be re-interpreted in order to demonstrate its compatibility with modernization. The most comprehensive attempt to formulate a synthesis between Islam and modernity in Turkey, however, was formulated by the Kurdish Muslim scholar Said Nursi (1878–1960). Said Nursi is considered to be one of the most important architects of Islamic thought in modern Turkey

(Abu-Rabi 2010). Taking Nursi's 6000-page opus magnum *Risale-i Nur* as its basis, the faith movement(s) founded by Nursi were an important factor in shaping the Islamic revival that gained momentum in Turkey from the 1970s and onwards.[9] Aside from the Qur'an, Said Nursi's *Risale-i Nur* is the most significant Islamic point of reference in the writings of Harun Yahya. The life and teachings of Said Nursi and the emergence of the Nur movement therefore warrants closer examination.

### 3.1.2. The life of Said Nursi

Said Nursi was born in 1876 in the Nurs Village in the Bitlis province of Eastern Anatolia. His life is generally divided into two periods: the Early Said (1876–1925) and the New Said (1925–1960), marking a transition from a more politically active Said to Said the religious reformer (Çakır 1990).[10] During his youth, Nursi studied at various *medreses* and received religious training from *şeyhs* of the Nakşibendi-Halidi branch.[11] He gradually gained a reputation as an independent mind and a learned religious scholar, earning him the nickname Bediüzzaman (the Wonder of the Age) at the age of 21. Although he never joined any Sufi *tarikat* and later declared that "this is not the time for *tarikat*, but the time for saving the faith",[12] he recognized the importance of Sufism for Islam in Turkey and was himself influenced by Sufi ideas. He was critical of the imitative learning aspect of traditional Sufism, however, and came to believe that modern times required the grounding of faith in reason and inquiry. He began to realize the insufficiency of traditional Islamic theology with regards to effectively responding to the challenges of the modern world, and therefore began to study modern science as well as current affairs (Vahide 2005, p. 27).

The "Early Said" was politically active and concerned with saving the Ottoman-Islamic state. Moving in the circles of the new Ottoman intellectuals, he initially supported the Young Turk movement and their work towards constitutional reform. He soon grew critical of the Committee of Union and Progress (CUP), however, and became instead involved with *İttihad-i Muhammedi* (Muhammedan Union), who staged a revolt against the CUP in 1909. Nursi was strongly critical of the British occupation of Istanbul (1918–1923), and initially mobilized behind the Turkish liberation struggle led by

---

[9] The collected corpus of Nursi's texts is titled the *Risale-i Nur Külliyatı* (Treatise of Divine Light). Nursi's followers are therefore referred to as *Nurcu* (Nurist). *Nurculuk* refers to the Nur movement or the current of thought. The term *Nur talebeleri* (students of light) is generally reserved for the closer circle of followers around Nursi.
[10] For more detailed accounts of Nursi's life and thought, see Tapper (1994, p. 2), Mardin (1989) and Vahide (2005).
[11] *Medrese* denotes a religious school (Ar. *madrasa*).
[12] "*Zaman tarikat zamanı değildir, imanı kurtarma zamanıdır*" (Nursi 2004a, p. 61).

Atatürk and the nationalist leaders. Nursi soon became aware of the radically secularizing plans of the new political elite, however.

The "New Said" turned to spiritual matters and was concerned with saving the faith. As it became increasingly clear that the new leaders intended to minimize the influence of religion in Turkey, Said Nursi became convinced that rather than challenging the political system, the way to go forward was to devote all his efforts on revitalizing and strengthening the faith of Muslim believers. He became convinced that the rejuvenation of Islam had to take place at the level of the individual rather than the state. Although the Turkish state saw Said Nursi as a threat to the secular regime, Nursi did not overtly try to reinstate the rule of sharia law or call for an overthrowing of the secular laws of Turkey. Instead, he believed that positive change could come about through the fostering of a Muslim consciousness among the broader population. He rejected the notion of using Islam as a tool to empower the state, and focused instead on the normative aspect of religion as the basis for morality and identity (Yavuz 2003, p. 156).

In what he describes as a spiritual awakening, Nursi decided that he should take the Qur'an alone as his "sole guide to the essence of reality", employing both heart and mind (Vahide 2005, p. 166). Nursi set out to prove the superiority of the Qur'an and at the same time refute materialist and positivist philosophy and show that they are both irrational and destructive for society. In Nursi's view, irreligion was the source of a host of societal problems. He argued that all virtues such as justice, love and peace come from faith, while the evils of the world – poverty, chaos, egoism – all come from lack of faith (Nursi 2004a, p. 1729 and pp. 1841–42).[13] He believed that the greatest threat to Islam was the eroding of religious belief as a result of materialist and positivist ideas from the West. He therefore set out to strengthen faith and counter the influence of positivist and materialist philosophy by creating an Islamic counter-discourse based on a synthesis of faith and science, and explaining the Qur'an in a manner adapted to the modern times.

### 3.1.3. The Risale-i Nur

This, then, became the path of the *Risale-i Nur,* the textual basis of the Nur movement. Nursi's texts were copied and distributed to emerging Nur communities around the country by a special postal system known as *Nur postacıları* (the Nurcu postmen). The Kemalist authorities were concerned over Nursi's growing influence and saw him as a potential threat. Nursi and his followers were therefore arrested and tried on charges of establishing a secret

---

[13] Most of the main volumes of the *Risale-i Nur* collection have been translated into English. There are no official translations of *Kastamonu Lahikası* and *Emirdağ Lahikası* however, which consist of letters written by Said Nursi to his students while he was in Kastamonu and Emirdağ respectively.

religious society, and Nursi spent a large part of his life in forced exiles and prisons in various places in Turkey. Most of the *Risale-i Nur* was produced between 1925 and 1933, when Nursi was in exile in Sparta for his religious activities. Consisting of 14 volumes and around 6000 pages, the *Risale-i Nur* is not a *tafsir* in the traditional sense, but rather an elaborate commentary on the Qur'an that aims to rejuvenate faith by explaining the basic principles and doctrines of faith to ordinary believers in modern terms. It is written in a language ripe with allegories, which Nursi claims are a form of "telescopes" that brings truth closer to view. According to Yavuz, the major objectives of *Risale-i Nur* were "first, to raise the consciousness of Muslims; second, to refute the dominant intellectual discourses of materialism and positivism; third, to recover collective memory by revising the shared grammar of society, Islam" (Yavuz 2003, p. 157).

In terms of theology, Said Nursi advocated classical Sunni Asharite *kalam* (Mermer & Ameur 2004).[14] The innovative element was the way in which he attempted to reformulate Qur'anic exegesis in the light of modern knowledge. The "Old Said" had sought the blending of science and Islamic studies through the establishment of a university. The method of the "New Said" however, was to apply a "Qur'anic vision" and reflect upon all things and beings in terms of their meaning (*mana-yı harfî*). Thus, Nursi developed a form of natural theology, whereby nature has meaning as attestation to "the truths of belief". Rather than casting doubt on the reality of the universe such as some Sufis and mystics, Nursi regarded "reading the book of the universe" as a way to knowledge of God the creator:

> I saw that rather than banishing or forgetting or not recalling the universe like the Sufis and mystics in order to gain permanent access to the divine presence, the universe gains a sense of the divine presence as broad as the universe, and that a sphere of worship opens up as broad and universal and permanent as the universe (Nursi 2004b, pp. 172–173).[15]

According to Nursi, belief is the only way to true happiness. He distinguished between imitative faith (*taklidi iman*) and faith by inquiry (*tahkiki iman*), arguing that by replacing the former with the latter, Muslims would be able to resist materialism and atheism. In his view, fulfillment and moral character emanate from the God-centered worldview that follows from internalizing "the

---

[14] *Ilm al-Kalam* refers to an Islamic discipline of systematic theology. Etga Uğur argues that although the majority of Turks are Hanafis and follow the Maturidi teachings on *kalam*, Asharite mentality dominated the Ottoman institutions after the 15th century. See Uğur (2004).
[15] English translation by Şükran Vahide.

truth of the Quran". As we shall see in Chapter 4, these ideas are carried forward in the works of Harun Yahya.

Nursi also wrote extensively on eschatology. He saw the present time as a dark period, but believed in a bright future for Islam. He made extensive use of apocalyptic themes, which he related to the present and current events. While these interpretations do not figure prominently in contemporary Nurcu discourse, they provide a framework for Harun Yahya's apocalypticism both in terms of content and method. As we shall see in Chapter 5, Harun Yahya employs Nursi's ideas concerning a coming Golden Age for Islam and the Mahdi as a blueprint for the efforts of the Harun Yahya enterprise.

### 3.1.4. The "Third Said" and the expansion of the Nur movement

Said Nursi sought to form a strong collectivity of pious individuals working towards the same aim: Serving the *Risale-i Nur* and Islam. From this emerged the Nur movement, or *Hizmet* (The Service), as the members commonly self-identify, which in its various manifestations would have an immense impact upon the Islamic revival in Turkey. The last 10-year period of Nursi's life is referred to by some as "Third Said" (Vahide 2005). This was a period where Nursi actively encouraged his followers to wage a "Jihad of the Word" (*cihad-i manevi*) against irreligion and atheism, and to step up the spreading of the *Risale-i Nur*, thus consolidating the missionary character of the Nur movement. Nursi also sought to spread the *Risale-i Nur* outside of Turkey, which the Nur movement still continues to do.[16]

In this "Third Said" period, Nursi's writings reflect a return to a preoccupation with politics and activism, which illustrates that the previously mentioned dividing line between faith-based and political Islamic activism is far from distinct. In this last period Nursi also began advocating cooperation between Christians and Muslims in combating atheism. This view of Christians as potential allies in the battle against irreligion has become an important element of contemporary Nurcu discourse, in particular the Gülen movement's emphasis on "inter-civilizational dialogue".[17] As we shall see, this ecumenical discourse is also appropriated by Harun Yahya.

The primacy given to the *Risale-i Nur* is one of the most striking features of the Nur movement. After Nursi's death in 1960, the Nur movement's distinctive character as a textual community was consolidated. Nurcu *dersanes*, study circles where the *Risale-i Nur* texts are studied and which still today constitute the core activity of the Nur movement, began cropping up all across the country.

---

[16] The Nur movement is continuously working to have the works of Nursi translated to other languages, and some Nur communities are actively setting up reading groups in other countries, in the Balkans among other places. See Solberg (2007).
[17] I will describe the Gülen movement further in section 4.5.

With time, the Nur movement split into various subgroups, with their own magazines and newspapers. The by far most influential of these is the Gülen movement, which is sometimes referred to as a "neo-Nur community" and differs markedly from the other groups both in terms of its approach and the prominent position of its leader, Fethullah Gülen (Yavuz & Esposito 2003).

The primary aim of the Nur movement is to revitalize and strengthen the faith. As a part of this, the movement has also sought to obstruct what they see as the two great dangers to the Turkish nation: Irreligion and communism (Işık 1990). In the 1970s, the Nur movement and particularly the influential Yeni Asya branch became a "nationalist-religious" (*milliyetçi-mukaddesatçı*) front against rising leftist activism. Many Nurcus became involved with "The Association to Fight Against Communism" (*Komünizmle Mücadele Derneği*) – among them Fethullah Gülen – and presented Islamic faith as an antidote to communism (Yavuz 2003, p. 174). The emphasis on Turkishness and anti-communism was a prominent element of the discourse of the Gülen movement, particularly in its early days. Generally shying away from overtly Islamist parties and instead tending to vote for rightist or center-right parties, the notion of "saving the nation and country from anarchy" (Nursi 2004a, p. 21) has continued to be an important aim of the Nur movement in addition to the primary aim of strengthening and renewing the faith (Abu-Rabi 2008, p. 4).

Representing a new form of religious community different from the traditional Sufi brotherhoods, the Nur movement can be seen as a form of prototype of contemporary Islamic revivalist movements in Turkey. It pioneered a type of Islamic activism focused on strengthening faith among ordinary believers and thus effecting change on the level of the individual and the society, rather than trying to change the political system or Islamizing the state. It has had a major impact on the Islamic revival and the trajectory of Islamic discourse in Turkey. The texts of Said Nursi and the Nur movement's engagement with these texts in Nurcu magazines and newspapers have contributed to the prominence of a "print-based Islamic discourse" in the Islamic revival in Turkey. Islamic magazines and newspapers became an important arena for the dissemination of ideas, and constituted an alternative discourse to both the official Islamic discourse of the Diyanet, as well as the Sufism of the *tarikats*. In the words of Hakan Yavuz, "spaces of knowledge thus were transferred from the *ulama* and the Sufi lodges to the printed text" (Yavuz 2003, p. 165). Yavuz understands the appeal and success of the Nur movement in terms of its ability to offer its followers a "conceptual bridge" for the transition from tradition to modernity, from oral to print culture, and from a rural to urban environment. It is an Islamic discourse that is directed towards an urban educated population, therefore stressing the importance of "evidence" for faith. According to Yavuz, the Nur movement has the largest number of educated people of any religious group in Turkey (Yavuz

2003, p. 177). Also targeting an educated, urban population, it is not surprising then, that Harun Yahya employs the Nurcu conceptual framework in his own discourse.

## 3.2. Islamic thought in Turkey between the state and civil society

Although Said Nursi and Nurcu discourse is arguably the most salient influence on the Harun Yahya enterprise, it is necessary to outline also other Islamic discourses in Turkey in order to present a more complete picture of the context in which Harun Yahya emerged. Of particular importance is the unique way in which the relationship between Islam and nationalism has been played out and configured both within Islamic movements and also at the level of the state. Political scientist Şerif Mardin distinguishes between three main clusters of Sunni Islam in Anatolia: The official Islam of the *ulama*, the mystical Islam of the Sufi orders, and the traditional Islam of the guilds and bazaars (Mardin 1989, p. 230). The legalistic Islam of the *ulama*, which became more and more part of the official Ottoman bureaucracy, is contrasted with the popularity of Sufi Islam of the various *tarikats*. Although the Kemalist elite dismantled the role of the *ulama* as part of the secularizing reforms, there is a certain continuity between the *ulama* of the Ottoman empire and the Ministry of Religious Affairs (Diyanet) in terms of representing official or "establishment Islam" in Turkey (Karpat 2000). As mentioned above, however, the Diyanet was set up to serve the modernization project of the Kemalist state, by promoting a nationalized and rationalized Islam as a form of national civic religion (Webb 2007). Due to these limiting parameters placed upon the Diyanet, Islamic thought and activism in Turkey in the 20$^{th}$ century has been developed mostly outside the state, by popular Islamic movements and Islamic intellectuals emerging out of the more orthodox of the Sufi orders, particularly the influential Mujaddidi-Halidi branch of the Nakşibendi order. The Sufi orders served as the social structures for Islamic mobilization, set against the official Islam of the Diyanet.

Another influential Turkish Islamic movement with roots in Nakşibendi Sufism aside from the Nur movement is the *Süleymancı*, a strictly pious *cemaat* with an estimated 4 million followers, founded by the *şeyh* Süleyman Hilmi Tunahan (1888–1959). Emerging as a reaction to the forced secularization and the closing of the medreses (traditional religious schools) in the 1920 in Turkey, the community focuses on traditional Qur'an education.[18] The Süleymancı movement established themselves among Turkish *Gastarbeiters* abroad long before the Diyanet began sending official religious representatives to these countries, illustrating the Diyanet's often passive role as a state institution compared to the activist approach of non-governmental Islamic groups. The

---

[18] For further reading on the subject of the Süleymancıs, see Jonker (2005).

Diyanet has at times taken a rather suspicious view of Islamic movements in Turkey.[19] However, the Diyanet has also been subject to the conjunctural changes in Turkey and the processes by which Islamic discourses has gained influence also on state level, and in recent decades there has been a gradual convergence in the discourse of Islamic civil society and the Diyanet (Solberg 2007, p. 454).

Thus, Islamic thought in Turkey has been formulated mostly outside the state, by Islamic movements and intellectuals, as dynamic responses to historical and political realities. As mentioned above, in the transition from Ottoman Empire to Turkish republic, Turkish nationalism replaced Islam as the unifying ideology of the republic. Islamism is sometimes presented as the antithesis to secular nationalism, as it emphasizes religious identity as the "imagined community" in Anderson's terminology, over ethnic or territorial identity (Anderson 2006). However, Turkish Islamism in most of its manifestations has been closely entangled with nationalism. Rather than rejecting nationalism, the Islamic movement in Turkey has sought to Islamize Turkish nationalism. Turkish political parties on the right have also appealed to Islamic values in order to garner votes and popular support, and as a buttress against growing leftist currents. Both among Islamic movements and on the part of the state, there have been efforts towards the "Turkification" of Islam. In the following, I will examine three periods or currents of Islamic thought in Turkey and their various configurations and engagements with nationalism, political rightism and Turkism. First, however, I will provide and an historical background for the broad appeal of nationalism in Turkey.

### 3.2.1. Nationalism, ethnicity and minorities in Turkey

Nationalism has been a powerful force in Turkey since the founding of the republic. As we shall see, nationalist idioms are frequently employed by the Harun Yahya enterprise. Giving a comprehensive account of the processes of nation building in Turkey and the shifting faces of Turkish nationalism lies beyond the scope of this dissertation. However, I will briefly touch upon some central themes in Turkish nationalism that are relevant as a background for the discourse of the Harun Yahya enterprise.

The republic of Turkey was established "during a grave crisis in which its very existence was threatened" (Bora 2003, p. 434). After World War 1, Western

---

[19] The Diyanet published a highly condemning report on Said Nursi and Nurculuk in 1964, commissioned by the 1960 coup government, which accuses the Nurcus of "attempting to establish a new religion", and charges that the *Risale-i Nur* collection "has no religious value" (Diyanet İşleri Başkanlığı 1964). However, this should be understood in relation to the political conjuncture at the time rather than reflecting the Diyanet's general view. The entry on Nurculuk in the Turkey Diyanet Foundation Encyclopedia, published in 2008, is a scholarly account of Nurculuk and contains no such critical remarks (Açıkgenç 2008).

forces planned to divide the Ottoman territories between them. According to The Treaty of Sevres (1920), the victorious powers of World War 1 would divide the former Ottoman heartland of Anatolia, create an Armenian homeland in the east and add Greek-speaking parts of Thrace and the Aegean coast to Greece and establish a Kurdistan. Much of the rest would be under British, French, Italian or International control, and the emerging Turkish state would be tiny. The harsh terms of this treaty threatened to crush the Turkish nationalist movement's vision of an independent Turkish state, and triggered the Turkish War of Independence, which led to the creation of modern Turkey. The humiliation of the Treaty of Sevres is often regarded as a national trauma for Turkey, and has had a significant impact on the Turkish nationalist imaginary both on state level and in the public. A concern with survival and territorial integrity are thus defining features of Turkish nationalism, and has at times manifested itself in what has been termed "Sevres paranoia", an obsessive fear of annihilation combined with the notion that "there are forces that seek to divide and destroy Turkey" (Akçam 2004, p. 230).

The nation builders of Turkey were faced with the challenge of carving a modern nation state out of the remains of a multiethnic empire. The process of nation formation is a complex and continuous process, often involving elements such as the construction of a mythic past; defining the members of the nation and a national identity, often in relation to a constructed "Other"; demarcating territory and homeland; and identifying enemies. Different nationalist discourses in Turkey have addressed these different issues in different ways. The relationship between the official nationalism of the state and various nationalist movements advocating Turkism, pan-Turkism, neo-Ottomanism and Islamist nationalism is complex. The official nationalism of the Turkish state is often called Kemalist nationalism, and is characterized by an emphasis on modernization and secularization. The official nationalism of the state is not a fixed entity, however, but has moved through various phases and incorporated elements of other nationalist discourses in Turkey.

Turkish nationalism has generally been of a defensive kind, concerned with preserving the state and maintaining territorial integrity (Bora 2010, p. 57). In the early stages of the Turkish nation building process, a number of different nationalist ideas competed for influence, some of them promoting more expansionist territorial conceptions. Turanism or pan-Turkism – the notion that all Turkic peoples should be united – was advocated by some segments of the Young Turk movement.[20] However, the founders of the republic eventually abandoned pan-Turkist ideas, and settled for secular nationalism as the official ideology and the notion of Anatolia as the Turkish motherland.

---

[20] See Özkırımlı and Sofos (2008, p. 124) for a discussion on the differences between Turanism, pan-Turkism and Turkism.

The nationalism of the Turkish state is officially a civic form of nationalism. However, the distinction between civic and ethnic nationalism is not clear-cut, and most nationalisms have elements of both (Uzer 2010). At various points in the history of modern Turkey, and especially the early Kemalist era, a strong emphasis on an ethnically defined Turkishness, or ethnocentrism, has dominated the nationalist discourse also at the level of the state (Özkırımlı & Sofos 2008, p. 69). This ethnocentrism had implications for the view of both Muslim and non-Muslim minorities, which were seen as citizens of Turkey, but not necessarily members of the Turkish nation. The Turkish republic pursued an assimilationist policy in the effort to create a homogenous nation out of the hodgepodge of different religious, ethnic and linguistic groups inherited from the Ottoman Empire (Özkırımlı & Sofos 2008, p. 162). The efforts to homogenize the Turkish nation have also included means such as expulsion, coercion and elimination, the most famous example being the deportation and massacre of Armenians in 1915, an issue that continues to haunt Turkey today.[21] In nationalist discourse, minorities were often scapegoated as a form of "fifth column" inclined to collaborate with enemies of the republic (Özkırımlı & Sofos 2008, p. 172).

Turkification policies did not merely affect non-Muslim minorities, but also non-Turkish Muslim minorities. Most of these groups integrated into the larger Turkish community, with the exception of the Kurds, the largest non-Turkish minority in Turkey. The Kemalist state denied the identity of Kurds, and thereby rejected the ethnic basis for Kurdish dissent (Özkırımlı & Sofos 2008, p. 174). Instead Kurdish dissent was framed in official discourse as an issue of socio-economic factors, regional backwardness and also the result of the plotting of foreign powers bent on dividing Turkey. This "explanation" became especially prominent in nationalist discourses in the 1980s and 1990s, during the military struggle between the Turkish state and the separatist PKK, a military conflict that has claimed an estimated 40,000 lives. As we shall see, the notion of foreign powers manipulating the Kurdish issue is also a theme employed by Harun Yahya. The Kurdish issue continues to haunt Turkey, and has arguably become the primary internal "Other" in Turkish nationalist discourse.

3.2.2. The alliance between Islam and rightist nationalism

One of the most salient features of contemporary Islamic discourses in Turkey is its entangled relationship with nationalism. In the 1950s, Islamic thought found its expression mainly through a form of conservative form of nationalism. The Democrat Party came to power in 1950 after the transition to multiparty politics,

---

[21] Özkırımlı and Sofos also mention the Thrace events in 1934, the wealth tax law in 1942, and the 6–7 September 1955 pogroms as examples of discriminatory practices against minorities (Özkırımlı & Sofos 2008, p. 171).

partly because it succeeded in appealing to the religious sensibilities of the largely Sunni Muslim population. The DP accommodated traditional and Islamic values as a prop to attract votes, but it was still firmly opposed to the politicization of Islam. Islamism was in a defensive position against the hegemonic ideology of secularism and Westernization, and therefore aligned itself with the political right against leftism, which they equated with atheism (Yildiz 2006). Some of the most influential Islamic thinkers of the time were Said Nursi, Necip Fazil Kısakürek, Süleyman Hilmi Tunahan and Süleyman Hilmi Işık. They shared the notion that Turkish identity had to be grounded in spiritual values, and thus advocated a conservative and religious nationalism as an alternative to secular nationalist ideology. This alliance between nationalism and Islam is expressed in the somewhat euphemistic phrase *milliyetçi-mukaddesatçı* ("nationalist-sacredist").[22]

With the outbreak of the Cold War, anti-communism became an increasingly central theme in both Islamic discourse and in the emerging far right movement in Turkey. As mentioned above, also the Nur movement adopted a conservative-nationalist discourse in the 1950s. The emergence of conservative nationalism during the DP rule paved the way for the development of a more radical right-wing politics (Kanra 2009). After 1960s, Turkist and pan-Turkist ideas re-emerged on the political map with the foundation of *Milliyetçi Hareket Partisi* (MHP – Nationalist Movement Party), an ultranationalist party that would come to be an important force in Turkish politics. The youth movement of the party called themselves *ülkücüler* (idealists) (Bora 2010, p. 74).

The relationship between Islamism and ultranationalism in Turkey is complex. A distinction is sometimes made between ultranationalist discourses that historically has emphasized *soydaşlık* (kinship based on ethnicity) and pan-Turkist ideas, and Islamist nationalist discourses that emphasize *dindaşlık* (kinship based on religion) and the notion of Turks as soldiers of Islam and the continuation of the Ottoman empire (Poulton 1997). However, the discourses of *dındaşlık* and *soydaşlık* have often converged. In the 60s and 70s, the Islamists and ultranationalists found common ground in a conservative nationalism that conglomerated around themes such as patriotism, anti-communism and the superiority of Turkishness (Kanra 2009, p. 84). The new far-right MHP and Islamists both saw communism as a threat, and there was an alignment of Sunni-conservative-Turkish nationalism that defined itself in opposition to the left, the Alevis, and growing Kurdish nationalism.[23] This alliance on the right between religious conservatism, anti-communism and Turkish nationalism has

---

[22] There is no good English equivalent for the Turkish term *mukaddesatçı*. It is defined in Turkish dictionaries as "a person who has extreme veneration for things understood as holy".
[23] Alevis are an ethno-religious minority in Turkey, closely associated with the Bektaşi Sufi order and Shi'a Islam. Politically the Alevis have generally aligned themselves with the left in Turkey.

shaped the development of Islamism in Turkey and is a discourse that has significant popular appeal (Poulton 1997, p. 199).

### 3.2.3. Neo-Sufism and political Islam

Before 1970 then, Islamic thought in Turkey was closely tied to conservative nationalism. From the 1970s onwards, Islamism began to emerge as a distinct political identity. The Nakşibendi Sufi order played a central role in this process. Islam in Turkey has historically been very much influenced by Sufism, and much of religious life have been organized around *tarikats* (Sufi brotherhoods or orders), ranging from heterodox Sufi orders such as the Bektaşi, and orthodox Sunni-Hanafi Sufi orders such as Nakşibendi and Kadiri.[24] The Nakşibendi grew especially influential in end of the 19$^{th}$ century due in particular to the Mujaddidi-Halidi revivalist movement instigated by Mevlana Halid-i Bağdadi (1776–1827). Emphasizing revitalization and preservation of the sharia and the Sunna of the Prophet,[25] the Nakşibendi order supported the Sultan, as they saw the continuation of the Ottoman Empire as the guarantor of the Islamic community (Özdalga 1998, p. 19). The Nakşibendi orders' orientation towards staying close to power and its well-organized structure has been suggested as one of the reasons why it was out of this order that the political Islam movement emerged. The majority of Islamic movements in Turkey have roots in Nakşibendi revivalism, including the Nur movement and the Süleymancı. The Iskenderpaşa lodge of the Nakşibendi order was instrumental in the establishment of the Milli Görüş movement, which provided the ideological and organizational framework for a succession of Islamist parties in Turkey (Yavuz 2003, pp. 207–237).

### 3.2.4. The ideology of the Milli Görüş

Islamic thought in the 1950s and 1960s had been articulated primarily in terms of conservatism and traditional values. From the 1970s onwards, a political Islam movement emerged and a period of more direct confrontation between the secular state and Islamism began. The development of political Islam in Turkey was not independent from global events, yet it followed its own unique trajectory. Although the works of Islamist thinkers like Said Qutb (1906–1966) were made available in Turkish in the 1960s, the ideas of Nakşibendi leaders such as Mehmet

---

[24] The use of the terms heterodoxy and orthodoxy here should not be understood as externally ascribed normative evaluations concerning "right" and "wrong" Islam, but merely as descriptive and heuristic terms reflecting inner-religious and socially constructed notions defined by power relations. For a theoretical discussion on the terms, see Schrode (2008).

[25] The way of life prescribed as normative in Islam, based on the teachings and practices of Muhammad and on exegesis of the Qu'ran.

Zahid Kotku had a much more direct influence upon Turkish Islamist discourse.[26] Kotku had a seminal role in the formation of the first Islamist party in Turkey, Milli Selamet Partisi (MSP – National Salvation Party), and the Milli Görüş movement. The founders of the MSP developed a new political ideology based on Islam to challenge the secular hegemony in Turkey. In 1969, Necmettin Erbakan, the leader of the MSP and other subsequent Islamist parties published a manifesto titled *Milli Görüş* (National View), which outlined their vision of change in Turkey. Milli Görüş thus became an umbrella term for the political wing of the Turkish pro-Islamic movement, which has been active also in Turkish diaspora communities in Germany and other countries.

Although it was a political movement, the primary aim was arguably not the establishment of an Islamic state, but rather to transform Turkish society and politics in accordance with Ottoman-Islamic ideals. The Milli Görüş movement ascribed the decline of the Ottoman Empire to Westernization, and called for a return to Islamic and Turkish national values. It focused on industrialization, religious education and social justice as a remedy for social problems. In terms of foreign policy it adopted an anti-European stance, frequently employing anti-Zionist, anti-Freemason and anti-communist conspiracy rhetoric. It also adopted the common political Islam idiom of representing the "real people".

Despite incorporating a transnational conception of an Islamic *umma*, the Islamic discourse of the Milli Görüş was still firmly rooted in the Turkish context and its ideology was based on the equation of the nation and Islam. This is also reflected in the use of the term *milli* in both the name of the movement and the two first political parties it spawned. *Milli* did not merely mean "national" in the conventional sense, but "connotes religious ethnos" (Yavuz 2003, p. 208). The Milli Görüş manifesto also refers to the "golden age" of the Ottoman Empire, emphasizing the importance of the Ottoman-Islamic heritage. The notion of Turkey as the leader of the Muslim world remained at the center of the Milli Görüş discourse. The idea of Ottoman-Islamic heritage as an essential part of Turkish national identity would be an increasingly influential discourse in Turkey throughout the 1980s, both in the Islamic movement and also at state level.

3.2.5. The Turkish-Islamic synthesis and the Turkification of Islam

Sectarian and political violence between rightwing and leftwing groups and Sunnis and Alevis escalated throughout the 1970s in Turkey. On the 12th of September 1980, military officers led by general Kenan Evren decided to end the cycle of violence and seized power in a military coup. The coup had wide-ranging repercussions and constitutes a watershed in modern Turkish history. It

---

[26] Said Qutb (1906–1966) was an influential Islamist theorist and a leading member of the Egyptian Muslim Brotherhood.

was primarily directed against the left, and in the wake of the coup followed a McCarthyesque purging of left-leaning intellectuals from universities, schools and state broadcasting. The coup leaders perceived communism as a great potential threat to the Turkish state, and therefore exploited Islamic symbols and discourses in an attempt to curb leftist ideology and activism. This strategy gave the Islamic movement legitimacy and a space to maneuver that it had not previously enjoyed, and is widely regarded as one of the primary reasons for the gradual Islamization of society that followed (Eligür 2010). One of the most striking developments of this period is the way in which the military, as a representative of the Kemalist establishment, redefined Kemalism and tried to merge it with Islam through the adoption of an ideology known as the Turkish-Islamic synthesis (Eligür 2010, pp. 88–102).

The Turkish-Islamic synthesis was formulated by a conservative nationalist advocacy group called *Aydınlar Ocağı* (Hearth of Intellectuals), who sought to consolidate the power of the ruling elite by constructing a new ideology based on the fusing of Turkish nationalism with Ottoman-Islamic myths and symbols (Poulton 1997, pp. 179–180). This new ideology was incorporated into the 1982 constitution, thus attaining the status as a semi-official ideology of the state. According to the Turkish-Islamic synthesis, there is an innate compatibility between the Turkish national character and Islam, so that the supposed character traits of pre-Islamic Turkish culture such as a strong sense of justice, monotheism and emphasis on family and morality were enhanced through the Turks' conversion to Islam, and that Turks were therefore "the soldiers of Islam". The 1985 curriculum for *imam-hatip* schools stresses among other things that Turks "were the leaders in the rise and spread of Islam in the world" (*Imam-Hatip Liseli Öğretim Programları* 1985, pp. 15–17). The position of the Diyanet was also strengthened during this period, and its role as a protector and preserver of Turkish nationalist ideology was highlighted, which boosted its legitimacy (Yavuz 2003, p. 70). The budget of the Diyanet was increased, as was the number of Imam-Hatip schools (religious high schools). This ideological shift also entailed a reappraisal of the Ottoman past. While the Kemalist ruling elite had previously sought to disassociate the Turkish republic from its Ottoman past, Turkey's Ottoman heritage was now lifted up as a source of pride and as a crucial part of Turkish identity (Yavuz 2003, p. 7).

These ideas where already a part of Islamist discourse in Turkey, and the co-option of these ideas by the military dictatorship provided increased legitimacy and strength to the Islamic movement. The transformation of the state also gave shape to the Islamic movement throughout the 1980s, and the dynamic interconnection between the state and Islamic movement helped transform the Islamic groups into a "complex amalgamation of sociopolitical networks" (Yavuz 2003, p. 38). One Islamic group in particular would benefit from the new political climate, and would develop the discourse of Turkish-Islamic synthesis further: The highly influential Gülen movement, which I will deal with in more detail below. The emphasis on Ottoman-Islamic heritage also entailed an "othering" of Arab Islam. The juxtaposition of Turkish Islam with Arab Islam, albeit not so explicitly, is a recurrent theme in Islamic discourse in Turkey, including the discourse of the Nur movement (Yavuz 2003, p. 196).

For the pro-Islamic movement in Turkey, Turkey is not merely one part of Islamic history and civilization, but rather the leading country of the Muslim world. The belief that Islam as it was represented and spread by the Ottoman Empire is the most authentic form of Islam is pervasive in Turkey. Although the Turkish-Islamic synthesis in time lost credibility both among Kemalists and Islamists, the notion of combining Kemalist nationalism and Islam has significant popular appeal, and no contradiction is seen between the two (Poulton 1997, p. 199).

## 4. Opportunity spaces: The Islamic revival post-1980s

The rise of the Islamist movement in Turkey began in the 1970s, but gained in strength during the 1980s after the military coup. This did not merely entail the development of a political Islamic discourse and the emergence of political parties with Islam as a main reference, but also entailed "a resurgence in religious consciousness and activity" (Tapper 1994, p. 2). Thus, "the Islamic revival" denotes the revitalization of Islam in a broader sense. Richard Tapper describes this revival as involving

> growth in the manifestations of popular religious sentiment, evidenced both in the building of mosques and religious schools and in the semi-clandestine activities of mystical groups, whether the older Sufi tarikats such as the Nakşibendi and Kadiris, or the more recent Nurcu and Süleymancı movements (Tapper 1994, p. 2).

The Islamic revival in Turkey is part of a worldwide trend: "Since the 1970s, latent Muslim identifications have begun to assert themselves in a worldwide Islamic revival" (Lapidus 2002, p. 823). According to historian Ira Lapidus, in religious terms the revival encompasses "schools of philosophical and religious thought, movements to promote personal piety and prayer, and educational movements dedicated to the reform of Muslim religious practice" (Lapidus 2002, p. 823). In the following I will describe key features of this revival in Turkey, focusing in particular on the aspects that constitute the setting for the emergence of the Harun Yahya enterprise. First, however, I will briefly introduce a number of theoretical approaches to Islamism and the Islamic revival in Turkey and position myself in relation to these.

## 4.1 Theoretical perspectives on the Islamic revival

The secularization thesis predicts that as societies are modernized, they will also become secularized, and religious institutions, practices and beliefs will decline (Berger 1990). The global resurgence of Islam since the 1970s is frequently cited as an example that illustrates the inadequacy of this thesis (Sutton & Vertigans 2005, p. 173). There is a plethora of scholarly literature that attempts to explain the Islamic revival and the emergence of political Islam. Some attribute the rise of Islamism to Islam itself, and regard the texts as the key to understanding the actions of Muslims. This may be referred to as the essentialist perspective, as it tends to see Islam as fixed and as having certain inherent characteristics. Bernard Williams is often mentioned as a scholar tending towards an essentialist perspective (Yavuz 2003, p 16; Tatari 2007, p. 96). Contextual approaches focus instead on contexts or structures as triggering factors that explain the emergence of Islamism. A prominent strand of these types of approaches is deprivation theory, which focuses on factors such as unfulfilled aspirations, low social mobility, high income inequality and poverty as explanations for the Islamic revival (Carvalho 2009).

In his influential work Islamic *Political Identity in Turkey* (Yavuz 2003), Hakan Yavuz instead proposes a constructivist approach. Constructivism regards human society and its institutions and concepts as socially constructed and therefore subject to constant interpretation, negotiation and transformation. In the constructivist view, individual actions are neither caused by social structure nor the outcome of individual choices (Yavuz 2003, p. 20). Instead, this perspective stresses how human agency is both conditioned by and involved in a reflexive construction of reality together with other individuals. One of the advantages of applying this approach to understanding the Islamic revival in Turkey is that it "does not confer agency to a reified Islam but rather to living Muslims whose actions are embedded in particular loyalties and networks" (Yavuz 2003, p. 21). A key analytical concept in Yavuz' approach is "opportunity spaces". Yavuz argues that

> reinvigorated Turkish Islam(s) in the political and social spheres cannot be explained by the failure of Kemalism but rather is an outcome of new opportunity spaces – social and economic networks and vehicles for activism and the dissemination of meaning, identity, and cultural codes [...] (Yavuz 2003, p. ix).

In *The Mobilization of Political Islam in Turkey*, Banu Eligür, another political scientist, sets out to explain the Islamic revival in Turkey by means of a variant of social movement theory called *the political process model* (Eligür 2010). Eligür approaches Islamist mobilization in Turkey as a social movement, and argues that its success must be understood in terms of the presence of favorable political conditions (political opportunity structures), and the presence of movement "entrepreneurs" who successfully frame their strategies according to the existing political context. Eligür identifies the incorporation of the Turkish-Islamic synthesis into the official state ideology as the political opportunity structure that explains the first phase of mobilization of political Islam from 1981–1990, and the malfunctioning of the state as the political opportunity structure of the second phase, 1990 to the present. I find the perspectives of both Yavuz and Eligür useful, as they recognize the fluidity and dynamic nature of Islamic discourses, and highlight the structural conditions that facilitated the Islamic revival while at the same time recognizing the embedded and reflexive agency of the actors involved. In the following, I will therefore draw on both these theoretical perspectives.

## 4.2 The scene in the 1980s

After a period of military rule (1980–83) and the implementation of a new constitution in 1982, Turkey returned to civilian rule. In 1983, the center-right Motherland Party won the majority vote and its leader Turgut Özal was elected prime minister. This marked the beginning of the Özal era (1983–93), which would transform Turkey economically, educationally, technologically and politically (Laçiner 2009). Yavuz identifies the neo-liberalism of Özal as a turning point in the reconfiguration of the political and intellectual landscape in Turkey (Yavuz 2003). Before the Özal era, economic power had mainly been concentrated in the hands of the bureaucracy and businessmen supported by the Kemalist state. Thanks to Özal's policies of opening up the economy to greater competition from both outside and within, a "Muslim *bourgeoisie*" of conservative businessmen from Anatolia emerged as a powerful economic force. Özal was not only a firm believer in economic liberalism, but also pro-Islamic and had strong ties with Nakşibendi Sufi orders. Both general Kenan Evren and Prime Minister Özal emphasized the importance of religious values in the fabric of Turkish nationalism (Salt 1995, p. 16). The Özal government encouraged religious expression, increased funding to religious institutions, and Islamicized the education system (Yavuz 2003, p. 75). The 1982 constitution had made religious instruction compulsory, and Özal's minister of education, Vehbi Dinçerler, prepared a new curriculum where the term *milli* was often used in a religious sense (Yavuz 2003, p. 75).

The liberalizing policies of Özal contributed to a burgeoning civil society. He removed the state monopoly on broadcasting and opened up for private education. This enabled Muslim entrepreneurs to establish their own schools, TV and radio stations, newspapers and magazines. There was an explosion in the publishing of Islamic books, newspapers and journals, and the growth in mass communication led to new modes of dissemination of religious knowledge

(Eickelman & Anderson 1997). A new generation of Muslim intellectuals emerged, representing alternative voices of Islam distinct from both the traditional *cemaats* and *tarikats* and the official discourse of the Diyanet. These new Muslim intellectuals are generally not Islamic scholars, but products of the secular state education system, and their newspaper columns and books often contain more references to Western scholarship than Islamic sources and authorities (Meeker 1994). They address contemporary issues relevant to their audience, and write in modern Turkish rather than employing Arabic or Islamic terminology, thus making the texts accessible to a wider audience. Muslim intellectuals such as Ali Bulaç played a significant role in formulating Islamic conceptions of Western ideals such as pluralism, fundamental liberties and human rights, thus contributing to the diversification of Islamic discourses throughout the 80s and 90s (Yildiz 2006). The growth of mass communication led to the emergence of new spokespersons for Islam, who contributed to shaping, vernacularizing and popularizing Islamic discourses. The 80s then, marked the beginning of a period in which Islam occupied a more prominent place in politics, but also in the social and cultural sphere.

## 4.3. Identity politics and the construction of difference

Although modern Turkey is often understood in terms of tensions between Islamist and secularist forces, there is no simple binary between Islamic and republican ideologies. Similarly, on the social and cultural level, it would be severely misleading to portray Turkey as consisting of committed Islamists on the one hand and staunch secularists on the other. People's identities and affiliations are often fluid, changing and conflicted. Nevertheless, one outcome of the Islamic revival throughout the 80s and 90s and the greater visibility of Islam in the urban sphere was an increasing emphasis on identity politics, and cultural polarization between a pro-Islamic segment and a secularist segment of society. Even though there was a shift to the right in the official ideology and despite a degree of popular acceptance of the Turkish-Islamic synthesis on one level, there was a high degree of suspicion towards Islamic groups among those who identified themselves as "modern" secular Turks. One consequence of this confrontational atmosphere was the creation of a situation whereby the polarities of "assertive secularists" and Islamists to a large degree set the parameters of public discourse, both of them contributing to a mutual process of "Othering".[27] Islamists often portrayed secularists as atheists and materialists, and defined what it means to be a Muslim in Islamist terms (such as wearing the headscarf if you are a woman). The secularists responded to the Islamist

---

[27] "Assertive secularists" is a term used by Ahmet T. Kuru to denote those who aim to remove religion from the public sphere, as distinct from "passive secularists", who support the secular system but who also tolerate the public expression of religion (Kuru 2007).

challenge by portraying the Islamists in negative terms, as fanatics, backwards, reactionary, anti-modern, ignorant and uneducated.[28]

The struggle between secularist and Islamists over what constitutes legitimate representations of Turkishness did not just play out in the political arena, but was also manifested in everyday life. In *Faces of the state: Secularism and public life in Turkey,* based on ethnographic study of public life in Istanbul in Turkey during the 1990s, anthropologist Yael Navaro-Yashin seeks to unravel the schism between secularists and Islamists, and examines how both secularists and Islamists narratively construe notions of what constitute the real and authentic Turkish identity (Navaro-Yashin 2002). Navaro-Yashin describes how this *Kulturkampf* is predicated upon key symbols such as attitudes to the headscarf, gender relations, and Atatürk, and how it is also linked to a growing consumerist culture.

> The politics of culture in the 1980s and 1990s developed in the context of a consumer market influenced by globalization. So central was consumerism to the social life of this period that political conflicts were organized, expressed, and mediated through this medium. [...] Commodification proved to be a context and activity that was historically shared by Islamists and secularists alike, rather than a domain that divided them (Navaro-Yashin 2002, p. 79).

Consumerist culture, with its emphasis on material wealth and financial success, hit Turkey full force in the 1980s under Turgut Özal's leadership. Secularist cultural constructions of Islamists were often intimately linked with notions of class, and the Islamic segment was conceived of as uneducated, poor and "low-class". However, throughout the 80s, the economic hegemony of the secular elite declined as the Islamic social segment moved from the cultural, political and economic periphery to the center. As the social mobility and economic power of the Islamic segment grew, so did the potential for Islamic-style consumerism. There was a growing market for Islamic products, including Islamic publiccations. Islamic circles produced its own elites and threatened the cultural hegemony of the secularists. Islamists came to construct identities in distinction from secularists, and develop contrasting patterns of consumption; their own shops, newspapers, clothes brands and so forth (Navaro-Yashin 2002, p. 80).

The public perception of businesses as representing either the Islamist or secularist "side" is illustrated by the following anecdote: During my time working in Turkey in the early 2000s, a secularist-identified Turkish colleague of mine would deride me for purchasing Ülker brand chocolate on the grounds that they are "Islamist", and suggested I buy the "secularist" competitor ETI's

---

[28] A term that figures particularly prominently in the secularists' anti-Islamist discourse is *yobaz*. Translated as bigot or fanatic, the term is used to denote the antithesis to all things modern and progressive.

chocolate instead (I did not comply, as I happened to prefer the taste of the allegedly Islamist chocolate). This illustrates the way in which patterns of consumption is linked to politics of identity. Some commodities became particularly potent emblems of identity, notably pictures of Atatürk for secularists and the veil for Islamists. Both secularists and Islamists were intent on communicating consumer power, status and wealth through consumption, but through different sets of symbols. Consumerism thus contributed to the cultural construction of secularist and Islamist identities in the urban space and to the consolidation of widely held notions of what constitutes secularist and Islamic lifestyles respectively.

The contestation over what constitutes legitimate representations of Turkishness has contributed to shaping the Islamic movement. One outcome is Islamist identity politics that emphasize difference and the cultivation of an alternative modernity as a counter to secularist lifestyles. However, despite the rise of a Muslim bourgeoisie in the 80s and 90s, secularist discourse retained a dominant position in the urban public space with regards to the right to defining "the modern". Navaro-Yashin argues that Islamism in Turkey is "imbued with the language of secularism" (Navaro-Yashin 2002, p. 7). Some Islamic groups therefore adopted a different strategy, appropriating the symbols and styles associated with secularist identity in order to communicate a modern image instead of employing Islamic symbols. As we shall see, the Harun Yahya enterprise is an example of the latter. This is also related to the increasing influence of Islamic discourses that instead of opposing secularism, seeks to redefine it. Especially after the 1997 coup, the mainstream Islamic discourse in Turkey began to shift from identity politics and Islamism to an emphasis on what Jenny White terms "Muslimhood" (White 2005). Two related developments are important here: The split in the Milli Görüş movement and the emergence of Justice and Development party, and the rise of the Gülen movement.

## 4.4. The failure of political Islam and the rise of the JDP

The heyday of political Islam in Turkey during the 1990s culminated in the appointment of Necmettin Erbakan as prime minister in 1996 in the coalition government of the Welfare Party and the True Path Party. The military grew increasingly uneasy over what they perceived as increasing influence of Islamism in Turkish politics, and in 1997, in what has often been referred to as the "soft coup", the military intervened and forced the coalition government to resign. In the aftermath of the soft coup, the political Islam movement split into a traditionalist and a reformist section. The reformist section founded the Justice and Development Party (JDP), which disassociated itself with the Islamist agenda of Milli Görüş. In 2003, Prime Minister Recep Tayyip Erdoğan famously declared, "we have shed the Milli Görüş shirt".[29] Appropriating a conservative-democrat identity, the JDP thus sealed the fate of political Islam in Turkey (Aras 2004).

Many scholars have pointed to the failure of political Islam globally, and the emergence of post-Islamism (Bayat 2007; Roy 2004). The transformation of the political Islam movement in Turkey and the success of the conservative democratic JDP is one example that is often mentioned to illustrate this shift (Dağı 2005). However, it is important to note significant differences between Islamist politics in Turkey and in many Arab countries. As argued by Asef Bayat, Turkey has barely experienced typical Islamist politics. Even before the reformist JDP, religious parties in Turkey have largely espoused "a post-Islamist disposition, advocating a pious society in a largely secular democratic state" (Bayat 2007, p. 189). The transition from the relatively moderate Islamism of the Welfare (Refah) party to the conservative democratic JDP is therefore not a dramatic shift.

The failure of Islamist party politics in Turkey, and the success of the reformist JDP, is paralleled by another major development in the relationship between Islam and secularism in Turkey in recent years, namely the success of the Gülen movement. Arguably, the evolution of the Gülen movement epitomizes a shift from an Islamist discourse critical of secularism to a consensus-based discourse that seeks to align itself with the state and negotiate the terms of liberal secular democracy rather than challenging it. In *Between Islam and the State: Politics of Engagement* (Turam 2007), Berna Turam argues that the success of both the Gülen movement and the JDP are a result of their ability to negotiate and cooperate with the secular state, and that this politics of engagement in turn has contributed to the democratization process in Turkey. Ahmet Kuru argues that mainstream Islamic discourse in Turkey underwent a transformation in the late 1990s towards endorsing secularism. Thus, he argues, the current struggle is not between Islamism and secularism, but rather of "a conflict between two types of secularism" (Kuru 2007). Kuru argues further that the Gülen movement played a key role in this shift and in the rethinking of Islamism and secularism in Turkey. The Gülen movement is thus a key factor in the transformation of Islamic discourse in Turkey that has taken place over the last decades. Moreover, as we shall see, there are significant points of convergence between the Gülen movement and the Harun Yahya enterprise in terms of their approach. I will therefore consider the hugely influential Gülen movement in some more detail.

---

[29] *"Milli Görüş gömleğini çıkardık"*, cited in "AKP'nin Yeni Zarfı" (Yüksek 2003).

## 4.5. The Gülen movement

Arguably, no other Turkish Islamic movement has been more successful in utilizing the opportunity spaces created in the wake of the 1980s coup than the Gülen movement. The Gülen movement denotes the followers of Fethullah Gülen, a retired Turkish Muslim preacher currently living in the Unites States. Over the last three decades, the Gülen movement has evolved into a vast transnational network that encompasses educational institutions, civil society organizations, media outlets and finance institutions. Fethullah Gülen was born near Erzurum in 1941, and received informal religious education there. In 1958 he started working as a *vaiz* (preacher) in Edirne, and in 1966 he was officially appointed by the Diyanet and started working in Izmir as an imam. His emotional and charismatic style of preaching won him followers, and he and the community gathering around him started developing a network of dormitories and religious summer camps for youth. In the 1980s, the movement started emerging in the public sphere, and Gülen wrote a number of books and articles putting forward his ideas and his vision of creating a "golden generation" of well-educated and committed Muslims. He developed close ties with Turgut Özal, Turkey's prime minister at the time, and the privatization of the education system in 1983 gave the community the opportunity to establish their own educational institutions.

In the years between 1983 and 1997, the community grew steadily, carrying out their activities in the education sector, the media and the market. A number of financial institutions and foundations were set up to finance the activities. The followers of Gülen opened hundreds of schools all over Turkey, the Balkans and the Turkic republic in Caucasus and Central Asia, preparatory courses for universities, and a network of dormitories. Today it is estimated that there are over 1000 of these Gülen-inspired schools in over 100 countries on 5 continents (Ebaugh 2009, p. v). The schools are not religious high schools, but non-confessional private schools that follow the curriculum of the countries they operate in. The community also bought the newspaper *Zaman* and turned it into one of Turkey's leading dailies, and established the national television station Samanyolu as well as several radio stations. The establishment of the Foundation for Journalists and Writers in 1994, with Fethullah Gülen as an honorary president, was a key factor in Gülen's widening appeal. The foundation established a forum for dialogue, the Abant platform, which invited some of Turkey's most prominent intellectuals, authors and journalists, liberals, conservatives, Islamists and seculars alike, to meet once a year to discuss social, cultural and political issues in Turkey and try to reach a common ground. As honorary president of the foundation, Gülen met with Pope John II and several other prominent leaders of Jewish and Christian communities in Turkey and abroad.

Gülen's early works contain a great deal of anti-communist, anti-West and anti-missionary discourse (Agai 2005). As Gülen's popularity rose, he shed his conservative rhetoric and turned more and more to a discourse of love, tolerance and dialogue. He became known as the moderate and caring *"hocaefendi"* (dignified religious teacher). Others were suspicious of the real motives behind his activities, and in the late 1990s, parts of the media launched an anti-Gülen campaign. The backlash against Gülen reached a zenith in 1999, when the press got their hands on some videotapes, allegedly intended for his core group of confidants, where Gülen makes explicit Islamist propaganda and instructs his followers not to disclose their real objectives. The authenticity of these tapes is disputed. In response to the videotapes, the Turkish state opened a court case against Gülen, but the charges were later lifted. In the wake of the anti-Gülen campaign, Gülen took refuge in the United States (allegedly for health reasons), and has stayed there since. The movement has continued to expand, and is now active all over the world, running schools, promoting Turkish-Islamic culture and organizing activities in the framework of inter-civilizational dialogue.[30]

### 4.5.1. Fethullah Gülen's vision

Gülen's ideas are heavily influenced by Said Nursi, and the *Risale-i Nur* was one of the main textual bases for the community in the early period. The community is therefore sometimes referred to as a Neo-Nur community (Yavuz & Esposito 2003, p. 19). Gülen's approach differs from that of Nursi and the other Nur communities in important respects, however. As with all the Nur movements, the root paradigm is "serving the faith" (*imana hizmet*), but whereas Nursi's emphasis was on personal transformation, Gülen emphasizes the transformation of society through fostering a "golden generation" (*altın nesil*) of conscientious, committed and well-educated Muslim individuals. A central term is *hizmet*, service, which is also the name by which the Gülenists refer to the movement themselves. Gülen teaches that Muslims have a duty to serve the nation and the community, an idea that has mobilized millions of followers and has transformed the movement from one Islamic community among many to a broadly based civic movement engaging with society on multiple levels. Elisabeth Özdalga borrows Weber's term "worldly asceticism" to describe Gülen's ideal of working hard and engaging in humble and ceaseless service, which she argues introduced a new feature in Turkish religious life (Özdalga 2000). Inspired by Weberian analysis, Gülen's strong emphasis on work ethic has been likened to a form of "Islamic Calvinism", which is seen as one of the

---

[30] For scholarly works on the activities of the movement, see for instance Esposito & Yilmaz (2010) and Özdalga (2000).

reasons for the Gülenists' entrepreneurialism and success in business.[31] Whereas Said Nursi was more ambivalent to capitalism, Gülen is a warm supporter of the free market and neo-liberal policies.

Another aspect that distinguishes Gülen from Nursi is that Gülen is much more of a Turkish nationalist. According to Bülent Aras, "Gülen's goals are simultaneously to Islamize Turkish nationalism and to Turkify Islam" (Aras & Çaha 2000). Gülen carried forward the idea of a Turkish-Islamic synthesis promoted by the state after 1980, which can be seen as part of the reason why Özal administration extended their support to the establishment of Gülen-inspired schools abroad. Gülen believes that Turks have achieved the highest understanding of Islam, and that this was manifested in Turkish-Ottoman culture and its tolerant state tradition (Yavuz 2003, p. 195). The Gülen movement frequently refers to Ottoman culture as an example of tolerance and harmonious co-existence of different religions. In the 1960s, Gülen joined the "Association for Fighting Communism in Turkey" (*Komünizmle Mücadele Derneği*), and continued to keep close relations to anticommunist and ultra-nationalist circles throughout the 80s (Özdalga 2000). However, in the late 90s, he shed his anti-communist and nationalist rhetoric in favor of a softer and more dialogue-oriented approach. Patriotism and Turkish nationalism remains an important aspect of the Gülen discourse, however, and in many of the movement's transnational activities the emphasis on promoting Turkish language and culture is often much more salient than the emphasis on Islam.

The Gülen movement is often described as a moderate or liberal Islamic movement (Akyol 2007; Aras & Çaha 2000; Ebaugh 2009). Although Gülen remains a theologically conservative Muslim (Eldridge 2007, p. 537), in practice he adopts moderate positions on issues relating to how Muslims should act in modern society. For instance, he takes a pragmatic approach to the headscarf, saying that it is not an essential of faith, and has advised women to remove it if necessary to gain access to the secular education system (Özgürel 1998).

The influence from Nursi is evident in the importance placed upon the relationship between science and religion in Gülen's thought. As mentioned, Nursi emphasized the compatibility between science and religion, and saw nature and knowledge of the natural sciences as a way to confirm the veracity of revelation (Mermer & Ameur 2004). Gülen also argues that God reveals himself in the "the book of nature", and the Gülen schools place much emphasis on teaching the natural sciences. Regarding Darwin's theory of evolution, however, Gülen takes a critical view. Already in 1975, Gülen organized conferences on Darwinism, and both Gülen himself and his followers have written extensively

---

[31] See "Islamic Calvinists. Change and Conservatism in Central Anatolia", a report published by the European Stability Initiative, which stirred much debate in Turkey (European Stability Initiative 2005).

on this issue, arguing that scientific evidence contradicts the theory. Creationist articles are regularly published in *Sızıntı*, a journal published by the Gülen movement and one of the top selling periodicals in Turkey.[32] Here then, is a parallel to Harun Yahya, and one I shall return to.

4.5.2. From political Islam to faith activism: Gülen vs. Milli Görüş

As the Nur movement in general, the Gülen movement explicitly rejects the politicization of Islam, and has always kept a distance to Islamist parties like the Refah party and instead developed ties to center-right and even and secular-left leaders such as former Prime Minister Bülent Ecevit. Particularly from the mid-90s onwards, the Gülen movement began adopting a more moderate Islamic discourse that differed markedly from the Islamist discourse of the Milli Görüş (Kuru 2007, p. 144). Whereas Erbakan and the Milli Görüş cadre were skeptical towards globalization and the EU and at times would engage in anti-Western, anti-American and anti-Israeli rhetoric, the Gülen movement adopted a pro-globalization approach, and advocated developing strong relations with both the US and Europe. More recently, Gülen criticized the Mavi Marmara flotilla, arguing that the activists' failure to seek accord with Israel is "a sign of defying authority", a move that elicited criticism from many pro-Islamic circles in Turkey who are strongly critical of Israel (Lauria 2010). This statement also reflect another prominent characteristic of Gülen, namely his pro-state attitude, the importance he places on stability and his distaste for any tendencies towards civil unrest and rebellion (Bilici 2006, p. 18). In contrast with the majority of pro-Islamic movements in Turkey, Gülen also supported the soft coup of 1997 (Kuru 2007, p. 145).

Since the mid-1990s, the key distinguishing feature of the Gülen movement has been their focus on dialogue-oriented outreach work. In addition to establishing schools, the Gülen movement has established organizations conducting activities in the framework of interfaith and inter-civilizational dialogue in numerous countries[33] In Turkey, the Gülen movement's dialogue-oriented approach and their emphasis on the necessity of tolerance and pluralism have also contributed to increased cultural interaction between Islamic and non-Islamic circles (White 2005, p. 91). In the framework of the Abant platform, the Gülen movement brings together intellectuals from all shades of the political spectrum in order to discuss contemporary key issue in Turkey, including the liberal left. Through their multi-faceted approach and a wide variety of activities that are not all explicitly religious in character, the Gülen movement is able to appeal also to liberal secularists. The

---

[32] The Gülen movement also publishes an English equivalent of *Sızıntı* called *The Fountain*.
[33] In Norway and Sweden for instance, followers of Gülen have established the organizations *En Verden i Dialog* (http://evid.no) and *Dialog Slussen* (http://www.dialogslussen.se) respectively, which conduct various activities in the framework of inter-civilization dialogue, the promotion of Turkish culture and the dissemination of Gülen's ideas.

movement's emphasis on promoting Turkish culture and language abroad also has appeal beyond traditional Islamic segments of Turkish society.

The Gülen movement is perhaps the most vivid example of the economic and cultural flourishing of the Islamic segment in Turkish society in the last decades. Out of the various Islamic groups that sought to avail of the opportunity spaces that opened up in the 1980s, the Gülen movement turned out to be the most successful, and part of the reason was arguably their ability to reach beyond the traditional Islamic segment as well as their profile as modern but pious Muslims. Far from the secularists' stereotypical image of old-fashioned, traditional, poor and rural Islamists, many Gülenists are modern, well-dressed and well-educated businessmen, journalists, teachers and students, who are seeking to mould hearts and minds through the movement's financial, educational and media empires. Presenting a modern, elite, pro-capitalist image and a moderate interpretation of Islam, the Gülen movement appealed to people who had bourgeois aspirations for upward social mobility (Turam 2007, p. 12).

The development of the Gülen movement epitomizes the transformation of Islamic discourse in Turkey over the last three decades from a political Islam discourse that asserts an Islamic identity as distinct from and in opposition to the secular system, to an Islamic discourse that seeks to relocate Muslim identity, piety and morality within the parameters of the secular system. The emergence of the Gülen movement also contributed to dissolving the stratification of Islamic and secularist lifestyles as described above. Although remaining a conservative Muslim and an ardent Turkish nationalist, Gülen championed a pragmatic approach. He came to believe that democracy and pluralism is not only inevitable, but that it is also a setting of opportunity in which Muslims can promote Islam and serve faith.

Today, the Gülen movement is referred to in the Turkish press, not merely as one Islamic community (*cemaat*) among many, but as "*the cemaat*".[34] In the 80s and 90s, however, they did not enjoy the same dominant position. There was another Islamic community active in Istanbul at the time that pursued a similar strategy, namely the circle around Adnan Oktar. Adnan and his associates shared the Gülen community's aspirations of being *the* cemaat for urban and upwardly mobile Muslims. In *Ayet ve Slogan*, Ruşen Çakır allocates a chapter to the *Adnancılar* (followers of Adnan) and examines them as 'modernist' Muslim proselytes who primarily address a Westernized audience in Turkey (Çakır 1990, p. 254). Until the late 90s, the *Adnancılar*, or the Harun Yahya enterprise as I refer to it, was able to establish themselves particularly among a segment of the educated middle class elite in Istanbul.[35] However, the Harun Yahya enterprise

---

[34] See for instance Ilıcak (2012) and Akyol (2012).
[35] According to former member "Mehmet", in some milieus in Istanbul at the time *the cemaat* referred to the *Adnancılar* and not the Gülenists (personal interview, 04.02.2012).

did not become a broadly based popular movement as the Gülen community did. The success of the Gülen movement makes it an important reference point and source of inspiration for the Harun Yahya enterprise, and as I will show, Yahya has in many respects followed the trajectory of the Gülen movement. Many elements of Fethullah Gülen's discourse can be traced to Said Nursi, and as we shall see, many of these also feature prominently in the discourse of Harun Yahya. In my later analysis, I will point to both similarities and differences between the discourse of the Gülen movement and Harun Yahya.

## 5. Concluding remarks

The purpose of this chapter has been to outline the socio-political conditions that constitute the context for the emergence of the Harun Yahya enterprise, as well as the discursive context of for Islamic and nationalist thought in Turkey, in order to enable me to locate Yahya's teachings and ideas within this framework in my later analysis. The broad context here is the modern Turkish state and the way in which secular nationalism came to be the official ideology of the Turkish republic that was founded after the decline of the Ottoman Empire. The dynamic relationship between secularism, nationalism and Islam has shaped the way in which the Islamic movement has developed in Turkey, and the Harun Yahya enterprise must be understood against this background. Harun Yahya may be further located within the tradition of one particular path of Islamic discourse in Turkey, namely the Nur movement founded by Said Nursi. A key feature of Nurcu discourse is the emphasis on strengthening the faith of Muslims in the face of unbelief and atheism by stressing the compatibility between Islam and modernity. The primacy of belief in Nursi's Islamic discourse is also present in Harun Yahya. Yahya has to a large extent modeled his own *da'wa* upon that of Said Nursi, and frequently refers to Nursi as a source of authority. Also, Yahya's targeting of materialism and communism as chief evils can be seen as rooted in both Nurcu discourse as well as Turkish contemporary Islamic discourse in general.

The Nur movement is a faith movement that strives for Islamization on the level of individuals and society rather than seeking to influence the state, and has generally rejected direct involvement in politics, believing it would weaken their aim of serving to the faith (*imana hizmet*). As such, it distinguishes itself from more overtly political Islam movements in Turkey such as the Milli Görüş movement. A distinction may thus be made between faith-based Islamic movements and Islamic movements with political aspirations, although this distinction is far from clear-cut. Although the Harun Yahya enterprise may be conceived of as a religious enterprise inspired by Said Nursi, its emergence must also be considered in light of the political Islam movement in Turkey, which arose in the 1970s and gained in strength throughout the 80s and 90s. As we shall see, there are points of convergence between the Milli Görüş ideology and the themes taken up by Harun Yahya in the beginning of his career.

The rise of the political Islam movement in Turkey is also important in terms of understanding the developments that took place after the military coup in 1980, and the way in which the coup leaders sought to ally themselves with Islamic and conservative forces in an attempt to curb leftist influence. In the above I have also discussed the entangled relationship between Islam and nationalism in Turkey, and how this is played out in the discourse of various Islamic movements. This is another key element of the Turkish context that is central to understanding the discourse of Harun Yahya. I have also focused on how the changes in Islamic discourse in Turkey over time. It should be noted, however, that this does mean that the emergence of new discourses have replaced others. To a large extent, various discourses co-exist within the contemporary setting. For instance, despite the success of the Gülen movement, there are also voices within the pro-Islamic community in Turkey today that reject Gülen's dialogue and consensus approach and favor a more confrontational line. Moderate, conservative and even militant jihadist Islamic discourses co-exist in the contemporary Turkish setting, although the latter is marginal.

I have argued that the Harun Yahya enterprise's emergence and initial success in Turkey in the 1980s must be understood as part of the Islamic revival that gained momentum during this time. This revival in turn, must be understood both as related to the rise of political Islam and Islamic revivalism as a global phenomenon, but also as understood as related to socio-political conditions in Turkey. In particular, I have found that Yavuz' concept "opportunity spaces" is useful in terms of describing various factors such as political and economical liberalization that facilitated greater visibility of Islam, a broader space for maneuvering for Islamic movements, and contributed to the emergence of an influential new Muslim *bourgeoisie*. This, in turn, gave rise to a growing market for Islamic publications.

The influence of Islamic discourses on the level of the state and the greater visibility of Islam in the urban space resulted in a growing polarization between self-identified secularists and Islamists. The 80s and 90s witnessed not only the cultural construction of an Islamic political identity, but also of secularist identity. The *Kulturkampf* between secularists and Islamists, both laying claim to representing the most legitimate and authentic form of Turkishness, was fought out within the context of an increasingly consumerist culture. Each group cultivated and developed their own patters of consumption, and commodities such as the headscarf and pictures of Atatürk became important cultural markers signifying belonging and identity. Additionally, in the public sphere, both Islamists and secularists engaged in aggressive polemics and a discourse of "othering" against each other, with secularists accusing Islamists of representing backwardness, ignorance and "Arab culture", and Islamists accusing the secularists of being atheists, communists, undemocratic elitists, and of eroding Turkish-Muslim values. Thus, one outcome of the Islamic revival was increased cultural and political polarization, culminating in the postmodern coup in 1997.

However, despite the cultural constructions produced and maintained by both assertive secularists and Islamists, large sections of Turkish society were neither committed Islamists devoted to challenging the secular system, nor committed materialists, but rather "ordinary believers" that consider themselves devoted to both Atatürkism, nationalism and Islam, and who aspire to be both Western and modern while cherishing traditional values. A group that became less visible in the contested environment of 'Islamists vs. secularists', were believers who were socialized within a secular sociocultural context and did not identify with the Islamic segment. This somewhat neglected segment came to constitute Harun Yahya's own "opportunity space" for establishing his enterprise. Yahya perceived a potential for a different kind of Islamic proselytism, directed towards urban secular young people. It was in this setting that Harun Yahya found a particular niche for Islamic proselytism.

However, the movement that would ultimately emerge as the most successful in profiling itself as "modern elite Muslims" was the Gülen movement. Through a moderate discourse that placed less emphasis on identity politics and sought to redefine secularism rather than challenge it, as well as a consensus- and dialogue-oriented approach, the Gülen movement was able to reach beyond the parameters of a traditional Islamic segment. The soft coup in 1997 marked the fall of political Islam in Turkey and the rise of a new Islamic discourse predicated upon "Muslimhood" rather than Islamism, represented by the Gülen movement and the Justice and Development party. This shift marked a departure from the Islamist-secularist divide, and precipitated new alliances in the 2000s and onwards between Islamic moderates and secular liberals predicated upon favoring Western-style democracy, capitalism and supporting Turkey's EU-bid an, against more insular nationalist secularists (*ulusalcı*), right-wing nationalists (*milliyetçi*) and hardliner Islamists (Akyol 2007).

Thus, the period from the early 80s till the present is a period of great transformations in Turkey. It is within this transformative period that the Harun Yahya enterprise emerged and developed. In my later analysis, I hope to demonstrate how the themes covered in this chapter bear relevance to both the emergence of the Harun Yahya enterprise as well as the developments and transformations it underwent from its emergence until today. I aim to show how Harun Yahya, as a religious entrepreneur, has both been shaped by various discourses in Turkey as well as contributed to the shaping of Islamic discourses by availing of the opportunity spaces that emerged after the 1980 coup.

Specifically, I hope to demonstrate the way in which Harun Yahya has framed and adapted his discourse to target a various audiences, and how his discourse has evolved over the course of the last three decades.

CHAPTER 3
# Nationalism and Conspiracism

## 1. Introduction

In the previous chapter I provided an historical account of the Turkish context in which Harun Yahya emerged, focusing on influential discourses and the rise of a political Islamic movement in Turkey. The purpose of this chapter is to examine how Yahya employs and incorporates various popular discourses in the Turkish context, and to look at *how* these discourses change over time and *why*. The focus is on how the Harun Yahya enterprise has sought to carve a place for itself within the multitude of Islamic communities in Turkey by attempting to appeal to various audiences. I will therefore concentrate primarily on works and activities directed towards a Turkish audience.

Following a discussion on "conspiracy theories" and "conspiracism", I will first examine Yahya's employment of Judeo-Masonic conspiracy theories and trace developments in this discourse over time, focusing in particular on how and why anti-Semitic ideas in his early works have been abandoned in favor of a more ecumenical discourse. The second part of the chapter examines nationalist and neo-Ottomanist themes in Yahya's works, focusing especially on how and why the Harun Yahya enterprise have sought to market itself both as pro-Atatürk and nationalist as well as appealing to neo-Ottomanist sentiments. I argue in this chapter that Harun Yahya's employment of these discourses and the way in which he has developed them must be understood in relation to changes within Turkey.

## 2. Conspiracism

"Conspiracy theories" and "conspiracism" are fuzzy terms, and it is sometimes difficult to draw a clear line between conspiracy theories that are put forward for rhetorical or political purposes, where the narrator does not necessarily believe in the theory narrated, and conspiracy theories as a form of paranoia (Gray 2008, p. 158). Middle East scholar Matthew Gray offers a working definition of conspiracy theory or conspiracism as the act of developing and sustaining a discourse, usually a counter-discourse, that challenges conventional or accepted explanations for events, and that uses weak, flawed or fallacious logic, seeks to convince through rhetoric and repetition rather than analytical rigor, and most often aims to develop a theory that is broad or even universal in scope (Gray 2008, p. 159).

A variety of theoretical perspectives have been proposed as explanations for the emergence and popularity of conspiracy theories in different cultural and political contexts. One of the first major scholarly works on conspiracy theories was Richard Hofstadter's *The Paranoid Style in American Politics* (1965). Hofstadter offers a psychological take on conspiracy theories as a form of fear or paranoia stemming from American group anxiety (now often referred to as "agency panic"). In *Hidden Hand: Middle East Fears of Conspiracies* (1996), one of the first major books to deal specifically with conspiracy theories in the Middle East, Daniel Pipes also gives pathological explanations for the prevalence of conspiracy theories in the Middle East. In more recent works, Middle East scholar Matthew Gray criticizes Pipes' work for being polemic, reductionist and Orientalist (Gray 2010, p. 23; Gray 2008, p. 157). Gray instead understands the prevalence of conspiracy theories on both the state and popular level in the Middle East, as elsewhere, as a complex phenomenon having multiple sources, "stemming from political structures, competition between political actors and interaction of social groups and forces with each other and the state" (Gray 2008, p. 157), which I find a more useful approach to conspiracy theories.

Michael Barkun defines conspiracy theories as "the belief that an organization made up of individuals or groups was or is acting covertly to achieve a malevolent end" (Barkun 2006). According to Barkun, conspiracy theories attempt to make sense of a confusing world by providing "an overarching explanation for contemporary politics by fitting all events into a single scenario" (Barkun 2006, p. 65), and tracing all evil back to a single source: The conspirators and their agents. Conspiracy theories are presented as special, secret knowledge, and Barkun also regards conspiracy theories as linked with millenarianism, which is a topic I will discuss more thoroughly in Chapter 5.

Conspiracism as a narrative genre has been a central feature of Harun Yahya's discourse since the first publication published in the name of Harun Yahya until the present day (2012). In this chapter I will focus in particular on anti-Zionist and anti-Semitic themes in Yahya's conspiratorial works produced for the Turkish market, and how they may be understood in relation to the Turkish context.

## 3. Harun Yahya's Jewish-Masonic conspiracy theories

### 3.1. Judaism and Freemasonry

The first work ever published in the name of Harun Yahya was a nearly 500-page long book titled *Yahudilik ve Masonluk* (Judaism and Freemasonry) (Yahya 1987b). This was the second edition of a book of the same title published by Adnan Oktar in 1986 in the name of *Araştirma Grubu* (The Research Group) (1986).[1] The central thesis of *Yahudilik ve Masonluk* is that Freemasonry is closely linked with Judaism, and that Zionists are using Freemasonry as a front to carry out Zionist agendas both in Turkey and globally. In *Yahudilik ve Masonluk*, Yahya claims that it is impossible to explain Freemasonry without explaining the worldview of those who believe in what Yahya terms "the distorted Torah" (Yahya 1987b, p. 6). The purpose of the first part of *Yahudilik ve Masonluk* is therefore to expose "racist Zionist ideology", which is something that Yahya claims stems from "the distorted Torah". The Torah of the Jews is not the original Torah, claims Yahya, but an altered, distorted version.[2] As proof that the Torah is distorted, Yahya quotes passages from the Torah which he claims are "obscene" (1987b, p. 26). He also provides verses from the Qur'an as "proof" that the Jews have distorted the Torah (1987b, pp. 130–131).

Yahya portrays the Torah as containing copious amounts of "hatred, brutality and massacres" (1987b, p. 97). He cites passages in the Torah which he interprets as referring to massacres performed by Jews in Canaan, and links them with contemporary actions by the Israeli army towards nations living in "the promised land" (1987b, pp. 102–103). Yahya also refers to what he claims are "orders to massacre" in the Torah, and juxtaposes these with newspaper headlines and graphic photos depicting results of "Israeli brutality" (1987b, pp. 109–124). Yahya claims further that Israel is a state governed by religion (1987b, p. 33). The book is richly illustrated with pictures of Jewish children performing Jewish religious rituals to underscore his point that religion is given much importance in the upbringing of Jewish children. He claims that Israeli children are indoctrinated into a militarist mindset from primary school to university (1987b, p. 91). Yahya also gives examples of Jewish animosity and violence against Muslims in history (1987b, pp. 125–129).

---

[1] I have only managed to obtain a physical copy of the second edition of *Yahudilik ve Masonluk*. The preface to the second edition states that it only contains minor corrections from the original first edition (Yahya 1987b, p. 7).
[2] Yahya uses the term *"muharref Tevrat"* (distorted Torah). *Muharref* is adjective form of *tahrif*, a term referring to the Islamic tradition which claims that Biblical manuscripts have been distorted by Jews and Christians. See "Tahrif" in *Encyclopaedia of Islam* (Lazarus-Yafeh 2013).

The second part of the book is devoted to showing the connection between Judaism and Freemasonry. Yahya argues that in addition to describing in detail "massacres and atrocities that the Jewish race are ordered to commit against the nations of the World", "the distorted Torah" also describes in detail various "inconspicuous methods" (1987b, p. 132). When these methods are employed, argues Yahya,

> nations will collapse from within, and neither will the targeted nations realize this, nor will it be known that Jews are behind these events. Freemasonry is one of these secret branches of Judaism, but it is only within their secret rituals that their connection with Judaism and the fact that they identify with the teachings Torah becomes apparent. The Freemasons see it necessary to hide their relationship with Judaism; because using charity organizations as a smoke screen and appearing as philanthropists gives better results in terms of serving this cause as far as they are concerned, than showing [openly] that they share aims with Zionism (Yahya 1987b, p. 132).

These shared aims are according to Yahya to erode religious and moral values. Yahya claims that Freemasonry represents an irreligious philosophy. He argues that the Masonic term "the Great Architect of the Universe" refers to an immanent force or "energy" and is at odds with the notion of God as Creator, and that it is merely "materialist philosophy camouflaged as pagan ideas [of pantheism]" (1987b, p. 189). As further "evidence" of the connection between Freemasonry and materialist philosophy, Yahya maintains that Freemasonry defends "the eternity of matter" and Darwin's theory of evolution (1987b, p. 193).

Allegedly relying on documentation obtained from Masonic lodges, Yahya devotes a large portion of the book to descriptions of Masonic rituals, symbols, and beliefs as "proof" of parallels between Judaism and Freemasonry. Close to a hundred pages of the book are devoted to documenting the activities of Freemasons in business, politics, journalism and education both in Turkey and globally. Yahya lists Turkish, Ottoman and International companies, statesmen, ministers, educators, journalists, authors and philosophers that he claims are either Jewish or Freemasons. Yahya claims that Jews and Masons played an important role in the French, American, Russian, and Turkish revolutions, and asserts that there is a strong connection between Freemasonry and communism.

Although *Yahudilik ve Masonluk* is currently out of print, it is available in a great number of second hand online bookstores, where it is advertised as a "famous classic" which has been printed in close to 100.000 copies.[3] Its publication created a stir in Turkey when it came out, and brought media attention to Adnan Oktar and the BAV group. The publication also indirectly led to Oktar's imprisonment and later transfer to the criminal ward of Bakırköy

---

[3] See for instance <www.kitapyurdu.com/kitap/default.asp?id=953> [Accessed 01.03.2013].

psychiatric hospital, where he was diagnosed with Paranoid Schizophrenia ("Adnan Hoca Paranoyak" 1987).

*Yahudilik ve Masonluk* is an example of what is often referred to as a Jewish-Masonic conspiracy theory, one of the most well known types of historical conspiracy theories, which merge anti-Semitic conspiracy claims with anti-Masonic conspiracy claims. *The Protocols of the Elders of Zion*, which was disseminated at the beginning of the 20th century and later revealed to be a hoax, is regarded as one of the main sources of this particular strain of historical conspiracy theories.[4] Yahya does not refer to *The Protocols of the Elders of Zion* in *Yahudilik ve Masonluk*, but instead claims to document the connection between Judaism and Freemasonry based on independent research and primary sources. The purpose of *Yahudilik ve Masonluk*, as well as a number of later similar publications by Yahya, is to reveal what Yahya claims are hidden forces in history. Yahya takes the role of a guide and teacher who through careful consideration of historical documents pieces together and explains to his readers "the truth behind" seemingly isolated historical events (Yahya 2009e). An excerpt from the introduction of a more recent conspiracy work by Yahya, *Global Freemasonry: The Masonic Philosophy Unveiled and Refuted*, serves as an example of the pedagogical approach taken by Yahya in these works:

> After reading this book, the reader will be able to consider many subjects, from schools of philosophy to newspaper headlines, rock songs to political ideologies, with a deeper understanding, and better discern the meaning and aims behind events and factors (Yahya 2010d, p. 17).

In Yahya's early conspiratorial works, Zionism takes a central stage as the villain behind the conspiratorial plot, and this is also accompanied by negative portrayals of Jews and Judaism. As we shall see, however, Yahya with time plays down his rhetoric on Zionism and Jews, focusing instead on the role of Freemasonry in sustaining an anti-religious and anti-materialist philosophy.

### 3.2. The *Holocaust Deception* controversy

Although *Yahudilik ve Masonluk* contains a great deal of anti-Jewish and anti-Zionist polemics, it was a later publication that caught the public's attention and brought accusations of anti-Semitism against Adnan Oktar. A booklet titled *Soykırım Yalani: Siyonist-Nazi İşbirliğin Gizli Tarihi ve "Yahudi Soykırımı" Yalanının İçyüzü* (The Holocaust Deception: The Hidden Story of Nazi-Zionist Collaboration and the Inner Story of the hoax of "Jewish Holocaust") was

---

[4] *The Protocols of the Elders of Zion* purports to be the proceedings of a secret meeting where Jewish leaders discuss their plans for world domination, but was revealed to be a Russian forgery. See "The 'Protocols of the Elders of Zion' and the Myth of a Jewish Conspiracy in Post Soviet Russia" (Hagemeister 2005).

published in the name of Harun Yahya in 1995 (Yahya 1995a).[5] As the title suggests, this booklet challenges the official account of the Holocaust. Featuring a book cover depicting Hitler marching under the flag of Israel, the book claims that the founders of the Israeli state were cooperating with the Nazis, and that a massacre of Jews never took place during the Second World War. This, claims Yahya, "is not a hypothesis, a guess or a 'conspiracy theory', but a factual reality emerging from the examination of historical and technical evidence" (Yahya 1995b, p. 4).

In the first part of the book, Yahya argues that Zionists who wanted to establish a Jewish state had difficulties persuading European Jews to emigrate to Palestine, and therefore formed an alliance with German Nazis. Yahya argues further that the Nazis signed an agreement with The Zionist Federation of Germany, which would isolate the Jews from German people, make them regain their "racial consciousness" and emigrate to Palestine. In the second part of the book, the author argues that what official historical accounts present as extermination camps were in fact labor camps where Jews were isolated because the shipping of Jews to Palestine was interrupted when the war broke out. What is presented as Holocaust, the author claims, was the death of some Jews due to a typhus plague during the war, and the famine towards the end of the war caused by the defeat of the Germans. The political purpose of "the myth of the Holocaust" according to Yahya, is for the state of Israel to appear as a victim and draw attention away from its wrongdoings in terms of occupation, massacres and depopulation (Yahya 1995b).

Denying the Holocaust is a serious affair and also a criminal offence in many countries, and *Soykırım Yalanı* attracted media attention both within Turkey and abroad (Institute for Jewish Policy Research 1999). In response to this criticism, Adnan Oktar has denied responsibility for the book, despite the fact that it was published in the name of Harun Yahya, which by 1995 was well established as Oktar's pen name. Instead Oktar claims that the book was penned by a friend of his, Nuri Özbudak (Bartholomew 2009c).[6] In a letter to scholar of religion and blogger Richard Bartholomew, Oktar's lawyers explains that Oktar uses a number of research assistants to prepare his books, and that materials prepared for another

---

[5] See image appendix, p. 2. My physical copy of this book, obtained from a private Turkish seller online, contains no information of publishing year, but is a "complimentary copy of *Akit*" (Yahya 1995b). *Akit* was a fervently Islamist newspaper in the 1990s in Turkey. The newspaper was closed in 2001 but reappeared under the name *Vakit* the same year. According to Ruşen Çakır, thousands of copies of *Soykırım Yalanı* were distributed for free and given as supplement by Islamist newspapers (Çakır 2005).

[6] Oktar also denies that an English edition of the book has been published, but pictures of the cover of a book titled *The Holocaust Deception* by Harun Yahya (See Bartholomew 2009c) as well as pdf-files of the book still linger on the Internet. See for instance <http://wnlibrary.org/Portabel%20Documents/H/Holocaust/?p=10> [Accessed 04.02.3103].

book, *Soykırım Vahşeti* (The Holocaust Violence), had been "misinterpreted" by Özbudak to create *Soykırım Yalanı* (Bartholomew 2009a).

As discussed in the introductory chapter, I approach Harun Yahya in this dissertation not merely as the pen name of Adnan Oktar, but as a constructed persona created by a collective under the leadership of Adnan Oktar. I define "the works of Harun Yahya" as those works that have been produced in the framework of this collective and been identified and promoted as such. There is much evidence to suggest that the book has been supported and promoted in the framework of the Harun Yahya enterprise. In the "About the Author" text printed on the booklet's cover, Yahya is not identified as Oktar, but a number of other books written in the name of Harun Yahya are listed. According to Michael Hopkins at the TalkOrigins Archive (2003), *Soykırım Yalanı* was listed among the works of Harun Yahya on the Harun Yahya enterprise's main Internet domain www.harunyahya.com. Hopkins also notes that Harun Yahya cites himself from *Soykırım Yalanı* in *Israil'in Kürt Karti* (Israel's Kurdish Card) (footnote 3, Yahya 2003k, p. 229), a book that is still listed and available for download on Harun Yahya's official website. Moreover, Oktar's friend Nuri Özbudak, who Oktar claims wrote the book without his permission, remained a part of the BAV group.[7]

Regardless of who wrote it, *Soykırım Yalanı* has been published in the framework of the Harun Yahya enterprise and I therefore consider it as a part of the discourse of Harun Yahya, although Yahya has later distanced himself from its highly controversial content. The Harun Yahya enterprise instead promotes a later publication, *The Holocaust Violence* (Yahya 2006a),[8] where Yahya maintains his thesis concerning collaboration between Nazis and what Yahya now refers to as "radical Zionists", but recognizes that "Jewish people, of whom 5.5 million died in concentration camps, were the worst victims of the Nazi barbarity" (Yahya 2006a, p. 13). We thus see a radical change in the discourse of Yahya with regards to the Holocaust.

## 3.3. Anti-Semitism and Harun Yahya

Even in these early works, Yahya claims that the theses he puts forward do not amount to anti-Semitism (Yahya 1995b). Instead Yahya claims that the works are "anti-Zionist", which he defines as opposing "racist and offensive elements in Judaism" and "racist, hostile and expansionist policies of the State of Israel" (Yahya 1995b, p. 4). Yahya links Jewish theology and Zionist ideology, and

---

[7] Nuri Özbudak was among the BAV members indicted and later acquitted in a court case against the *Adnancılar* group in 2007. See "Adnan Hocacılar Grubu Davasında 5 Sanık Beraat Etti" (2007).

[8] The original Turkish edition was originally published in 2002 under the title *Soykırım Vahşeti* (Yahya 2002p) and is currently only available in a later edition (Yahya 2005a).

claims to document Zionist agendas involved in both Turkish and global affairs. Following the working definition of anti-Semitism adopted in 2005 by the EUMC (now called the European Union Agency for Fundamental Rights), such claims in themselves give sufficient grounds for characterizing Yahya's early works as anti-Semitic (European Forum on Antisemitism 2012).

According to many scholars of Islam and the Middle East, the kind of racist and theologically based anti-Jewish attitudes that have characterized European anti-Semitism have until recently been much less prominent in the Muslim and Arab world (Lewis 1998; Ma'oz 2010; Cohen 2010). Historically speaking, Jews generally fared better under Muslim rule as *Ahl al-Dhimma* (protected people) than they did in Christian Europe (Ma'oz 2010, p. viii). The attitudes of Muslim states and many Muslims began to change with the advent of the Jewish-Zionist national movement in the Palestine in the late 19th century (Ma'oz 2010). As the Arab-Israeli conflict has escalated throughout the 20th century, Arab and Muslim political opposition against Zionism and the Israeli occupation have at times been accompanied by an increased antagonism against Jews in general among many Muslims, particularly in the Arab world. European anti-Semitic conspiracy theories became popularized through for instance the Islamist ideologue Sayyid Qutb, who in his works referred to the *Protocols of the Elders of Zion* (Cohen 2010, p. 41).

### 3.4. The Islamist movement of the 1990s and the Harun Yahya enterprise

Yahya's anti-Zionist and anti-Masonic conspiracy theories found particular resonance with the political Islamic movement led by Necmettin Erbakan, which rose to power in Turkey in the 1990s. Anti-Jewish rhetoric was never part of the mainstream political discourse in Turkey, and Turkey's foreign policy vis-à-vis the Arab-Israeli conflict has generally been one of caution. Turkey has sought to strike a balance between maintaining good diplomatic relations with Israel, while also supporting UN resolutions against Israel as well as recognizing Palestine (Giray 2010). The publication of *Yahudilik ve Masonluk* coincided with the outbreak of the Palestinian intifada in 1987, which led to rising sympathies with the Palestinian people in Turkey (Giray 2010, p. 171). Throughout the 1990s, the growing Islamist movement in Turkey sought to mobilize political discontent over the plight of the Palestinian people by intensifying their anti-Israel and anti-Jewish rhetoric. The polemic of the Islamist newspapers became harsher, often failing to distinguish between Israelis, Zionists and Jews. The Welfare Party sought to appeal to Islamist sentiments by combining anti-Western and anti-Zionist rhetoric (Eligür 2010, p. 150). Necmettin Erbakan, the leader of the Milli Görus, was known for harboring anti-Zionist views bordering on anti-Semitism (Akyol 2011). According to Turkish scholar Rıfat Bali, two main themes in Necmettin Erbakan's anti-Zionist rhetoric were the notions that international Zionism aims for world domination and that Zionism is a source of anarchy in Turkey (Bali 1999).

Claiming to provide hard evidence for Zionist and Masonic plots both in Turkey and globally, the books of Harun Yahya therefore caught the interest of Erbakan and laid the ground for amicable and mutually beneficial relations between Erbakan and the Harun Yahya enterprise in the 1990s. After the "soft coup" and the backlash against political Islam in 1997, the Welfare Party was banned and remerged as the Virtue (Fazilet) Party. Adamant to show that the new party's platform remained Islamist, the secularist press published news reports indicating close ties between the Virtue Party and Oktar, who had recently been scandalized by an extensive and widely covered police operation in 1999 during which Oktar and many of his associates had been arrested. *Cumhuriyet* daily alleged that prominent executives of the Virtue Party had tried to protect Oktar by attempting to halt the police operation in 1999 ("Fazilet Partisi Adnan Hocacıların Koruyucusu" 2000). Another Turkish daily, *Milliyet*, reported that Erbakan had summarized the content of *Yahudilik ve Masonluk* during an *iftar* dinner (the breaking of the fast during Ramadan) with Islamic civil society organizations close to the Virtue Party ("Adnan Hocacı Erbakan!" 2001).[9] There were even speculations that the real author behind the books published under the name of Harun Yahya was not Oktar, but Erbakan himself ("Harun Yahya Erbakan Mi?" 2001; "Harun Yahya Oymuş" 2000).

In addition to the works on Darwinism, the anti-Zionist and anti-Masonic conspiracy works published in the name of Harun Yahya thus contributed to Oktar and his group winning sympathy within Islamist circles in the 1990s. Islamist newspapers associated with Milli Görus such as *Milli Gazete* have generally given the efforts of the Harun Yahya enterprise favorable press coverage. However, in the wake of Oktar's recent TV appearances featuring scantily clad women and disco dancing, circles close to Erbakan appear to have distanced themselves from Adnan Oktar. An article published on Erbakan's official website criticizes Oktar harshly for the content of his TV programs. The article praises the books published in the name of Harun Yahya, but asserts that Oktar's behavior shows that Oktar could not have been the real author behind these books (Eraydin 2012).

---

[9] The news article also claims that Erbakan had made speeches to his party executives citing segments of Yahya's books on evolution, and urged that Fazilet Party should attend the conferences of Bilim Araştırma Vakfi with full cadre ("Adnan Hocacı Erbakan!" 2001).

## 4. Yahya's shift towards ecumenism

### 4.1. The evolution of Yahya's conspiracism

The turn of the decade and the beginning of the 2000s marked a new phase, in which the Harun Yahya enterprise transitioned from a religious community operating in the Turkish context to a global publishing enterprise. The first English translations of Yahya's works were published in 1999, and were followed by a series of publications in English and other languages in subsequent years. It was also around this time that the Harun Yahya enterprise began utilizing the marketing possibilities of the Internet and build up a network of websites online. This global expansion was accompanied by a gradual shift in the discourse of Harun Yahya, which was also reflected in the works published in Turkish for the domestic market. After being subject to accusations of anti-Semitism and the backlash against *Yahudilik ve Masonluk* and *Soykırım Yalanı*, Harun Yahya began to modify his conspiratorial discourse on Judaism and Zionism.

In 1996, Yahya published a massive volume of nearly 1000 pages titled *Yeni Masonik Düzen* (New Masonic Order) (Yahya 1996b), which to date has been published in eight editions. This ambitious work aspires to providing a comprehensive account of the development of secularism in Europe as the result of a Masonic conspiracy, drawing on elements of New World Order conspiracy theories as well as anti-Zionist conspiracy theories. Yahya presents a grand conspiracy theory regarding the secret workings of Freemasonry from the Middle Ages until the present:

> This book investigates events which may appear quite different from one another from an historical perspective. From the discovery of America by Christopher Columbus to Nazi Germany, from the Protestant Reformation to the Muslim bloodshed in Bosnia-Herzegovina, the author investigates his topics in an orderly manner [...]. The main idea that this book proposes – and proves – is that, behind historical events, there are some secret realities that cannot be grasped by a superficial view (Yahya 2002s, p. 12).

This 4th edition from 2002 also includes an introduction emphasizing the difference between Zionism and Judaism.

Another work titled *Global Masonluk* was also published in 2002 (Yahya 2002j). Here Yahya claims to "unveil Masonic philosophy and the Masonic war on religion". The book's thesis is largely based on a book titled *The Hiram Key* (Knight & Lomas 1997), which traces the origins of Freemasonry to the Knights Templar. Yahya traces the roots of Freemasonry to the Knights Templar and Pharaonic Egypt. Yahya holds that the Knights Templar, which he claims were the precursors to Freemasonry, was heavily influenced by Kabbalah (Jewish mysticism). According to Yahya, the teachings of Kabbalah are rooted in pagan idolatry and ancient Egyptian paganism. These themes have been developed further in *Tapınak Şövalyeleri* (The Knights Templar) (2002q) and *Tapınakçılar ve Masonlar* (Templar and Masons) (Yahya 2006b).

From the late 2000s onwards, Yahya began taking further measures to try to disassociate himself from anti-Semitism. A later edition of *Global Masonluk* (2008) includes an added preface emphasizing that Masons have misunderstood certain elements of Kabbalah and interpreted it according to their own prejudices, and that Jewish beliefs and practices are not responsible for the superstitious interpretations of Freemasons:

> Masons' misinterpretation of certain information in the Kabbalah in the light of their own interests stems from their own prejudice and flawed perspective. Judaic belief and practice is not responsible for the false Masonic interpretation. The criticism made when considering the connection between Freemasonry and Kabbalistic teaching is not, therefore, aimed at Judaic belief (Yahya 2008b, p. 8).

The 8th edition of *Yeni Masonik Düzen* (2009j) includes an added special preface titled "Important Statement about Judaism and Zionism", where Yahya not only distinguishes between Judaism and Zionism, but also explains that there are two varieties of Zionism. Muslims are not opposed to "the Zionist conception of the devout Jewish people, who wish to live in peace and security in Israel alongside Muslims, seeking peace and wishing to worship in the lands of their forefathers and engage in business", claims Yahya, but oppose "radical, atheist Zionism, a social Darwinist and occupying ideology" (Yahya 2009j, p. 10). The same disclaimer has been added to many of the recent editions of Yahya's works referring to Zionism and Judaism. A work titled *Siyonizm Felsefesi* (Yahya 2002o) was renamed *Ateist Siyonizm Felsefesi* in the latest edition (Yahya 2009c). In *Ateist Siyonizm Felsefesi* (Atheist Zionism Philosophy), Yahya explains that the main reason behind war and conflict in the Middle East is "Atheist Zionist Ideology" (2009c). Here Yahya writes that "the Torah does not command Jews to occupy, shed blood and cause corruption; on the contrary it commands them to ensure peace and serenity" (p. 178). This, then, is a major departure from *Yahudilik ve Masonluk*, where Yahya explained the actions of the Israeli state with reference to passages in the "distorted Torah". In *Ateist Siyonizm Felsefesi*, Yahya instead underlines that Islam and Judaism share beliefs and morals, and gives examples of how Jews were given refuge in the Ottoman Empire (2002o, p. 178).

Thus, there has been a gradual transformation in Yahya's discourse on Jews and Zionism from 1987 to the present. In the first work, *Judaism and Freemasonry*, Yahya makes little effort to distinguish between Judaism and Zionism. Instead he explicitly attributes "Zionist racism" to the Torah, which Yahya refers to as "the distorted Torah". In more recent works, Yahya has modified the anti-Semitic rhetoric and instead refers to how "some radical Zionists" and "atheist Freemasons" have misinterpreted some elements of the Kabbalah. Furthermore, early and overtly anti-Jewish works such as *Yahudilik ve Masonluk* (1987b) and another book titled *Yehova'nin Oğulları* (Bilim Araştırma Grubu 1993) have been removed from Yahya's official website.[10] Conspiracy theories still play an important part in the discourse of Harun Yahya, but anti-Jewish and anti-Zionist themes have been toned down and modified in favor of a focus on "atheist Freemasonry" and how materialist and irreligious philosophies have been carried forward by various forces in history.

## 4.2. The turn to ecumenism

Parallel with Yahya's effort to disassociate himself from anti-Semitism, a gradually more positive and affirmative attitude towards "the people of the book" began taking shape in the works of Yahya in the 2000s. After the 9/11 terror attacks, Yahya published *Islam Terörü Lanetler* (Islam Denounces Terrorism) (Yahya 2001e), which has been published in six editions and been translated to 12 languages.[11] In *Islam Terörü Lanetler,* Yahya argues that there is no such thing as Islamic, Christian or Jewish terror, because "there is no place for terror in neither Islam nor in the two other divine religions" (Yahya 2001e, p. 8). Instead Yahya identifies irreligion, barbarism and Darwinism as the sources of terrorism. European colonialism was not born out of Christian morality, claims Yahya, but out of "an irreligious current that opposed Christian morality, and whose greatest atrocities were carried out with the support of 19$^{th}$ century Social Darwinist ideology" (2001e, p. 42).[12] "Actually", argues Yahya, "the main clash in the world is not between the West and Islam, but between religious people in both the West and Islamic world and those opposed to religion (materialists, atheists and Darwinists)" (2001e, p. 42).

Yahya explains that the Qur'an refers to Jews and Christians as "the people of the book" because they abide by the divine books revealed by God. He emphasizes that Islam's outlook on "the people of the book" is one of justice and mercy (2001e, pp. 52–53), and that anti-Semitism is a form of racism completely contrary to Islam (2001e, p. 55). He emphasizes that Islam shares many beliefs and moral values with Jews and Christians (p. 53), and that the Qur'an instructs Muslims, Jews and Christians to live in friendship (p. 57). According to Yahya,

---

[10] Another book, *Kabala ve Masonluk* is according to Yahya "an updated version of our book *Yehova'nin Oğulları*" (Yahya 2007e, p. 16). Both books are also listed among Yahya's works on a website from 2007. See <http://harunyahyakitaplari.blogspot.se> [Accessed 04.02.3013].

[11] It is worth noting that the publication date of the book is October 2011, less than two months after the 9/11 attacks. The book refers to the attacks in the introduction and appears to have been written in response to it.

[12] This is in all likelihood a reference to Samuel P. Huntington's thesis of a "clash of civilizations".

Muslims, Christians and Jews are also drawn together by having common opponents, namely "irreligious philosophies" and "harmful ideologies" such as "materialism, communism, fascism, anarchism, racism, nihilism and existentialism", which Yahya claims have "dragged people, societies and nations into great crises, conflicts and wars" (2001e, p. 54).

In *Gelin Birlik Olalım* (A Call for Unity) (Yahya 2003f), Yahya further develops this theme of Muslims, Jews and Christians sharing beliefs and values, and declares that the time has come for Muslims, Christians and Jews to bring forward and highlight these shared values, and to unite against Darwinism and irreligious ideologies. Later works highlight positive aspects of Judaism and Christianity, such as *Tevrat'tan Hikmetler ve Güzel Öğütler* (Wisdom and Sound Advice from the Torah) (Yahya 2008g) and *İncil'den Güzel Sözler* (Pleasant Words from the Gospel) (Yahya 2010f).

The emphasis on dialogue and "a union of faiths" became central features of the Harun Yahya enterprise's other outreach activities from 2009 onwards.[13] The Harun Yahya enterprise developed links with a Jewish group from Israel called "the re-established Sanhedrin", and had a meeting with them in Istanbul in July 2009.[14] In 2011 the enterprise invited another delegation of religious leaders from Israel to Istanbul and held a joint press conference ("Joint Press Conference of Mr Adnan Oktar with Israeli Delegation" 2011). The event was reported in the *Jerusalem Post* (Mandel 2011), and videos from these meetings were published on the Harun Yahya enterprise's websites. When the Harun Yahya enterprise established their own satellite TV channel in 2011, a program titled "Building Bridges" became a regular show featuring Jewish leaders, Christian evangelists and even Freemasons.[15]

### 4.3. Yahya's ecumenical discourse and the Gülen movement

Harun Yahya's discourse on Jews and Zionism started to change after the Harun Yahya enterprise began shifting its focus from an exclusively Turkish to a global market in the 2000s. This change of focus must be understood partly on the background of the Harun Yahya enterprise targeting a wider and more global audience, including non-Muslims. However, the embracement of ecumenism was not only a feature of English-language publications, but also of publications published in Turkish. The turn to ecumenism must therefore be understood not

---

[13] The Harun Yahya websites <www.kitapehli.com> and <www.unionoffaiths.com> (English version) are devoted to showcasing the Harun Yahya enterprise's ecumenical and interfaith activities [Accessed 03.03.2013]. See image appendix, p. 10.

[14] An official statement from the meeting is available on the Sanhedrin's website: <www.thesanhedrin.org/en/index.php/Hachrazah_5769_Tamuz_9> [Accessed 11.02.2013]. The Sanhedrin and their links to Adnan Oktar are also discussed in one of Richard Bartholomew's blog posts (Bartholomew 2009b).

[15] See image appendix, p. 5.

merely as an aspect of the global expansion of the Harun Yahya enterprise, but also as related to changing dynamics in the Turkish Islamic discourse and Harun Yahya's positioning within the religious market in Turkey.

As described in Chapter 2, Islamic discourses in Turkey have undergone a gradual transformation in the last three decades. The 80s and 90s were dominated by the political Islamic discourse of Erbakan and the Milli Görüş, which also included anti-Western and anti-Zionist Islamist rhetoric. However, especially after the "soft coup" in 1997 where the military clamped down on Islamist politics, which it saw as a threat to the secular order in Turkey, these types of discourses have been increasingly marginalized. Instead a more moderate Islamic discourse developed, which sought to align itself with the state and negotiate the terms of secularism. Avowedly turning its back on Islamist politics, a reformist wing of Milli Görüş formed *Adalet ve Kalkınma Partisi* (Justice and Development Party – JDP), which came to power in 2002 and whose political identity may be characterized as conservative-Islamic nationalist and neo-liberal rather than Islamist.

While the JDP rose to political power, the Gülen movement developed into the most influential Islamic civil society movement in Turkey. In its earliest phase, the discourse of the Gülen movement contained anti-communist and anti-Western elements. With time it developed a more inclusive approach, emphasizing dialogue and tolerance as necessary for solving conflicts and problems both in Turkey and globally, and thereby gained sympathizers also among secular liberals in Turkey (Yavuz 2003, p. 184). Arguably, the Gülen movement spearheaded the change towards a more pluralistic, moderate Islamic discourse in Turkey. From the mid-90s onwards, the Gülen movement began advancing interfaith dialogue, and Fethullah Gülen had meetings with Jewish and Christian leaders, including John Paul II in 1998 (Yavuz 2003, p. 201). It was only after the Gülen movement's efforts that the Diyanet also began promoting interreligious dialogue and eventually also established its own unit for interreligious dialogue (Yılmaz 2003, p. 233). Inter-civilizational dialogue is today one of the core bases of the Gülen movement's transnational activities, together with activities in the field of education (Pandya & Gallagher 2012).

This change in Yahya's discourse must therefore be understood not merely as a result of global opening, but also as reflecting the changing Zeitgeist in Turkey and the marginalization of the Islamist agendas of the old Milli Görüş and Erbakan in favor of the moderately Islamic and conservative nationalist JDP–Gülen axis. As the Gülen movement grew increasingly more influential in Turkey, the Harun Yahya enterprise disassociated itself with the anti-Zionist discourse of the old Milli Görüş, and instead aligned itself increasingly with a modernist neo-Nurcu dialogue-friendly "liberal Islam".[16] Yahya has taken to emphasizing the commonalities between Islam and the people of the book in a similar manner to Fethullah Gülen.

Although this dialogue-oriented discourse now appears to be the dominant one in Turkey, there is still a certain tension between the modernist Nurcus and the Gülen movement on the one hand, and certain conservative Nakşibendi groups more aligned with the old Milli Görüş view on the other. An example of the latter is the well-known preacher Ahmet Mahmut Ünlü a.k.a Cübbeli Ahmet Hoca, one of the leaders of the conservative Ismailağa *cemaatı*.[17] Cübbeli Ahmet Hoca receives much media attention and is known for his humorous and entertaining style of preaching. He is one of Yahya's most vocal critics, and has among other things criticized Yahya for his inclusivist attitude to Jews and Christians.[18] Ironically, some conservative nationalist critics seeking to discredit Oktar have also "accused" Oktar of being crypto-Jewish.[19]

## 4.4. Yahya's conspiracism and nationalist discourses in the 1990s

Although the themes of Zionism and Israel have been toned down both in Turkish and English publications, Yahya's main website still lists conspiratorial works in Turkish which express anti-Israel and anti-Zionist attitudes. In *İsrail'in Dünya Egemenliği Politikası* (Israel's Politics of World Hegemony) (2003j), Yahya claims that Israel's domestic and foreign policy is dominated by "irreligious, racist and aggressive" Zionist ideology (Yahya 2003j, p. 10). The third edition of a book titled *İsrail'in Kürt Kartı: İsrail'in Ortadoğu Stratejisi ve "Kürt Devleti" Senaryoları* (Israel's Kurdish Card: Israel's Strategy in the Middle East and "Kurdish State" Scenarios) is also still available on Yahya's official webpage (Yahya 2003k)[20]. In this book, Yahya claims that Israel supports Kurdish separatism and aims to establish a Kurdish state as part of their foreign policy strategy. Yahya here explains "imperialist" Israel's foreign policy as stemming from an irrational fear rooted in

---

[16] I had my first encounter with the Harun Yahya enterprise in 2005, when I met with the then head of Bilim Araştırma Vakfı, Sedat Altan. During this meeting, Altan criticized the prevalence of anti-Western and anti-American attitudes among certain circles in Turkey, and was careful to emphasize that Bilim Araştırma Vakfı did not entertain such ideas.
[17] The Ismailağa *cemaat* is a Nakşibendi community revolving around the Ismailağa mosque in the conservative Çarşamba neighborhood of Fatih municipality, Istanbul. Considered to be a particularly conservative Turkish Muslim community, the women usually wear full-covering *çarşaf* (similar to the Iranian chador), and the men usually sport beards, baggy trousers and skull caps, which is not very common in Turkey. See Çakır (1990).
[18] Cübbeli Ahmet says that anyone who believes Yahya's statement that "Jews and Christians are friends of God" will be *muşrik* (polytheist) and *mürted* (apostate). Available at <www.dailymotion.com/video/xh1s1o_cubbeli-ahmet-hoca-adnan-oktar-ve-yahudiler_shortfilms> [Accessed 04.02.2013].
[19] See for instance <http://a9tvizlemeyin.blogspot.se/2012/08/bunlar-musluman-degiller-adnan-oktar.html>[Accessed 04.02.2013].
[20] The first edition was published in 1997 (Yahya 1997b).

the history of the Jewish people, especially the siege of Jerusalem in 1187. Yahya terms this fear *Hıttin korkusu;* the fear of [the battle of] Hattin, and claims that "Jewish ideology" is characterized by constant hatred and animosity towards non-Jews (Yahya 2003k, p. 33).[21]

These books appear to conflict with Yahya's new ecumenical line and his effort to dissociate himself from political Islam. The fact that such books are still available on Yahya's official website could be interpreted as reflecting an effort to continue to cater to anti-Zionist sentiments within the Islamist movement in Turkey. However, it must also be understood within a broader framework of the resurgence of nationalism in Turkey during the 1990s.

Turkish nationalism gained momentum in the late 1980s and 1990s. Left nationalism in Turkey has generally been anti-imperialist and secularist. With the rise of Islamist and Kurdish nationalism, however, a harsher and more fanatic variety of left secular nationalism known as *ulusalcılık* developed. Staunchly secular and opposed to the conservative, neo-liberal JDP with its Islamist roots, *ulusalcılık* is often juxtaposed with *milliyetçilik,* which is associated with conservative or right-wing nationalism (both words translate as nationalism). However, the discourse of *ulusalcılık* shares common ground with Turkism and right-wing nationalism in terms of containing xenophobic elements and a perception that Turkey is under threat from both external and internal forces wishing to divide Turkey. In this neo-nationalist discourse, both Kurdish cultural demands and Islamic identity are perceived as threats to the unity and territorial integrity of the state, and minorities' claims and demands in Turkey are suspected as really being a part of "foreign agendas".

Tanıl Bora argues that a number of factors related to globalization incited Turkish nationalism during this time, and contemporized the perceptions of external and internal threats which has given shape to Turkish nationalism since the establishment of the republic (Bora 2010). Transnational processes upset the structures of the nation state, and the position of minorities and Turkey's human rights record became diplomatic issues. The Kurdish issue and the conflict between the military and the PKK between 1984 and 1999 also played a central role in triggering nationalist responses.

Turkey entered the beginning of the 1990s with confidence. There was an economic boom, and optimism with regards to the prospects of Turkey joining the EU. The newly independent Turkic republics fueled a new wave of pan-Turkism. However, self-confidence started to fade with the Gulf war. There was growing fear that Western hegemony would increase in the region. The rise of the Kurdish nationalist movement and the pressure Turkey was faced with from Europe with regards to its treatment of minorities, its failure to solve the

---

[21] The Battle of Hattin in 1187 was the battle in which the Crusader Kingdom of Jerusalem was defeated by Muslim forces under the leadership of Saladin.

Kurdish issue with democratic means was used by nationalists to support the argument that Turkey was faced by a conspiracy. The theme of national survival thus remerged in the nationalist discourse of the 1990s and early 2000s.

The rise in nationalist discourses and a re-actualization of Turkey's "ontological insecurities" (Nefes 2012) were factors conducive to the proliferation and widening appeal of conspiracy theories in the 1990s, argues Bora (Bora 2010). Along with the rise of *ulusalcılık* from the 1990s onwards, conspiracy theories became more widespread and popular in Turkey, also among the secular left (Bora 1994). This new conspiracism in the 1990s in Turkey also included elements of suspicion against Jews, more specifically Sabbateans/crypto-Jewish *dönmes*.[22] Conspiracy theories regarding Jewish "hidden hands" had previously mainly been confined to ultra-right and conservative segments in Turkey (Bora 1994). The involvement of *dönmes* in the Young Turk movement and the fact that the Committee for Union and Progress (CUP) met in Freemasonry lodges contributed to conspiracy theories among conservative critics of the CUP regarding Jewish involvement in the Turkish modernization movement (Nefes 2012, p. 417). When the CUP cadres became the founders of the republic, the conspiracy theories began to focus on the founders of the Turkish republic, including Atatürk (Nefes 2012, p. 418). There were also a few works published by Islamist or right-wing authors in the second republican period, which portrayed *dönmes* as a secret and closed community like the Freemasons, causing moral decay in Turkey (Nefes 2012).

Conspiracy theories regarding *dönmes* re-emerged in the 1990s and 2000s in the writings of *ulusalcı* conspiracists who saw the *dönmes* as part of a neo-liberal conspiracy. In 2004, a book titled *Efendi: Beyaz Türklerin Büyük Sırrı* (Efendi: The Great Secret of the White Turks) became a bestseller in Turkey (Yalçın 2004). Its author, Soner Yalçın, claims that prominent and powerful families in Turkey are Sabatteans or *dönme* (crypto-Jewish).[23] Yalçın is now chief editor of the *ulusalcı* TV channel Oda TV.

Much of the opposition from Kemalists and the *ulusalcı* against the JDP has been framed not merely in terms of accusations that the JDP threatens the secular order in Turkey, but also that it compromises the national autonomy of Turkey. The government is accused of "selling out" Turkey, and letting its

---

[22] Sabbateans refers to followers of Sabbatai Sevi, a leader of a Jewish messianic movement in the 17th century. Due to his growing popularity, Jewish religious authorities requested the Ottoman Empire to take action. Sevi was forced to convert to Islam, and was subsequently employed by the Ottoman Sultan. Many of Sevi's followers followed his example. The *dönme* (convert), as they became known, acted as Muslims in public but retained Jewish identities in private. This practice and the *dönme* community's connections with the Turkish modernization movement gave rise to conspiracy theories regarding *dönmes* and Jews. See Nefes (2012) about the scapegoating of *dönmes* in Turkey.
[23] See Rıfat Bali's article "What is Efendi telling us?" (2005) for an analysis of Yalçın's anti-Semitism and the context in which the book was received.

destiny be controlled by foreign interests, such as the US, the EU or Israel. Some of this opposition has been expressed in terms of conspiracy theories claiming that central figures in the government secretly work for foreign interests rather than for Turkey. Ergün Poyraz has written a series of condemnatory works about the JDP and the Gülen movement, including the bestseller *Musa'nin Çocukları* (The Children of Moses), which contains claims that Prime Minister Recep Tayyip Erdoğan ascended to power as part of a "Zionist conspiracy" (Poyraz 2007).

Türkay Nefes understands this new wave of conspiracy theories among the nationalist left in the 90s as reflecting nostalgia for the "solid modernity" of the early republican era, in the face of the "liquid modernity" that characterized the 1990s and 2000s (Nefes 2012, p. 431).[24] Globalization and an emerging multiculturalist discourse in the 1990s challenged the exclusionary character of Turkish nationalism.

In the neo-nationalist discourse the 1980s and 1990s, the Kurdish issue was also often approached from a conspiratorial perspective. There was widespread disillusionment that the PKK continued to exist in spite of the efforts of the Turkish military. In nationalist discourse, Kurdish identity claims and demands for rights were dismissed and instead external factors and were sought as explanations for the Kurdish issue. There was a proliferation of conspiracy theories surrounding the PKK, claiming for instance that the US supported PKK as a part of a its Greater Middle East project. Yahya's thesis in *Israil'in Kürt Kartı* is thus a variation of this type of nationalist conspiracy theory. Yahya combines the propensity in neo-nationalist discourse to ascribe Kurdish separatism to external factors with antagonism towards Israel.

Yahya's conspiracism must thus be considered in a broader light than merely a certain type of political Islamic rhetoric. As we shall see in the second half of this chapter, Yahya did not merely seek to appeal to a narrow Islamist segment through employment of anti-Zionist rhetoric, but also sought to appeal to a wider audience in Turkey by employing a broad range of nationalist discourses.

## 4.5. Conspiracism and ecumenism in the English works

The focus of this chapter is on Yahya's changing discourses in the Turkish context, and I have therefore concentrated on Turkish editions of Yahya's works. From the 2000s onwards, the Harun Yahya enterprise expanded its activities beyond Turkey to include a global market, and began publishing works in English and other languages. The themes of conspiracism and ecumenism are also carried forward in Yahya's English-language works. The works dealing with ecumenism published in the 2000s are available in both Turkish and English,

---

[24] A term coined by Zygmunt Bauman, "liquid modernity" refers to a chaotic continuation of modernity characterized by feelings of uncertainty and alienation.

and many of the works on conspiracy theories referred to above are also available in English. It is difficult to obtain publishing details for some of the earlier editions in English, however, since they are no longer listed on Yahya's websites. For example, *The Complete Works of Harun Yahya*[25] refers to an English edition of *Yeni Masonik Düzen* titled *The New Masonic Order*, but this publication is no longer available from Yahya's official website.

Apart from the exceptions that I have discussed above, in both the Turkish and the English works on conspiracy theories published in the 2000s, there is a general tendency away from anti-Zionism and political themes towards a focus on the history of irreligious ideas, materialism and Darwinism. While earlier works assign blame to Zionists and vilify the state of Israel, more recent works claims to trace broader lines in the history of irreligious and materialistic ideas, from ancient pagan religions via the Knights Templar, some "atheist Freemasons", and Darwinist ideology as the current manifestation of irreligious ideas. Recent works focus on a historical conspiracy of irreligious, materialist and Darwinist forces against theistic religion, and therefore something Jews, Christians and Muslims should work against together. As we shall see in Chapter 5, this conspiracy is not merely framed in historical terms, but is also placed into a cosmological and eschatological framework.

## 6. Atatürkism, nationalism and neo-Ottomanism

As I have outlined in Chapter 2, nationalist idioms have played a major role in contemporary Islamic discourses in Turkey. In the present section, I will look closer at how Yahya engages with and appropriates various nationalist discourses in his works. Specifically, I will examine Yahya's ideas about Atatürk, nationalism, Turkishness and Turkish foreign policy in his politically themed works. Although the themes overlap, the works considered in this section may be divided broadly into two categories: Works dealing with Atatürk and Turkish nationalism; and works dealing with neo-Ottomanism, pan-Turkism and the notion of Turkish leadership.

## 7. Appropriating Atatürk

### 7.1. The cult of Atatürk and politics of identity

Kemalism or Atatürkism refers to the ideology of Mustafa Kemal Atatürk as embodied in the six founding principles of the Turkish state. However,

---

[25] No publication year is available for this book, but it can be downloaded from http://harunyahya.com/en/works/965/the-complete-works-of-harun/chapter/2533 [Accessed 04.02.2013].

sometimes Atatürkism or *Atatürkçülük* implies not merely the official Kemalist ideology, but also has connotations to the personality cult surrounding Atatürk (Zürcher 1992, p. 239). Anthropologist Yael Navaro-Yashin describes how the image of Atatürk, an emblem of the state and a symbol of Turkish sovereignty, took on a different dimension in the 1990s, which she studies as "Atatürk fetishism" or "the cult of Atatürk". In the context of the politics of identity between secularists and Islamists, the image of Atatürk was employed in the making of various items such as posters, badges, portraits, photographs, busts and statuettes, which were extensively circulated at public and private secularist events and demonstrations (Navaro-Yashin 2002, pp. 188–201). The framing of Atatürk as a symbol of opposition to Islamism by the secularists was mirrored, in turn, by large sections of the pro-Islamic segment portraying Atatürk as an enemy of religion. Against this background, I will examine Harun Yahya's move towards the promotion of a particular interpretation of Atatürkism from the 1990s onwards.

## 7.2. Harun Yahya's turn towards Atatürkism

Due to the existence of a special law in Turkey often referred to as the Atatürk Protection Law (law nr 5816), explicit criticism of Atatürk or Kemalism has potential legal repercussions, and it is therefore difficult to find examples of this in writing.[26] However, there are indications that until the late 80s, Oktar's attitude to Atatürk was more or less in line with the Islamist circles at the time; that is, highly critical. In a column in the daily newspaper *Yeni Şafak* in 2000, Nazlı Ilıcak writes:[27]

> I know Adnan Oktar from the early days. In the beginning of the 80s, he got a foothold into the high schools of wealthy kids. There, he would preach to youngsters who were feeling a sense of emptiness and try to draw them into a religious community life. At that time, he was an opponent of Atatürk. Later he understood that his anti-Atatürk position made these children of wealthy families uncomfortable. [...] In Bulvar newspaper, we organized a panel where Adnan Oktar and his followers participated. I was the panel moderator. Due to Oktar's anti-Atatürk statements, we were both tried by the State Security Court (Ilıcak 2000).

An editorial titled "Taktik Atatürkçülük" (Tactical Atatürkism) in *Hürriyet* daily cites an interview with Oktar from June 2nd 1986, where Oktar allegedly had said

---

[26] Law 5816 has been in effect since 1951.
[27] Nazlı Ilıcak is a well-known conservative journalist in Turkey. In an interview Ilıcak did with Adnan Oktar in *Bulvar Gazetesi* in 1986, Oktar declared "Türk kavmindenim, İslam milletindenim" (I am of the Turkish tribe and the Islamic nation), a statement for which he was charged with "making propaganda with the aim of weakening or destroying national sentiments" by the Istanbul State Security Court, and subsequently arrested and imprisoned at the criminal ward of Bakırköy psychiatric hospital (Güner 1986).

that "there are ideas of Atatürk that I disagree with, such as theories resembling Darwin's theory" ("Taktik Atatürkçülük" 1999).

In the beginning of the 1990s, however, Oktar and his associates began promoting Atatürk and *Atatürkçülük* (Atatürkism) on a large scale.[28] In 1990, they established Bilim Araştırma Vakfı (BAV). From the mid-90s onwards, BAV functioned as the organizational framework around the Harun Yahya enterprise's various creationist activities. Initially, however, BAV was established as a *hizmet kuruluşu* (service foundation or volunteer organization) with nationalist goals, as reflected in its mission statement:

> The aim [of BAV] is to protect the national and moral values that are keeping the Turkish State and society on its feet, and to create strategic solutions to the country's problems. With its identity as Atatürkist, democratic, modern, nationalist, progressive and sacredist,[29] BAV aims to raise enlightened generations that will light the future of our Turkey. It is clear that in order to transcend the contemporary level of civilization, we need generations that love their country and their state, and have been sanctified by Turkish-Islamic ethics. Our organization believes that only a young generation in line with this can bring forth a Turkey that will lead the Turkish-Islamic world under the umbrella of peace, security, love and mercy (Bilim Araştırma Vakfı 2013).

BAV became Adnan Oktar's primary platform for profiling himself and the community around him as "real Atatürkists" working for Turkish nationalist aims, thus dissociating themselves from the Islamist label. BAV began publishing the journal *Rönesans* in 1991, mostly containing articles about Atatürk and featuring pictures of Atatürk on the front page. Throughout the 1990s, BAV launched extensive advertising campaigns that featured full-page ads in daily newspapers and huge billboards and street banners in designated high-traffic areas of Istanbul, with pictures and quotes of Atatürk juxtaposed with the name and logo of BAV. In 1995, they established another foundation, *Milli Değerler Koruma Vakfı* (Foundation for the Protection of National Values). Also promoting Atatürkism, MDKV's activities have a more exclusively national focus.[30]

In the early 2000s, Yahya published a number of books on Atatürk in Turkish, partly based on the articles that had been printed in *Rönesans* in 1991: *Gerçek Atatürkçülük* (Real Atatürkism) (Yahya 2001d), *Samimi Bir Dindar Atatürk* (The Genuinely Devout Man Atatürk) (Yahya 2002n), *Asker Atatürk* (Atatürk The Soldier) (Yahya 2002a), *Atatürk ve Gençlik* (Atatürk and Youth)

---

[28] In an editorial titled "Notes of the Month" in *Altınoluk*, a religious journal published by the Erenköy cemaatı branch of the Nakşibendi Sufi order, the author writes that after being released from the criminal ward in Bakırköy Hospital, Adnan Oktar "became more Atatürkist than anyone" and the journal *Rönesans* published by Yahya and his colleagues "was filled with Atatürkism back to front" ("Ayın Notları" 1990).
[29] See Chapter 2 section 3.2.2.
[30] Website available at <www.mdkv.org> [Accessed 01.03.2013].

(Yahya 2002c), *Atatürkü'ü İyi Anlamak* (Understanding Atatürk Well) (Yahya 2002d), *Atatürk'ün Vatan ve Millet Sevgisi* (Atatürk's Love for Nation and Homeland) (Yahya 2002e), and a two-volume *Atatürk Ansiklopedisi* (Atatürk Encyclopedia) (Yahya 2002b; Yahya 2003a). Following the distinctive graphical style of Harun Yahya's works, the books are ornate and richly illustrated. In an interview included in the 3rd edition of *Atatürk'ün Millet ve Vatan Sevgisi*, Yahya proudly proclaims: "My books are the most beautiful and high-quality works on Atatürk in the history of the republic. With regards to both design, decoration, content, technique and style, they are the most perfect" (Yahya 2002e, p. 23).

## 7.3. Harun Yahya's Atatürk

One of the principal aims of these books published by Yahya is to demonstrate by reference to Atatürk's words, actions and biographical sources that Atatürk was both a devout man who promoted Islamic values as well as a fervent Turkish nationalist, and thus that there is no contradiction between the two:

> For more than a century, certain ideological circles have attempted to present the Turkish public with a profoundly distorted reasoning. According to this reasoning, the founder of the Turkish republic, Atatürk, was against religion and a defender of materialist ideas. What's more, being religious and being religious was presented as opposing concepts (Harun Yahya 2002n, p. 9).

Yahya argues that examination of the biographical sources on Atatürk's life shows that he was not a materialist, but on the contrary "a devout Muslim who believed in Allah and took the Qur'an as the guide for his life" (Yahya 2002n, p. 12). Rather than rejecting Atatürk, Yahya seeks to reclaim Atatürk from the trappings of assertive secularism and to (re)-interpret him as an emblem of Turkish nationalism as well as a "genuine Muslim" who fought against both materialism and communism (2001d, p. 7). As arguments for the devout Atatürk, Yahya presents quotes attributed to Atatürk about Islam in order to show that he was attached to Islam and that he had great respect and affection for the Prophet Muhammed (Yahya 2002n, p. 20). He quotes statements about Islam made by Atatürk during the Turkish War of Liberation (2002g, pp. 43–44).[31] He claims that Islamic ethics was manifest in Atatürk's personality (2002g, p. 23) and points to parallels between Atatürk and the ideal Muslim as Yahya interprets it from the Qur'an (2002g, p. 59). He devotes a chapter to Atatürk's anticommunism, which he regards as evidence of Atatürk's nationalist and antimaterialist stance (Yahya 2001d, p. 67). Yahya also addresses Atatürk's idea of

---

[31] As mentioned in Chapter 2, Atatürk and his supporters sought to appeal to Islam in the struggle against the Greeks. Statements made by Atatürk during this period therefore lend themselves easily to interpretations of Atatürk as a deeply devout Muslim.

*laiklik* (secularism). He claims that the main purpose of the principle of *laiklik* is to ensure the freedom of religious belief and worship in society, an interpretation that is rather different from how *laiklik* is generally understood. Following this definition, Yahya argues that *laiklik* is compatible with Islam, because Islam emphasizes that faith must be adopted by free will and not coercion (2002g, p. 110).

These books are ripe with praise and idealization of Atatürk as an exceptional leader as well as a superior person. Yahya describes him as a as "a stylishly dressed Ottoman gentleman" with impeccable table manners (2001a, p. 7), a humble genius with superior personal qualities (2001a, p. 17), and an extraordinarily strong and decisive leader with exceptional love for his country who held the interests of his nation before his own (Yahya 2002e, p. 9). Yahya's idealized representation of Atatürk as an exemplary human being and an embodiment of nationalist and Turkish-Muslim values mirrors in many ways the notion of the Prophet Muhammed as the role model for Muslims.

The Harun Yahya enterprise's turn towards promoting Atatürkism began after a period in which Adnan Oktar was first imprisoned and later transferred to a criminal ward in Bakirköy hospital. It is therefore possible to read the intense promotion of Atatürk and the emphasis on loyalty to the state as a purely tactical move sprung from fear of persecution from the authorities.[32] However, although tactics may be an important factor, Harun Yahya's engaging in Atatürkism must be understood as not merely an attempt to avoid trouble with the state and the army, but also as an important part of his *da'wa* mission. Instead of rejecting Atatürk as an enemy of religion, Yahya reconfigures Atatürk to fit his own purposes. His preoccupation with Atatürk underscores the uniqueness of Yahya's approach and how it differs from much pro-Islamic discourse in Turkey. The emphasis on Atatürk, Turkish nationalism and loyalty to the secular state can be understood as part of an attempt to reach a secular audience in Turkey. He seeks to disassociate Atatürk from the trappings of positivism and anti-religion, and portrays him as a pious man that embodies both the greatness of the Turk and the moral superiority of Islamic values. Yahya's Atatürk is modern, secular, fervently nationalist, conservative, anti-communist and deeply religious. He thus utilizes Atatürk to communicate that there is no contradiction between being modern, secular, nationalist and religious at the same time, and to signal distance to "bad" Islamists who according to Yahya misrepresent Atatürk as anti-religious. He interprets and frames his interpretation of Atatürk, the state and nationalism in ways that is compatible with his wider worldview. For instance, he stresses Atatürk's preoccupation with fighting communism and preserving national and religious

---

[32] It is also not entirely unlikely that Yahya's change of mind regarding Atatürk is genuine and not merely tactical, although this is of course impossible to determine.

values, thus creating the impression that Yahya's ideas are not only compatible with Atatürkism, but that serving Atatürk's ideals and serving the Islamic *da'wa* of Yahya is essentially converging causes.

Furthermore, Harun Yahya's efforts to integrate Atatürk and secular nationalism into an Islamic framework may also be understood in terms of the way in which the Islamic segment as a whole has moved from the periphery to the center of Turkish politics and society. As the state itself has come to redefine secularism, it is becoming less and less politically expedient to promote an Islamic discourse predicated upon dissent and opposition. Thus, in so far as Harun Yahya can be seen as part of the Nurcu tradition in Islamic thought in Turkey, he has also followed the neo-Nurcu Gülen movement's move towards aligning itself with the state, as I have discussed in Chapter 2.

## 8. The nationalist discourse of Harun Yahya

In addition to praising Atatürk as a great leader who was both a fervent nationalist and a devout Muslim, Yahya outlines his views on the concepts of the nation, the homeland, the state and the army. He devotes *Asker Atatürk* (Yahya 2002a) to the importance and value Atatürk attached to the Turkish army. The focal point of *Atatürk'ün Millet ve Vatan Sevgisi* is the idea of nationhood and homeland. Yahya stresses that the notion of homeland is not merely the lands in which a nation lives, but "one of the most important treasures a person may be in possession of in life" (Yahya 2002e, p. 8). Yahya here promotes nationalist ideas:

> The basis that gives strength to the individual is elements such as the accumulation of culture, the history and the traditional characteristics of the nation it belongs to. The key factor that ensures the continuation of the nation is the safeguarding of the indivisible territorial integrity of the homeland. The loyalty and affection of the Turkish nation to the homeland is an historical reality, and is one of the principal characteristics that makes our nation superior among other nations. Additionally, every Turk has a deep love for the nation and an understanding that holds the interests of the nation above own interests and the future of the nation above one's own future (Yahya 2002e, p. 8).

This reads as a whole-hearted embracement of Turkish nationalism, complete with key elements such as "indivisible territorial integrity" (*vatanın bölunmez bütünlüğü*), the notion of the interests of the nation as surpassing the interests of the individual, and chauvinist ideas of the superiority of the Turkish nation. It is clearly addressing a Turkish audience with the intent of appealing to nationalist sentiments.

In the booklet entitled *Devlete Bağlılığın Önemi* (The Importance of Loyalty to the State) (Yahya 2000a), Yahya takes an explicitly pro-state stance, and calls upon Turks to support the state. He identifies the currents that go against the state as primarily consisting of currents based in Marxist ideology, but also some who erroneously believe that weakening the state is necessary in order to achieve democracy, and lastly some Islamic groups who think that the state is anti-religious. Against this he claims that "our State has never led anti-religious politics" (Yahya 2000a, p. 12). He advocates the notion of a strong state, arguing that it gives protection against external enemies and preserves domestic stability, peace and order (Yahya 2000a, p. 21). Here he also links Turkish nationalism with the struggle against materialism:

> All irreligious and materialist ideologies, and fascism and communism especially, target spiritual/moral values. Materialists are bound to their personal interests, not to their homelands, flags and nations. They are not nationalists, but internationalists. They work for their own happiness, not the happiness of their nations. [...] Our Father [Atatürk] wants our and future generations to be people who puts their life on the line for their homeland and their flag, who works all their lives for the happiness of their nation, and who defends the sanctity of the family. The materialist mindset, however, is opposed to all the sacred values taught to us by our Father. Therefore, it is crucial for all patriotic and nationalist people to back the intellectual struggle against all materialist systems and ideologies [...] (Yahya 2000a, p. 49).

Thus, according to Yahya, it is the duty of all real Atatürkists to protect the country from harm, including ideological harm such as communism and fascism, and all materialist ideologies.

## 9. Turkish-Muslim moral superiority and Neo-Ottomanism

Yahya has published a number of works that give rather glorifying accounts of Turkish culture as morally superior, arguing for instance that

> the Turkish culture is predicated upon an exceptionally honorable history and a superior character. [...] Throughout history, [the Turks] have been known for their bravery and honesty, and with a character remote from tyranny and injustice, they have been admired even by their enemies (Yahya 2000b, p. 15).

*Türk'ün Yüksek Seciyesi* (The High Moral Disposition of the Turk) is devoted in its entirety to outlining the alleged superiority of the Turk as evidenced through Ottoman history, under headlines such as "The Turk's superior morality", "Justice and Tolerance", "The Importance Given to Honor" and "The Turks are Honest People" (Yahya 2001k). As described in Chapter 2, an ideology referred to as "the Turkish-Islamic synthesis", which seeks to blend Turkish nationalism and Islam, became influential after the military coup in Turkey in 1980. Drawing on these ideas, Yahya writes in *Türk'ün Şanlı Tarihi* (The Glorious History of the Turks) (Yahya 2002r) that "the synthesis of the core values of the Turkish Nation with Qur'anic morality led to developments that deeply affected world history" (Yahya 2002r, p. 9).

Yahya's nationalism does not stop at the Turkish national border. Yahya refers to "the geography of Turkish national culture" as encompassing a vast area of Turkish-Muslim populations from China to the Balkans and parts of the Middle East (Yahya 2000b, p. 11). Elsewhere he also espouses pan-Turkish ideas, arguing for the unification of all Turkic states under a single roof.[33] Yahya contends that "the Turkish world" represents a unique opportunity for Turkey to assume leadership:

> Having been the flag bearers for Islam for centuries, the Turkish Muslim Nation, with its modern, enlightened and powerful composition, its pure concept of religion that is far from extremism and obscurantism, has the most suitable makeup for undertaking this mission. The Turkish Muslim Nation harbors all the attributes and merits necessary for being an example to the world (Yahya 2000b, p. 50).

Yahya argues further that "it is the profession of the Muslim Turk to establish super states", and that the Turkic states are "waiting breathlessly" for Turkey to take steps towards a union (Yahya 2000b, p. 50). This prospect, he claims, represents a "light of hope" for the whole world. Yahya concludes by asserting "both in history and today, hundreds of signs have appeared of Muslim Turks assuming guardianship for peace and justice in real terms" (Yahya 2000b, p. 50).

*Türkiye İçin Milli Strateji: Türk Dış Politikasına Osmanlı Vizyon İle Yeni Bir Bakış* (A National Strategy for Turkey: A New Perspective on Turkish Foreign Policy with an Ottoman Vision), published in 1996, was the first full-length book published in the name of Harun Yahya to deal specifically with Turkish foreign policy (Yahya 1996a). Here, Yahya advocates a distinctly neo-Ottoman foreign policy, formulating strategies for how Turkey can utilize the current political conditions in the Balkans, the Caucasus and Central Asia to its advantage and thus expand its "living space" from the Adriatic to China. Yahya focuses on how Turkey can use its historical influence, ethnic and religious kinship and the present political situation to its advantage and increase its power and influence.

Similar ideas are brought forward in *Türkiye'nin Geleceğinde Osmanlı Vizyonu* (The Ottoman Vision in Turkey's Future) (Yahya 2003s). In contrast to the rather dry and non-illustrated work from 1996, the latter is written in a more opulent prose and is richly illustrated with maps and Ottoman imagery. Arguing

---

[33] In a press conference with international journalists on June 8th 2007, Oktar declared that the Turkic states and Turkey should have united long ago. Transcript excerpt available at <http://harunyahya.com/en/works/10361/The+impact+of+the+announcements+headed+%27Azerbaijan+and+Turkey+must+unite+as+two+states,+one+nation,%27+based+on+the+works+of+Adnan+Oktar> [Accessed 19.03.2013].

that Turkey must lay claim to its Ottoman legacy, the focus here is not merely on Turkey's strategic interest, but also its potential positive role in ensuring peace in the region. In the framework of Bilim Araştırma Vakfı (BAV), the Harun Yahya enterprise has organized a number of foreign policy-themed conferences, including a conference titled *Osmanlı Vizyon ile Balkanlara Bakış* (Approaching the Balkans with an Ottoman Vision), where a number of prominent politicians from Bosnia, the Sancak and Kosovo and Turkey were present.[34] The final words of the speech made by Tarkan Yavaş, a representative of BAV speaking at the conference, reflect the neo-Ottoman outlook: "Not only the Muslims, but the West too needs a new Ottoman. The Ottoman model lies before us as a solution to the authority void of the Turkish and Muslim world. The world needs a new Ottoman".[35] In *Türkiye'nin Geleceğinde Osmanlı Vizyonu,* Yahya claims

> Turkey may gather Albanians, Bosnians, Pomaks, Georgians, Azeris and even Croats, Serbs, Romanians and Bulgarians under a new 'Ottoman Nations Community'. In fact, most of these societies today aspire to achieve a new order in which they can experience the peace and security they experienced during the Ottoman period, and are looking to Turkey with hope (Yahya 2003s, p. 105).

The works mentioned above address a Turkish audience, and are mainly written from the perspective of the interests of the Turkish state and the Turkish people. Yahya presents a full endorsement of Atatürk, Turkish nationalism and the Turkish state, and claims that it is in the strategic interest of Turkey to assume a leading role in a union both with Turkic Muslim nations and with nations in the Ottoman "hinterland". Furthermore, Yahya claims that Turkish leadership is both beneficial for and also desired by these nations. Yahya elaborates on how the glorious history of the Ottoman Empire shows that Turks and Turkey are destined for leadership. The qualities of Turkish culture combined with Islamic morality, make the Turks natural leaders, Yahya argues.

As we shall see in Chapter 5, Yahya also begins to formulate these political ideas of Turkish leadership in terms of an Islamic Union, and publish books promoting these ideas also on the global market in the 2000s. He increasingly emphasizes that Turkish leadership is not only in Turkey's interest, but also in the interest of regional and global peace and stability. There is thus a gradual shift in emphasis from Turkey's political interests to the notion of Turkey as a solution to regional and global problems. As will be discussed in Chapter 5, in

---

[34] *Osmanlı Vizyon ile Balkanlara Bakış,* conference 22t[h] of September 2003 at Çırağan Palace in Istanbul. See Bilim Araştırma Vakfı (2003, pp. 72–81). BAV also organized a series of conferences on the Cyprus question, Musul-Kerkük and the Türkmen, and the Kosovo question.
[35] Speech made by Tarik Yavas, cited in *Bilim Araştırma Vakfı Dış Politika Konferansları* (Bilim Araştırma Vakfı 2003, p. 72).

more recent works this solution is presented not merely in terms of political guardianship in the sense of Turkey assuming responsibility for its Ottoman "hinterland", but is also formulated in more explicitly religious terms as being a matter of spiritual guardianship and Turkey's destiny.

## 11. Concluding remarks

In this chapter I have examined works of Harun Yahya that address a Turkish-speaking domestic audience, and looked at how Yahya employs different types of popular discourses that were on the rise in Turkey in the 1990s and 2000s: Conspiracy theories, anti-Zionism, Atatürkism, nationalism, neo-Ottomanism and ecumenism. By placing Yahya's works into a Turkish historical and sociopolitical context, I have sought to offer explanations both for why Yahya have focused on these particular themes in his works, as well as explaining changes in his discourse over time.

Conspiracism features prominently in the works of Harun Yahya. In the first part of this chapter, I have examined anti-Semitic and anti-Zionist themes in Yahya's early works. I have showed how these conspiratorial works won the Harun Yahya enterprise favor among the Islamist circles around Necmettin Erbakan. In the late 80s and 90s, the Harun Yahya enterprise appeared to align itself with Islamist discourses that were gaining momentum during this time.

Yahya's anti-Zionist conspiracy theory rhetoric must be understood not merely in terms of its relationship with 1990s Islamism in Turkey, but must also be considered in a broader framework of Turkish nationalist discourses gaining momentum from the 90s onwards, especially after the Gulf War. As noted by Tanıl Bora, conspiracy theories became more widespread in the 1990s, also in secular nationalist discourse (Bora 1994). Processes of globalization and the Kurdish issue reignited the "ontological insecurities" that arguably characterize Turkish nationalism, and led to a widened appeal of conspiracy theories identifying "foreign factors" behind Turkey's problems, as well as a resurgence of nationalist themes in popular culture.[36]

One function of conspiracy theories is to offer cognitive maps for locating blame. While some types of conspiracy theories target the state as the villain, Yahya's conspiracy theory rhetoric dissolves Turkey of responsibility and instead locates the blame for social and political problems elsewhere. In their early formulations in particular, Yahya's conspiracy theories targeted foreign powers and forces and "enemies within" – Masons, Zionists, communists and atheists – as the causes of conflict and immorality. In Yahya's worldview, terror is committed by Darwinists, not Muslims, and the insurgency of PKK is due to the influence of materialist ideology and the plotting of Israel, not the politics of the Turkish state.

---

[36] See Einar Wigen (2011) for an analysis of nationalist themes in Turkish popular culture.

As we shall see in Chapter 5, Yahya offers redemption through his proposed solution to both domestic and global problems: The Turkish-Islamic union.

I have also examined how the anti-Zionist elements of Yahya's conspiracy theories are gradually modified, and how a more ecumenical discourse emerges. In the late 2000s, interfaith dialogue and the theme of "a union of faiths" against materialism began assuming an increasingly prominent role in the discourse of the Harun Yahya enterprise. This development accompanies the Harun Yahya's entry into a global market, and is linked with the emphasis on waging an intellectual struggle against Darwinism, which will be dealt with in Chapter 4, and also with eschatological themes, which I will examine in Chapter 5.

However, I argue that this turn towards ecumenism and a more moderate discourse also can be understood against the background of developments in Turkey. In the wake of the "soft coup" in 1997 there was a backlash against the political Islam of Erbakan, and instead a reformist wing of the Islamist movement formed the JDP, which rose to power in 2002. This initiated a discursive shift from Islamism to what Jenny White terms "Turkish Muslimhood" (White 2005) as discussed in Chapter 2. This changing political context provided an opportunity space for the Gülen movement, which repositioned itself and developed closer engagement with the state (Turam 2007).[37] The shift in the discourse of the Harun Yahya enterprise may therefore partly be understood as an attempt to take part in the highly successful franchise of the Gülen movement: Interfaith dialogue and "modern", state-aligned Turkish Islam.

The second part of the chapter examines the development of nationalist themes in Yahya's works. In 1990, the Harun Yahya enterprise launched a large-scale marketing campaign in 1990 in order to promote itself as Atatürkist and nationalist, and in the early 2000s, Yahya published a number of political works advocating Atatürkism, Turkish nationalism as well as Ottoman-Turkish historical and moral supremacy. In these works, Yahya reinterprets Atatürkism within an Islamic framework in order to communicate that there is no contradiction between being modern, secular, nationalist and religious at the same time, and to signal distance to "bad" Islamists who according to Yahya misrepresent Atatürk as anti-religious.

The themes in Yahya's works produced for the Turkish market reflect the resurgence of secular nationalism and "Atatürk fetishism" (Navaro-Yashin 2002), Turkism, pan-Turkism and neo-Ottomanism in the 1990s and early 2000s. Yahya taps into a variety of popular discourses that has the potential to appeal to a broad spectrum of nationalist sensibilities in Turkey. He attempts to appeal to an urban middle class of "white Turks" through works that glorify Atatürk and secular Turkish nationalism, and by appropriating the secularist

---

[37] Fethullah Gülen supported the "soft coup" in an effort to appease the military coup plotters (Yavuz 2013, p. 97).

discourse that portray Islamists as *yobaz*.[38] He attempts to appeal to ultranationalists and pan-Turkists through works that glorify Turks and emphasize kinship with Turkic peoples and nations outside Turkey. He also attempts to appeal to neo-Ottoman sensibilities through works that glorify Turks and the Ottoman Empire.

Two parallel tendencies may be identified in the works I have considered in this chapter. Firstly, Yahya concurrently engages in apparently conflicting discourses. In the 90s, Yahya both aligned himself with Islamist circles through works espousing anti-Zionist conspiracy theories, while at the same time embracing Kemalist secularism and promoting the Harun Yahya enterprise as Atatürkist. As discussed in Chapter 2, however, in practice the ideological distinction between nationalism and Islamism is not clear-cut, and changing political circumstances have often produced new ideological alliances, such as in the case of Kemalist nationalism and right-wing nationalism in the 1990s.[39] Moreover, Yahya does not merely adopt various discourses, but also adapts and reconfigures them, as in the case of Atatürkism where Yahya's Atatürk is not an enemy of religion, but on the contrary a deeply religious Muslim nationalist.

Secondly, one may detect a gradual change in Yahya's discourse over time, which corresponds to the changing dynamics of these different types of discourses in Turkish politics and society. The Harun Yahya enterprise gradually disassociates itself with Islamism, and aligns itself with the ecumenical, pro-Western and moderate "modern Muslim" discourse of the Gülen movement. In line with this, recent works of the Harun Yahya enterprise also display a more pro-Western form of nationalism that differs from the isolationist nationalist discourses of *ulusalcılık* and ultranationalism, and is more in line with what Özkırımlı and Sofos terms "liberal nationalism":

> Associated with neoliberalism and the political and economic aspirations of the urban middle and upper classes, [liberal nationalism] has maintained a secular, yet not secularist, outlook. Although open to globalization, the European Union, consumerism and Western tastes, it maintains a strong sense of pride around Turkish identity and displays strong elements of class racism that has been associated in the media and popular discourse with the term "White Turk" (Özkırımlı & Sofos 2008, p. 191).

As I have argued in Chapter 2, the primary target group for the proselytizing activities of the Harun Yahya enterprise in Turkey is a wealthy secular urban middle class segment referred to as the "White Turks" (Navaro-Yashin 2002).

---

[38] The terms "white" and "black" Turks are often used to contrast social groups in Turkey. "White Turks" denote a privileged urban middle class elite consisting primarily of the military, media, bureaucracy and the *bourgeoisie*, who see their lifestyle, values and tastes as standards of what is good and civilized, and who set themselves apart from "black Turks", who are seen to represent rural values and low class. See Demiralp (2012).

[39] Often referred to in the media as the "red apple coalition" (*kızıl elma koalisyonu*).

Moreover, the shift in Yahya's discourse also reflects changing perceptions of Turkey's role in the region and globally. The rise of Turkey as a regional power and the increasing self-confidence of Turkey are reflected in a more triumphant tone in Yahya's works, as we shall see in Chapter 5. The shift from anti-Semitism to an emphasis on unity with other faiths is also linked with the broader development of the Harun Yahya enterprise and how it fits in with the struggle against creationism and millennialist ideas about the coming of the Mahdi and the End Times, which is also the focus of Chapter 5.

Although the anti-Zionist elements are gradually downplayed, conspiracy theories remain an important element of Yahya's discourse both in the Turkish and global context. Yahya's conspiracy theories are of the grandest sort: He draws sweeping historical lines from pagan Greece to current Israeli foreign policy, and as Chapter 5 illustrates, ultimately places these theories into an eschatological framework. Over time, the focus shifts from a political focus on concrete Zionist and Masonic conspiracies and their activities in Turkey, to a focus on irreligious and materialist forces in history. In Yahya's most recent formulations of conspiracy theories, it is not Zionists and Masons in general, but rather "some atheist Zionists and Masons" who are culpable.

In the mid-90s, the Harun Yahya enterprise began focusing its attention on the topic that it would eventually be closely associated with, and which would come to define its profile and niche, first in Turkey and later internationally: The campaign against the theory of evolution and the formulation of a distinct form of Islamic creationism. The next chapter therefore deals with the origin of creationism, and locates Harun Yahya's campaign against the theory of evolution within a wider global context of creationism as a particular type of religious discourse.

CHAPTER 4
# The Islamic creationism of Harun Yahya

## 1. Introduction

No scientific theory has created as much controversy in the 20th century as the theory of evolution put forward in Charles Darwin's *The Origin of Species* (1859). The creation-evolution debate, as the dispute over the origin of life has come to be known, has religious, philosophical, theological, political and legal dimensions. The debate is above all associated with the United States, where it is regarded as one of several battlegrounds in an alleged "culture war" between conservative and progressive values (Chapman 2010, p. 128). One camp in this struggle is the creationist movement and its attempts to discredit the theory of evolution on scientific grounds and to have creationism taught in schools alongside the theory of evolution. Although the creationist movement mainly emerged and developed in the United States, it is not exclusive to the American context. A development that has received attention in recent years is the growing influence of an Islamic variety of creationism that has emerged from Turkey but has a global impact, namely the creationism of Harun Yahya.

The purpose of this chapter is to contextualize, describe and analyze Harun Yahya's creationist discourse. The chapter is divided into two main parts. The first part provides a background to Harun Yahya's creationism by locating it into a broader context. My starting point is the recognition that Harun Yahya is both a local and global creationist actor, and the roots of Harun Yahya's campaign against evolution must therefore be sought within both a global and local context. One the one hand, it takes its inspiration from a global creationist movement that has emerged out of conservative evangelical Christianity. As we shall see, Yahya employs many of the strategies and arguments of the Christian creationist movement. I will therefore briefly outline the historical emergence and the spread of this movement. On the other hand, creationism also has its own history in Turkey, which I will outline in this chapter. This history is closely linked with Said Nursi and the Nur movement, which, as we shall see, Harun Yahya is greatly influenced by. This Turkish discourse in turn, must be grasped within a broader framework of Islamic discourses on modern science, which therefore also will be discussed. In the second and empirical part, Harun Yahya's creationism will be described and analyzed, taking *The Evolution Deceit* (Yahya 2002g) as the main point of departure.

## 2. The evolution of creationism in local and global contexts

### 2.1. What is creationism? Taxonomy and definitions

Creationism is a term with multiple meanings (Numbers 1999). In the broadest sense, creationism is the belief that God created the universe and life out of nothing. Within the monotheistic religions, the origin of life and the cosmos is regarded as the product of the creative act of God. However, in current use, creationism has a more restricted meaning as an umbrella term for various doctrines of divine creation that rejects or disputes the theory of evolution on the grounds that it conflicts with divine revelation and the notion of God as a divine creator of the world. It is in this sense, as anti-Darwinism or anti-evolutionism, that I will use the term creationism in the following.

There are a number of different types of creationist positions. The most important aspect for our discussion, however, is the emergence of Creation Science as a particular approach that argues that creation is supported by scientific evidence.[1] Furthermore, creationism as it is commonly used does not merely refer to a passively held doctrine. A creationist denotes someone who is actively involved in promoting creationist views in various arenas, employing a number of strategies. Today, a global creationist movement exists, which consists of various organizations and individuals involved in organized efforts to discredit the theory of evolution and/or to assert the literal truth of a religious account of origins over and above mainstream science. Creationists are active participants in the production and dissemination of literature and other material refuting or criticizing the theory of evolution. Creationists promote these ideas through publishing and other outreach activities, one of their primary goals being the introduction of creationist ideas in schools. Creationism as a movement emerged in the United States, and most studies on creationism focus on Protestant creationism in the American context (Numbers 2006). However, although creationism in some senses is a "peculiarly American" phenomenon,[2] it has with time become a global phenomenon, emerging not only from Christian but also from Muslim perspectives.[3]

---

[1] I have chosen to capitalize Creation Science and Young Earth creationism as proper nouns referring to relatively distinct schools, while creationism in general is approached as a common noun and therefore not capitalized.

[2] Stephen Jay Gould cited in Numbers (2006, p. 399).

[3] Ronald Numbers also documents Jewish creationist activism emerging in Israel at the end of the 20th century. However, it has limited relevance for the current discussion (Numbers 2006, pp. 427–430).

Numerous Christian, Muslim and Jewish believers accept the theory of evolution, and see no conflict between the modern scientific paradigm of evolution and their religious beliefs. A religious worldview does not necessarily lead to antievolutionism. Antievolutionism is rather a particular religious stance that has emerged in response to specific concerns, and must be understood as emerging from specific cultural and political contexts. In a broader sense, the debate between creation and evolution can be regarded as the current manifestation of an old conundrum: How to reconcile revelation and science? Christian and Muslim thinkers grappling with questions regarding the relationship between faith and science have emerged out of different concerns and contexts, and antievolutionist discourses have therefore followed quite different historical trajectories in Muslim and Christian contexts. Below I will outline and compare these different developments, as a background to Harun Yahya's creationism. First, however, I will give a brief introduction to the source of the trouble.

## 2.2. The source of the trouble: Darwin's theory of evolution

Creationism as defined above emerged as a reaction to Charles Darwin's theory of evolution, put forward in *The Origin of Species* (1859). However, it was not primarily evolution itself that was new and controversial about Darwin's theory. The idea that species change over time has roots in antiquity and can, for example, be found in medieval Islamic science (Khaldun 1967, p. 195).[4] What was contentious about Darwin's theory was firstly the idea of *common descent*, meaning that all species have evolved from one or more common ancestors, and particularly the idea that humans have evolved from lower primates. This challenges the idea of *special creation*, the notion that humans were specially created by God, and that there is a special relationship between God and humanity. Secondly, Darwin introduced *natural selection* as the mechanism behind evolution. Natural selection explains how the organic world developed without reference to a designer outside of nature itself, and is therefore regarded as challenging or threatening the understanding of life and the universe as created by God. In the first 80 years after *The Origin of Species*, there was disagreement among scientists on some elements of the theory. Developed between 1936–1942, the Modern Evolutionary Synthesis brought widespread consensus and acceptance of the theory among scientists, by synthesizing the idea of natural selection as the evolutionary mechanism with the discovery of genetics (Mayr 2001, p. x).

---

[4] Jean-Baptiste Lamarck introduced a theory on the transmutation of species in 1809, but it lacked the evidence and the explanatory mechanism of evolution that Darwin introduced (Lamarck 1809).

## 2.3. The emergence and evolution of creationism in the US

The term creationism is above all associated with a particular variety of creationism that emerged in the United States, namely Biblical or Young Earth creationism. Young Earth creationists interpret the Biblical creation narrative literally and believe that the world was created by God only between 5.700 and 10.000 years old (Numbers 2006, p. 11). This variety of creationism is by far the most influential in the United States. Public opinion polls indicate that almost half of Americans subscribe to the Young Earth creationist account of human beings as created by God in their present form less than 10.000 years ago.[5] Young Earth creationists do not only reject Darwinian evolution, but also other elements of modern science, such as geology, when they conflict with the Biblical narratives. Even though this variety of creationism differs from Islamic creationism in many respects and has emerged out of a different historical context, it has relevance for the present study because the creationist arguments and strategies employed by a small but powerful segment of conservative American Protestantism have provided inspiration for the creationist movement in Turkey.

The history of Christian responses to the theory of evolution in the United States can be divided into four phases, which I will outline below: Accommodation, Fundamentalism, Creation Science and Intelligent Design. It should be noted that these different responses also co-exist today.

### 2.3.1. The response to Darwin: From accommodation to confrontation

Within a few decades after Charles Darwin's *Origin of Species* was published, the scientific communities both in North America and Britain had largely accepted the evolutionary origin of species, some of them albeit reluctantly (Numbers 2006, p. 17). The empirical evidence for evolution seemed overwhelming, and many pious naturalists felt compelled to accept evolution, while still clinging to a belief in the notion of special creation for humans. The response to evolution among Christian clericals came late, and it would take many decades before the idea of the earth being 6000 years old and the deluge as an explanation for fossil records became a part of the creationist opposition to Darwin's theory. Biblical literalist opposition to evolution emerged with the ascendancy of the fundamentalist movement in the beginning of the 20th century.

### 2.3.2. Creationism and fundamentalism

At the end of the 19th century, there was a growing concern among Protestant Christians over the increasing influence of liberal theology and higher criticism,

---

[5] 46 % in 2012 (Gallup.com 2012).

which they saw as a threat to true Christian faith.[6] The emergence of Biblical creationism in the United States is regarded as closely linked with the emergence of the fundamentalist movement, which was launched by the publication of *The Fundamentals,* a series of essays published between 1910 and 1915 and edited by the Presbyterian reverend Amzi C. Dixon. According to intellectual historian Arthur McCalla, "the creation–evolution controversy is at bottom a conflict over the status and authority of the Bible in the modern world" (McCalla 2007, p. 547). Historian of science Ronald Numbers, one of the foremost experts on creationism, also links creationism to the fundamentalist reaction to higher criticism. He reports how one of the authors of *The Fundamentals* identifies evolution as "the inspiration of higher criticism" and an enemy of the Christian faith (Numbers 2006, p. 53).

The creationist movement grew in strength during the course of the first decades of the 20th century, culminating in the first eruption of the creation–evolution struggle into the public sphere: The Scopes trial in 1925. Schoolteacher John Thomas Scopes was tried in court for breaking a recently passed Tennessee law banning the teaching of evolution in schools (Numbers 2006, p. 88). Presbyterian statesman William Jennings Bryan was brought in as a prosecutor. Bryan believed that Darwinism was responsible for moral decay both in the nation and abroad, and had launched a nationwide crusade against evolution. He was joined by a number of conservative Christians from different Protestant denominations, such as William B. Riley, the fundamentalist pastor of the First Baptist Church of Minneapolis. Both Jennings and Riley were Biblical literalists, but they did not view the six days in Genesis as six 24-hour periods and they conceded that the world was older than 6000 years.[7] The highly publicized trial pitted science against religion and brought national as well as international attention to the creation–evolution controversy. The play *Inherit the Wind* (1955) and later a film by the same name (1960) were made based on the events of the 1925 Scopes Trial.

2.3.3. Scientific creationism

After the Scopes trial in 1925, the creationist movement went into decline in the United States. However, the fundamentalist campaign did have a lasting effect. As the theory of evolution was regarded as controversial, mention of evolution was omitted from many textbooks. Things started changing in the late 1950s, when the Soviet Union launched the Sputnik satellite program. This sparked worry in the United States that the country was lagging behind in the field of

---

[6] Higher criticism is the branch of Biblical criticism that studies the Bible in its historical context, and is today generally referred to as historical criticism.
[7] Like many creationists at the time, Bryan and Jennings were Day-Age creationists, holding that the six days mentioned in the Bible refer to time periods of thousands or millions of years.

science. More emphasis was put on the teaching of science in schools, and the teaching of evolution was reintroduced in biology textbooks. This is widely regarded as a contributing factor and impetus for the rekindling of the creationists' efforts (Numbers 2006, p. 256). The creationist movement reemerged, this time helped by individuals with academic credentials and the desire to make creationism scientific.

The 1960s marked the beginning of what came to be known as "Creation Science" or "scientific creationism" (Numbers 2006, p. 269). It also marked a shift from the Old Earth creationism of the 1920s fundamentalists, to Young Earth creationism. In 1961, Henry M. Morris and John C. Whitcomb published *The Genesis Flood: The Biblical Record and its Scientific Implications* (Whitcomb & Morris 1961), which was to become the "new Bible" of the Biblical creationists. *The Genesis Flood* was based on a simple premise: The Bible is God's word, and God does not make mistakes. Hence, if the Bible and science do not correspond, there must be something wrong with the science. Whitcomb and Morris rejected the findings of modern geology, claiming instead that the Genesis flood was a worldwide event that accounts for the fossil record and the geological column. *The Genesis Flood* provided a "scientific" basis for Young Earth creationism – an interpretation of scripture that allows for "no life on earth before Eden and no death before the fall" (Numbers 2006, p. 10). The book was a success and has been translated into a number of languages. It popularized Young Earth creationism, and many of the arguments against evolution put forward in the book are still used by creationists today. Morris and Whitcomb became household names among conservative Christians both in and outside of the United States.

After the publication of *The Genesis Flood*, the creationist movement became more organized in their efforts, and a series of creationist organizations were founded, such as The Institute for Creation Research (ICR), which was established in 1970. The primary goal of these organizations was to win acceptance for creation science as an alternative to evolution science, and ensure that creationism be taught in schools. These creationist ministries lobbied for legislation mandating the teaching of creationism in schools, and brought creationism to the attention of the wider public and the scientific community. Some states passed legislation mandating the teaching of creationism in the early 1980s, but these "Creationist Acts" were later challenged and deemed unconstitutional as the courts ruled that Creation Science was essentially promoting particular religious ideas and therefore had no place in public schools (Scott & Eldredge 2009, p. 113). In the late 1980s, the creationists therefore changed strategy, removing religious references to Creation and Creator from the texts, and instead focusing on presenting "scientific alternatives to evolution" or "evidence against evolution". This new strategy is often referred to as "neo-creationism" (Scott & Eldredge 2009, pp. 113–130).

### 2.3.4. Intelligent Design

One brand of neo-creationism that developed and consolidated during the 1990s was the Intelligent Design (ID) movement, which attempted to restore creationism by uncoupling it from its religious connotations. ID gained a broader appeal beyond the conservative Protestant constituency of Creation Science, and received more attention in the media. ID does not explicitly refer to a Divine Creator, but argues that some aspects of nature are impossible to explain through natural causes. It therefore posits that the universe must have been designed by some "intelligence". The argument from design, also called the teleological argument, is a common theological argument for the existence of God within both Islam and Christianity (Van Huyssteen 2003, p. 876). Proponents of Intelligent Design, however, present their claims as scientific rather than theological.[8]

The question of whether Intelligent Design is a type of creationism is a debated one. Michael Ruse refers to ID as "creationism light" and argues that there is "an evangelical Christian motive setting the agenda on origins" both in Creation Science and Intelligent Design (Ruse 2007). Many proponents of ID accept common descent and the notion of an ancient earth. However, there are also ID proponents who joined the ID movement from Creation Science and reject evolution altogether (Scott and Eldredge, 2009, p. 126). One might argue that it is the strategy more than the ideas and aims that make ID proponents different from (other) creationists. After Creation Science was discredited as unscientific religious propaganda by the courts, Intelligent Design became a new strategy for the inclusion of alternatives to evolution in school curriculums. The Discovery Institute, the main advocacy institute for Intelligent Design established in 1994, launched the campaign "teach the controversy", a PR strategy that emphasized that students should be given the opportunity to critically evaluate the full range of scientific views with regards to evolution. The scientific community responded that there is no controversy over the validity of evolution (Scott & Branch 2003). In 2004, in a trial known as *Kitzmiller vs. Dover Area School District*, the judge ruled that Intelligent Design is not science (Goodstein 2005).

One might distinguish between "hard" creationists who refuse to accept the transmutation of species, and "soft" creationists like ID proponents, who accept

---

[8] The two most prominent ID arguments are two complementary ideas put forward by biochemist Michael Behe and philosopher/mathematician William Dembski. Behe contends that intelligence is required to produce irreducibly complex cellular structures (the irreducible complexity argument). Mathematician Dembski argues that probability theory can prove irreducible complexity, which Dembski calls specified complexity (Scott & Eldredge 2009, pp. 117–120).

evolution, but criticize what they regard as the naturalist or materialist assumptions in modern science. While Biblical creationists are more concerned with protecting their particular interpretation of the Christian faith and defending the truth of scripture, ID proponents are chiefly concerned with opposing what they consider to be materialist biases in science and defend the idea of a purposeful universe. As we shall see, this is also the main issue for many Muslim antievolutionists.

### 2.3.5. Creationism goes global

Creationism in the sense described above, is predominantly an American phenomenon. As argued by McCalla, its emergence is closely related to the emergence of a particular form of conservative Protestantism in the United States (McCalla 2007). Although it is in the United States that the creation–evolution debate has been played out the most vociferously, Numbers describes in a chapter entitled "Creationism Goes Global" how in the last few decades antievolutionism "has quietly spread from America throughout the world and from evangelical Protestantism to Catholicism, Eastern Orthodoxy, Islam, Judaism, and even Hinduism" (Numbers 2006, p. 399). Under the heading "The Islamic World", Numbers gives ample attention to Harun Yahya's creationism. However, although the Harun Yahya enterprise has had contact with the ICR and Harun Yahya's creationism undoubtedly takes inspiration from American-style creationism, Yahya's creationism is far from just an American import. Antievolutionism has its own history in Turkey that for the most part has developed independently from American Protestant creationism. The emergence of antievolutionism in Turkey must also be considered as part of a broader context of Islamic discourses on science and responses to the theory of evolution in the Muslim world, which therefore will be discussed in the next section.

### 2.4. Islam and science

Creationists share the belief that the theory of evolution is essentially atheistic and constitutes a threat to religion. How closely related is Christian and Muslim creationism? Because creationism is commonly identified with the American Protestant variety, it is associated with fundamentalism. Fundamentalism in the Christian context is usually regarded as having developed as a reaction to modernist theology. The influential historical-critical approach to Christianity that developed within Christian theology did not have a parallel in the Islamic context, and hence there was no "fundamentalist reaction" in the strict sense. However, fundamentalism can also be understood in a more general sense. Historian of religion Torkel Brekke argues that fundamentalism is a special reaction to certain developments in the modern world that have taken place in many religious traditions (Brekke 2012, p. 6).[9] A major argument in Brekke's book is that "fundamentalism is a movement mainly driven by lay people under circumstances where traditional religious elites are seen to be impotent in the struggle to adjust religion to the modern world" (Brekke 2012, p. 194). Brekke examines science as one of several fundamentalist areas of struggle. Acknowledging that there is no one shared Muslim fundamentalist position on the question of the relationship of religion to science, Brekke notes that "one recurring issue has been the search for ways to demonstrate how science encompasses scientific truths" (Brekke 2012, p. 194). Muslim responses to the theory of evolution and the emergence of Islamic creationism must therefore be grasped within a broader framework of Islamic discourses on modern science.

2.4.1. Searching for harmony between Islam and science

The emergence of Islamic modernism is closely linked with the challenges posed by the dominance of the West and its technological advances. In the 19th century, science was increasingly regarded as a vehicle for progress and power, and there was a growing realization in the Islamic world that it was lagging behind the West with regards to science and technology (Kalın 2002, p. 43). In addition to these practical concerns, there was an emerging intellectual debate regarding the compatibility between Islam and modern science. The first major manifestation of this debate was the exchange between French scholar Ernest Renan (1823–1892) and Jamal al-Din al-Afghani (1838–1897) (Stenberg 1996, p. 32; Iqbal 2007, p. 150), often referred to as one of the founding fathers of Islamic modernism (Esposito 2003, p. 354). Al-Afghani wrote a refutation of Renan's criticism of Islam, and argued that contrary to Renan's charge, there is no incompatibility between science and Islam. The foremost representative of Islamic modernism in the Ottoman Empire was Namık Kemal (1840–1888), a contemporary of al-Afghani who also sought to synthesize Islam and science. However, it was in the works of Said Nursi that the ideas about the compatibility of Islam and science would find its most forceful expression in the Ottoman Empire and the subsequent Turkish republic.

2.4.2. Said Nursi

The urge to demonstrate the compatibility between science and religion arises out of a context where science is perceived to challenge religious worldviews. Discourses on Islam and science in the colonial era had a defensive character, seeking to both proclaim the compatibility of Islam and science and to protect religion against potential attacks. However, encounters between Islam and

---

[9] This is also the understanding of fundamentalism that underlies the Fundamentalism Project, an interdisciplinary study sponsored by the American Academy of Arts and Sciences, which resulted in five encyclopedic volumes, published 1991–1995 (Marty & Appleby 1991).

modern science did not merely engender defensive apologetics, but also offered the opportunity to utilize science as a means of strengthening the basis of faith. Said Nursi's approach is an example of the latter.

Nursi was more knowledgeable of modern science than many of his contemporaries (Iqbal 2007, p. 150; Kalın 2002, p. 52), and saw in Western science a possibility in which to renew and substantiate faith. He did not merely assert the compatibility between science and Islam, but regarded science as a decoder of the sacred language of nature (Kalın 2002, p. 55). He believed that a careful and honest inquiry of nature would reveal its purposefulness, harmony and order so clearly that it would inevitably lead to faith. Nursi's ideas have had a major impact in Turkey through the followers of Nursi, the Nur movement. The most influential Nurcu leader today, Fethullah Gülen (b. 1941), has inspired a global network of schools which place particular emphasis on the natural sciences.[10]

The view of nature as the cosmic book of the universe is a common idea in Islamic *kalam* and not unique to Said Nursi.[11] Nursi, however, sought to merge the classical *kalam* arguments of design and harmony as a proof of God with a Newtonian mechanistic cosmology (Kalın 2002, p. 52). He did not regard the prevalent metaphors of nature as a machine favored by secularists as conflicting with a theistic worldview, but embraced these metaphors as confirming the existence of God. However, Nursi's relatively pro-science attitude was not without reservations. From the late 19th century onwards, Western ideas of positivism and materialism began to gain influence among parts of the Ottoman elite, and Nursi saw these ideas as a serious threat to faith and to the Muslim community. While "the early Said" attempted to synthesize Islam and modern forms of knowledge and sought to establish a university that would teach both Islam and modern sciences, "the later Said" immersed himself in the Qur'an and set out to explain and defend "the truths of faith" (*iman hakikatleri*) against materialist philosophy and positivism.

The legacy of Nursi's approach to science is therefore equivocal. On the one hand, Nursi's science-conscious modernism and his attempt to integrate science with a theistic perspective have had a major influence on Islamic discourses on science in modern Turkey. It also laid the foundations for the development of more explicit attempts to confirm the Qur'an through science, which I will discuss below. On the other hand, Nursi's strong antipathy towards positivist and materialist ideas laid the foundations for active opposition to one central

---

[10] Fethullah Gülen is a Turkish preacher and the leader of the Gülen movement, the most prominent Nursi-inspired Islamic movement in Turkey today (see Chapter 2).
[11] Kalam (Ar. *'ilm al-kalam*), often translated as theology, is a branch of the Islamic religious sciences that is concerned with establishing belief and providing arguments for the existence of God.

aspect of modern science, namely Darwin's theory of evolution. As we shall see, both of these legacies are present in the works of Harun Yahya.

### 2.4.3. Science in the Qur'an

The view of the Qur'an as an ultimate source of knowledge is a widespread notion in Islamic traditions. The notion that the Qur'an contains references to scientific discoveries, however, is a relatively modern idea. There is an extensive amount of popular Muslim literature that puts forward claims that the teachings of the Qur'an are confirmed by modern science. The most well known exponent of this view is the French doctor Maurice Bucaille (1920–1998). In *The Bible, the Qur'an, and Science: The Holy Scriptures Examined in the Light of Modern Knowledge* (first published in 1976), Bucaille states: "The Qur'an does not contain a single statement that is open to criticism from modern science" (Bucaille 2003, p. 218). Bucaille claims that the Qur'an makes references to modern scientific discoveries that were not known at the time of revelation, and that it is impossible to explain these statements if one assumes that the Qur'an is a text written by humans (Stenberg 1996, p. 218). Thus, according to Bucaille, there is a correspondence between the Qur'an and modern science that proves that the Qur'an is a divine revelation.

Bucaille was not the first to make these types of claims, but the fact that he was a Western convert, a French doctor with a high position in society as well as a command of Arabic, increased his status as a Muslim and contributed to his popularity (Stenberg 1996 p. 226; Edis 2007, p. 94). Bucaille's books have been translated to many languages, but "Bucaillism", as his approach has been pejoratively termed by his opponents, has also been much derided. Ziauddin Sardar (b.1951), a Muslim intellectual engaged in current debates on Islam and science, criticizes Bucaille for using modern science in order to legitimize the Qur'an, a type of legitimization that revealed scripture does not need according to Sardar (Stenberg 1996, p. 277).

This kind of popular discourse regarding correspondences between modern science and the Qur'an also has its counterpart in the Turkish context, emerging especially from the Nur movement. Said Nursi himself alluded to how verses in the Qur'an anticipate modern technology, but he also acknowledged that such Qur'anic references were obscure (Edis 2007, p. 93). As the Nur movement continued to develop after Nursi's death, his followers did not only reproduce and spread Nursi's opus *Risale-i Nur*, but also wrote their own articles which developed these themes even further. Popular Nurcu magazines such as *Sızıntı* (the Leak (of truth)) and *Zafer* (Victory) published articles drawing comparisons between the Qur'an and scientific discoveries, treating every new discovery as proof of the miracle and credibility of the Qur'an (Kalın 2002, p. 9). The Nur movement thus produced its own form of "Bucaillism", which, as we shall see, is also manifested in the works of Harun Yahya. Aside from this form of popular Muslim apologetics that centers on the harmony between the Qur'an and modern science, another legacy of the Nur movement is the development of a more confrontational form of Muslim apologetics, namely an increasingly vocal antievolutionism.

## 2.5. The emergence of Islamic creationism in Turkey

### 2.5.1. Early Muslim responses to Darwin's theory of evolution

As is the case with the Christian context, Muslim responses to Darwin's theory of evolution have been shaped by a number of social and political conditions (Iqbal 2009). At the time Darwinian ideas were introduced, there was limited knowledge of modern science in the Muslim world (Iqbal 2009). The first Arabic translations of Darwin's works came as late as 1918, and both favorable and critical responses were thus mainly based on interpretations by others (Iqbal 2009). Some of the first Muslims to accept Darwinian ideas were reform-minded Ottoman intellectuals who were interested in materialist and positivist ideas. They became familiar with Darwin's ideas through French translations of the works of the German materialist Ludwig Blüchner (Riexinger 2011). From the very beginning, then, Darwin's theory of evolution was associated with materialist and positivist ideas. Due to the lack of knowledge of the theory beyond a small elite, however, there was little debate and little active opposition to it in the late Ottoman Empire.

Prominent members of the Westernized and secular segments of the Young Turk movement continued to admire Darwin, including Mustafa Kemal Atatürk, who reportedly became interested in Darwin as a student of the Ottoman War Academy (Kazdağlı 2001). Their interest was primarily ideological, however. Blending evolutionary ideas with Comtean positivism, the emerging secular elite provided justification for their radical social engineering program (Riexinger 2011, p. 246). After the founding of the new Turkish republic, the theory of evolution was introduced into the school curriculum in accordance with the Kemalist emphasis on rationalism and science, and remained there until the late 1970s. The theory of evolution thus became part of the ideological package of Kemalism.

### 2.5.2. Antievolutionism in Turkey

Until the 1970s, there was little opposition to the teaching of evolution in schools from religious circles in Turkey. Presumably, evolution remained a minor issue among a host of other secularizing measures that were perceived by many as repressive against religion (Edis 2007, p. 122). One of the first extensive attacks on the theory of evolution in Turkey was formulated by a religious conservative intellectual, Ismail Fenni Ertuğrul, in 1928 (Riexinger, 2011, p. 487). In comparison with much other antievolution literature, Ertuğrul's criticism is written in a neutral and non-polemical tone. He presented a combination of scientific, moral and theological arguments against the theory of evolution. Many of Ertuğrul's arguments can also be found in later antievolutionist tracts, such as the idealist concept of species, the lack of fossil proofs and the gap between the capabilities between apes and humans (Riexinger, 2011, p. 488).

The main origin of ideologically based creationism in Turkey, however, was the Nur movement. Said Nursi never mentioned Darwin explicitly, but frequently referred to the perfect harmony in nature as a proof of God, and emphasized that all events are continually directed by God (Riexinger 2011, p. 489). Furthermore, Nursi wrote extensively on the need to fight against the influence of Western naturalist and materialist ideas (Özervarli 2003, p. 320). It is therefore not surprising that it was among Nursi's followers that a more polemical and vigorous antievolutionism would emerge. Fethullah Gülen delivered a series of lectures arguing against the theory of evolution in the early 1970s, and soon articles denouncing the theory of evolution began appearing in religious publications associated with the Nur movement. These articles included typical creationist arguments, some of which appears to have been developed independently of Protestant creationist movements, and others that were Turkish translations of the arguments of prominent Protestant creationists such as Duane Gish and John Morris (Edis 2007, p. 122).[12] The Nurcu campaign against evolution was also joined by other writers, such as theologians Haluk Nurbaki (1924–1997) and Zekeriya Beyaz (b.1938).

During the 1970s, the theory of evolution began generating more controversy. It was after the military coup in 1980, however, that Islamic creationism in Turkey entered a new phase and began to have a considerable political impact. After the election in 1983, a conservative segment of the ruling Motherland party took control of the Ministry of Education. The American Institute for Creation Research (ICR) received a surprising phone call from the Turkish Minister of Education Vehbi Dinçerler, requesting literature dealing with scientific evidence for creation (Edis 2007, p. 124). Dinçerler also asked Adem Tatlı, a prominent Nurcu creationist, to prepare a report on evolution. On Tatlı's recommendation, scientific creationism was included in the school curriculum. In *Biyoloji 1* (Güven 1986), the biology textbook used in Turkish high schools between 1986 and 1998, creationism is presented as a scientific theory about the origin of life. A report prepared by the State Planning Organization in 1983 where they endorsed the Turkish-Islamic synthesis, also included attacks on

---

[12] Martin Riexinger provides an extensive list of the main scientific and moral/theological arguments employed by Turkish Islamic creationists in (Riexinger 2011).

Darwinism (Edis 2007, p. 123). Hence, the conservative turn in Turkish politics after the coup in 1980 that I described in Chapter 2 provided an opportunity space for Islamic creationism.

With its science-oriented Islamic discourse, the Nur movement had laid the foundations for the development of a Turkish Islamic creationism that on the one hand emphasized the compatibility between the Qur'an and modern science, but on the other hand regarded the theory of evolution as representing dangerous and damaging Western materialist ideas. It was not until Harun Yahya launched his own campaign against the theory of evolution in the mid-1990s that Islamic creationism started to gain significant influence in both Turkey and globally.

## 3. The Islamic Creationism of Harun Yahya

### 3.1. *The Evolution Deceit*: Yahya's attack on Darwinian evolution

Against this background, I will now describe and analyze the Islamic creationism of Harun Yahya. What does the Islamic creationism of Harun Yahya contain, and which of Yahya's works should such an analysis take as its starting point? As I have discussed above, creationism is a complex concept. There are different types of creationism, and the term is used in different senses. Furthermore, the trajectories of creationist discourse are somewhat different in Christian and Muslim contexts. In the United States, creationism is associated not merely with anti-Darwinism, but also with efforts to discredit other fields of modern science which are perceived as conflicting with the Biblical narrative of creation, such as geology. However, as mentioned, the notion of an ancient earth is not perceived as conflicting with the Qur'an. Instead, Islamic creationism is linked with efforts to assert the compatibility between science and Islam in popular Muslim apologetics. In the Muslim context, then, the closest cousin of creationism is not flood geology, but claims regarding scientific miracles in the Qur'an. In the following, I will therefore also include a discussion about this theme in the works of Harun Yahya. As is the case with Islamic creationism in general, the core of Yahya's creationism is the perceived link between Darwinism and materialist philosophy or atheism. In Yahya's creationist discourse, the theme of anti-materialism takes a particularly central stage, and it is in his approach to and understanding of materialism that we find the most original element of his creationist discourse.

With this in mind, I take *The Evolution Deceit: The Scientific Collapse of Darwinism and its Ideological Background* (Yahya 2002g), which I will henceforth refer to as *The Evolution Deceit* for short, as the empirical point of departure for the analysis of Yahya's antievolutionism. First published in April

1997 in Turkish as *Evrim Aldatmacası: Evrim Teorisi'nin Bilimsel Çöküşü ve Teorinin İdeolojik Arka Planı* (Yahya 1997a), *The Evolution Deceit* may be considered the bedrock of the campaign that Harun Yahya launched against Darwinian evolution. It includes all the central elements of Yahya's anti-Darwinist discourse, which he has expanded upon in later works. *The Evolution Deceit* therefore serves as a useful starting point for an examination of Harun Yahya's creationism. It lays out the basic framework of his case against Darwin, and also exemplifies the particular jargon-free, plain and self-assured style in which the Harun Yahya works are typically written.

The first English edition of *The Evolution Deceit* was published in July 1999 (Yahya 1999a). Written for a global audience, the English edition omits references to Atatürk and other Turkey-related references that are present in the Turkish original edition. For instance, the introduction to the Turkish edition cites Atatürk's dictum "*hayatta en hakiki mürşid ilimdir*" (the truest mentor in life is science) and argues that "spreading this truth [that the theory of evolution is invalid] is a requirement of the way Atatürk has shown us" (Yahya 1997a, p. 3).[13] Besides, a section in the original Turkish version on what Yahya denotes as Darwin's racism and anti-Turkism (Yahya 1997a, pp. 18–19) has been altered in the English edition and references to Darwin's anti-Turkism has been removed (Yahya 2002g, p. 44). In 2002, a revised 7th Edition of *The Evolution Deceit* was published which included a special preface about terrorism titled "The Real Ideological Root of Terrorism: Darwinism and Materialism", most likely prompted by the September 11th attacks.[14] My analysis will be based on the edition from 2002. I will first present a brief synopsis of Yahya's anti-Darwinist critique as presented in *The Evolution Deceit*, before making a closer examination of the targets of Yahya's critique, the types of argumentative strategies Yahya employs in order to discredit the theory of evolution, and how Yahya places the battle against the theory into a broader framework.

### 3.2. A brief synopsis of *The Evolution Deceit*

The basic premise of *The Evolution Deceit* is that the theory of evolution is scientifically invalid, and that the real reason why it continues to hold its sway is that it serves to underpin materialist philosophy. Harun Yahya claims that the theory of evolution leads people away from God because it provides the false notion that materialism is a scientific idea. According to Yahya, materialist philosophy is responsible for social ills like war, violence and terror. The pro-

---

[13] *Hayatta en hakiki mürşid ilimdir* is one of many dictums attributed to Atatürk, and the phrase decorates the walls of many schools and universities in Turkey.
[14] The 8th and currently latest (2012) English edition contains only minor revisions and a new front cover. The 5th and latest Turkish edition also contains the mentioned special preface on terrorism.

fessed purpose of the book is therefore to help the reader realize "that Darwinism is not a scientific theory but a pseudo-scientific dogma upheld in the name of materialist philosophy" (Yahya 2002g, p. 29), in order to break the influence of materialism and turn people towards God. The book consists of three main parts. In the first part, Yahya makes a moral and religious case against Darwinism and materialism, claiming that as the pseudo-scientific underpinning for materialism, Darwinism leads to social evils and turns people away from God. In the second and lengthiest part of the book, Yahya seeks to present a full refutation of the theory of evolution on scientific grounds. In the third part, he makes a philosophical and scientific case against materialism, and concludes that both science and logic points to the truth of creation, the truth of God's existence and the truth of the Qur'an.

## 3.3. The targets of critique

The chief target of Yahya's critique is Charles Darwin's theory of evolution. The opening lines of the introduction to *The Evolution Deceit* sets the tone of the work:

> For some people the theory of evolution or Darwinism has only scientific connotations, with seemingly no direct implication in their daily lives. This is, of course, a common misunderstanding. Far beyond just being an issue within the framework of the biological sciences, the theory of evolution constitutes the underpinning of a deceptive philosophy that has held sway over a large number of people: Materialism (Yahya 2002g, p. 27).

As implied in the above citation, for Yahya "the theory of evolution" and "Darwinism" is essentially the same thing, and both expressions are employed in *The Evolution Deceit*, although the term Darwinism is preferred. In distinction from some other detractors of the theory of evolution, Yahya's focus is not that Darwin's theory is "only a theory" (Miller 2008), but rather that it is an ideology, reflected in the use of terms such as "Darwin*ism*", "Darwin*ist*" and "evolution*ist*".

In scientific discourse, a distinction is often made between the *fact* and the *theory* of evolution. Evolution is widely considered among biologists to be a fact that can be observed today, and for which there exists overwhelming evidence. There exists several theories of the *mechanisms* of evolution, that is, *how* evolution has occurred. Harun Yahya rejects both the *fact* of evolution, e.g., the claim that species have evolved from a common ancestor, as well as the *theories* of the mechanisms of evolution. Scientists also distinguish between *the Darwinian theory of evolution* as it was proposed by Charles Darwin in *The Origin of Species* (where he advocates natural selection as the mechanism behind evolution), and what is often referred to as *the modern evolutionary synthesis* or *the neo-Darwinian synthesis*. The modern evolutionary synthesis incorporates scientific discoveries after Darwin, most importantly genetics, and also recognizes other mechanisms of evolution than natural selection (Mayr 2001).

Yahya's arguments are directed at both Darwin's original theory and the modern synthesis, which Yahya refers to as neo-Darwinism. Moreover, Yahya does not merely target Darwinian explanations for why evolution has occurred, but also rejects the *fact* of evolution, namely the idea that living species have evolved over time from a common ancestor. He devotes considerable time on attempting to disprove the evolution of species as a means to weaken the scientific credibility of the theory of evolution in general. This argument is for instance the main focus of the *Atlas of Creation* (Yahya 2007a), the spearhead for Yahya's global campaign against evolution. However, evolution itself is arguably not Yahya's main grievance about the theory of evolution. Rather, Yahya is concerned in particular with two alleged aspects of Darwinism that he perceives as conflicting with a religious understanding of human existence and morality, namely the notion that life originated by *chance*, and the notion that existence is based on *conflict*.

> The answer to the question "What is a human being?" has changed. People who used to answer: "God creates human beings and they have to live according to the beautiful morality He teaches", have now begun to think that "Man came into being by chance, and is an animal who developed by means of the fight for survival" (Yahya 2002g, p. 14).

The second part of *The Evolution Deceit* is devoted to refuting a philosophy Yahya claims is closely linked with Darwinism, namely "materialism" or "materialist philosophy". Yahya defines materialist philosophy as the view that "matter has always existed, and everything that exists consists of matter" (Yahya 2002g).[15] He equates materialism with "irreligion" (Yahya 2002g, p. 26) and argues that materialism "makes belief in a Creator impossible, of course, because if matter has always existed, and if everything consists of matter, then there can be no supramaterial Creator who created it" (Yahya 2002g, p. 180). According to Yahya, materialistic philosophy produced the theory of evolution in the middle of the 19th century (Yahya 2002g, p. 41). In Yahya's view, then, "Darwinism" and "materialism" are two sides of the same coin: They are both the expressions of an atheistic worldview that denies the existence of a creator (Yahya 2002g, p. 20).

---

[15] The theory that physical matter is the only or fundamental reality is referred to as *philosophical materialism*, as distinct from *economic materialism* (a preoccupation with material things and consumption) and *historical materialism* (the doctrine that economic or social change are materially caused). Routledge Encyclopedia of Philosophy defines materialism in the philosophical sense as "a set of related theories which hold that all entities and processes are composed of – or reducible to – matter, material forces or physical processes. […] Since it denies the existence of spiritual beings or forces, materialism is typically allied with atheism or agnosticism" (Stack 1998).

## 3.4. Methods of critique

The main purpose of *The Evolution Deceit* is to convince the reader that neither Darwinism nor materialism has any scientific basis, and the focus is therefore on arguments aiming to demonstrate this. However, Yahya also presents a moral case against Darwinism and materialism as an explanation for why an intellectual struggle against them is paramount.

### 3.4.1. The moral case against evolution

Moral arguments are a common line of argumentation against the theory of evolution among creationists in general (Isaak 2005). It is a form of *argumentum ad consequentiam*, in that it appeals to alleged negative consequences of the theory regardless of whether the theory reflects empirical reality or not. *The Evolution Deceit* posits a causal connection between materialism/Darwinism and a whole range of social and political problems. According to Yahya,

> Ideologies based on materialism [...] have brought permanent violence, war and chaos to the world. Communism, responsible for the death of 120 million people, is the direct outcome of materialistic philosophy. Fascism, despite pretending to be an alternative to the materialistic world-view, accepted the fundamental materialist concept of progress though conflict and sparked off oppressive regimes, massacres, world wars and genocide. Besides these two bloody ideologies, individual and social ethics have also been corrupted by materialism (Yahya 2002g, p. 27).

This, he explains further, is because materialism is "reducing man to an animal whose existence is coincidental and with no responsibility to any being, demolished moral pillars such as love, mercy, self-sacrifice, modesty, honesty and justice" (Yahya 2002g, p. 27).[16] Darwinism promotes the view that life is essentially based on a conflict of interests, thereby justifying a social system based on "the law of the jungle", he argues further (Yahya 2002g, p. 28).[17] According to Yahya, "humanity has paid a heavy price in the 20th century for the dissemination of these callous views [of Darwinism] which lead people to acts of ruthlessness and cruelty" (Yahya 2002g, p. 16). These themes are expanded upon in greater detail in *Fascism: The Bloody Ideology of Darwinism* (Yahya 2002h).[18]

What is perhaps most striking about Yahya's version of this argument is the way in which he blames Darwinism and materialism for not only precipitating political ideologies like communism, fascism and Nazism, but also all forms of

---

[16] This argument is presented as claim CA001, "Evolution is the foundation of an immoral worldview", in Isaak (2005).
[17] American creationists Ken Ham and Henry Morris have made similar arguments. See also Claim CA002.1: "Evolution Leads to Social Darwinism" in Isaak (2005, p. 3).
[18] See image appendix, p. 4.

terrorism, including terrorism committed in the name of Islam. In the special preface added to editions published after 2001 titled "The Real Ideological Root of Terrorism: Darwinism and Materialism", Yahya argues that Darwinism justifies a view of life based on conflict and violence, and "man as a fighting animal" (Yahya 2002g).[19] According to Yahya, Islam, Christianity and Judaism all oppose violence, while "Darwinism sees and portrays conflict and violence as natural, justified and correct concepts that have to exist" (Yahya 2002g, p. 19). For this reason, argues Yahya,

> if some people commit terrorism using the concepts and symbols of Islam, Christianity or Judaism in the name of those religions, you can be sure that those people are not Muslims, Christians or Jews. They are real Social Darwinists. They hide under a cloak of religion, but they are not genuine believers (Yahya, 2002g, pp. 19-20).

Thus, according to Yahya, those who commit acts of terror in the name of religion are Social Darwinists and under the spell of materialism, whether they are aware of it or not. This is a line of argumentation that Yahya develops further in subsequent books on the subject, such as *Islam Denounces Terrorism* (2002k).[20]

### 3.4.2. The scientific case against evolution

The main bulk of *The Evolution Deceit* is devoted to showing that Darwinism is "a fallacy completely contrary to scientific facts" (Yahya 2002g, p. 196). In the following, I will outline the main types of argument that Harun Yahya presents in order to try to show that the theory of evolution is unsupported on scientific grounds. As mentioned earlier, Adnan Oktar does not have any particular scientific expertise. It is therefore reasonable to assume that most of the arguments and examples presented have been adapted from other sources. As the following examination will show, the scientific creationism of Harun Yahya is an eclectic blend of arguments.[21] The fact that many of the arguments can be found in a wide range of both Christian and Muslim creationist literature makes it difficult to ascertain their exact source, and that is also not the main objective in this dissertation. As mentioned, Adnan Oktar has a team of researchers who

---

[19] It should be noted that Yahya invariably assigns masculine gender to generic antecedents ("man", "mankind", "he", "him"). I have retained this gendered language in instances where it appears justified in order to reflect the general tone of the text.
[20] See for instance the chapter entitled "The Real Roots of Terrorism: Materialism and Darwinism" (2002k). The argument that Islam is a religion of peace and that a real Muslim therefore cannot be a terrorist, is a claim that has been put forward by many others as well, including Turkish Muslim preacher Fethullah Gülen. See (Akman 2004).
[21] I use the term "scientific" here not in a normative sense as based on the methods and principles of science, but merely to refer to arguments that are presented by Yahya as being scientific.

collects material for the books published in the name of Harun Yahya. When I asked Oktar in 2009 where his researchers find the material, he simply replied, "the Internet".[22]

Most of the time Yahya does not explicitly acknowledge the origin of the arguments he is using, but rather presents them as the product of his own inquiry. He does make references, however, to Western scientists who advocate Intelligent Design theories such as Michael Denton (b. 1943), Michael Behe (b. 1952) and Jonathan Wells (b. 1942). He makes no reference, however, to Muslim scientists who defend creationist views. He could for instance have cited Adem Tatli, who is a biologist. Instead a number of Western scientists and creationists are referred to and cited as authorities. This may be interpreted as reflecting the notion that "Western" scientists lend more authority to the arguments. Martin Riexinger observes that a typical discourse in Islamic apologetics is references to Western "crown witnesses" who "serve to highlight the superiority of Islam and/or the moral failure of the West on the basis of his scientific of philosophical knowledge" (Riexinger 2011, p. 505). Leif Stenberg also brings up this point in relation to the popularity of Maurice Bucaille (Stenberg 1996, p. 226). Another possible reason is that Yahya aspires to be *the* authority on creationism, particularly in the Muslim context, and therefore sees no reason to acknowledge other voices of Islamic creationism.

*The Evolution Deceit* was originally written in Turkish for a Turkish audience. Notably, several Turkish authors are cited in the text, but then as representatives of the evolutionist view that Yahya's polemics are directed against. Although Yahya makes no reference to other Islamic creationists, this does not preclude the possibility that the arguments might originate from Nurcu sources. Riexinger claims that most of the arguments put forward by Yahya can also be found in Nurcu tracts (Riexinger, 2011, p. 496).

Although there is disagreement over particular elements of the theory of evolution, there is no major disagreement in the scientific community over the fact that evolution has occurred. According to evolutionary biologist Ernst Mayr, the evidence for evolution is so overwhelming that today's biologists "consider it a fact – as well-established as the fact that the Earth rotates around the sun and that the Earth is round and not flat" (Mayr 1997, p. 178). The arguments against the theory of evolution put forward by Yahya in *The Evolution Deceit* are mostly well-known creationist arguments that mainstream science rejects as based on misunderstandings or misconstructions of scientific facts and theories. *The Counter-Creationism Handbook* (Isaak 2005) offers a comprehensive and systematic overview over common creationist claims. Most of the arguments presented by Harun Yahya are covered in Isaak's handbook, which mainly refers to Protestant creationist sources. Some elements of

---

[22] Personal interview with Adnan Oktar, 07.01.2009.

Protestant creation science are completely absent in Yahya's works however, notably what is known as flood theology, since Yahya – as most Muslim creationists – accepts the notion of an ancient Earth and can thus be defined as an Old Earth creationist. Yahya concentrates on arguments that fall into one of the following categories, which will be outlined below:

- Paleontological arguments against evolution itself
- Arguments regarding neo-Darwinism and the mechanisms of evolution
- Arguments regarding the origin of life
- Arguments for creation

*3.4.2.1. Rejection of evolution itself: Paleontological arguments*

Many Muslim critics of Darwinian evolution accept some forms of evolution of species while remaining critical to other aspects of Darwinism. Maurice Bucaille, for instance, accepts that animals have evolved, but posits a separate evolution for humanoids (Hameed 2008, p. 1638). Harun Yahya, however, holds that all species were created in their present form and denies that evolution has occurred. He devotes considerable attention to denying the validity of the paleontological evidence for evolution, and claims instead that the fossil record proves that the theory of evolution is wrong. This is the main line of argument in the richly illustrated grand opus of Yahya's antievolution campaign, the three-volume *Atlas of Creation*. Yahya presents various arguments familiar from creationist literature:

1. Arguments regarding the fossil record: Yahya claims that the so-called Cambrian explosion shows that life emerged on earth suddenly and in complex forms (Yahya 2002g, p. 61).[23]

2. Arguments regarding transitional fossils: Yahya claims that in order for the theory of evolution to be true there should exist "transitional forms" (half-fish, half-reptile), but that no such forms have ever been found (Yahya 2002g, p. 46).[24] Yahya repeats the accusation of astronomer and science fiction writer Fred Hoyle (Hoyle & Wickramasinghe 1986), often quoted by creationists, that the London *archaeopteryx* specimen was a hoax (Yahya 2002g, pp. 70–71).[25]

3. Arguments regarding physical anthropology. Yahya claims that all hominid fossils are either fully human or fully ape, and points out

---

[23] The Cambrian explosion is a term used to describe the appearance of many forms of life in a relatively short time some 542 million years ago. See Claim CC300, "The Cambrian explosion shows all kinds of life appearing suddenly" in Isaak (2005, p. 128).

[24] Claim CC200, "There are no transitional fossils" in Isaak (2005, p. 113).

[25] The *archaeopteryx* is a fossil of a primitive bird presented as an intermediate form between dinosaurs and modern birds.

actual and alleged forgeries of "missing link" fossils in physical anthropology.[26] He claims that there are "unbridgeable anatomical gaps" (Yahya 2002g, p. 122) between different groups of species, such as amphibians and reptiles, reptiles and birds, and also humans and apes:

> Comparative anatomy revealed that species that were supposed to have evolved from one another had in fact very different anatomical features and that they could never have been ancestors or descendants of each other (Yahya 2002g, p. 46).

Yahya thus concludes that contrary to what the majority of paleontologists, physical anthropologist and biologist claim, the fossil record does not present us with evidence for species evolving, but quite the contrary, evidence that species have not evolved.

*3.4.2.2. Rejection of the neo-Darwinian synthesis*

According to Harun Yahya, Darwin's theory of evolution through natural selection was not based on scientific discovery or experiment, but simply the product of his imagination (Yahya, 2002g, p. 42). The mainstream view is that scientific discoveries made after Darwin, particularly in the field of genetics, actually strengthened the theory (Mayr, 2001, p. x). Yahya claims the opposite. According to him, "Darwin's theory entered into a deep crisis because of the laws of genetics discovered in the first quarter of the 20th century" (Yahya 2002g, p. 45). Neo-Darwinism was a desperate attempt to salvage the theory, claims Yahya, and rejects both Stephen Jay Gould's notion of "punctuated equilibrium", which Yahya claims was introduced as a solution to a gap in the fossil record, as well as the famous example of industrial melanism as presented by Douglas Futuyama in *Evolutionary Biology* (1986), which is erroneously referenced as *The Biology of Evolution* in Yahya (2002g, p. 51).

Yahya also claims that mutations are harmful, and that they can therefore not be the mechanism of evolution: "No useful mutation has been so far observed. All mutations have proved to be harmful" (Yahya 2002g, p. 57).[27] Yahya concludes, "It is impossible for living beings to have evolved, because there exists no mechanism in nature that can cause evolution" (Yahya 2002g, p. 57). Yahya also rejects a number of the biological phenomena that are presented as evidence for evolution. Under the heading "The Fallacy of Vestigial Organs", Yahya rehashes Henry Morris' claim that vestigial organs, contrary to the claim of

---

[26] Claim CC050, "All hominid fossils are fully human or fully ape" in Isaak (2005, p. 106).
[27] Claim CB101 "Most mutations are harmful" in (Isaak 2005, p. 52). This argument is also made by Henry Morris (Morris 1974, pp. 55–57).

evolutionists, do have definite uses (Yahya 2002g, p. 170).[28] Citing biophysicist and Jewish creationist Lee Spetner (1998), Yahya also claims that contrary to the claims of evolutionists, antibiotic resistance is not evidence for evolution (Yahya 2002g, pp. 167–170).

*3.4.2.3. Arguments regarding the origin of life*

Harun Yahya places much emphasis on rejecting what he perceives as the theory of evolution's claim that life and living things have come about by *blind chance*. In the chapter titled "The Molecular Impasse of Evolution", Yahya argues that the theory of evolution implies that life came about by chance, and that the accidental formation of life is not only improbable, but also impossible. He repeats the common creationist argument that the statistical probability of a cell forming spontaneously is close to zero.[29] Also in concurrence with other creationists, Yahya claims that the Miller-Urey experiment – which sought to prove that amino acids could form on their own in conditions close to that of a primordial earth – was invalid.[30] Yahya claims that abiogenesis, the process by which life rose from inorganic matter, is scientifically impossible:

> Research has revealed that the mere combination of all the materials essential for life is not enough for life to get started. Even if all the essential proteins for life were collected and put in a test tube, these efforts would not result with producing a living cell. All the experiments conducted on this subject have proved to be unsuccessful. All observations and experiments indicate that life can only originate from life. The assertion that life evolved from non-living things, in other words, "abiogenesis", is a tale only existing in the dreams of the evolutionists and completely at variance with the results of every experiment and observation (Yahya 2002g, p. 149).

Yahya thus concludes that evolution is unable to explain how life began.

*3.4.2.4. The argument from design*

Most of the above arguments are presented by Harun Yahya as evidence specifically against various elements of Darwin's theory of evolution. However, *The Evolution Deceit* is also devoted to arguments *for* creation, more specifically arguments that the design in nature is proof of a creator. This is known as "the argument from design" or the teleological argument, and is one of Yahya's favored lines of creationist argumentation. Varieties of this argument are common both in Christian traditions where it is often identified with Christian apologist William Paley who set forth the famous watchmaker analogy, and in

---

[28] Claim CB360 "Vestigial organs may have functions" in Isaak (2005, p. 70). See also Henry Morris (1974, pp. 75–76).
[29] Claim CB010 "The odds of life forming are incredibly small" in Isaak (2005, p. 43).
[30] Claim CB025 "Not all amino acids needed for life have been formed experimentally" in Isaak (2005, p. 46).

Islamic *kalam*.³¹ In recent years, the Intelligent Design movement has promoted a variant of the argument from design, maintaining that the existence of irreducibly complex biological systems cannot be accounted for by means of evolution.

Yahya employs both general design-arguments regarding the harmony in nature that are familiar from both *kalam* and from the works of Said Nursi and his followers, as well as more specific Intelligent Design arguments regarding complexity.³² In chapter 12, titled "Design and Coincidence", Yahya presents the standard argument from design: "A complex system like the cell is no doubt created by a superior will and wisdom" (Yahya 2002g, p. 157). In line with numerous other creationists, Yahya also uses the eye as the chief example of something that is too complex to have evolved and could not have come about "by chance" (Yahya 2002g, p. 160).³³ The "architectural wonders of honeycombs" and "the design in bird feathers" are also used as examples of design that could only have been created. Yahya claims that science is continuously discovering new miraculous structures in nature, and that these are too complicated to have come about by chance. However, whereas Intelligent Design proponents focus on aspects such as mathematic improbability (William Dembski) and concepts like *irreducible complexity* (Michael Behe), Yahya often speaks in terms of "miracles" and "divine order". In Yahya's view, nature does not merely reveal intelligence, but also beauty and wisdom:

> All the millions of living species on the earth possess miraculous features, unique behavioral patterns and flawless physical structures. Every one of these living things has been created with its own unique detail and beauty. Plants, animals, and man above all, were all created with great knowledge and art, from their external appearances down to their cells, invisible to the naked eye (Yahya 2002g, p. 32).

This is a wisdom that only a benevolent God could have created, according to Yahya:

> The great wisdom, design and plan that prevails overall in nature, provides solid evidence for the existence of a supreme Creator dominating over the whole of nature, and this Creator is God (Yahya 2002g, p. 196).

---

³¹ *Kalam* refers to an Islamic discipline of systematic theology. The watchmaker analogy argument proposes the following: When I see a complex object such as a watch, I know that it has been designed; therefore, when I see a complex object such as a tiger, I should infer that it has been designed as well.

³² The argument that the complexity of organisms necessitates a designer has also been brought forward by other Turkish creationists. See for instance Akbulut (1985) and Beyaz (1978), cited in (Riexinger forthcoming).

³³ Claim CB301 "The eye is too complex to have evolved" in Isaak (2005, p. 65).

Although Yahya cites Intelligent Design proponent Michael Behe at length in *The Evolution Deceit* (p. 37, p. 54), and even uses the term "intelligent design" to describe creation (p. 152), in a later article he criticizes both Christian and Muslim Intelligent Design proponents for omitting references to Allah. According to Yahya, anyone of normal intelligence must understand that the intelligence in question is "none other than God" (Yahya 2007d). In another article, Yahya claims that the theory of Intelligent Design is "another kind of deism" and a "New Age theory" which "accepts neither revealed religions nor the existence of Allah" (Yahya 2008d). According to Yahya, New Age theories have been devised by atheist masons in order to distract those people who are abandoning materialist ideas away from revealed religion, and to establish a new system "ornamented with metaphysical language" (Yahya 2008d). The message of Yahya is thus that science does not only confirm the existence of an intelligent designer, but divine creation as revealed by Allah. Yahya has devoted a whole series of books to the notion that nature is full of miracles that could only have been created by God, including titles such as *Miracle in the Atom* (Yahya 2001i), *The Miracle in the Ant* (Yahya 2000c), and *Miracle in the Eye* (Yahya 2006c).

*3.4.2.5. The secret behind matter: Yahya's anti-materialism and idealism*

Yahya sets out to scientifically disprove, not just the theory of evolution, but the philosophy he claims underpins it, namely materialism:

> We can therefore investigate by means of scientific methods the materialist claim: that matter has existed for all eternity and that this matter can organise itself without a supramaterial Creator and cause life to begin. When we do this, we see that materialism has already collapsed, because the idea that matter has existed since beginning of time has been overthrown by the Big Bang theory which shows that the universe was created from nothingness (Yahya 2002g, p. 180).

Yahya not only rejects the materialist idea that the material world is the only reality, but also questions the reality of matter itself:

> We are so conditioned to suppositions about the existence of matter that we never think about whether or not it does exist or is only created as an image. Modern science demolishes this prejudice and discloses a very important and imposing reality (Yahya 2002g, p. 216).

Yahya argues that modern scientific explanations of how our senses work confirm that we have no access to the external world except as perceptions in our brains. Yahya declares that "the universe we occupy and the body we possess [...] have no material reality" (Yahya 2002g, p. 227). He explains that everything we see, touch, hear and perceive as "matter" or "the external world" is nothing but electrical signals occurring in our brain, and that "the qualities we ascribe to the objects are inside us and not in the external world" (Yahya 2002g, p. 225). He cites Western philosophers such as Ludwig Wittgenstein (1889–1951) and Bertrand Russell (1872–1970) and scientists such as the German biochemist Frederic Vester (1925–2003) to support the view that we only have access to an image of the world. There is no distinction between dreams and our perceptions of the external world, claims Yahya, as both are experienced in the brain.

Yahya then goes on to reflect on a well-known question in the philosophy of mind, namely the mind/body problem, or how to account for "the ghost in the machine" in the words of British philosopher Gilbert Ryle (1900–1976):"Within the piece of meat we call our 'brain', there is nothing to observe the images, to constitute consciousness, or to create the being we call 'myself'" (Yahya 2002g, p. 227). What is real then, according to Yahya, is the soul, and "the aggregate of perceptions we call the 'material world' is a dream observed by this soul" (2002g, p. 227). The perceptions perceived by our soul must have been caused by another power, namely God. Yahya concludes: "It is very evident that there exists a supreme Creator, Who has created the entire material universe, that is, the sum of perceptions, and Who continues His creation ceaselessly" (Yahya 2002g, p. 228). Matter, then, is an illusion created in our minds by Allah, according to Yahya: "It is a scientific and logical fact that the 'external world' has no materialistic reality and that it is a collection of images God perpetually presents to our soul" (Yahya 2002g, p. 231). From neurological explanations of how perceptions works via philosophical reasoning on the mind-body problem, Yahya thus arrives at a theological defense for continuous creation or the idea that the one, real productive cause of all things is God. In Islamic philosophy this view is associated with the early Asharite theological school and al-Ghazali in particular (Griffel 2012).

The struggle against materialist philosophy is a prominent theme in Nurcu thought. Said Nursi himself emphasized that the spiritual world is as real as the physical world, and wrote that "this material and manifest world is but a lace veil strewn over the inner and spirit worlds."[34] Yahya not only affirms the reality of the spiritual world against materialist worldviews, but goes as far as denying the reality of the external world itself. In *The Evolution Deceit,* Yahya refers to Muslim scholars and mystics such as Imam Rabbani, Muhyiddin Ibn Arabi and Mevlana Cami as philosophers who have understood this "secret" about our existence.[35] He also refers to Anglo-Irish idealist philosopher George Berkeley (1685–1753) as an example of a Western philosopher who has understood this

---

[34] Nursi cited in Yunus Çengel (2008).
[35] Imam Rabbani/Ahmad Sirhindi (1564–1624) was an Indian Hanafi jurist and Nakşibendi *şeyh*. Muhyiddin Ibn Arabi (1165–1240) was an Andalusian Sufi mystic and philosopher. It is not entirely clear who Yahya means by Mevlana Cami as there is no further reference or citation, but presumably it is the Persian Sufi mystic Jalaluddin Rumi (1207–1273), generally referred to as Mevlana in Turkish.

reality. Yahya develops these mystical ideas regarding "the secret of matter" in a number of other works, such as *Matter: The Other Name for Illusion* (Yahya 2002m) and *Idealism, the Philosophy of the Matrix and the True Nature of Matter* (Yahya 2003i). In the latter, Yahya examines popular science fiction films such as *The Matrix, Vanilla Sky, The Thirteenth Floor* and *Total Recall,* and makes the case that these films capture important truths about our existence, namely how created dream worlds can appear as reality. Much like in these films, in reality we are "only watching a copy of our lives", argues (Yahya 2003i, p. 19).

3.4.3. The religious case against evolution

The main bulk of *The Evolution Deceit* is devoted to arguments which truth claims appeal to "scientific discoveries, logic and reason" as its authority (Yahya 2002g, p. 164). Throughout the book, Yahya attempts to convince the reader that scientific facts, logic and reason all point away from Darwinism and materialism, and that careful consideration of the arguments he presents inevitably points to the existence of a Creator. In a sense, Yahya turns the evolutionary biologist Theodosius Dobzhansky's famous statement that "nothing makes sense in biology except in the light of evolution" on its head (Dobzhansky 1973). *The Evolution Deceit* is designed to demonstrate that nothing in the natural world makes sense except in the light of divine creation. However, Yahya also appeals to another form of authority, namely revelation. Yahya applies a technique that he uses in many of his works, namely to employ verses from the Qur'an to illustrate or support his arguments.

In the special preface on terrorism, Yahya cites verses of the Qur'an that deal with morality as "proof" that Islam and terrorism is incompatible. He cites for instance sura 5:32 in order to show that the killing of innocent people is unlawful, and therefore terrorism is also unlawful (Yahya 2002g, p. 22).[36] In the foreword Yahya cites sura 6:111 in order to illustrate what he calls "the psychology of the unbelievers" who "ignore the clear signs and evidences of creation" (Yahya 2002g, p. 38). There are also a couple of references to the Qur'an in the main body of the book, which focuses on scientific arguments against evolution and for creation. In the section titled "Honey Bees and the Architectural Wonders of Honeycombs", Yahya explains why the hexagonal structure of the honeycomb is the most appropriate form the bee could possibly use to store its honey. Yahya's point is that the structure of the honeycomb is so perfect that it could only have been designed by a creator. This line of argumentation is then supplemented with verses from the Qur'an about bees (16:68–69), which according to Yahya's interpretation declare that it is God who "inspires" the bees to make honeycombs (Yahya 2002g, p. 197). Yahya thus

---

[36] Cited as "Suratal-Ma'ida: 32" in Yahya. For the sake of consistency I refer to the sura by number.

juxtaposes "evidence from nature" with "evidence from revelation". In another section, Yahya claims that science confirms that the first life on earth must have originated from other life. This insight, Yahya argues, is reflected in God's epithet of "Hayy" (The Owner of Life), and the notion that "life can only start, continue, and end by His will" (Yahya 2002g, p. 149).[37]

It is in the last part of *The Evolution Deceit*, however, that Yahya more explicitly places his arguments for creationism into an Islamic apologetic framework. Having established that all science and logic inevitably points to a divinely created world, Yahya answers the rhetorical question, "who is this creator of all things?" by declaring that "This Creator is God and the name of His Book is the Qur'an" (Yahya 2002g, p. 229). Yahya maintains that the secret of matter that, according to him, is now confirmed by modern science has already been revealed in the Qur'an. He insists that evidence does not only point towards theistic creation, but to creation as revealed by the Qur'an. Yahya concludes that it is "only God that exists: everything except Him are images", and that "God is surely 'everywhere' and encompasses all". He asserts that this is explained in the Qur'an in 2:255 (Yahya 2002g, p. 229).

Yahya employs both the Qur'an as a context for illuminating science, and science as a context for understanding the Qur'an. The argumentative structure of *The Evolution Deceit* is designed not merely to disprove evolution, but to show that reason and science confirm the Qur'an. As discussed above, appealing to science to show the veracity of the Qur'an is a prominent theme in the Nurcu school of thought. A popular variety of this type of discourse is also the science-in-the-Qur'an discourse associated with Maurice Bucaille. In another work, *Miracles of the Qur'an* (Yahya 2001j), Yahya engages in a Bucaillist science-in-the-Qur'an discourse. Citing from the Qur'an, Yahya claims that scientific discoveries that were only discovered in modern times such as the Big Bang, the orbits of the earth and moon, and the formation of rain and identity in fingerprints, are all featured in the Qur'an. This book and 64 similar types of books such as the above-mentioned *Miracle in the Atom* (Yahya 2001i) are listed on Yahya's main website under the category "Signs Leading to Faith".[38]

Arguing against evolution then, is one of several methods Yahya employs to convince his audience of the existence of God, the factuality of creation and the truth of the Qur'an. Antievolutionism nevertheless remains at the core of the Harun Yahya enterprise. Regardless of the topic, most of the works published by

---

[37] Al-Hayy is one of the 99 names that according to some Muslim traditions denote the attributes of God. See for instance Gardet (2013).
[38] See book section at harunyahya.com. Another Yahya website, <www.miraclesofthequran.com> (image appendix, p. 9), features an article about the miracle of the number 19 in the Qur'an, which appears to be inspired by the works of Rashad Khalifa as mentioned in the introduction chapter. Available at <http://www.miraclesofthequran.com/mathematical_03.html> [Accessed 19.03.2013].

Yahya from the early 2000s and onwards therefore contain a special preface or afterword on "the evolution deception".[39]

The next section deals with how Yahya accounts for the hegemony of Darwin's theory of evolution, and how he places the struggle against Darwin's theory of evolution into a broader Islamic cosmological framework.

### 3.4.4. Conspiratorial and cosmological framework

According to Harun Yahya, the claims of those supporting the theory of evolution are absurd in the face of scientific evidence. The central thesis of *The Evolution Deceit* is that it is not science that keeps the theory of evolution alive, but the dogma of materialist philosophy (Yahya 2002g, p. 180). After presenting his "scientific evidence" against the theory of evolution, Yahya insists that logic and reason inevitably leads one to conclude that the theory of evolution is false:

> It needs to be made clear that anyone free of prejudice and the influence of any particular ideology, who uses only his reason and logic, will clearly understand that belief in the theory of evolution, which brings to mind the superstitions of societies with no knowledge of science or civilization, is quite impossible (Yahya 2002g, p. 162).

If the theory of evolution is so blatantly and obviously wrong, as Yahya claims, how come it is so widely accepted? In *The Evolution Deceit*, Yahya accounts for the continued prevalence and influence of the theory of evolution in three different but interrelated ways, and it is within these explanations that the specificities of his creationist position become apparent. Firstly, Yahya claims that those scientists who believe in evolution are blinded by the philosophy of materialism, and that "Darwinism is a false religion" (Yahya 2002g, p. 186):

> [The evolutionist scientist's] attitude can be explained with a single word: "faith". Yet it is a blind superstitious faith, since there can be no other explanation for one's disregard of all the facts or for a lifelong devotion to the preposterous scenario that he has constructed in his imagination (Yahya 2002g, p. 35).

Yahya here appropriates a common popular discourse on science and religion which portrays creationists as dogmatic and evolutionists as rational, and inverts it through a form of semantic reversal. Belief in evolution is described as "irrational", "dogmatic", "blind faith" and "indoctrination", and juxtaposed with acceptance of creation, which is described as based in reason, logic and science. These ideas are developed further in other works, such as *The Religion of Darwinism* (Yahya 2003o). Here Yahya claims that Darwinism is an ancient pagan doctrine originating in Greek and Sumerian religion: "Darwinist beliefs

---

[39] See for instance Communist China's Repression of East Turkestan (Yahya 2010b).

were first encountered a few thousand years ago in the polytheistic and materialistic religions of Greece and Sumeria" (Yahya 2003o, p. 24).

Secondly, Yahya argues that "Darwinism is a deceit" that is "belied by science at every step but is upheld to veil the fact of creation" (Yahya 2002g, p. 40). According to Yahya, some of those who defend the theory of evolution are not just irrational and prejudiced, but also dishonest and willfully deceitful. Yahya does not expand upon this in *The Evolution Deceit*, but in a later publication, *The Dark Clan* (Yahya 2003b), he develops conspiratorial ideas regarding this alleged deceit. He claims that there is a "dark clan" operating in the world who orchestrates moral degeneration, and that this dark clan is also working to safeguard the theory of evolution because it serves their aims of spreading immorality:

> The comprehensive brainwashing and indoctrination campaign fought on behalf of the theory of evolution is presided over by the clan and its ideological partner: Darwinism. The theorists of the dark clan are well aware that the irreligious and selfish world they have created is "scientifically" based on Darwinism and for this reason, they use any means of propaganda to keep this defective theory alive (Yahya 2003b, p. 49).

Finally, Darwinists, together with all materialists in history, are placed into an Islamic framework as the "unbelievers" referred to in the Qur'an:

> The psychology of the unbeliever has existed throughout history. In the Qur'an it is described thus: "Even if We did send unto them angels, and the dead did speak unto them, and We gathered together all things before their very eyes, they are not the ones to believe, unless it is in God's plan. But most of them ignore (the truth)" (Sura 6:111) (Yahya 2002g, p. 37).

Yahya assures that unbeknownst to themselves, Darwinists and evolutionists are actually a part of God's plan. According to Yahya, they fulfill a divine purpose by providing a way in which to separate "the traditionalist and bigoted thought" that poses in the name of Islam, with the rational and science-compatible "real religion" or as revealed in the Qur'an (Yahya 2002g, p. 186):

> In accordance with [the Darwinists'] fate, they become the means whereby the decree of God about His upholding His true religion by causing the antagonists of religion counteract against each other is made true. God's law is stated in the Qur'an as follows; "And did not God check one set of people by means of another, the earth would indeed be full of mischief" (Sura 2:251) (Yahya 2002g, p. 187).

Within the conflict between evolutionists and creationists lies an opportunity created by God, according to Yahya. It is precisely this opportunity that Harun

Yahya has seized, namely to utilize the theory of evolution and its defenders as a means to promote what he regards as "the true religion", namely Islam. Yahya thus places the intellectual struggle he wages against the theory of evolution and materialism into an Islamic cosmological framework. In Chapter 5 of this dissertation, we shall see how Yahya develops this cosmological framework by drawing from Islamic apocalyptic traditions.

### 3.4.5. The narrative and visual rhetoric of scientificity

*The Evolution Deceit* is designed to persuade it readers of the existence of God and the truth of creation through appealing to the authority of reason and science. Although the existence of God at times is postulated rather than argued, most of the time Harun Yahya arrives at "the truth of Qur'an" in *The Evolution Deceit* by way of argumentation. Stefano Bigliardi (forthcoming 2013) terms this approach used by Yahya "argumentative theology". Another characteristic strategy of persuasion employed by Yahya is *scientification* (Riexinger 2011; Bigliardi forthcoming 2013). Both visually and in terms of narrative structure, *The Evolution Deceit* resembles a popularized work on science. It follows a logical structure, footnotes are provided (if incomplete), and Yahya's claims are followed with examples and scientific "facts" and "data" that appear to provide "proof" for his arguments. Yahya frequently uses a common creationist argumentative strategy known as *quote mining*. This involves taking words or passages from their original context in a way that distorts the source's intended meaning. For instance, Yahya cites evolutionary biologists and places their citations in a context that gives the impression that these biologists are conceding that the theory of evolution as such is in major trouble.[40]

Scientific "facts" are also represented visually.[41] Illustrations in the form of animals and stock photos of scientists doing science (Yahya 2002g, p. 31) do not only make the book more appealing to read, but also contribute to the general impression of "professional" merit and quality. These various factors contribute to giving the works of Yahya an air of trustworthiness. It is presented as science, it looks like science, and for many who are not very familiar with evolutionary biology or other fields referred to in the book, it probably also reads like science. Rather than using scientific methods, Yahya employs the symbols and language of science as rhetorical devices to persuade his readers of the falsity of the theory of evolution and the truth of creation.

---

[40] For example, Yahya includes a quote by former paleontologist at the British museum Colin Patterson which gives the impression that Patterson claims that there is no evidence for evolution (Yahya 2002g, p. 50). Patterson has been quote mined by other creationists as well, and rejects creationist interpretations of his statements. See for instance Theunissen (1997).

[41] This strategy of visual representation is used in particular in *The Atlas of Creation* (Yahya 2007a), which consists mostly of photos of fossils and living animals.

### 3.4.6. The creationist campaign of Harun Yahya

The above examination focuses on the content of Yahya's creationism as published texts. These texts form the core of what Harun Yahya terms "the intellectual struggle against Darwinism". In order to understand what sets Yahya's Islamic creationism apart from other forms of Islamic creationism in Turkey, it is necessary to also briefly look at how Yahya went about spreading and marketing this material, and to examine the development of Yahya's large-scale creationist campaign. Harun Yahya was influenced by the teachings of Said Nursi and the Nurcu antievolutionist writings of the 1970s and 1980s. Nurcu antievolutionist material published in *cemaat* magazines and presented in sermons attended by the Nurcu followers rarely reached beyond these Nurcu communities. Inspired by the "creationist ministries" in America, however, Yahya professionalized the campaign against evolution and brought Nurcu-style creationism to a wider audience first in Turkey and later globally.

In 1986, Adnan Oktar and his associates published a book on evolution titled *Canlılar ve Evrim* (Living Things in Evolution) in the name of Bilim Araştırma Grubu (The Science Research Group) (1986). It was not until a decade later, however, that the Harun Yahya enterprise decided to launch a massive campaign against evolution.[42] Harun Yahya aspired to present a comprehensive and definite refutation of the theory of evolution, with whatever means available. Members of the group around Oktar who had qualifications such as foreign language skills were given the task of finding material and arguments to use in the effort to debunk evolution. Some were sent to the US to meet with the Institute for Creation Research (ICR). This work resulted in the first Turkish edition of *The Evolution Deceit* in 1997 (*Evrim Aldatmacası*). In 1998, Bilim Araştırma Vakfı (BAV) held a series of international conferences on creationism in Istanbul and Ankara, which were attended by major figures in American creationism such as Duane Gish and Henry Morris. The last chapter of *The Evolution Deceit* is devoted to these conferences, and includes photographs of the most prominent international guests as well as excerpts from their speeches. The Harun Yahya enterprise organized hundreds of such conference all over Turkey between 1998 and 2002.

In March 2006, the Harun Yahya enterprise opened a creation museum – allegedly the first of its kind in the world – in a shopping center in Beylikdüzü Istanbul ("Milyonlarca Yıllık Fosiller Yaratılış Müzesinde" 2006). Another museum was opened later the same month in a shopping center in Üsküdar, Istanbul. These free-entrance museums featured exhibitions using the type of visual argumentation employed in the *Atlas of Creation*: Million-year-old fossils are displayed together with photos of modern-day animals which, it is claimed,

---

[42] According to "Mehmet", a former member of the Harun Yahya enterprise, this decision was taken some time in the mid-90s (personal interview, 04.02.2012).

are these fossils' current equivalent, and thus that no evolution has taken place. The opening of the museum was widely publicized, and BAV also invited school classes to visit the museum. When a group of 80 primary school students from a public school nearby visited the museum, it was described as "a scandal" in secular/Kemalist-oriented newspapers such as *Radikal* and *Cumhuriyet* (Salman & Saymaz 2006). These museums were eventually discontinued as permanent features, but the Harun Yahya enterprise continues to display fossil exhibitions at street stands and in shopping centers both in Turkey and abroad.

The publication of the first English edition of *The Evolution Deceit* in 1999 marks the start of the global expansion of Yahya's campaign. The book has been translated to at least 18 languages to date (2013). Already with the second revised edition of *The Evolution Deceit* in 2001, Yahya's Islamic creationism began attracting attention from science educators outside of Turkey (See Koenig 2001). It was with the mass distribution of the *Atlas of Creation* in 2007, however, that Yahya's Islamic creationism began eliciting considerable international attention. Aside from *The Evolution Deceit* and the *Atlas of Creation,* Yahya has also published a great number of other works on the same theme. Currently 78 works are listed on Yahya's website in the category "The collapse of the theory of evolution". As indicated by this title, the theory of evolution is increasingly presented as an already discredited theory. Yahya's continued struggle is focused on reiterating and fortifying the arguments against evolution, and also to show how successful Yahya's campaign has been. This dissertation is not a reception study, and a detailed account of the influence of Yahya's creationist campaign both in Turkey and on a global scale therefore lies beyond its scope. It is relevant to note, however, that Harun Yahya with time incorporates the perceived success of his campaign into his discourse. In works such as *The Global Impact of the Works of Harun Yahya* (2002i), Yahya aims to show how the impact of his works in terms of convincing people of the falsity of the theory of evolution. I will return to this aspect in Chapter 5.

Apart from this increasing emphasis on the success of the creationist campaign in terms of disproving the theory of evolution, Yahya's books on evolution are very similar. New editions sometimes include recent and topical material. In *A Definitive Reply to Evolutionist Propaganda* (2003d) for instance, Yahya reiterates the claim that evolution is false by addressing claims made in science and nature television documentaries aired on the BBC, National Geographic, Discovery Channel and History Channel, and published in scientific journals such *The New Scientist* and *Scientific American.* In general, however, these works just rehash the arguments put forward in *The Evolution Deceit.* Islamic creationism then, is a field in Yahya's production where there has been little change in the discourse over time.

## 4. Why antievolutionism?

The reasons why antievolutionism became such a central theme in the discourse of the Harun Yahya enterprise must be sought both within the Turkish and global context. From the start, the theory of evolution had become tainted by its association with Western materialism. At the same time, Islamic modernism in Turkey found its most influential expression through Said Nursi and the Nur movement. The Nurcu tendency towards the scientification of theology must in turn be understood on the background of the hegemony of Turkish secular positivist modernism and its emphasis on science.

As in the American context, the theory of evolution became an increasingly politicized issue in Turkey. The ideological polarization in Turkey that I described in Chapter 2, which carries similarities with the so-called "culture wars" in America, became more pronounced in Turkey during the 1990s. However, in contradistinction to the American context, creationism was partly co-opted by the state. Creationism was already taught in schools in Turkey from the 80s onwards, and the pro-evolution scientific community was small and marginalized and had little resources to oppose it. The statement made by previous minister of education Hüseyin Çelik defending the continued teaching of creationism in school is telling in terms of the government's attitude: "There are many theories concerning creation. It's in the name; the theory of evolution" (Kotan 2006).[43] Thus, the conservative turn in Turkish politics provided a political opportunity space for creationist activism. Harun Yahya had the human and financial recourses to seize this opportunity and market creationist ideas on a large scale, eventually also outside of Turkey.

In one sense, it would seem that the battle against evolution had already largely been won in Turkey, and that Yahya was "preaching to the converted". There was poor knowledge of and widespread skepticism towards the theory of evolution in the Turkish population as a whole.[44] Those few who openly embraced the theory of evolution and criticized creationism were often associated with the secularist leftist political segment. Yahya incorporated this into his polemics by labeling critics as "communists" or "Maoists" (Sayın & Kence 1999), thus perpetuating the idea that the creation–evolution debate is not about science, but about ideology. Also beyond the assertively Islamic segment, the theory of evolution suffered from an "image problem" as a radically antireligious or communist theory.

---

[43] "Yaratılışla ilgili birçok teori var. Adı üstünde, evrim teorisi". Scientists argue that the "it's only a theory"–argument reflects a misunderstanding or misconstruction of what theory means in scientific terms (Moran 1993).

[44] According to a global survey on the public acceptance of evolution conducted in 2005, more than half of the adults from Turkey surveyed believed that the theory of evolution is false (Miller et al. 2006).

These conditions made antievolutionist polemics a comparatively easy product to market in Turkey, and an opportune strategy for the preaching of Islam also beyond Islamic circles. Yahya targeted an audience that had been socialized through the Turkish secular education system and who had been taught science as an ideal and a measurement of truth. Moreover, the low public acceptance of the theory of evolution meant that Yahya's arguments appeared convincing to many. Creationist activism thus represented a relatively untapped market for gaining credibility. Creationism can therefore be understood as a strategy for Yahya to gain authority as much as an actual effort to convince.

Aside from theological reasons, the widespread skepticism to the theory and the relative absence of a vocal pro-evolution opposition may also explain why Yahya did not shift to ID and the "teach the controversy"-strategy like the creationist movement in the US did: The lack of a vocal opposition provided little incentive to wrap the message in a more sophisticated "creationism 2.0".

Around the turn of the millennium, the Harun Yahya enterprise began to avail of an opportunity space for Islamic creationism in the global context. Yahya's lavish and well-produced antievolutionist works in particular found an audience among diaspora Muslims, who welcomed these works from a Muslim scholar who appeared to offered scientific arguments against evolution against a Western materialist elite (Arda 2009).

## 5. Concluding remarks

Harun Yahya's Islamic creationism must be grasped both within the context of American Protestant creationism and antievolutionism in Turkey. An important development in American Protestant opposition to the theory of evolution was the emergence of scientific creationism, which boosted creationism in America and gave rise to the so-called creation–evolution struggle. This trend also has its counterpart in the Turkish context. The theory of evolution was closely associated with materialist ideas in Turkey from the outset. Especially from the 1970s onwards, opponents of the theory of evolution in Turkey began to counter the theory of evolution using scientific arguments familiar from American creationist literature (Riexinger 2011). This rising opposition against the theory of evolution coincided with Islamic discourses becoming more vocal in Turkey.

In the American context, the scientification of theology in the form of scientific creationism emerged as a response to the re-introduction of the teaching of evolution in schools in the 1960s. In Turkey, evolution was introduced into the school curriculum already in the late 1920s, but it was not until the 1970s and especially after the military coup in 1980 that Turkish detractors of the theory of evolution became vocal and adopted the scientific discourse of Protestant creationism.

It was especially within the modernist Nur movement that Islamic creationism emerged in Turkey. Against the influence of materialist philosophy and positivism, Said Nursi emphasized correspondence between modern science and "the truths of faith". It is therefore not surprising that it was within Nurcu circles that a trend towards the scientification of theology became influential (Riexinger 2011). Harun Yahya was not the first Muslim voice to employ scientific arguments against the theory of evolution in Turkey. Many of the arguments and strategies used by him can also be found in other antievolutionist literature in Turkey.

It was with Harun Yahya, however, that Turkish Islamic creationism developed into a major phenomenon. Drawing on both Turkish and protestant creationist material, Yahya developed his own brand of Islamic creationism. One the one hand, Yahya appropriates a particular modernist Islamic discourse that centers on the harmonization of faith and science and which has been influential in Turkey through the teachings of Said Nursi. According to this discourse, there is no disagreement between Islam and science. While some Islamic thinkers invoke postmodern critiques of the epistemic hegemony of science and call for an Islamization of knowledge (Stenberg 1996), Yahya does not question the epistemological foundations of modern science. His understanding of science as it transpires in *The Evolution Deceit,* is a straightforward Newtonian notion of science, as a set of facts about the world. Thus Yahya does not question the authority of science in itself, but the way in which materialists, in his view, have "hijacked" science.

One the other hand, Harun Yahya rejects one of the most well-documented and most strongly supported theories of modern science, namely the theory of evolution. Sharing Said Nursi's idea that materialism poses the greatest danger to faith in our time, Yahya targets the theory of evolution as the root of contemporary materialism, and therefore regards fighting it as a primary intellectual task. As the above examination of *The Evolution Deceit* shows, Yahya employs a variety of methods and strategies in order to convince his readers that the theory of evolution is invalid. He equates the theory of evolution with "the ideology of Darwinism" and "the philosophy of materialism", which he in turn blames for a host of past and current evils in the world. He therefore rejects all attempts to reconcile Islam and theory of evolution. Moral arguments against the theory of evolution are common creationist arguments, but in the special preface added to editions of *The Evolution Deceit* published after the 9/11 terror attacks, Yahya also links Darwinism directly to terrorism, thus using anti-evolutionism as a way of criticizing post-9/11 Islam-critical discourse.

The bulk of *The Evolution Deceit* is devoted to trying to show that scientific evidence disproves evolution. It is designed to persuade, through the use of a science-like language. There is no room for doubt: Harun Yahya's case against

Darwinism and materialism is put forward with absolute certitude and conviction. Although many of the arguments are familiar from other creationist works, Yahya's Islamic creationism also contains some idiosyncratic elements. One of the most characteristic features of Yahya's creationism is the emphasis on "the secret of matter". Yahya does not stop at merely trying to disprove the theory of evolution by reference to modern science, but also philosophical materialism. He also attempts to refute "philosophical materialism" by reference to science.

Through these methods, Yahya strives to show that reason and scientific evidence not only speaks against evolution, but also in favor of creation and the existence of God. The attempt to prove that creation is supported by scientific evidence is a common creationist strategy. Harun Yahya thus partakes in a global creationist discourse with shared aims and strategies. However, aside from the effort to prove the existence of God, creationist discourse may also be utilized to promote a specific religious tradition, as well as a specific interpretation of a religious tradition. Yahya places standard creationist argumentation into an Islamic discursive framework. Throughout the text, Yahya cites verses from the Qur'an to underscore his points and to show that there is correspondence between modern science and the Qur'an. Yahya explains the hegemony of evolution as the product of indoctrination and blind, irrational faith in "the myth of materialism", a "false religion" which he juxtaposes with "the true religion" as revealed in the Qur'an. Ultimately, Darwinists are cast as "the unbelievers" referred to in the Qur'an. Yahya thus "Islamicizes" creationist discourse by placing the struggle against Darwinism into an Islamic theological framework. As we shall see in the next chapter, this cosmological framework gives Yahya's creationist campaign a special significance within his entire enterprise, as the struggle is also placed within an eschatological and political framework.

The prominence of antievolutionism in the works of Harun Yahya may be understood on the background of the Turkish context in which Harun Yahya emerged, and in particular the influence of the ideas of Said Nursi. However, the fact that the Harun Yahya enterprise launched a creationist campaign in the 1990s in Turkey and later in the global context, can also be understood as Harun Yahya availing of opportunity spaces and utilizing antievolutionist polemics as both a way in which to preach Islam for a wider audience, and as a strategy for Harun Yahya to establish authority and credibility in both in Turkey and globally. While earlier creationist writings in Turkey were mainly "preaching to the choir", addressing a traditional and conservative segment, Harun Yahya aimed for a broader readership with well-produced, lavishly illustrated and attractive books distributed cheaply or free of charge. Yahya thus became the new, modern and well-funded media-savvy face of creationism in Turkey, and

Turkey became the center of a confrontational Islamic creationism that was to become influential throughout the Muslim world.

CHAPTER 5

# The Mahdi, the End Times and the Turkish-Islamic union

## 1. Introduction

In the two previous chapters, I have examined how the Harun Yahya enterprise has marketed itself in the Turkish and global context through the employment of conspiracy theory rhetoric, nationalist discourses and anti-Darwinism. The purpose of this chapter is to examine Harun Yahya's use of eschatological themes. The chapter describes *what* Yahya teaches regarding the Mahdi and the End Times, *how* he argues and what sources and strategies he employs to support his interpretations. The chapter also analyzes *why* the messianic figure of the Mahdi and the notion of an imminent End Times occupy such a pivotal position in the discourse of the Harun Yahya enterprise.

In the first part of this chapter, I outline a context for Yahya's apocalyptic and messianic ideas. As this chapter will show, Yahya's apocalyptic teachings regarding the Mahdi and the End Times are based on his interpretations of three main sources: Allegorical verses in the Qur'an; hadiths and other Islamic sources; and the teachings of Said Nursi. I will therefore briefly outline the main themes prevalent within Islamic eschatology discourse in general as well as the teachings of Said Nursi pertaining to eschatological ideas. In more recent works, Yahya also utilizes Christian and Jewish scriptures and themes from Christian millennialism to find support for his apocalyptic interpretations. Yahya's apocalypticism and messianism must therefore be understood against the background of a global resurgence of millennialism and apocalyptic themes both in popular culture and in religious discourses, including a general resurgence of apocalyptic themes in contemporary Islam as argued by several scholars (Amanat 2009; Cook 2005). In the second and empirical part of the chapter, Yahya's millennialist works advocating apocalypticism are analyzed and the methods he uses to arrive at his apocalyptic interpretations of eschatology are examined. In the third part of this chapter, the rhetorical function of Yahya's use of apocalyptic and messianic themes and their role in framing the efforts of the Harun Yahya enterprise is probed into.

## 2. Eschatology, apocalypticism, millennialism and messianism

Eschatology, ideas concerning "the last things", such as death, the afterlife and the end of the world, are features of most religious traditions. The Islamic eschatological tradition shares many commonalities with that of Christianity and Judaism. All three traditions feature the notion of a judgment day, the resurrection of the dead and a messianic figure whose arrival marks the ushering in of the end times. Arguably, both Islam and Christianity started out as apocalyptic movements, but over time the aspirations that the world would soon come to an end dwindled, and the apocalypse was largely relegated to a distant future within both mainline Christian denominations as well as "establishment" Islam. Throughout history and around the world, however, apocalyptic movements have emerged from within these traditions that have evoked eschatological beliefs concerning the end times and temporalized them into the present or into a near imminent future.

*Apocalypticism*, derived from the Greek *apokalypsis*, meaning revelation or unveiling, can be defined as a discourse that reveals or makes manifest a vision of ultimate destiny (O'Leary 1994). More specifically, it is a type of religious discourse that argues for the imminence of the Last Days and the Final Judgment, either in prophetical or exegetical terms. In the following, I will thus use the term apocalypticism to describe the discursive act of temporalizing eschatological beliefs into a near imminent future, including making calculations and interpreting current events in the light of the purported signs foretold in the scriptures.

Apocalypticists attempt to predict when the end times will occur on the basis of certain signs described in the eschatological traditions. These prophecies are applied to a contemporary setting, thus creating a sense of urgency. In addition to this temporalizing aspect, apocalypticism also often entails *millennialism*, which *The Encyclopedia of Millennialism and Millennial Movements* defines as "the idea that the world can, and will, be transformed or improved or saved" (Landes 2000, p. xi). Although the term millennialism derives from the Christian notion of a thousand year kingdom on earth, in a wider sense the term applies to the vision or promise that the imperfect and degenerated present will be succeeded by a new and better world; a Golden Age (in this wider sense, the term *millenarianism* is often used).

Lastly, many millenarian movements are also *messianic* movements. The word "messiah" is derived from a Hebrew word meaning "the anointed one". Originating in ancient Israeli traditions about a Davidic king who will deliver Israel from its enemies, *messianism* is associated with Judaic and Christian religious traditions. In more general terms, however, messianism denotes "a person chosen by God to play a crucial role in an end time scenario. The messiah heralds the advent of an utopian epoch – the 'messianic age'" (Landes 2000, p.

245). Although we do not find in Islam the notion of the Messiah as a deliverer in the sense that we do in Judaism and Christianity, and although Messiah (al-Masih) and Mahdi is generally believed to be two different characters in Islamic tradition, there are also Islamic traditions that conceive of the Mahdi as someone who will set things right and usher in a Golden Age and the final judgment. Mahdism and Mahdist movements may therefore be characterized as messianic. Mahdism entails not merely speculations or prophecies about how and when the eschatological drama will begin, but also often entails launching a figure as the Mahdi who will take the centre stage in this drama. As we shall see, Yahya's eschatology contains both millennialist, messianic, apocalyptic and Mahdist elements, and I will therefore use the terms interchangeably to describe various aspects of Yahya's teachings.

## 2.1. Islamic eschatology

The apocalyptic tradition in Islam is not unified or codified, but consists of a number of verses from the Qur'an as well as the Sunna. The belief in *al-Qiyamah* (The Resurrection or The Last Judgment) when all humans – living and dead – will be held accountable for their deeds, is an essential part of Islamic doctrine. However, there is little consensus regarding the nature and sequence of events that will occur prior to *al-Qiyamah*. A number of characters and events, trials and tribulations described in the Qur'an and the hadiths are interpreted as related to the end times, and elaborated and commented upon by Islamic traditionists. Some of these events are interpreted as foreshadowing the Day of Judgment, and classified in tradition as Lesser and Greater signs of the Hour (Cook 2005, p. 8). The return of Jesus is considered one of these major signs, based on a common interpretation of certain verses of the Qur'an.[1]

The key character in the Muslim eschatological drama is not Jesus, however, but the Mahdi (Madelung 2010). No reference is made to the Mahdi, "the rightly guided one", in the Qur'an, but he figures prominently in the hadith literature and in speculations of Islamic scholars regarding the end of times. Many early Islamic traditionists doubted or rejected the notion of the Mahdi, which may account for the absence of any traditions about him in the most revered canonical collections of hadiths: al-Bhukari and Muslim (Madelung 2010). However, other canonical Sunni *hadith* collections contain numerous Mahdi traditions, which have formed the basis for a popular belief in the Mahdi.[2] In the Shi'a traditions, where the Mahdi tradition plays a more central role than in Sunni Islam, the Mahdi has come to be identified with the "hidden imam", who

---

[1] Qur'an 43:61: "And indeed, Jesus will be [a sign for] knowledge of the Hour, so be not in doubt of it, and follow Me. This is a straight path" (Trans. Sahih International).
[2] Notably Abu Dawud, Tirmidhi, Ibn Madja, al-Nasa'i, and the Musnad of Ibn Hanbal (Madelung 2010).

is expected to return when Muslims are in great need. Belief in the Mahdi never became an essential part of Sunni doctrine, however, and is a topic that has often been avoided by prominent Sunni *ulama* (Madelung 2010; Cook 2005).

The earliest traditions of the Mahdi portray him as a great leader who will bring justice to the Muslim community and lead it in victory. With time the Mahdi's eschatological role and his association with the return of Jesus became more pronounced, and the beliefs that the Mahdi will appear before the return of Jesus, that the Mahdi will assist Jesus in the slaying of the *Dajjal* (the False Messiah or the Antichrist) and that Jesus will eventually pray behind the Mahdi, became more widespread. Treatises dealing specifically with the Mahdi were produced by later traditionists, which often attempted to harmonize earlier diverging traditions (Madelung 2010). The Mahdi is often predicted in these traditions as someone who will restore justice and reinstate the true worship of God. In Sunni traditions the Mahdi figure is also closely associated with the notion of a *mujaddid*, a renewer who according to certain hadiths will come every century to renew the Muslim community (Landes 2000, p. 188).[3]

Islamic messianic expectations regarding the Mahdi are often linked with the notion of an ultimate battle between the Forces of Good, represented by the Mahdi and Jesus, and The Forces of Evil, represented by the Dabbat al-Ardh (the Beast of the Earth), the Dajjal (The False Messiah), the Sufyan and Gog and Magog.[4] According to Shi'a traditions, the Mahdi will revenge the blood of Hussain and initiate an apocalyptic battle of cosmic proportion that precedes the Day of Resurrection and the End of Time (Amanat, p. viii). In both Shi'a and Sunni Islam, Mahdi traditions have inspired a number of revolutionary Mahdist movements throughout Islamic history, which have tapped into the messianic tradition in Islam and proclaimed the arrival of the awaited Mahdi. In recent history, one of the most well known examples of Sunni Mahdism is the proclaimed Sudanese Mahdi of the 19th century, Muhammad Ahmad (1845–1885).[5] In Turkey, a Nakşibendi dervish named Mehmet also proclaimed himself Mahdi in 1930, and

---

[3] Due to the widespread belief that a *mujaddid* will come every hundred years, Landes suggests that the term *centennialism* might be more appropriate to the Islamic context than *millennialism* (Landes 2000, p. 187).

[4] Dabbat al-Ardh, "the Beast of the Earth" is associated with the Last Days and mentioned in the Qur'an 27:85. The Dajjal is "the Deceiver" who according to Muslim apocalyptic traditions is one of the signs of the End Times (Abel 2013). Al-Sufyan is "a descendant of the Umayyad Abu Sufyan figuring in apocalyptic prophecies as the rival and opponent of the Mahdi and ultimately overcome by him" (Madelung 2013). Gog and Magog (Ar: Yajuj wa-Majuj) are apocalyptic characters in both Biblical and Qur'anic eschatology. Qur'an 18:93-98 refers to Dhu'l-Karnayn ("a great and righteous ruler") erecting a barrier against them (van Donzel & Ott 2013).

[5] Muhammad Ahmad was a Sufi Muslim religious reformer, revivalist, and militant who proclaimed himself as the Mahdi. His messianic resistance movement mobilized Northern Sudanese Muslims to fight against the Ottoman Egyptians (Pandya 2012).

instigated a rebellion against the Kemalist government in what has been known as "the Menemen incident" (Kadıoğlu 1996; Bozarslan 2000).

## 2.2. Contemporary Islamic apocalypticism

There has been a global resurgence of apocalyptic themes both in religious discourses and popular culture in the latter half of the 20th century (O'Leary 1994, p. 7). Especially in the run-up to the millennium, apocalyptic themes surfaced in popular culture and culminated in the fears of the millennium bug. Several authors have also pointed to a renewed interest in Mahdism and apocalypticism in the Islamic world in recent times (Amanat 2009; Cook 2005; Landes 2000). Attempts to temporalize or contemporize apocalyptic prophecies have generally remained marginal within "establishment" Islam (Amanat 2009 p. 21).[6] Sunni *ulama* have generally tended to be critical of apocalyptic interpretations of Islamic tradition. An oft-quoted Qur'an verse states "Allah [alone] has knowledge of the Hour" (Qur'an 31:34). Hence, Sunni *ulama* have tended to merely reproduce and comment on the classical texts on the End Times without relating the material to events taking place within the contemporaneous setting of their readers (Cook 2005, p. 15). However, observes David Cook, a new generation of popular Muslim apocalyptic authors in the 20th century began relating the tradition to current events much in the same manner as evangelical Christians (Cook 2005, p. 15). This new generation attempts to update the meaning of the hadiths as referring to the present rather than the time of classical Islam as more conservative scholars would be inclined to do. Drawing upon themes from Christian apocalypticism and conspiracy theories regarding Jews, they re-interpret tradition in light of current events and politics (Haddad & Smith 2010).

Focusing specifically on contemporary Shi'ite apocalypticism, Abbas Amanat sees apocalyptic and millennial currents as alternative interpretations to the readings of "orthodox" traditions, contrasting the prevailing legalistic theological norms of the time (Amanat 2009, p. 24). There is a messianic revival in Iran today, Amanat argues, with much speculation regarding the advent of the Mahdi (Amanat 2009, p. x). This revival is exploited by the regime for political purposes. Ahmadinejad often frames political messages in an apocalyptic language, interpreting current events as heralding the advent of the Mahdi.[7]

---

[6] David Cook writes that apocalyptic literature is often viewed as an "embarrassment" and claims that "the faculty of al-Ahzar University – the most respected Muslim institution of higher learning in the Sunni world – generally publish books rebutting popular apocalyptic writers, even when those writers received their education at al-Ahzar" (Cook 2005, p. 2).
[7] In response to the death of Venezuelan leader Hugo Chávez, Ahmadinejad declared that Chávez will return to earth on resurrection day along with Jesus and Imam Mahdi (Siddique 2013).

Many theories of apocalypticism seek to address the appeal of apocalypticism and apocalyptic movements to its adherents. For my purposes, however, I am not primarily interested in the appeal of these ideas, but their rhetorical function within the religious enterprise of Harun Yahya. In his influential work on apocalypticism, Stephen O'Leary focuses on contemporary apocalypticism as a particular form of rhetorical discourse (O'Leary 1994). Apocalyptic predictions are often associated with prophetic visions that take place outside the realm of rationality. However, as noted by O'Leary,

> Examining the discourse of most modern apocalyptic evangelists, one finds that their claims are founded not on the charismatic authority of the prophet granted a divine vision, but on the (ostensibly) rational authority of one who interprets canonical scripture (O'Leary 1994, p. 13).

As we shall see, Harun Yahya does not claim prophetic power. The apocalyptic literature of Harun Yahya is an exercise in exegesis, an attempt to persuade the audience that The Last Days are near by interpreting current events in the light of tradition. As mentioned, Yahya claims to find support for his apocalyptic interpretations both in the Qur'an, the hadiths and other Islamic sources. The main source of Yahya's ideas regarding the advent of the Mahdi and the End Times, however, are the works of Said Nursi, which will be presented next.

## 2.3. Said Nursi's ideas about a coming Golden Age for the Mahdi

Particularly in the "New Said" period, Said Nursi withdrew from worldly matters and had his eyes on a brighter future. In letters to his followers, Nursi laid out the purpose of the *Risale-i Nur* and advised them to concentrate on the task of strengthening faith and to stay away from politics. He perceived the time he lived in as a period of regression and darkness for Islam, but believed that "the spring of Islam" and a Golden Age would come (Vahide 2005, p. 91). He argues in *The Damascus Sermon* that since "the truths of Islam possess a perfect capacity to progress both materially, and in moral and nonmaterial matters", consequently "the future shall be Islam's and Islam's alone, and the truths of the Qur'an and belief shall be sovereign" (Nursi 1996, pp. 26–27). He believed that the West had departed from true Christianity and come under the influence of Greek and Roman philosophy, and that it therefore would be dispersed and give way to Islamic civilization. This was also related to Nursi's eschatological views and his understanding *Risale-i Nur* as a "Renewer of Religion":

> It can be understood from Nursi's letters that during [the time around the Second World War] he was concerned with the end of time, and related the war and dreadful events of this century to those foretold to occur at those last times. He placed the Risale-i Nur and its mission within this perspective (Vahide 2005, p. 239).

Nursi's most comprehensive apocalyptic treatise is found in the "Fifth Ray" of the *Rays* collection in the *Risale-i Nur* collection. Here Nursi argued that apocalyptic hadiths can be likened to allegorical (*müteşabih*) verses of the Qur'an, meaning that their true meaning is hidden and that they thus should not be understood literally but must be interpreted. For instance, a hadith refers to al-Sufyan (which Nursi refers to as the "Islamic Antichrist") as having the mark of *Kafir* (unbeliever) on his forehead. Nursi suggests that this could mean that he wears the headgear of the unbelievers and forces others to do the same (Stowasser 2003). This could be interpreted to refer to Atatürk and his famous Hat Law of 1925, which decreed that the *Fez* should be replaced with Western-style hats. In the trial against Nursi in Afyon in 1948, an expert committee did indeed conclude in favor of the authorities' accusations that the references to the Sufyan and the Dajjal in "The Fifth Ray" were referring to Atatürk, and as such constituted an attack on Atatürk and his reforms (Vahide 2005).

Said Nursi believed that God will send a renewer, a *mujaddid*, every century to renew faith (Saritoprak 2011). Nursi's followers pointed to parallels between Nursi and Mevlana Halid-i Bağdadi (1777–1826), the founder of the Halidi branch of the Nakşibendi order, and regarded Mevlana Halid-i Bağdadi as the renewer of the 12$^{th}$ century AH, and Nursi as the renewer of the 13$^{th}$ century AH.[8] In the context of the notion of a renewer for every age, Nursi also links to the idea of the coming of the Mahdi and the End Times. In *Emirdağ Lahikası* (The Emirdağ Letters), written after the Second World War, Nursi outlines three important functions that he claims the Great Mahdi will carry out: Firstly and most importantly, silencing the idea of materialism (the stage of belief); secondly, reviving the Sunna of the prophet (the stage of life); and thirdly, strengthening the Islamic world and bring about Islamic Unity (the stage of sharia) (Nursi 2004a, p. 259). In the following passage from one of Nursi's letters to his students, it transpires that he regards the collective personality of *Risale-i Nur* as the *mujaddid* of the 13$^{th}$ century AH, while indicating that the Great Mujaddid, the Mahdi, will come at the end time and perform all of these three duties:

> It does not appear to be possible for these three duties to be performed all together perfectly by one person or community at this time and for them not to impede one another. They can only be brought together at the end of time by the Mahdi and the collective personality of his community, which represents the luminous community of the Prophet's Family. Endless thanks be to Almighty God that in this century He has

---

[8] Nursi here uses the Islamic calendar, which commemorates the Hijra, the emigration of Muhammed and his followers to the city of Medina in 622. I use the abbreviation AH (After Hijra) and BH (Before Hijra) to refer to the Islamic calendar.

given the duty of renewal and preservation of the truths of belief to the Risale-i Nur and to the collective personality of its students (Nursi 2004b, p. 139).[9]

In another letter, Nursi writes that the Mahdi will come in the next century (Nursi 2004b, pp. 57–58).

## 3. Harun Yahya's apocalyptic works

Against this background I will examine the eschatology of Harun Yahya, taking his earliest work on this topic, *Mehdi ve Altin Cag: İslam'ın Dünya Hakimiyeti* (Mahdi and the Golden Age: The World Supremacy of Islam) (Yahya 1989), as my point of departure.[10] Harun Yahya's preoccupation with apocalyptic themes has been a feature of his publishing enterprise from the earliest days. In 1987, Yahya published a brief pamphlet titled *AIDS Kuranda Bahsi Geçen Dabbet-Ül Arz mı?* (Is AIDS the Beast mentioned in the Qur'an?) (Yahya 1987a). The first book published by Yahya on the subject of the Mahdi and the End Times was *Mehdi ve Altın Çağ: Islam'in Dünya Hakimiyeti* (Yahya 1989). It was published in 1989, nearly a decade before *The Evolution Deceit*, Yahya's first integrated attack on the evolution theory.

The next book published dealing with the end times was *Hz. İsa Gelecek* (Yahya 1999b), published in English as *Jesus Will Return* (Yahya 2001g), thus being one of the first of his books in English to deal with this topic. A host of other books on the subject followed, such as *Ölüm Kıyamet Cehennem* (Yahya 2000d), published in English as *Death, Resurrection, Hell* (Yahya 2002f); *Altınçağ* (Yahya 2001b) published in English as *The Golden Age* (Yahya 2003g); *Ahir Zaman ve Dabbetü'l-Arz* (The Last Days and the Beast) (Yahya 2001a);[11] *Kehf Suresi'nden Ahir Zamana İşaretler* (Yahya 2001h), published in English as *Signs of the End Times in Surat al-Kahf* (Yahya 2003p); *Mesih Müjdesi* (Yahya 2003n), published in English as *The Glad Tidings of the Messiah* (Yahya 2004b); *Kıyamet Alametleri* (Yahya 2002l), published in English as *Signs of the Last Day* (Yahya 2003q); *Hz. İsa (as)'in Geliş Alametleri* (Yahya 2003h),[12] published in English as *The Signs of Jesus' Second Coming* (Yahya 2004c); *Kıyamet Günü* (Yahya 2003m), published in English as *The Day of Judgment* (Yahya 2003c); *The End Times and the Mahdi* (Yahya 2003e) (a reworked version of *Mehdi ve Altın Çağ*); *Mehdi'nin Çıkış Alametleri ve Özellikleri* (Demir 2005),[13] published in English as *Portents*

---

[9] English translation by Şükran Vahide.
[10] See image appendix, p. 2.
[11] This book is no longer available for download at <www.harunyahya.com>.
[12] (as), which appears in many titles of Harun Yahya's books, is short for "'alayhi al-salam" (Ar.), which means "peace be upon him". The expression is used after naming a prophet other than Muhammed or angels.
[13] The author title of the pdf-file of this book available for download at harunyahya.com is Ahmet Demir, which appears to be a pen name used instead of Harun Yahya in this instance

*and Features of the Mahdi's Coming* (Yahya 2007g); *Hz. İsa (a.s.) Ve Hz. Mehdi (a.s.) Bu Yüzyılda Gelecek* (Yahya 2009g), published in English as *The Prophet Jesus (as) and Hazrat Mahdi (as) Will Come This Century* (Yahya 2010g);[14] *Hz Mehdi (as) Hz. İbrahim Neslindendir* (Yahya 2009f), published in English as *Hazrat Mahdi (PBUH) Is a Descendant Of The Prophet Abraham (PBUH)* (Yahya 2010e);[15] *Deccal Nasıl Öldü?* (Yahya 2010c), published in English as *How Did the Dajjal Die?* (Oktar 2011); *İsa Mesih (as), Hz. Mehdi (as) ve İttihad-i Islam* (Yahya 2012e), published in English as *The Prophet Jesus (as), Hazrat Mahdi (as) and the Islamic Union* (Yahya 2012c). Based on these publications, the Harun Yahya enterprise has made a number of documentaries that are available both as DVDs and online video files for download and streaming, as well as a vast number of websites devoted to the Mahdi and the End Times.[16]

## 4. The Mahdi and the Golden Age

Published in Turkish in 1989, *Mehdi ve Altın Çağ: İslam'ın Dünya Hakimiyeti* (Mahdi and the Golden Age: The World Domination of Islam) is the first full-length book of Harun Yahya to deal with Islamic eschatology, and indeed one of his first publications overall (Yahya 1989). As such, it provides an opportunity to survey Yahya's earliest formulations of apocalyptic ideas. It deals with most of the apocalyptic themes that he has expanded upon in later works, and the topics covered in it forms the basis for later books dealing with segments in detail. Although Yahya has updated and altered some of his interpretations in the course of time, his approach to the subject, the sources used, the main ideas and the interpretive strategies employed in it are by and large the same as used in later works on the topic.

The book is divided into four sections, dealing with the Mahdi, Jesus, Dabbat al-Ardh (The Beast) and ad-Dhukan (The Smoke) respectively.[17] Each section is subdivided according to the three sources Yahya employs in his exposition: The Qur'an, hadiths, and the *Risale-i Nur* corpus. Yahya deals with each topic in the light of these sources respectively. The sections dealing with hadiths typically

---

only. The English translation of the book published in 2007, however, is published in the name of Harun Yahya.
[14] The term Hazreti (Ar. *Hadra*), abbreviated as Hz., is an honorific title used to express respect.
[15] PBUH is an abbreviation for "peace be upon him".
[16] See, for instance <www.awaitedmahdi.com>, <www.mahdineversheddsblood.com>, <www.endoftimes.net>, <www.jesuswillreturn.com> [Accessed 15.03.2013]. See image appendix, pp. 6–7.
[17] Yahya uses Turkish spellings and translations of Qur'anic terms: Mehdi, Deccal (Dajjal), Dabbet-ül Arz, and Duman (the Smoke). However, in later works in English, Yahya generally uses Arabic transliteration, often with the English translation in parenthesis. To avoid confusion, I will give the Qur'anic and Islamic terms in Arabic transliteration rather than the Turkish transliteration employed by Yahya.

feature several shorter and longer excerpts from various hadith collections and other Islamic sources, followed by Yahya's interpretation and commentary. At the end of each section Yahya includes Qur'an verses, which he interprets as allegorically related to the subject at hand, under the caption "verse interpretation in the indicated meaning".[18]

Many of the hadiths that refer to the signs or portents of Mahdi's appearance are considered weak hadiths in the traditional Sunni schools of jurisprudence. Applying an idiosyncratic interpretive strategy, Harun Yahya argues that weak hadiths become reliable once the events described in them transpire (1989, p. ii). The references given by Yahya to hadiths and other Islamic sources are often incomplete or obscure. In many cases it is therefore difficult to ascertain whether Yahya's claims regarding the content of various sources are correct. This is also not my objective. From my perspective, and as I will discuss later in this chapter, the references he makes to various sources should be understood as rhetorical devices.

## 4.1. The Mahdi

The first part of the book is devoted to the Madhi. In the preface, Yahya states that rather than hushing up the subject of the Mahdi, it is important to inform Muslims on this topic as it presents a source of great joy for Muslims. When the Mahdi appears and rules the world, Yahya writes, the *umma* will break free from the hardships befalling them and reach prosperity: "In short, a second Golden Age (*asr-ı saadet*) will be experienced" (Yahya, 1989, p. ii). According to the hadiths, claims Yahya, the Mahdi will assume leadership of the Islamic world as a caliph and rule the whole world both politically and religiously. The appearance of the Mahdi will mark the beginning of a new *asr-ı saadet* ("the era of bliss"; the time of the Prophet) where Islam will rule the world. "The age of Islamic dominance under the leadership of Mahdi and Jesus, in other words the Golden Age, is in the hadiths described as an 'era of bliss' which will last for more than half a century", writes Yahya (Yahya 1989, p. 16). Quoting from the six canonical hadith collections, he lists the attributes of the Golden Age, describing it as a time of plenty, security, social justice, welfare, peace and prosperity. He specifically quotes a hadith indicating that a few handfuls of seed will generate 700 handfuls of produce. This quote is then followed by facsimile images from contemporary newspaper articles about modern agricultural technology, in order to show how that is in fact happening now. This, then, is the first example of how Yahya interprets the signs of the last days as corresponding to current events. Based on a number of various hadiths and also the writings of Said Nursi, Yahya concludes that the Mahdi's time of appearance

---

[18] Orig. "*İşari manada Kuran mealleri*".

will be between 1400–1500 AH (1979–2076 CE), and more specifically at the beginning of the 15th century AH.

The next section deals with the signs of the appearance of the Mahdi. Yahya lists 18 signs, quotes various hadiths relevant for each sign, comments upon them, and presents examples from recent and current history that he interprets as the actual fulfillment or possible fulfillment of the signs. Hadiths understood to describe the negative atmosphere in the world before and at the time of Mahdi's appearance are juxtaposed with headlines from Turkish newspapers. Thus, for example, hadiths concerning "the proliferation of temptations (*fitna*)" and "the prohibited being regarded as lawful" are followed by Turkish newspaper headlines about gambling, prostitution, alcohol consumption and divorce being on the rise. Another purported sign, "the open denial of God", is followed by newspaper clippings where well-known Turkish left-wing intellectuals describe themselves as atheists (Yahya 1989, p. 47).[19] In addition to these more general features, he also interprets a number of hadiths as referring to concrete events in recent history such as the Iranian revolution in 1979, the outbreak of the Iran-Iraq war in 1980, the Soviet occupation of Afghanistan in 1979, the Keban Dam ("the halting of the river Euphrates"), the storming of the Kaaba in 1979, Halley's comet in 1986, the burning of a Romanian oil tanker in the Bosporus in 1979 ("a sighting of a flare in the east"), and the Taksim Square massacre on May 1st 1977 ("a major occurrence") (Yahya 1989, pp. 50–83).

Citing a number of hadiths and complementing them with verses from the Qur'an, Yahya subsequently lists what he claims are the attributes of the Mahdi according to the hadiths. These include among others that he will be of good moral character; that he will be much loved; that he will be a fighter; that he will have great preaching powers; that he will be knowledgeable (including knowledge of numerology); that he will encounter trials and tribulations; that he will be spied on; that the Dajjal will attempt to torment him, and that he will be the victim of negative propaganda (Yahya 1989, p. 98). In terms of personal and physical characteristics, Yahya writes that the Mahdi will be a *sayyid* (from the bloodline of the Prophet Muhammed); that he will be beautiful; that he will have the seal of prophet on his shoulder; that he will be of "Arab" complexion ("a mixture of white and red"); that he will resemble "the children of Israel" (majestic and sturdily built); that he will be of medium stature, and that he will between 30–40 years old and have a copious and thick beard (Yahya 1989, pp. 99–102).

The final portion of the section on the Mahdi in the hadiths deals with a number of topics regarding the circumstances of the Mahdi's appearance, including the location in which he will appear. Here, for the first time, Yahya makes a connection between the Mahdi and Turkey. He cites a great number of

---

[19] I translate Allah in the original Turkish text to God. In his English texts, Yahya himself uses both God and Allah.

hadiths regarding the Mahdi's conquering of Kostantiniyye (Constantinople).[20] Yahya argues that the place referred to in these hadiths is in fact modern Istanbul, and that the conquering in question is a spiritual one. Under the caption "The Mahdi Being In The Same City As Sacred Relics", he cites hadiths that allude to the Mahdi appearing with various relics of the Prophet Muhammed, and explains:

> These sacred relics [...] of Rasulullah (saas) are today in the Topkapı Palace in Istanbul. The hadith above also refers to a banner that has never been unfurled. According to the museum's Sacred Relics Department, the Topkapı Palace Museum holds two holy banners belonging to the Prophet (saas). One of these was stitched subsequently and contains parts taken from an old banner. The other is not on public display. This may well be the banner referred to in the hadith, which will be unfurled by Hazrat Mahdi (as) (Yahya 1989, p. 108).

In more recent works, the interpretation of these hadiths is formulated in a less tentative manner: "Since the sacred relics are in Istanbul, it is clear that Hazrat Mahdi (as) will be in Istanbul, too" (Yahya 2010g, p. 116).

Yahya also refers to hadiths indicating that Mahdi's struggle will be bloodless, and that the conquering of Kostantiniyye will occur through the recitation of *takbir*.[21] Yahya interprets this to mean that the conquering will take place through the explaining of "the being and unity of God using a knowledge-based (*ilmi*) method" (Yahya 1989, p. 110). He links this with the Mahdi's struggle against the Sufyan as mentioned in the hadiths, and assures that the Mahdi's killing of the Sufyan should be understood to refer primarily to the destruction of his idea system, "or with a more contemporary expression, [the Mahdi] will destroy [the Sufyan's] philosophy and ideology by disproving it with scientific methods" (Yahya 1989, p. 110). In later texts, Yahya is careful to emphasize that the struggle is an ideological one, and that the Mahdi will never shed blood.[22]

The next point discussed by Yahya appears at first sight to be somewhat off-topic. Under the caption "The Turkish Nation and the Years Between 700–1400 (AH)", Yahya writes that the year 700 and its derivatives are particularly important for Turks, and lists important events in the history of the Turks which he claims took place 1400 and 700 BH, and 350 and 700 years AH. He quotes 15:87, a Qur'an verse where the number 7 is mentioned. In most English and Turkish translations, "the often repeated seven" is interpreted as the seven verses of al-Fatiha: "And We have certainly given you, [O Muhammad], seven of the

---
[20] Constantinople was referred to as Kostantiniyye in Arabic and Ottoman Turkish.
[21] The *phrase "Allahu akbar", often translated as "God is Greater"*.
[22] The Harun Yahya enterprise runs a webpage titled "The Mahdi Never Sheds Blood" <www.mahdineversheelsblood.com>[Accessed 19.03.2013].

often repeated [verses] and the great Qur'an".²³ However, Yahya omits the reference to verses, and interprets this Qur'an verse as referring to the importance of the number seven in general. He claims that

> Great Islamic scholars like Said Nursi and al-Suyuti have explained that [...] the Mahdi will appear in 1400 AD (1979-80), and thus the first steps of world domination of the Mahdi and Islam under his leadership will be taken in these years. That the Mahdi will appear in 1400, that he will form his first army from Turks, and that he will send this army to the Turks and conquer Kostantiniyye (today's Istanbul) spiritually, gives a distinct meaning to the subject we touch upon above (Yahya 1989, p. 112).

Thus, according to Yahya, the Mahdi will conquer Istanbul, and from there lead his struggle against figures appearing in apocalyptic prophecies such as the Dajjal and the Sufyan.

The sections following deal with how the Mahdi will be known after he appears, and who his enemies and supporters will be. Yahya cites a hadith and comments that everyone will recognize the Mahdi when he appears. In more recent publications, however, Yahya emphasizes that "Hazrat Mahdi (as) will initially not be recognized by the great majority of people" (Yahya 2010g, p. 267). Yahya also cites hadiths alluding to a hand appearing out of the sky as a sign of the Mahdi's coming. Yahya argues that this hand should be understood symbolically as representing the power of God. He then suggests that the waves emanating from the sky from TV antennas are a kind of hand that has the power to reach almost every home and thus be seen by everyone. Another hadith cited alludes to a voice from the sky that "will call him by name" (Yahya 1989, p. 114). This, suggests Yahya, may be radio, which spreads the Mahdi's voice all over the world. This was written in 1989, before the age of Internet, when TV and radio still represented the main mass media. Yahya finally concludes, "it is understood from the hadith reports that when the Mahdi appears, he will be broadcast to the whole world through medias like TV and radio, and each nation will hear it in their own language" (Yahya 1989, p. 115).

A major topic in the Shi'ite Mahdi traditions is the occultation of the Mahdi. Yahya argues that the conception of occultation in the Shi'ite tradition is based on a misunderstanding stemming from an error in the transmittance of the hadiths (Yahya 1989, p. 119). Contrary to the Shi'ite notion, claims Yahya, the Mahdi will not be hidden for hundreds of years. Instead, he argues, the disappearance of the Mahdi refers to periods in his life when he will be away from the public eye. The Mahdi will disappear twice from sight, one long disappearance and one short, and the long one will be under difficult conditions and against his own will, claims Yahya.

---

²³ The Qur'an (Sahih International). Available at <www.quran.com> [Accessed 15.03.2013].

Interpreting other hadiths, Yahya writes with regards to the Mahdi's struggle that his enemies are the Sufyan, The Dajjal and "a man with a limp". According to Yahya, the Sufyan will try to impede the growing *da'wa* of the Mahdi. Yahya links a hadith alluding to the Sufyan appearing in Damascus with the then Syrian president Hafez al-Assad and his repressive policies against Muslims. He further quotes hadiths declaring that the *Masih ad-Dajjal* will be Jewish, and comments that "[the Dajjal] will gather many followers through encouraging irreligion and all manners of immorality" (Yahya 1989, p. 123) before being killed by Jesus and the Mahdi. According to Yahya, the man with a limp probably refers to the leader of an atheist group who will vilify the Prophet Muhammed. In the hadiths, continues Yahya, it is notified that many bigots (*yobaz*) and reactionaries (*gerici*) will turn against the Mahdi.[24] According to Yahya's interpretation, these bigots will not be happy with the Mahdi's efforts: "In fact they go as far as to say that 'this man [The Mahdi] is destroying our religion'" (Yahya 1989, p. 124). He then lists twelve characteristics of the *yobaz*, such as ignorance; making religion difficult by emphasizing details that have no support in the sources; being superficial and formalist; being against all forms of innovation and degrading women.

Yahya also cites hadiths concerning Mahdi's "close helpers" (Yahya 1989, p. 136). The term employed in the hadiths is "army", but this term might refer to the Mahdi's students or close assistants, Yahya suggests. Although the size of this army varies in the hadiths cited, Yahya emphasizes the number 313. Citing hadiths, he comments further that these assistants will be superior, that various gossips will be spread about this army, that some individuals will leave Mahdi's community (*cemaat*) but that this will not affect the struggle, and that this community will continue to fight the Dajjal until doomsday (Yahya 1989, pp. 136–143).

## 4.2. The End Times in the Qur'an

The next section of the book deals with the End Times in the Qur'an. Yahya claims that "the world domination of Islam is the most important event after the death of the Prophet and will last until doomsday. The Mahdi is the most important person of this event from its beginning till its end" (Yahya 1989, p. 146). The Mahdi is not mentioned in the Qur'an, but, according to Yahya, there are many allegorical verses in the Qur'an about the Mahdi: "There are several hadiths of the prophet that connects these verses to the Mahdi, and hadiths that points us to relevant verses that we should look to in the Qur'an" (Yahya 1989, p. 146). Yahya focuses in particular on the story of the cave in sura al-Kahf, the

---

[24] Both *yobaz*, used in the sense of "religious fanatic" and often denoting lack of sophistication, and *gerici* (reactionary) are terms commonly used by secularists to criticize Islamists in Turkey.

story of King Talut (Saul) and the stories of Dhul-Qarnayn and Sulayman (Solomon). He argues that there is a close connection between sura al-Kahf and the End Times, and that one can therefore assume that there are many parallels between the *Ashab al-Kahf* (the people of the cave) alluded to in sura al-Kahf and the companions of the Mahdi. Based on Qur'an verses and hadiths, Yahya describes the parallels between the people of the cave and the companions of the Mahdi as follows: They are a small community of young people; their faith is strong; they live in a time that is anti-religion; they work against the system of the Dajjal; they are prudent and discreet; they will meet in a closed space on a hillside overlooking the sea, with a wide space in the middle, a guard at the door and a mosque in the vicinity.

Commenting on a hadith regarding Talut (Saul), Yahya argues that the number nine which is mentioned in the hadith is hardly accidental, and that it may refer to 1979, the year when the Mahdi will appear according to Yahya. Finally he interprets the story of Dhul-Qarnayn as told in the sura al-Kahf in the Qur'an, suggesting that the two mountains mentioned in the Qur'an 18:93 might refer to the contemporary Islamic and Christian world. Due to the uncongenial relations between these two worlds, writes Yahya, they have not joined together to fight irreligion and communism. Thus evil forces, taking advantage of this divide, are trying to take over the world (Yahya 1989, p. 165). As discussed in Chapter 3, the urging to join forces with (some) Christians and Jews against the unbelievers is a reoccurring theme in later writings of Yahya.

### 4.3. The Mahdi in *Risale-i Nur*

The final portion of the section on the Mahdi deals with the Mahdi in Said Nursi's *Risale-i Nur* corpus. Nursi writes that God will send a *mujaddid* at the start of every century. Yahya argues that the *mujaddid* that will come at the start of 1400 AH will be the awaited Mahdi. In a cited portion of the *Risale* collection, one of Nursi's scribes compares the life of Nursi to that of Mevlana Halid-i Bağdadi and identifies four *tawafuq* (harmonies or similarities) between the two (Yahya 1989, p. 171). Yahya argues that we understand from this quotation that Mevlana Halid- i Bağdadi was the *mujaddid* of the 12$^{th}$ century AH and that Said Nursi was the *mujaddid* of the 13$^{th}$ century AH. He also cites from Nursi's *Words*, "Eight Principle":

> Thus, unfair people who do not know this truth say: "Why did the Companions of the Prophet with their vigilant hearts and keen sight, who had been taught all the details of the hereafter, suppose a fact that would occur one thousand four hundred years

later to be close to their century, as though their ideas had fallen a thousand years from the truth?"[25]

Here, according to Yahya, Nursi clearly indicates that the Mahdi will appear in the 14th century AH. He also cites Nursi's *Damascus Sermon* (from 1951), where Nursi speaks of eight obstacles that have "eclipsed the sun of Islam", and which will have been dispatched "in thirty to forty years time".[26] Although Nursi does not refer specifically to the Mahdi in this sermon, Yahya interprets this to mean that the Mahdi will fight his war in 1981–1991, and win against the unbelievers in 2001. Under the caption "Islam will rule the world under the leadership of the Mahdi", Yahya cites excerpts from Nursi's *Rays* and *Letters*, and contends that Nursi clearly refers to the Mahdi as an individual. In a Q&A section on a prominent Nurcu website, however, it is explained that Nursi refers to the Mahdi as a *cemaat* (community), not a person, and that he uses the term close to the meaning of a *mujaddid*.[27] Yahya has recently criticized the Nurcus (the followers of Said Nursi) for what he claims is a failing on their part to acknowledge that Nursi clearly refers to the Mahdi as an individual (Allah Sevgisi 2011). He devotes much effort to argue this point both on websites and in his TV programs (Yaratilistr 2012d).

In the last point of the section, Yahya deals with the tasks of the Mahdi. He cites Nursi's *Emirdağ Lahikası*, where Nursi refers to the *cemaat* of the Mahdi having three great tasks. According to Nursi, the first and most important task of the Mahdi is to silence materialist philosophy. Yahya comments "Nursi here advises that since the Mahdi will be short of time, in his effort to silence the materialists he will benefit from [...] the works put together by his students as a result of comprehensive research" (Yahya 1989, p. 178). The second task of the Mahdi, according to Nursi, is to revive the customs and practices of Islam. The third task, according to Nursi, is to revive and apply the provisions of the Qur'an and "the sharia of the Prophet", with the help of all Muslims and those who come from the bloodline of Muhammed (Nursi 2004a, p. 259). Yahya interprets this further to denote the uniting of the world's Muslims. Nursi also writes that each age has its *mujaddid*, but that only the Great Mahdi of the End Times will complete all of these three tasks and thus earn his title as Mahdi. Citing Nursi's *Kastamonu Lahikası*, Yahya writes that Nursi explains that the Mahdi will first concentrate on solving the most important problem of saving the faith (*iman*), particularly in the enlightened part of the population. After sorting out this first task, he will complete the two other tasks.

---

[25] English translation available at <www.saidnur.com/en/index.htm>[Accessed 19.03.2013].
[26] Translated from the Turkish original *Hutbe-i Şâmiye* by Şükran Vahide (Nursi 1996).
[27] See <http://risale-inur.org/yenisite/moduller/arama/haber.php?sid=2816&keyword=herbir%20fesad-%FD%20%FCmmet%20zaman%FDnda>.

The section ends with musings on the disintegration of morality with a distinctly local flavor: Yahya bemoans people picking their noses, laughing loudly and acting rowdily on the streets of Istanbul; people being impolite and selfish, people pushing on the bus and not offering their seats to elders and so on. He sees this development in his local environment as the "ground work for communism" (Yahya 1989, p. 182). He sees the influence of materialism in the decline of family ties, giving the example of "young people in Europe who leave their families as soon as they gain economic independence and start living together with someone of the opposite sex without being married" (Yahya 1989, p. 183). When the Golden Age comes, Yahya assures, all this will change.

## 4.4. Jesus, Dabbat al-Ardh and ad-Dukhan

The last third of the book deals with the return of Jesus, and with characters from Islamic apocalyptic traditions such as Dabbat al-Ardh (the Beast), ad-Dukhan (the Smoke) and the Dajjal (the Antichrist), which Yahya relates to current events. Since the gist of the book is devoted to the Mahdi, I will only briefly discuss the main points of these passages. Based on his interpretations of the hadiths, the Qur'an and Nursi's works, Yahya outlines the role of Jesus in the End Times. According to Yahya's interpretations of the hadith and the Qur'an, Jesus did not die but was taken up to God, and will return to restore the real Christianity. Together with the Mahdi, Jesus will destroy the Dajjal. Citing hadiths from Sahih Muslim alluding to the Antichrist being Jewish, Yahya comments that the Antichrist will "encourage immorality, homosexuality and sexual perversion, which is still considered legitimate in Europe, America, Russia and Israel and many other places" (Yahya 1989, p. 195). He also emphasizes that Jesus will not bring a new religion, but rather that he will confirm the sharia of the Prophet Muhammed.

Yahya finds support for his view on Jesus in Said Nursi, and cites the following passages from Nursi's *Letters*:

> A tyrannical current born of Naturalist and Materialist philosophy will gradually become strong and spread at the end of time by means of materialist philosophy, reaching such a degree that it denies God. [...] And the greatest of them, the Dajjal, who will come to lead them, will manifest awesome wonders – a sort of spiritualism and hypnosis. [...] At that point when the current appears to be very strong, the religion of true Christianity, which comprises the collective personality of Jesus (Upon whom be peace), will emerge. That is, it will descend from the skies of Divine Mercy. Present Christianity will be purified in the face of that reality; it will cast off superstition and distortion, and unite with the truths of Islam. Christianity will in effect be transformed into a sort of Islam. [...] Although defeated before the atheistic

current while separate, Christianity and Islam will have the capability to defeat and rout it as a result of their union (Yahya 1989, pp. 204–205).[28]

Thus, according to Nursi, it is only when Christianity is purified and unified with Islam that the atheistic current will be defeated. Commenting upon Nursi's writings on the materialist current growing stronger and Jesus' return, Yahya explains that Judaism will be astonished by the new civilization emerging from the unified Islamic world led by Mahdi, and will thus launch an alternative to the Mahdi, namely the False Messiah. It should be noted that in this work, Yahya generally writes about Judaism and Jews in a pejorative manner. In addition to the quotes mentioned above, later in the book he writes, "Jews will become firmly attached to the False Messiah with the joy of accepting a Messiah that is just like they dream of: Immoral, cruel, sadistic" (Yahya 1989, p. 195). In more recent works, however, Yahya's negative attitude to Jews has been modified, as I have examined in Chapter 3.

The last sections of *Mehdi ve Altın Çağ* is devoted to Dabbat al-Ardh (The Beast) and Ad-Dhukan (The Smoke). Under the caption "Is AIDS the Beast Mentioned In The Qur'an?" Yahya goes to great lengths to try to show that Dabbat al-Ardh, the creature mentioned in sura al-Naml (27), refers to the AIDS epidemic. Citing hadiths alluding to Dabbat al-Ardh, Yahya suggests for instance that there are similarities between the Beast as described in the hadiths and the green monkey thought to be the source of the AIDS virus (Yahya 1989, p. 244). He dwells in particular on the connection between homosexuality – which he regards as a perversion – and AIDS. The section includes graphic pictures of AIDS patients with various visible ailments such as black spots, which he claims corresponds to the way the Beast is described in the hadiths. He concludes that the AIDS virus, the monkey that spread it, and its effects on those affected by the disease, must be considered in sum as the Beast. The book was published in 1989, when the AIDS epidemic was high on the global agenda. The moral panic triggered by the AIDS epidemic has been the topic of several social studies analyses.[29] Yahya published a short booklet on this topic in 1987 (Yahya 1987).[30] The last few pages of *Mehdi ve Altın Çağ* is devoted to the Smoke mentioned in Qur'an 44:10–11, which he suggests might refer to the Chernobyl nuclear disaster in 1986.

---

[28] This English translation of these excerpts from the 15th letter of Nursi's *Letters* are obtained from <www.saidnur.com/en/> [Accessed 15.03.2013].
[29] See for instance Dowsett (2009).
[30] Hannelore Schönig analyses this booklet in an article in 1990 (Schönig 1990).

# 5. Themes in Harun Yahya's apocalypticism and their development

As I have shown above, Yahya finds a template for the apocalyptic scenario in sources from the Islamic tradition and the works of Said Nursi, on the basis of which he develops his own and distinct interpretation. The themes introduced in *Mehdi ve Altın Çağ* that have been presented above are developed further in works published by Harun Yahya during the 2000s, and many of them are made both more elaborate and more explicit over time. In the following, I will first examine these themes and how they are developed and integrated with other themes in Yahya's more recent works. I will also compare Yahya's apocalypticism with other examples of contemporary Muslim apocalypticism, as well as apocalypticism in the works of Said Nursi. I will then address the question of *why* these themes come to take such an important place in the discourse of Harun Yahya. Drawing on Stephen O'Leary's theory of apocalyptic rhetoric, I will approach Yahya's apocalypticism as a form of rhetoric, the intention of which is to persuade. I will examine how he legitimizes his apocalyptic interpretations and the role these interpretations play in terms of framing the *da'wa* of the Harun Yahya enterprise, and placing the Harun Yahya enterprise itself into a cosmic framework.

## 5.1. Targeting a global audience: Jesus Will Return

After the Harun Yahya enterprise began aiming for a global market around the turn of the millennium, Harun Yahya picked up the apocalyptic themes from *Mehdi ve Altın Çağ*. The first book published in English dealing with these themes was *Jesus Will Return* (Yahya 2001g).[31] In this book, Yahya does not concern himself with the Mahdi, but with hadiths and passages from Said Nursi dealing with the return of Jesus. This book thus appears to aim for a broader global audience, by tapping into millennial expectations that reached a peak around the turn of the millennium. To date, this book has been published in seven editions, and has been translated to 10 languages besides Turkish and English. In the following, I will refer mainly to Yahya's English publications, since they are mostly direct translations of Turkish editions, as indicated by the overview of works provided earlier in this chapter.

## 5.2. Temporalizing the apocalypse

Abbas Amanat writes; "In any given situation, the millennialists tend to engage in some form of temporalizing past prophecies and demonstrate the imminence, or near imminence, of the End in their own time and place" (Amanat 2009, p.

---

[31] The first Turkish edition was published as *Hazret İsa Gelecek* (Yahya 1999b).

21). This is clearly the case with Harun Yahya. Throughout *Mehdi ve Altın Çağ*, Yahya attempts to show that many of the signs alluded to in the Qur'an and the hadiths in fact correspond to events that have happened shortly before or were happening at the time he wrote the book, and that we are thus currently living in the initial phases of the end times. He particularly focuses on the year 1979 as the year in which the Mahdi will begin his struggle. As we have seen above, he takes a number of events that happened in and around 1979 and interprets them as corresponding to signs foretold in the hadiths, and he uses both Said Nursi and al-Suyuti as authoritative sources underscoring his claims that the Mahdi will appear in 1400 AH (1979).

Yahya continues this practice of temporalizing signs of the End Times in more recent publications. The notion that Jesus will return and assist the Mahdi in providing salvation from the degenerate present constitutes an important part of Yahya's eschatology. In *The signs of Jesus' Second Coming* (2004), Yahya focuses on the portents of Jesus' second coming.[32] In the same manner as in *Mehdi ve Altın Çağ*, Yahya interprets current events as corresponding to signs of the End Times both in Islamic and Biblical sources, and concludes that we are now living in the time of the second coming of Jesus. Some of the signs mentioned in *Mehdi ve Altın Çağ* are given a more global interpretation, however. For instance, "the sighting of a flare in the East", which Yahya in his work from 1989 suggested might refer to a rather local event, namely the burning of an oil tanker in the Bosphorus, is here interpreted as referring to the burning of oil wells in Kuwait following Iraq's invasion of Kuwait in 1991 (Yahya 2004c, p. 127).

In line with Yahya's increasingly ecumenical focus, which I have discussed in Chapter 3, he also turns to Judaism and Christianity to find support for his millennial views. In *Hazrat Mahdi (PBUH) is a descendant of the Prophet Abraham* (Yahya 2010e), Yahya considers signs of the End Times in both the Bible and the Qur'an, and claims that "the coming of the Hazrat Mahdi is announced in all the holy scriptures" (Yahya 2010e, p. 18).

## 5.3. The Golden Age and the redemption of a Turkish-Islamic union

In addition to Yahya's endeavors to show that the End Times are imminent, Yahya's apocalypticism is also millennialist in the sense that it contains the promise of a better world that will replace the degenerate present. In much of his writings, Yahya juxtaposes what he regards as the immorality, injustice and chaos of the present (for which he blames irreligion, communism and Darwinism), with the peace, harmony and prosperity of the Golden Age to come. The first part of *Mehdi ve Altın Çağ* is devoted to hadiths that describe the

---

[32] Image appendix, p. 4.

features of this promised final stage of the End Times. These features are elaborated upon in detail in *The Golden Age* (Yahya 2003g), summed up as follows on the book's back cover:

> [The Golden Age] will be marked by the abundance of every type of goods and crops, the establishment of security, justice, peace, and happiness; and the use of advanced technology for humanity's comfort, ease, joy, and peace. No one will be in need, for all goods and services will be available to satisfy all people's material needs (Yahya 2003c).

*The Golden Age is* richly illustrated with images representing abundance, aesthetic pleasure and harmony.

This redemptive notion of a coming Golden Age is linked with another key theme in Yahya's writings, which I examined in Chapter 3, namely neo-Ottomanism and the notion of Turkish world leadership. In this section, I will look at how these themes are fused with two other ideas: The notion of an Islamic union, and the theme of the advent of the Mahdi.

A central theme in millennialism is the notion of establishing justice and promising redress for past injustices. The beneficiaries of such a divine redress in Yahya's teachings are first and foremost Muslims. *Islam'in Kışı ve Beklenen Baharı* (The Winter of Islam and the Spring to Come) (Yahya 2001f) deals specifically with this. Yahya here presents a wide variety of recent and current conflicts in which Muslims have been victims of violence and oppression, taking the cases of Palestine, Chechnya, Kashmir or East Turkestan as examples. He claims that the present dark reality for Muslims in fact heralds good news, namely the coming of the Golden Age.

As argued in Chapter 3, Yahya's political works in Turkish in the 1980s and 90s sought to appeal to nationalist sentiments and a burgeoning pride in Turkey's Ottoman past. In 2003, Yahya began to formulate these political ideas of Turkish leadership in terms of an Islamic union. In an appendage to *Türkiye'nin Geleceğinde Osmanlı Vizyonu* (The Ottoman Vision in Turkey's Future) (Yahya 2003s), Yahya makes a call for an Islamic Union led by Turkey, claiming that such a union is in the interests of Muslims worldwide, and that Turkey, as the heir to the Ottoman Empire, is its natural leader.

The eschatological promise of redemption for the world's Muslims through an imminent End Times and the arrival of the Mahdi is synthesized with both the call for Muslim unity as well as the political themes of Turkish-Ottoman moral and historical supremacy in Yahya's vision of a Turkish-Islamic Union, presented first in *Türk-Islam Birliğine Çağrı* (A call for a Turkish-Islamic Union) (Yahya 2003r). An English translation was published the following year titled *A Call to an Islamic Union*, where all references to a "Turkish-Islamic Union" has been substituted for merely an "Islamic Union" (Yahya 2004a)[33]. Citing both Qur'an verses and passages from Said Nursi's works that he interprets as referring to the importance of Muslim unity, throughout the book Yahya promises that the establishment of an Islamic Union will resolve all current ills and conflicts, defeat irreligious ideologies and bring justice, peace and happiness to the world (Yahya 2004a, p. 132). Yahya assures that the purpose of this Islamic Union is to unite behind common policies and interests, but that it must have a structure that preserves the independence of the member states (Yahya 2004a, p. 155). This proposed Islamic union will not only be of benefit to Muslims, argues Yahya, but will bring peace and prosperity to all people since it will be based on the love, affection, brotherhood and compassion required by the moral values of the Qur'an. He presents examples from the history of Islam of Christians and Jews being treated with compassion, and argues that

> Remodeling the Islamic world according to the Qur'an's values is not only important for Muslims, but also for all members of other religious denominations living here as well as for members of all civilizations, especially those living in the West. The existence of strong nations based on the Qur'an's values will remove the West's concerns about the Islamic world and become one of the cornerstones of world peace (Yahya 2004a, p. 313).

He claims further that there has been a series of changes in the last decades that have paved the way for an Islamic union, such as the end of colonial rule and communism, irreligious ideologies losing their hold, and growing global interest in Islam, increasing dialogue and solidarity due to globalization and the Internet, and finally "Westerners search for the Ottomans" (Yahya 2004a, p. 348). Yahya refers to a number of articles written in Western media, which he interprets as signs that the West favors a reviving of the Ottoman model in order to solve problems, for instance in the Balkans (Yahya 2004, pp. 348–350).

In the concluding chapter, Yahya connects the call to an Islamic Union with his messianic interpretations of the hadith literature as heralding an imminent bright future:

> [...] the Islamic world is ripe for great and fundamental change. The Qur'an and the hadith literature suggest that the approaching period will be a bright one for the world's Muslims, Allah willing. Setting up the Islamic Union will speed up the process and begin a new era of plenty and prosperity for humanity in general (Yahya 2004a, p. 357).

The characteristics of the present time such as war, destitution, famine, oppression, and tyranny against Muslims correspond to the signs of the End Times, Yahya argues. He devotes the last section to reiterating his interpretations

---

[33] Image appendix, p. 4.

of the hadiths and Nursi as predicting the appearance of the Mahdi and the return of Jesus in this century. Islam and Christianity will be united into one faith, Yahya maintains, and the world will enter a golden era in which peace, happiness, security, contentment, and prosperity will rule.

Intended for the global market, this 2004 edition does not overtly refer to the Islamic Union as a Turkish-led union. Nevertheless, in the book's foreword, Yahya argues that Turkey is particularly suitable as a candidate for leading the Islamic Union:

> It must be remarked here that out of all Islamic nations, Turkey in particular has an important role to play, as it is the heir of the Ottoman Empire, the founder of such an Islamic Union which it ruled successfully for over 5 centuries. Turkey has the social infrastructure and state tradition necessary to fulfill the requirements of this important responsibility. Furthermore, of all Muslim states, it has the best-developed relations with the West and is therefore ideally placed to mediate the differences between the West and the Islamic world. Turkey also has a tradition of tolerance and harmony, and represents the Ahl as-Sunnah belief as the majority of Muslims believe, rather than a certain sect. All of this makes Turkey the most qualified candidate for leading the envisaged Islamic Union (Yahya 2004a, pp. 13–14).[34]

Published in 2010, the second edition of this book is retitled *A Call to a Turkish-Islamic Union*. This edition includes a new preface where the moral supremacy of the Turkish nation is further emphasized:

> Turkey will be the natural leader of this Union. All Turkic and Muslim countries sincerely accept and desire Turkish leadership. At the root of this lie Turkey's historic experience and the moral virtues of the Turkish nation, which have been proved over and over again (Yahya 2010a, p. 10).

However, the basis for Turkey's leadership is not only moral supremacy and historical experience. According to Yahya, Turkey's crucial role is also predicted in the hadiths:

> One of the main proofs that the Turkish Nation will fulfill this historic responsibility is the way that in the hadith about the end times our Prophet (may Allah bless him and grant him peace) makes particular reference to Istanbul and to Turkey (Yahya 2010a, p. 10).

---

[34] Here, as many other places, Yahya emphasizes the importance of *ahl al-Sunna* (see for instance *The Importance of Ahl al-Sunnah* (Yahya 2007c)). Oktar/Yahya is often accused by Muslim critics of straying from the Sunna, and his emphasis on the Sunna must be understood in the context of this criticism. In *Idealism, the Philosophy of the Matrix and the True Nature of Matter*, Yahya proclaims, "Let us state, before all else, that the author of this book is a believer strictly abiding by the doctrine of Ahlus Sunnah and does not defend the view of Wahdatul Wujood" (Yahya 2003i).

Yahya refers to a number of hadiths that he interprets as indicating that the Mahdi will appear in Istanbul, several of which he also alludes to in *Mahdi ve Altın Çağ* (1989). He cites hadiths which he interprets to the effect that the Mahdi will "spiritually capture Istanbul", "serve among the Turks", and "unite the fragmented Turkish states" (Yahya 2010a, pp. 11–17). In this recent work then, written for a global market, Yahya emphasizes that the notion of a Turkish-Islamic union as not merely desirable, but also divinely predicted. While his previous works in Turkish argue for Turkey's special merits in providing leadership and guidance due to its history and the moral superiority of the Turks, in this work Yahya claims that Turkey's special role is foretold in the hadiths concerning the end times. The political themes of neo-Ottomanism and pan-Turkism are thus synthesized with Yahya's messianic notions of the Mahdi appearing to redeem the world's Muslims and usher in a Golden Age of peace and prosperity.

## 5.4. Forces of evil: Materialism, Darwinism and atheist Freemasonry

Yahya also integrates anti-Masonic conspiracy theories into his apocalyptic eschatology. Referring to Said Nursi's understanding of the Antichrist as a system, Yahya identifies the Dajjal as the system of Darwinists, materialists and atheist Freemasons: 'Today the heretical ideology of Darwinism has been spread across the world by the system of the Dajjal, Freemasonry, and has become a false religion" (Yahya 2009i). Turning to tradition to find support for his view of Freemasonry as the Dajjal, Yahya writes that "in compliance with the Antichrist descriptions in the hadith and the New Testament, Freemasons have claimed that they have come out in the name of Allah" (Yahya 2009d). Yahya also refers to a hadith from the *Sahih* of the hadith collector Muslim (d. 875CE), according to which the Antichrist only will have one eye. He writes: "Since Freemasonry represents the system of the Antichrist and directly worships Satan, it has adopted this distinguishing characteristic of the Antichrist as its own symbol. That symbol is the 'single eye', which appears before us in just about all Masonic institutions".[35]

## 5.5. Yahya's apocalypticism and contemporary Arab apocalyptic literature

Harun Yahya is not unique in his efforts to interpret Islamic sources in the light of current events. As mentioned in the outset of the chapter, there has been a resurgence of popular Islamic apocalyptic literature in the last half of the 20th

---

[35] This quote is taken from an article on <Freemasonsandtheirerrors.blog.com>, a blog which links to harunyahya.com ("The Masons' Single Eye Is the Symbol of the Antichrist" 2009). In 2012 the article was available directly from harunyahya.com, but has since been removed.

century. Much of the contemporary Arab apocalyptic literature surveyed by Cook (Cook 2005) and Haddad & Smith (Haddad & Smith 2010) is strongly anti-American and anti-Semitic. Cook understands the proliferation of popular Muslim apocalypticism as related to the rise of "radical Islam" (Cook 2005, p. 15), which he does not define, but appears to identify with certain intellectuals striving to develop "new interpretations of Islam [...] that would build a complete system separate from any European-derived political or social system" (Cook 2005, p. 14). Yahya shares with these authors the propensity to incorporate Christian apocalyptic themes into his eschatology, but differs in other respects. Both the context from within which Yahya and his associates write as well as their target audience is quite different from that of the mainly Egyptian popular authors that David Cook has analyzed.

Conspiracism, defined as "a narrative form of scapegoating" where a stigmatized "Them" is blamed for societal problems and accused of plotting against the good "Us" (Landes 2000, p. 102), plays a central role in both Christian and Muslim contemporary apocalypticism. However, while the evil "Them" in the writings examined by David Cook and Haddad & Smith are Jews and Americans, the evil "Them" in Yahya's account are materialists, Darwinists and "Atheistic Freemasons". As examined in Chapter 3, Yahya also has a history of Holocaust revisionism and anti-Semitism, and this is also reflected in *Mehdi ve Altın Çağ*. After the turn of the millennium, however, Yahya has largely abandoned his previous anti-Semitic rhetoric for an ecumenical discourse and an inclusive approach towards Jews.

Islamic apocalyptic traditions concerning the Mahdi contain references to the previously unattainable goal of conquering Constantinople and the Byzantines. In the contemporary Islamic apocalyptic literature surveyed by David Cook, this has often been interpreted to refer to a Muslim conquering of the Christian West or the United States (Cook 2005, p. 127). In Yahya's works, the Mahdi's enemies are not Western armies, but rather materialist philosophy and those who defend it. Yahya interprets references to Constantinople to mean modern Istanbul, which he claims the Mahdi will conquer spiritually and intellectually, without bloodshed. Some of these Arab authors refer to Turkey as a country which will resist the Mahdi, and which therefore will be defeated by Muslim armies (Cook 2005, p. 133). In Yahya's account, the rising star of Turkey is a sign of the heralding of the messianic age.

The Arab-language popular apocalyptic literature examined by Cook display a vitriolic animosity towards the West and Jews. Muslim dominance and supremacy is projected into the future, as the present offers little in terms of reassurance, where the world is ruled by an overwhelmingly powerful conspiracy, and Muslims are suffering. While Muslim suffering is also a theme in Yahya's works, the tone is triumphant, especially in his more recent works.

Yahya comes across as confident in terms of the success of his own project as well as on behalf of the advent of Turkish-Islamic world leadership. As far as Yahya is concerned, everything is going according to plan, and Turkey's rise as a regional power only attests to this in his interpretation.

## 5.6. Harun Yahya and the use of Nursi's teachings as a template

Throughout history, both Sunni and Shi'ite revolutionary activists have employed the Islamic apocalyptic framework for political purposes. But, as noted by Barbara Freyer Stowasser, in the teachings of Said Nursi, the notion of the apocalypse was not a political tool, but a "paradigmatic and kerygmatic device" (Stowasser 2003, p. 232).[36] According to Stowasser,

> the apocalyptic Hadith provided for Nursi a language of powerful symbols and metaphors that he used to underline the seriousness of the confrontation between good and evil, faith and unbelief, spirituality and materialism, and religion and secularism, which was the central message of his work (Stowasser 2003, p. 232).

Modeling his *da'wa* enterprise upon Nursi's revivalist faith movement, Yahya too employs eschatology in a manner that serves to place his call to faith into a symbolic and emotively evocative context. However, although Nursi also used apocalyptic themes from the hadiths metaphorically to highlight elements of Turkish society, and associated the figure of the Dajjal with atheism and secular ideologies from the West, Yahya goes much further in contemporizing the portents of the Last Days by providing concrete interpretations of the Mahdi's character traits. Nursi warned that only God knows the exact time of the End Times and that all predictions of its imminence are therefore faulty (Stowasser 2003, p. 232). Yahya on the contrary, emphatically states that the End Times have already begun, and that the Mahdi has already arrived.

In *The End Times and the Mahdi* (Yahya 2003e), Yahya sums up the Mahdi's crucial and redemptive role as follows:

> During the terrible chaos of the final times, Allah will use a servant having superior morality known as the Mahdi (the guide to the truth), to invite humanity back to the right path. The Mahdi's first task will be to wage a war of ideas within the Islamic world and to turn those Muslims who have moved away from Islam's true essence back to true belief and morality. At this point, the Mahdi has three basic tasks:
> 
> 1. Tearing down all philosophical systems that deny Allah's Existence and support atheism.

---

[36] "Kerygmatic" is a theological term denoting preaching or proclamation.

2. Fighting superstition by freeing Islam from the yoke of those hypocritical individuals who have corrupted it, and then revealing and implementing true Islamic morality based on the rules of the Qur'an.

3. Strengthening the entire Islamic world, both politically and socially, and then bringing about peace, security and well-being in addition to solving societal problems (Yahya 2003e, p. 33).

These three tasks are Yahya's interpretation of the three tasks of the Mahdi as taught by Said Nursi. Nursi's teachings thus serve as a template for the *da'wa* of the Harun Yahya enterprise. Since the late 1990s, the Harun Yahya enterprise has focused on trying to demolish thought systems of materialism, targeting in particular Darwinism, which Yahya regards as the most serious threat to faith. While Yahya's creationist activism is still ongoing, he has in later years focused also on the Turkish-Islamic Union and the unification of Muslims. The Turkish-Islamic union is Yahya's version of the vision of Islamic unity, one of the tasks of the Mahdi as presented by Said Nursi (Saritoprak 1997).

## 6. The rhetoric of apocalypticism

In his influential work *Arguing the Apocalypse: A Theory of Millennial Rhetoric* (1994), Stephen O'Leary undertakes a rhetorical analysis of apocalyptic discourse. He proposes that the appeal of apocalyptic belief should be understood not merely in terms of the dispositions of its adherents or as a literary genre, but also in terms of the rhetorical power of the apocalyptic discourse itself. O'Leary writes that much study on apocalyptic discourse have focused mainly on the dispositions of the followers and the conditions that predispose them towards being partial to believing in an imminent apocalyptic scenario, such as material deprivation, anomie or natural catastrophes. However, argues O'Leary, apocalyptic discourse may also be understood as a form of rhetoric. According to O'Leary, the *topoi* of apocalyptic discourse are time, evil and authority. O'Leary analyses apocalyptic discourse as argument and rhetorical strategy, suggesting that apocalyptic eschatology "functions as a symbolic theodicy, a mythical and rhetorical solution to the problem of evil, and that its approach to this problem is accomplished through discursive construction of temporality" (O'Leary 1994, p. 14). Apocalyptic discourse proposes a resolution to evil in the world by proposing that the end of time is near.

### 6.1. Apocalypticism as a framework for the *da'wa* of Harun Yahya

Both apocalyptic discourse and conspiracy theories can be employed in order to represent history as a dramatic contest of good and evil, where evil is defined as an outside threat, something that exists exterior to the true community. Both function as *theodicies*, rhetorical and mythical solution to the problem of evil, by developing "symbolic resources that enable societies to define and address the problem of evil" (O'Leary 1994, p. 6). Applied to Yahya's works, we have seen how materialism and Darwinism are presented as the prime evils, and both apocalyptic and conspiratorial discourses are employed as symbolic resources. Yahya places the present-day intellectual struggle against Darwinism and materialism into the eschatological framework of Islamic tradition. O'Leary argues that whereas generic conspiracism "strives to provide a spatial self-definition of the true community as set apart from the evils", apocalyptic conspiracism on the other hand "locates the problem of evil in time and looks forward to its imminent resolution" (O'Leary 1994, p. 6).

In Chapter 3, I suggested that Yahya's conspiracy theories provide a cognitive map for locating blame. Yahya presents a reading of history where dark forces, such as "atheistic Freemasonry," are responsible for upholding and spreading materialist philosophy and Darwinist ideology. Drawing from apocalyptic traditions, Yahya places these alleged political and historical conspiracies into a religious context and identifies them as the evil forces that have been identified and predicted in sacred texts. The apocalyptic cosmology, with its emphasis on imminent redress and justice, provides the framework from within which the problem of evil is resolved rhetorically.

In O'Leary's view, "The story of the apocalyptic tradition is one of community building, in which human individuals and collectivities constitute their identities through shared mythic narratives that confront the problem of evil in time and history" (O'Leary 1994, p. 6). Arguably, Yahya can be seen to employ apocalyptic discourse as a "mythical framework" for his and his associates' battle against Darwinism. In this sense, the rhetorical function of the apocalyptic narrative developed by Yahya can be analyzed in terms of framing analysis. According to Snow and Benford (1988), the three core framing tasks of a movement are to identify a problem and identify who is to blame (diagnostic framing), articulate solutions (prognostic framing) and urge others to act (motivational framing). The *diagnostic frame* in the discourse of Harun Yahya can be summarized as follows: Due to the influence of Darwinism and materialist philosophy and the worldwide conspiracy that upholds it, the current state of the world is one of conflict and terror. Said Nursi's teachings regarding the Mahdi provide a *prognostic frame* for the Harun Yahya enterprise. The solution is articulated in terms of the tasks of the Mahdi as Yahya interprets them: To wage an intellectual struggle against Darwinism, to free Islam from the superstitions of the *yobaz*, and calling for an Islamic Union, which in time is articulated in terms of a Turkish-Islamic union.

The *motivational framing*, what is intended to serve as a call to arms for the associates of Harun Yahya, is that these tasks are presented as predicted in scripture. The current situation is presented as the first stage of the End Times, and atheistic Freemasons and Darwinists are understood as representing the forces of evil in apocalyptic traditions. For the apocalyptic argument to be convincing, it is essential to create an impression of a situation where the community is under siege, and promise vindication. The community under siege in Harun Yahya's discourse has developed over the years, from a relatively exclusive focus on Turks and Muslims, to a more inclusive concept of "true believers" in his works produced for the global market (Yahya 2004c, p. 397). The promised vindication is the victory of Islam. Yahya's readers and associates are called on to support the cause of the Mahdi and the forces of good against the forces of evil.

As mentioned above, the first work in English calling for an Islamic Union do not stress the Turkish element, perhaps because the appeal of such an emphasis is perceived to be limited vis-à-vis a global audience. However, by the end of the 2000s, there is an increasing emphasis on the role of Turkey and Turkish leadership also in Yahya's works geared towards a global audience. From making a call to Muslims to unify under Turkish leadership, Yahya is increasingly emphasizing that Turkish-Islamic leadership is predicted in the hadiths and thus inevitable.

This increasing emphasis coincides with political trajectories in Turkey and worldwide which Yahya interprets as confirming his idea that the world awaits Turkish-Islamic leadership. Turkey's rising power under the rule of Erdoğan through economic growth and a reorientation of its foreign policy, has led to increased confidence in Turkey and its geo-strategic importance. The notion of Turks as morally upright heroes who "saves the world" has emerged as a key theme in Turkish popular culture, through books such as *Metal Fırtına* (The Metal Storm) (Uçar & Turna 2004) and the film *Valley of the Wolves: Iraq* (*Valley of the Wolves: Iraq* 2006).

In a regular feature on Yahya's website titled "What he said, What happened", Yahya's proclamations concerning the Turkish-Islamic union is juxtaposed with news articles on Turkey's rising influence, giving the impression that Yahya's predictions are gradually becoming reality.[37] Statements made by both Turkish and foreign leaders on the potential important and positive role of Turkey are interpreted as confirming Yahya's ideas regarding a Turkish-Islamic Union as a solution to regional and global problems.[38] The theme of redress for the world's Muslims is thus combined with redress for the fallen Ottoman Empire. Yahya's writings on Turkey and Turks are strongly informed by a sense of "imperial

---

[37] A list of these types of articles is available at <http://harunyahya.com/list/type/42> [Accessed 19.03.2013].

[38] See for instance this article that juxtaposes Adnan Oktar's statements with statements by Turkish Prime Minister Recep Tayyip Erdoğan: <http://harunyahya.com/en/What-he-said-What-happened/101775/turkish-leadership> [Accessed 13.03.2013].

nostalgia". As discussed in Chapter 3, the trauma of the Treaty of Sevres has had a significant impact on popular nationalist discourse in Turkey. There is a perception in the nationalist imaginary by which Turkey – after having been a great imperial power – was humiliated and reduced to a continuously denigrated *enfant terrible* knocking on the doors of Europe. What greater redress than casting Turkish Muslims as the glorious locomotive for the good and morally upright in a cosmic battle between good and evil forces? In Yahya's teachings, then, the solution to the world's problems is the establishment of a Turkish-Islamic Union, which will usher forth the era of the Mahdi. The Ottoman era thus comes to represent both a nostalgic past and a utopian future in Yahya's apocalyptic vision.

The synthesis between messianic ideas concerning a soon-to-appear Mahdi and the Turkish-Islamic union has become the lens through which Yahya perceives and comments on current events. In interviews and in TV show, Yahya regularly comments on current conflicts, arguing that the Turkish-Islamic Union is the solution to all these various problems, including the Palestinian question, Iraq, Afghanistan, and PKK terror in Turkey (Yahya 2010i; HarunYahyaEnglish 2011b). Thus a circular logic is at work, whereby the hadiths are interpreted as confirming Yahya's claims, and events happening are interpreted as forecast by Yahya and Yahya's interpretation of the hadiths and of Said Nursi.

## 6.2. Yahya's apocalypticism and the question of interpretive authority

The act of engaging in apocalyptic interpretations of tradition raises the question of authority. The apocalyptic author announcing the imminent end is inevitably faced with the question: How do you know? Max Weber's famous typology of authority distinguishes between traditional, rational/legal and charismatic authority. Most apocalyptic authors rely on rational authority in the sense that they appeal to tradition and engage in exegesis. However, some also rely on charismatic authority by claiming for instance prophetic powers. In the following, I will argue that both rational and charismatic authority play a role in Yahya's attempt to convince his audience.

### 6.2.1. Sources and strategies: Yahya's apocalypticism as a form of exegesis

As observed by Amanat, millennialists employ "various strategies to make evidence speak out the anticipated End and the events preceding it" (Amanat 2009). Harun Yahya bases his interpretations and predictions on three sources: Hadiths and other Islamic sources, the Qur'an and the *Risale-i Nur* collection. As mentioned above, there is no explicit mention of the Mahdi in the Qur'an, but the Mahdi is mentioned in various hadiths attributed to Muhammed. The hadiths concerning the Mahdi referred to by Yahya are taken from the works of a handful of Sunni scholars, in order to claim that his interpretation is authoritative and based on reliable and authentic sources.[39] Yahya writes in *Mehdi ve Altın Çağ*:

> The Mahdi, Dabbat-ul Ardh, the Smoke, Jesus and Dajjal; events generally known as signs of the Last Days, are only given limited treatment in books surveying strong hadiths. Other accounts on the subject are characterized as weak hadiths. That does not mean, however, that they cannot be used as evidence. It is near impossible to ascertain the veracity of weak hadiths. But when the hadith in question concerns the future, it is different. Because when an event that is foretold happens as described, the veracity of that hadith is confirmed; that is, it becomes a *sahih* hadith. That means, when it comes to the End Times, it does not matter whether a hadith is weak or strong (Yahya, 1989, p. ii.).

Thus, Yahya argues that weak hadiths become reliable as the events described in them "come true". Consequently, he justifies his use of the sources by making the distinction between strong and weak hadiths irrelevant, and this becomes an important precondition to one of the main rhetorical strategies throughout both *Mahdi ve Altın Çağ* and subsequent apocalyptic works, namely to temporalize scriptural prophecies by identifying current or past events as identical to events prophesized in scripture.

Yahya's credentials as an Islamic scholar or interpreter of tradition are neither discussed in *Mehdi ve Altın Çağ* nor in his later works. His later works do however include an "About the Author" section where – although his educational background in art and philosophy is mentioned – the focus is primarily on the aims of his works:

> Under the guidance of the Qur'an and the Sunnah (teachings of the Prophet), the author makes it his purpose to disprove each fundamental tenet of godless ideologies and to have the "last word", so as to completely silence the objections raised against religion. He uses the seal of the final Prophet, who attained ultimate wisdom and moral perfection, as a sign of his intention to offer the last word (Yahya 2003l).

The emphasis is on how Yahya is being "guided" by the Qur'an, but the issue of interpretation and interpretive authority is not dealt with explicitly. Both in the apocalyptic works and other works, Yahya depicts himself as someone who is merely bringing these issues to people's attention. Yahya takes the role of a particularly perceptive "humble servant of God" that explains and brings clarity

---

[39] The references given by Yahya are often incomplete, and it is therefore difficult to identify the source. On the Harun Yahya main website, an article titled "The sources of some hadiths about Hazrat Mahdi (as)" lists various Islamic scholars and simply states that these sources contain a number of reliable hadiths about the Mahdi (Yahya 2011b).

to matters using scientific and rational methods.[40] In the preface to *Mehdi ve Altın Çağ*, Yahya emphasizes how his method is based on evidence:

> The difference between this book and other books on the subject is that this book presents the evidence showing that a great portion of the signs of the coming of Mahdi foretold in the hadiths of the prophet has already happened as described (Yahya 1989, p. 8).

Yahya emphasizes that the evidence Yahya brings forward speaks for itself, so that the reader must necessarily draw the same conclusions as Yahya: "You will see for yourself how closely those portents of the age prior to the coming of Hazrat Mahdi (pbuh) match conditions of this present day" (Yahya 2010e, p. 17).

Elsewhere, however, Yahya acknowledges that the majority of hadiths regarding the End Times are *müteşabih* (they are allegorical or their meaning is not apparent) and that they therefore must be interpreted (Yahya 1989, p. 40). In a section that draws heavily on Said Nursi's work *The Rays* (Şualar) (Nursi & Vahide 1998), Yahya explains:

> Since the world is a place of competition where one's accountability and beliefs are put to the test, theoretical issues that are obscure, profound, and in need of careful study and experiment cannot be obvious. Individuals must be able to decide using their reason, conscience and will, for in this way their true nature will become manifest. If the hadiths concerning the end times had been unequivocal, everyone would have had to accept them. But then accountability and the ability to discern would be rendered meaningless. The highest person and lowest person would be on the same level (Yahya 1989, p. 40).

The fact that the hadiths are open to interpretation provides an opportunity for individuals to demonstrate their skill and competence, Yahya emphasizes. Here then, Yahya acknowledges in a sense that he takes part in a struggle for interpretive supremacy.

6.2.2. Charismatic authority: The Harun Yahya as the center of a cosmic drama

Following Weber's typology of legitimation, O'Leary holds that rational authority refers to authority deriving from rationally created rules. Charismatic authority, in contrast, is based on an "extraordinary and personal *gift of grace*" and appeals to "the absolutely personal devotion and personal confidence in revelation, heroism, or other qualities of individual leadership" (O'Leary 1994, p. 52). O'Leary argues that "from a rhetorical perspective, charisma is best

---

[40] In a recent interview, Oktar declares "Ben de ne hocayım, ne alimim. Allah'ın aciz bir kuluyum sadece" (I am neither a *hoca* (religious leader) nor an *alim* (religious scholar), I am merely a humble servant of God) (Akkaya 2013).

conceived as a property *attributed by the audience*. By this definition, a prophet 'has' charisma when he or she succeeds in attracting a following" (O'Leary 1994, p. 53). O'Leary has argued that apocalyptic discourse should be understood as argument that is intended to persuade, but also that

> Argumentative analysis by itself is insufficient, however, for this discourse is produced by human beings who view themselves not only as rational creatures, but as actors in a cosmic drama. The "logical" form of the discourse thus takes shape within the structure of the participants' dramatic worldview. Insofar as rhetors and audiences perceive history and human action in terms of the dramatic narrative of myth, their discourse will exhibit dramatic, as well as argumentative, form (O'Leary 1994, p. 16).

Yahya is clearly concerned with providing evidence for his interpretations and to persuade his audience of his adequacy as an interpreter of tradition. However, Harun Yahya's apocalyptic interpretations of hadiths and the writings of Said Nursi do not merely have the function of framing the activities of the Harun Yahya enterprise and to constitute Yahya's legitimacy as an interpreter of tradition, but also appear to point towards Yahya/Oktar himself and the Harun Yahya enterprise as participants in a cosmic drama.

Yahya reinterprets the apocalyptic struggle against evil as the struggle against Darwinism and materialism, the struggle he himself claims to be waging. The emphasis on the imminent appearance of the Mahdi and Jesus in this century serves not merely as a reminder of the importance of faith, but serves to give a sense of urgency and cosmic importance to the Harun Yahya *da'wa* effort in itself. In Yahya's worldview, anyone who is on the side of belief in God is on the side of the Mahdi, and anyone defending Darwinism is serving the system of the Antichrist. Harun Yahya repeatedly emphasizes that, as a result of his endeavors, the belief in Darwinism worldwide is in decline: "All contemporary movements of denial are now ideologically defeated, thanks to the books written by Harun Yahya" (Yahya 2003l).

Furthermore, the apocalyptic scenario painted up by Yahya bears a striking resemblance to Adnan Oktar's own persona, his own life, his own *da'wa* efforts and his community of associates. Since Yahya's first work dealing with apocalypticism was published in 1989, he has increasingly been striving to draw attention to congruities between his own persons' – that is Adnan Oktar's – life and physical appearance, and that of the Mahdi. Already in *Mehdi ve Altın Çağ*, Yahya interprets the sources in a manner that appear to fit the description of Oktar and his community. According to Yahya, the Mahdi will appear in this century, he will appear in Turkey, he will fight against materialism and he will have a small community of followers. Yahya specifically claims that the Mahdi will appear in 1979, the same year Oktar came to Istanbul and enrolled at Mimar Sinan University, and which is identified as "the year in which Oktar began his great intellectual struggle against Darwinism" (Yahya 2008f). He claims that the Mahdi will conquer Istanbul spiritually, the city where from where Oktar leads the activities of the Harun Yahya enterprise. The description of the meeting place of the Mahdi and his followers as interpreted by Yahya also appears to fit the description of Yahya's mansion on the Asian side of Istanbul.

These hints become increasingly more explicit from 2009 onwards. They are especially blatant in *The Prophet Jesus (as) and Mahdi Will Come This Century* (2010g), a more than 1000-pages long work which, among other things, details the characteristics of the Mahdi and his community in ways that all appear to correspond with Oktar and his community. For example, Yahya here writes that "the Mahdi will have around 300 followers" (Yahya 2010g, p. 909), the same number that Oktar estimates his own community of followers to count,[41] and "a working group of 30" people (Yahya 2010g, p. 366), which according to the harunyahya.com FAQ is also the size of Yahya's group of assistants who help him write the books.[42] According to Yahya "Hazrat Mahdi (as) will appear in Turkey and be active in Istanbul" (p. 290), and 1956, Oktar's birth year, has a special significance in terms of the end times (Yahya 2010g, p. 458). He emphasizes that "one of Hazrat Mahdi's names will be 'Arslan' (Lion)" (Yahya 2010g, p. 125). Adnan Oktar's family name from birth is Adnan Arslanoğulları (sons of the lion). The book also lists 38 physical characteristics of the Mahdi, which appear to correspond with Oktar's physical appearance. Oktar claims to be a *sayyid*, a descendant of Muhammed, as the Mahdi is reported to be according to many hadiths to which Yahya refers.[43]

These parallels have naturally led to suspicions that Oktar is hinting that he is the Mahdi, and have sparked ridicule and criticism both in Islamic online debate forums, as well as from other religious leaders.[44] Oktar has never openly declared that he is the Mahdi. When confronted with this question in interviews, Oktar often emphasizes that making such a claim would amount to apostasy. At the same time, however, Oktar says that he cannot deny that he shares the physical characteristics of the Mahdi. In an interview with *Wall Street Journal* in 2009, Oktar responded

---

[41] In an interview with Australian TV channel ABC, Oktar estimates the size of his community to around 300 people (Yahya 2009a).
[42] http://harunyahya.com/bilgi/sss [Accessed 19.03.2013].
[43] Oktar's authorized biography states that he is *sayyid* with ancestry from the Caucasus, and claims to present documentation showing that Oktar's great-great-grandfather is recorded as a *sayyid* in Russian archives. Available at <www.harunyahyaimpact.com/biyografi.php> [Accessed 19.03.2013].
[44] In particular Cübbeli Ahmet Hoca, one of the leaders of İsmailağa *cemaatı*, has entered into polemics with Oktar. In his own televised sermons (www.cubbeliahmethoca.tv), Cübbeli accused Oktar of misleading people by claiming that he is the Mahdi. These videos were previously available on YouTube [Accessed 2 July 2012], but has since been removed, after Oktar responded by filing a claim of damages against Cübbeli Ahmet Hoca of 20.000 Turkish Lira for defamation ("Cübbeli Ve Adnan Hoca Davalık Oldu!" 2011)

There may be such a suspicion [that I am the Mahdi] stemming from certain physical characteristics. There is indeed a resemblance when one looks at the features described in the hadith, but that does not presuppose any claim to be Hazrat Mahdi (pbuh), of course (2009h).[45]

In the same interview, Oktar also declared that he is *not* the Mahdi. At the same time, however, Oktar preserves the ambiguity by frequently emphasizing that "Hazrat Mahdi (as) will accept no claims regarding his being the Mahdi" (Yahya 2009k). In one of his recent TV shows, Oktar remarked that

People will insist on telling the Mahdi, 'You are the Mahdi'. In huge numbers. In response, he will say, 'I am not the Mahdi'. They will keep forcing him to deny he is the Mahdi. They will say he is, and he will insist that he is not (Yahya 2012b).

Without speculating on whether Oktar and/or his followers actually believe that Oktar is the Mahdi, it is very likely that Harun Yahya deliberately interprets the sources regarding the Mahdi in such a way as to be consistent with Adnan Oktar. The intention of Yahya's accounts of the Mahdi and Oktar's statements in interviews is most probably to persuade the readers and viewers that Adnan Oktar, at the very least, *might* be the Mahdi. Yahya writes: "Hazrat Mahdi (AS) will not say 'I am the Mahdi (AS)', but he will permit them to grasp the truth of the Mahdi by lifting the fog of awareness from their eyes" (2010, p. 268). Under the pen name Harun Yahya, Oktar appears in the garb of a scholar interpreting hadiths and conveying the ideas of Said Nursi regarding the Mahdi and the End Times. At the same time, however, these interpretations contribute to creating an impression that Oktar/Yahya is not merely a commentator, but in fact the lead protagonist of these eschatological events. Yahya's apocalyptic discourse thus operates rhetorically by "linking the 'rational' with the 'oracular' voice" (O' Leary 1994, p. 13). Through this discourse, Yahya's seeks to establish not just rational, interpretive authority, but also charismatic authority.

## 6.3. Framing the hardships and successes of Adnan Oktar

Yahya's teachings regarding the Mahdi and the End Times do not only provide a framework that integrates the various themes of Yahya's works into a coherent worldview, but also come to function as an interpretive framework within which the experiences of Oktar and the Harun Yahya enterprise itself is provided

---

[45] In another interview conducted by the Turkish TV channel Kon TV 29 January 2008, the interviewer points to the similarities between the Mahdi and Oktar as described by Oktar, and asks Oktar if he is the Mahdi. Oktar replies that saying "I am the Mahdi" would amount to apostasy. However, he confirms that he shares the physical characteristics of the Mahdi: That he has a broad forehead, thick hair and a small nose, that he has a stamp on his back, and so on. (AdnanOktarRoportaj 2009).

meaning. Both the hardships and successes of Oktar and his associates are interpreted within a religious framework. In the apocalyptic works of Harun Yahya, it is emphasized that the Mahdi will encounter difficulty and hardship, and be the victim of plots and conspiracies (Yahya 2010g, p. 276). Oktar and his associates have experienced a row of legal troubles over the last few decades. On several websites run by the Harun Yahya enterprise, it is claimed that these legal troubles are the result of plots, conspiracies and "psychological warfare methods" employed against Adnan Oktar:[46]

> Under the influence and direction of the circles involved in prosecuting this psychological war, there have to date been many plots against Adnan Oktar, and he has been slandered many times and many smear campaigns against him have been set in motion.[47]

Oktar has claimed that the criminal charges against himself and his associates are part of a "Masonic and communist conspiracy" ("Komünistlerle Mason Locaları Komplo Kurdu" 2000). After an official investigation was launched against the Ergenekon network in 2007, Oktar began referring to the alleged Ergenekon organization as being behind these plots (Yahya 2009b). At a press conference held by Oktar and Bilim Araştirma Vakfı (BAV) in 2008, Oktar claimed that there are connections between the Ergenekon network and the courts and the press in Turkey, and that the Ergenekon network is controlled by Masons ("Ergenekon'da Mason Şühpesi" 2008).[48] On the Harun Yahya websites, the alleged "psychological warfare" against Oktar is juxtaposed with verses from the Qur'an regarding prophets who were the victims of slander, thus creating an associative connection between Oktar and the prophets (Yahya 2010h). The troubles encountered by Oktar are presented in such a way as to seemingly confirm that Oktar's struggle is a religious struggle, predicted by tradition.

In addition to depicting criminal charges as part of a Masonic atheist conspiracy, Oktar frames his religious critics as *yobaz*; bigots or fanatics. Already in *Mahdi ve Altın Çağ*, Yahya emphasized that the Mahdi will be met with opposition from the *yobaz*. Oktar has been much derided for his TV shows where he appears with his entourage of sexy women and dances to pop music, as well as for his Mahdi intimations. In an interview with Oktar conducted by the Turkish TV channel Beyaz TV, Oktar again describes the Mahdi in terms that

---

[46] The Harun Yahya enterprise has especially focused on what they refer to as "the cocaine conspiracy". In 1991, Oktar was taken into custody by Turkish security forces and charged with using cocaine. However, he was acquitted of the charges in 1994 due to insufficient proof. Oktar has since claimed that the security forces put cocaine in his food.
[47] <http://psychologicalwarfaremethods.com> [Accessed 19.03.2013].
[48] At the same press conference, it was announced that the Harun Yahya enterprise would publish a book titled *Ergenekon: The Sword of Masonry*, but the book has so far not been published.

appear to describe Oktar himself. The interviewer then asks in a mocking tone, "will the Mahdi play music and dance?" Oktar replies, "Contrary to what you may think, the Mahdi will not be a fanatic. The Mahdi will make religion easier and less demanding, and therefore all the bigots will go against him" (Izlevideoo2 2013).

The apocalyptic works of Yahya also emphasize that, despite these attacks, the Mahdi will not falter but be successful in his struggle (Yahya 2010g, p. 287). A significant portion of the activity of the Harun Yahya enterprise is centered on emphasizing the successes of the Harun Yahya enterprise, through books such as *The Global Impact of Harun Yahya* (Yahya 2007b) and a great number of articles and websites (Yahya 2009e).[49] Oktar announced in one of this TV performances in 2011 that:

> The way of the Dajjal has two arms, and it attacks from both. One is direct atheism, Darwinism and materialism. The other way it attacks is through fanaticism. But I have broken both of the Dajjal's arms. Both the fanatic arm and the atheist one (Yahya 2011a).

In one of Yahya's most recent works, *How Did the Dajjal Die?* (Oktar 2011), Yahya claims that Darwinism has been defeated, and even declares that the Dajjal is now dead:

> According to the hadiths of our Prophet (saas), Hazrat Mahdi (pbuh) has already appeared. The time when he will be recognized by people is very close. Again as can be seen from the hadiths, the coming of the Prophet Jesus (pbuh) will also take place very soon. Darwinism, the worst corruption of the global system of the Dajjal, has suffered the greatest defeat in history. The Dajjal is now dead. By Allah's leave, the plenty and abundance, the peace and security of the Golden Age, which is now close at hand, will reign over all mankind and enfold the whole world (Oktar 2011, p. 13).

Since Adnan Oktar assumed a more public role in the late 2000s, the author title of the published works began appearing as "Harun Yahya (Adnan Oktar)". It is interesting to note that the order is reversed in this very recent publication, where the author appears as "Adnan Oktar (Harun Yahya)". This, then, may indicate that Adnan Oktar is gradually replacing Harun Yahya as the brand name of the enterprise also in the global context, as the efforts of the Harun Yahya enterprise increasingly focus not just on the promotion of certain ideas, but also the promotion of the individual Adnan Oktar. Emphasizing the success of the Harun Yahya enterprise is an important part of the framing process, seeking to convince the audience of its religious importance.

---

[49] E.g. <www.byvirtueofharunyahya.com> and <www.harunyahyaimpact.com>. See image appendix, p. 6 and 11.

Outside of Yahya's inner circle, however, the intimations that Oktar might be the Mahdi are met with both ridicule and indignation. At the end of the abovementioned interview, which turns into a heated argument between Oktar and the interviewer, the interviewer finally loses his temper, and shouts: "You can make yourself believe it, you can make your associates believe it, but this country will never believe that you are the Mahdi!" before abruptly taking Oktar off the air (Izlevideoo2 2013). Thus, to the extent that the rhetorical intention of the apocalyptic themes in Yahya's works is to place Oktar and the Harun Yahya enterprise in the middle of a cosmic struggle, it appears to be a strategy that has backfired as far as the general public is concerned. The Harun Yahya enterprise has achieved some measure of success both in Turkey and globally through the publication of attractive and easy-to-read works dealing with the basics of Islam, creationism, Masonic conspiracy theories, Atatürkism and neo-Ottomanism. As the Harun Yahya enterprise has become increasingly more insistent upon drawing attention to parallels between Oktar and the Mahdi, however, the scholarly authority Yahya has achieved as a prominent Muslim debunker of Darwinism may be compromised. The ego of Adnan Oktar, it seems, is increasingly undermining the perceived religious authority of Harun Yahya.

## 7. Concluding remarks

Apocalyptic eschatology exists as part of Islamic tradition, and throughout history Mahdist movements have emerged that tap into this tradition. In the latter half of 20th century, there has been a resurgence of Muslim apocalyptic literature, drawing on Christian apocalyptic traditions and apocalyptic themes in popular culture. Heavily inspired by the teachings of Said Nursi, apocalypticism has been a theme in Yahya's works from the outset. Although Nursi also employed eschatological themes as metaphors for the confrontation between faith and unbelief, neither Nursi himself nor his present Nurcu followers place much emphasis on contemporalizing apocalyptic predictions. Yahya, however, interprets current events as fulfilling prophecies related in hadiths. He argues that the portents of the End Times as described in the hadiths have been fulfilled, and claims that the Mahdi has already appeared and that we are presently living in the End Times. Harun Yahya's eschatology is thus distinctly *apocalyptic*.

Moreover, Yahya's apocalyptic eschatology is *millennialist* in character in so far as he elaborates upon a forthcoming Golden Age where the allegedly current state of war and chaos will be replaced by the "the system of the Mahdi", where everything will be good and beautiful. Finally, his apocalyptic vision also has *messianic* aspects, since in Yahya's account it is the Mahdi who will be the key individual in effectuating this transformation. In *Mehdi ve Altın Çag*, relying on his own interpretations of the Qur'an, Sunni hadiths and the works of Nursi,

Yahya seeks to convince his readers that the appearance of the Mahdi and the Last Days is imminent. Yahya envisions the apocalyptic confrontation between good and evil forces as an ideological one: Without shedding a drop of blood, the Mahdi will triumph over materialism through faith and science and unify all believers in a Golden Age of peace and prosperity. This first work also contains more conventional representations of Islamic eschatology, such as the notion of the first period of the End Times as a time of conflict, immorality, and oppression for Muslims, and the promise of vindication for Islam.

Yahya's more recent apocalyptic works reflect the general development of themes in the discourse of Harun Yahya that I have documented in previous chapters. While Yahya cites hadiths that portray Jews in an unfavorable light in *Mehdi ve Altın Çağ*, works published after the global opening of the Harun Yahya enterprise in the 2000s are intended for a global audience and incorporates ecumenical themes. The evil forces described in apocalyptic traditions are interpreted as referring to Masons, communists and Darwinists rather than Israel and the West as in some of the Arab works surveyed by Cook and Haddad & Smith.

Furthermore, Yahya interprets hadiths as indicating that the Mahdi will emerge in Istanbul. As this chapter has demonstrated, Yahya's neo-Ottoman ideas are blended with Islamic eschatology to form his vision of a Turkish-Islamic Union. The idea of Turkish regional leadership from Yahya's political works is merged with the religious notion that the solution to the oppression of Muslims worldwide is Islamic unity. In Yahya's interpretation, the hadiths do not only predict a bright and imminent future for Islam, but also indicate that it is precisely in Turkey that the Mahdi will appear and lead the world into a bright and better future. Thus, in addition to providing historical and moral justification for Turkish leadership, Yahya also appeals to revelation and Islamic tradition and claims that Turkey's unique role is confirmed by the hadiths. He utilizes the perceived rising star of Turkey as proof that Turkey is the center where the supremacy of Islam will begin, and that it therefore makes sense that the Mahdi will emerge there.

As certain themes are made more explicit over time, it becomes increasingly clear *why* apocalypticism is part of the discourse of Harun Yahya. In general terms, the apocalyptic discourse of Harun Yahya functions rhetorically as both a form of theodicy and a kerygmatic device. Like conspiracy theories, the apocalyptic narrative explains and defines evil. Apocalypticism also brings urgency and cosmic importance to the struggle against evil because it predicts an imminent End Times. However, Yahya does not merely employ perform exegesis in order to substantiate an imminent end, but also to place his own apologetic project and arguably himself in the center of this eschatological drama, thus combining rational authority with charismatic authority.

The apocalyptic framework serves to integrate the various themes in Yahya's discourse that I have examined thus far, namely Turkish nationalism, the notion of a modern, urban Islam, conspiracism, creationism and ecumenism into a whole that is rhetorically anchored in tradition. Yahya gives his own distinct interpretation of Nursi's teachings regarding the three tasks of the Mahdi, and takes these as the template for the Harun Yahya enterprise: Fighting Darwinism, ridding Islam of the influence of the *yobaz,* and calling for an Islamic union led by Turkey. Thus, the Harun Yahya enterprise appears to be doing exactly what the Mahdi is supposed to be doing according to Yahya's interpretation. At the very least then, it seems justified to conclude that Yahya identifies with the struggle of the Mahdi as recounted in the hadiths and Nursi texts to which he refers, and that this has shaped his whole endeavor from the outset.

However, from 2009 onwards, it becomes increasingly clear that the Mahdi serves as more than mere inspiration for the Harun Yahya enterprise. In the late 2000s, Adnan Oktar steps into the limelight as the central figure of the Harun Yahya enterprise. The features and signs of the Mahdi as described in *The Prophet Jesus (as) and Hazrat Mahdi (as) Will Come This Century* (2010g) correspond with Oktar and his associates in ways that are unmistakable. It is highly probable that the parallels are deliberate and that the rhetorical intention is to create an impression in the reader that Oktar is, or might be, the Mahdi. It appears then, that the ultimate purpose of Yahya's apocalypticism is to promote Adnan Oktar as a central figure in a battle for Islam, and to convince the audience that the *da'wa* of Harun Yahya is not just any *da'wa,* but *the* cosmic struggle that has been predicted in Islamic tradition. In the discourse of Harun Yahya, Mahdism, creationism and neo-Ottomanism are fused into a particular form of Islamic apocalyptic discourse that places Turkey – and indeed Oktar/Yahya himself – at the center of a cosmic battle against the Forces of Evil, ultimately leading Muslims and the world at large into a Golden Age in which Islam will rule.

CHAPTER 6
# Concluding Analysis

## 1. Summarizing discussion

In this study, I have examined the emergence and evolution of the Harun Yahya enterprise by describing, analyzing and contextualizing the texts of Harun Yahya. I have traced the development of Adnan Oktar and his associates from an Istanbul-based religious *cemaat* targeting in particular urban, wealthy, secular middle-class youth, to a global enterprise promoting Islam through a particular brand of Islamic creationism, and increasingly also promoting Adnan Oktar and the Harun Yahya enterprise itself.

I have focused on four main themes that have been part of the discourse of Harun Yahya since the 1980s and early 1990s: Conspiracism, nationalism/neo-Ottomanism, creationism and apocalypticism/Mahdism. Additionally, I have identified a fifth theme, ecumenism, which has acquired an increasingly prominent role in Yahya's more recent work. I have sought to address the following research questions: Why has Harun Yahya focused on these themes in particular? How has Yahya's discourse changed over time and why? What argumentative strategies are employed by Yahya?

One way in which to understand the ideas promoted by the Harun Yahya enterprise is to take them at face value: According to Harun Yahya, the aim is to promote Islamic values and the "oneness of Allah", to convince people that the theory of evolution is wrong, to bring the good news of a coming Mahdi and an imminent Golden Age, to promote an understanding of Islam that is compatible with Kemalist principles and nationalism, and – as in Yahya's more recent works – to encourage peaceful relations with Christianity and Judaism. However, I argue that these ideas can be understood as *products*, both in the sense of *result* and *commodity*. They can be understood as springing from the local and global contexts in which Harun Yahya emerged, but also as commodities created by the Harun Yahya enterprise and adapted to specific markets. Harun Yahya can be understood as a *religious entrepreneur*, and his ideas can be understood as a form of *rhetoric*, the purpose of which is to convince the readers and promote not merely a certain interpretation of Islam, but also Adnan Oktar and the Harun Yahya enterprise.

## 1.1. The Turkish context, Islamic revival and opportunity spaces

Although the Harun Yahya enterprise with time has become a global enterprise, it emerged in Turkey, and must therefore be understood within the context of the Islamic revival and the complex web of convergences and divergences between Islam, modernity and nationalism that characterizes the history of modern Turkey. While other Muslim-majority countries have also undergone state-enforced secularization programs, nowhere else were these programs as radical as in Turkey, and this reality has given shape to the Islamic movement in Turkey. Two recurrent themes in Islamic discourses in Turkey are of particular importance: Firstly, the attempt to counter irreligion and materialism by synthesizing religion and science and presenting an evidence-based faith, represented most comprehensively by Said Nursi and the Nur movement. Secondly, both on state level and in the Islamic movement there has been a strong tendency towards the nationalization and Turkification of Islam. As seen above, the influence of both these currents is evident in the discourse of Harun Yahya.

Yahya's ideas regarding the importance of waging an intellectual struggle against materialism and communism, the notion of strengthening faith by providing rational arguments for the existence of God and a created universe, and the emphasis on uniting with Jewish and Christian "true believers" against materialism can be traced to Said Nursi and the Nur movement(s) that have developed Nursi's ideas after his death. Additionally, Harun Yahya employs Said Nursi to lend legitimacy and authority to his interpretations regarding the Mahdi. Aside from the Qur'an, Said Nursi's *Risale-i Nur* constitutes the most significant Islamic point of reference in the writings of Harun Yahya.

Turkish Islamism in most of its manifestations has been closely entangled with nationalism. Rather than rejecting nationalism, the Islamist movement in Turkey has sought to Islamize Turkish nationalism. Despite incorporating a transnational conception of an Islamic *umma*, the ideology of the Milli Görüş was based on the equation of the nation and Islam, and on the notion of the Ottoman Empire as the locus for Islamic civilization. As we have seen in Chapter 3 and 5 especially, the influence of these ideas is evident in the works of Harun Yahya.

I have argued that the emergence of the Harun Yahya enterprise must be considered in the context of how *opportunity spaces* for Islamic activism opened up in the post-coup environment of the 1980s, and the Islamic revival that followed in its wake. The coup leaders sought to align themselves with Islamists against what they perceived as a growing communist threat, and sought to amalgamate Islam and nationalism through an ideology known as the Turkish-Islamic synthesis. The Harun Yahya enterprise emerged at a time when economic, political and cultural power was gradually shifting hands from an urban secular elite to an emerging "Muslim *bourgeoisie*", and when a broad variety of Islamic movements became more visible, confident and diversified. The economic liberalization and privatization in the Özal era led to a growth in mass communication, and there was a growing market for Islamic publications.

The rise of political Islam in Turkey engendered growing polarization between increasingly assertive Islamic and secularist segments, and an ongoing cultural and political struggle over the right to define both Turkishness and modernity. This struggle contributed to shaping the discourse of the Islamic movement in Turkey. Hakan Yavuz describes these processes as *the vernacularization of modernity* and the "internal secularization of Islam in terms of rationalization, nationalization, and the accommodation of faith to the overriding exigencies of reason and evidence" (Yavuz 2003, p. 5). In the polemics of the secularist urban elites in Turkey, Islam became associated with backwardness, *yobazlık* (fanaticism), *gericilik* (reactionism), poverty and ignorance. Oktar and his associates were not alone in terms of seeking to counter this dominant secularist discourse by emphasizing the importance of forging an elite of well-dressed, well-educated and modern Muslims. However, to a greater extent than for instance the Gülen movement, Oktar and his associates specifically sought to target a secular segment and mobilize a young urban middle class in Istanbul who were open to religious proselytism, but who did not feel at home in more traditional Islamic circles.

The Harun Yahya enterprise thus emerged first as a *cemaat* led by Adnan Oktar, recruiting young, wealthy, well-educated people for the cause of spreading faith and fighting materialism. Gradually, this *cemaat* developed into an enterprise that promoted various ideas through its outreach and publishing activities, first in Turkey and later globally, under the brand name "Harun Yahya". In the three empirical chapters, I have examined the key themes in this outreach and publishing activity and their development over time.

## 1.2. Nationalism and conspiracism

I have examined how the Harun Yahya enterprise positioned itself in Turkey in the 1980s and 90s through the employment of nationalist idioms, but also anti-Semitic, anti-Zionist and anti-Masonic conspiracy rhetoric. The first major work published in the name of Harun Yahya was *Yahudilik ve Masonluk* (Judaism and Freemasonry) (1987b). In this and subsequent works, Yahya claims that Freemasonry is closely linked with Judaism, and that Zionists are using Freemasonry as a front to carry out Zionist agendas and erode religious values both in Turkey and globally. This type of conspiracy polemic as well as the anti-Darwinist publication activity conducted in the framework of BAV won Adnan Oktar and his associates favor among sections of the Islamist movement. The Harun Yahya enterprise thus appeared to align itself with Islamist discourses that were gaining momentum in the 1990s. However, this conspiratorial rhetoric must also be considered in a broader framework of Turkish nationalist discourses gaining momentum from the 1990s onwards. Processes of globalization and the Kurdish issue re-actualized the "ontological insecurities" that arguably characterize Turkish nationalism, and led to a widened appeal of conspiracy theories identifying "foreign factors" behind Turkey's problems.

After Adnan Oktar's release from prison in 1990, the Harun Yahya enterprise launched a campaign to profile itself as an Atatürkist and nationalist outfit. I have suggested that while this shift may be read as tactical move to avoid further trouble with the authorities, it can also be understood in terms of the resurgence of secular nationalism and "Atatürk fetishism", Turkism, pan-Turkism and neo-Ottomanism in the 1990s and early 2000s. If the aim is mass appeal, propagating nationalism is a fairly safe bet in Turkey. As noted by historian Holly Case:

> Turkey is a country with two right wings. One is nationalist and secular, built on the oversized legacy of Mustafa Kemal Atatürk, the nation's first president. The other is nationalist as well, but rooted in Islam and a renewed interest in the legacy of the Ottoman Empire (Case 2013).

In his works produced for the Turkish market, Yahya taps into a variety of popular discourses that has the potential to appeal to a broad spectrum of nationalist sensibilities in Turkey. He attempts to appeal to an urban middle class of "white Turks" through works that glorify Atatürk and secular Turkish nationalism, and by appropriating secularist symbols and discourses. Yahya does not merely adopt these idioms, however, but also adapts and reconfigures them, as in the case of Atatürkism. Yahya's Atatürk is a deeply religious Muslim nationalist, who fought against communism and upheld Turkish Muslim values. Yahya also attempts to appeal to ultranationalists and pan-Turkists through works that glorify Turks and emphasize kinship with Turkic peoples and nations outside Turkey, and to neo-Ottoman sensibilities through works that glorify the Ottoman Empire and imply its continuity through Turkey's allegedly increaseingly central role in the Muslim world.

## 1.3. Creationism

It was creationism, however, that would bring the Harun Yahya enterprise into prominence both in Turkey and globally. Although Oktar had been publishing booklets arguing against the theory of evolution as early as 1986, in 1997 the Harun Yahya enterprise launched its large-scale campaign against the theory of evolution, with the publication of *Evrim Aldatmacası* (The Evolution Deceit) and a series of conferences in Turkey, the first of which was organized in Istanbul in 1998.

Creationism as a form of "scientification" of theology is above all associated with evangelical Protestantism in the US, but also had its counterpart in the Turkish context, especially within Nurcu circles. I have argued that Yahya's creationism must be understood in a broader framework of modernist efforts to harmonize Islam and science, especially the Nurcu discourse of utilizing science to fortify faith and combat materialism. Inspired by the "creationist ministries" in America, however, Yahya professionalized the campaign against evolution and brought Nurcu-style creationism to a wider audience.

The creationist works of Harun Yahya are designed to convince the reader that the theory of evolution is false, and that nothing makes sense expect in the light of creation. Yahya employs a combination of scientific, moral and religious arguments, many of which are familiar from both Nurcu tracts and Protestant creationist literature. Yahya does not just present arguments *against* evolution, but argues *for* creation. Juxtaposing "evidence" from nature with "evidence" from revelation, Yahya insists that the evidence does not only point towards theistic creation, but positively to creation as revealed in the Qur'an.

Characteristic of Yahya's brand of Islamic creationism is its radical anti-materialism. Yahya combines mystical notions of "the secret of matter" with scientific rhetoric. Yahya does not only employ scientific arguments against the theory of evolution, but also seeks to discredit materialist philosophy on scientific grounds, arguing that "matter is an illusion". While moral arguments against Darwinism are common in creationist rhetoric, Yahya goes a step further in blaming Darwinism and materialism for all evils of our times, including terrorism, war and conflict. For this reason, it is paramount to wage an intellectual struggle against Darwinism and expose its falsehood, argues Yahya.

Yahya also places this struggle into an Islamic framework by identifying Darwinists as the "unbelievers" referred to in the Qur'an. According to Yahya, the conflict between evolutionists and creationists is an opportunity created by God in order to enable the distinguishing between "true religion" and "false religion", where the former is understood as Islam as revealed in the Qur'an, and the latter as both "materialist philosophy" and "bigoted thought posing as Islam". It is precisely this opportunity that Harun Yahya has seized, namely to utilize the theory of evolution and its defenders as a means to promote his modernist interpretation of Islam as both rational and science-compatible.

Although the Nur movement had also engaged in anti-Darwinian discourse, it was the Harun Yahya enterprise that pioneered a systematic form of creationist activism in Turkey, benefiting from political conjunctures after the 1980 coup. The conservative turn in Turkish politics provided a political opportunity space for creationist activism, as creationism was included in the school curriculum. The Turkish context shares certain commonalities with the American context in the sense that the theory of evolution has become a highly politicized issue and a culture war flashpoint. However, a significant difference is arguably the fact that while creationism remains marginal outside protestant evangelist segments in the US, in Turkey, on the contrary, evolution has few vocal defenders outside of marginal scientific and political circles with little leverage. Hence, popular acceptance of evolution in Turkey is relatively low. These conditions made antievolutionism an opportune strategy for the preaching of Islam without necessarily alienating audiences that identify as "secular" and "modern". By presenting the critique of Darwinism as science rather than religion, the Harun Yahya enterprise sought to present evidence for faith and gain credibility beyond the Islamic segment.

The Harun Yahya enterprise also realized the potential for promoting Islamic creationism globally, and had the human and financial resources to do so on a large scale. The Harun Yahya enterprise published *The Evolution Deceit* as its first English-language publication in 1999, but it was the mass mailing of the *Atlas of Creation* to thousands of addresses worldwide in 2007 that set Yahya's creationist campaign in motion on a global scale. The Harun Yahya enterprise appeared to find a market especially among diaspora Muslims looking for evidence against the theory of evolution placed within an Islamic framework.

Antievolutionism remains at the center of the effort of the Harun Yahya enterprise, as reflected in the fact that almost all of Yahya's works published from the mid-2000s onwards that deal with other topics include a special appendix on the "evolution deceit".

## 1.4. Ecumenism

In this dissertation I have documented both change and continuity over time in the discourse of the Harun Yahya enterprise, as well as highlighted differences between the works available in Turkish and English respectively. After the transition of the Harun Yahya enterprise from a Turkish to a global enterprise in the 2000s, the enterprise started to render written publications as well as online material available in English and other languages. Publications targeting the domestic market, such as the nationalist works on Turkey and Atatürk, have not been translated to English, however. In the works that have been translated, references to Atatürk and Turkey have generally been omitted. In the works published in English that contain references to Turkey and Turkish leadership, the emphasis is shifted from a patriotic focus on Turkey's national interests, to a focus on the beneficial role of Turkish leadership for all Muslims, and also non-Muslims.

The most dramatic shift in the discourse of the Harun Yahya enterprise, which is evident in both the Turkish and foreign-language works, is arguably the shift from anti-Semitism to ecumenism. From publishing works that contained anti-Jewish rhetoric in the late 80s and 90s, Yahya gradually sought to distance himself from anti-Semitism, first by emphasizing the difference between Judaism and Zionism, and later qualifying his condemnations further by speaking of "some atheist Zionists" rather than Zionists as a whole. Similarly, Yahya has also modified his anti-Masonic polemics by speaking in terms of "atheist Freemasons" rather than all Freemasons. Moreover, since the late 2000s, the Harun Yahya enterprise has actively pursued an agenda of interfaith unity, by publishing books calling for a union of faiths against materialism and Darwinism, organizing meetings with Jewish groups, and inviting Jewish religious leaders, evangelical Christians and even Freemasons as guests in Oktar's televised talk shows.

This shift may be understood as a consequence of the Harun Yahya enterprise orienting itself towards a global market with aspirations of appealing to a wide audience of both Muslims and non-Muslims. However, Yahya's emphasis on interfaith unity can also be seen as rooted in Nurcu discourse. Said Nursi emphasized the importance of cooperating with "righteous" Christians and Jews in the struggle against materialism. This approach is above all reflected in the activities of the neo-Nurcu Gülen movement, whose appeal outside of Turkey to a large extent rests on their success in promoting interfaith dialogue and presenting a moderate face of Islam. The shift in the discourse of the Harun Yahya enterprise may therefore be understood not merely as a result of its global expansion, but also as an attempt to take part in the highly successful franchise of the Gülen movement, and as reflecting the changing Zeitgeist in Turkey and the marginalization of the Islamist agendas of the old Milli Görüş in favor of the moderately Islamic and conservative nationalist JDP–Gülen axis.

### 1.5. Apocalypticism, Mahdism and a Turkish-Islamic union

The final key theme that I have examined in this dissertation is apocalypticism and Mahdism. Yahya's first major work dealing with the Mahdi and the End Times, *Mehdi ve Altın Çağ* (Mahdi and the Golden Age), was published as early as 1989. Throughout the 1990s, it was nationalist and creationist activism that preoccupied the Harun Yahya enterprise, but the topics dealt with in *Mehdi ve Altın Çağ* began to resurface in the works of Harun Yahya in the beginning of the 2000s. From 2009 onwards, the themes of an imminent Mahdi and a Turkish-Islamic union began to take prominence in the Harun Yahya enterprise's outreach activity.

*Mehdi ve Altın Çağ* contains most of the elements that have been developed and made more explicit in Yahya's later apocalyptic works. The aim of the book is to convince its readers that prophecies in Islamic sources regarding the End Times and the arrival of the awaited Mahdi have been fulfilled. Yahya bases his interpretations on the Qur'an, hadiths and other Islamic sources, and the works of Said Nursi. According to Yahya's interpretations of these sources, we are currently living in the first phase of the end times, a time marked by wars, conflict and immorality. The Mahdi has already appeared and begun his struggle; he has just not been recognized as such yet. According to Yahya, the Mahdi will struggle against both materialist philosophies and the superstitions of the *yobaz*.

*Mehdi ve Altın Çağ* can be characterized as an apocalyptic, messianic and millennial work, since it contemporalizes apocalyptic Islamic traditions and predicts the imminence of a messianic age of peace and prosperity ushered in by the Mahdi. While such contemporalizations of apocalyptic prophecies have generally been shunned by Sunni *ulama*, several scholars have pointed to a resurgence of apocalyptic and messianic themes in contemporary Islam, where popular Muslim authors employ themes from apocalyptic Islamic tradition to comment on current issues, often also drawing on apocalyptic themes from Christian traditions.

Harun Yahya picked up the themes from *Mehdi ve Altın Çağ* a decade later in *Jesus Will Return* (2001g), incorporating apocalyptic themes from Christian traditions and tapping into millennial expectations that began to peak around the time of the millennium. In works published subsequently, Yahya puts forward the idea of a Turkish-Islamic union that will bring peace and usher the world into a Golden Age, thus merging millennial themes with both the themes of neo-Ottomanism and ecumenism. In Yahya's interpretation, the hadiths do not only predict a bright and imminent future for Islam, but also indicate that it is precisely in Turkey that the Mahdi will appear and lead the world into a bright and better future. Thus, in addition to providing historical and moral justification for Turkish leadership, Yahya also appeals to revelation and Islamic tradition and claims that Turkey's unique role is confirmed by the hadiths. Yahya also uses the alleged rise of Turkey as a regional and global power as evidence that Turkey is the center where the supremacy of Islam will begin.

The main source of Harun Yahya's ideas regarding the Mahdi is the works of Said Nursi. While Nursi's teachings regarding the Mahdi do not figure prominently in contemporary Nurcu discourse, they serve important functions for Harun Yahya, in particular Nursi's claim that the Mahdi will carry out three important functions: 1) silence materialism 2) revive the marks of faith, and 3) restore sharia with the assistance of all believers and the support of Islamic unity. These duties are often shortened as the stage of belief, the stage of life and the stage of sharia in Nurcu sources (Saritoprak 2011). This becomes the template or *action frame* for the Harun Yahya enterprise. With time Yahya gives these tasks his own particular interpretation, as 1) tearing down the philosophical systems that support atheism; 2) fighting superstition by freeing Islam from the yoke of those hypocritical individuals who have corrupted it; and 3) strengthening the Islamic world and bringing about peace (Yahya 2003e, p. 33). The tasks of the

Mahdi as interpreted by Yahya thus appear to correspond with the efforts of the Harun Yahya enterprise: To wage an intellectual struggle against Darwinism, to promote a "modern" understanding of Islam, and calling for a Turkish-Islamic Union. The apocalyptic framework thus serves to integrate the various themes in Yahya's discourse into a whole that is rhetorically anchored in Islamic tradition.

Apocalypticism is a form of religious rhetoric that brings urgency and cosmic importance to the struggle against evil because it predicts an imminent End Times. I have suggested that the apocalyptic discourse of Harun Yahya can be understood in terms of offering "collective action frames for mobilization" (Meyer 2003) for those involved in the enterprise. Yahya identifies materialist ideology, which according to Yahya causes conflict, war, chaos and immorality, as the problem, thus providing a *diagnostic frame*. The solution to this problem is to expose those who according to Yahya perpetuate this ideology (e.g. Freemasons); to wage an intellectual war against Darwinism as well as asserting the truth of the Qur'an and Allah as the Creator; and to call for the uniting of Muslims under Turkish-Islamic leadership. This thus represents a *prognostic frame*. Yahya presents this particular form of *da'wa* as predicted both in scripture and in the works of Said Nursi as the tasks of the Mahdi: By participating in the *da'wa* effort of Harun Yahya, one is participating in "team Mahdi" against the forces of evil. This, then, can be understood as providing a *motivational frame*.

While Harun Yahya's early apocalyptic works were focused on convincing the readers that current events correspond with the signs of the End Times, by the end of the 2000s, the focus shifts even more towards the figure of the Mahdi. This coincides with Adnan Oktar assuming an increasingly public role. In *The Prophet Jesus (as) and Hazrat Mahdi (as) Will Come This Century* (2010g), the features and signs of the Mahdi are described in ways that appear to correspond in every respect with Oktar himself, and Oktar also concedes to these similarities in interviews. While Oktar has never openly claimed that he is the Mahdi, it seems reasonable to conclude that the Harun Yahya enterprise is deliberately seeking to create an impression in the reader that Oktar is, or at least might be, the Mahdi. Moreover, the successes and hardships of Oktar and his associates are framed by the Harun Yahya enterprise as corresponding with apocalyptic prophecies. Thus, it seems that the primary purpose of Harun Yahya's apocalyptic works is to convince the audience that the *da'wa* of Harun Yahya is not just any *da'wa*, but *the* cosmic struggle that has been predicted in Islamic tradition.

## 2. General discussion

### 2.1. Rhetoric and framing

In this dissertation, I have suggested that the discourse of Harun Yahya may be conceived of in terms of diagnostic, prognostic and motivational *frames* that mobilize action and construct meaning for the participants in the Harun Yahya enterprise, and as *rhetoric* that aims to persuade a wider audience of readers and sympathizers. I have highlighted the way in which the Harun Yahya enterprise has adopted and adapted popular discourses and utilized political and market opportunities in local and global contexts. This focus on the strategic and rhetorical aspects of the discourse of the Harun Yahya enterprise may lead the reader to suspect that I am implicitly charging the Harun Yahya enterprise with *opportunism*. Firstly, while I do not wish to speculate on the motivations behind the Harun Yahya enterprise, I would contend that opportunism does not necessarily preclude idealism. That is to say, although the Harun Yahya enterprise appears to be willing to go to great lengths in its efforts to gain appeal and influence, this does not speak to the "sincerity" of the effort, whatever that may entail. The question of whether popularity for the Harun Yahya enterprise is an end or a means to an end remains unanswered. The use of opportunism and marketing strategies is not unique to the Harun Yahya enterprise, but is arguably a feature of many religious communities aiming to increase their reach and influence.

In conclusion, the discourse of the Harun Yahya enterprise may be interpreted as serving both the purpose of promoting Islam and the Harun Yahya enterprise, and there need not be a contradiction between the two. The key themes in Harun Yahya's *da'wa* enterprise can be seen as serving the twin purpose of both promoting a particular interpretation of Islam, as well as constructing Harun Yahya as a central figure within an Islamic eschatological framework.

### 2.2. Argumentative strategies and authority

Harun Yahya utilizes a wide range of argumentative strategies in his effort to persuade the readers of both the validity of his arguments and his legitimacy as an interpreter of Islam. The works are presented as scholarly works that are based on research and careful consideration of evidence. Yahya does not claim to be an Islamic scholar, however. He circumvents established principles of interpretation, and instead attempts to legitimize his account of Islam in other ways. Especially when writing for a Turkish audience, he draws on the established influence of Said Nursi by placing himself in the Nurcu tradition and presenting his ideas as sanctioned by Nursi. Citing a section from Nursi's *The*

*Rays*, Yahya argues that the fact that *müteşabih* (allegorical) hadiths are open to interpretation provides an opportunity for individuals to demonstrate their skill and competence. Yahya appears to use the Nursi quotation to support a view of interpretive legitimacy that is not based on formal credentials, but on merit. Harun Yahya utilizes his purported success in debunking Darwinism and convincing people of the truth of creation as a testimony to the legitimacy of the efforts of the Harun Yahya enterprise. Put differently, in terms of establishing authority, the aim of the Harun Yahya enterprise is not only to convince the audience that the theory of evolution is wrong, but also to convince the audience that it is through the efforts of the Harun Yahya enterprise that the theory of evolution has been proven wrong. Thus, much of the publishing activity of the Harun Yahya enterprise revolves around parading the alleged successes of the enterprise under the guidance of Adnan Oktar.

## 2.3. Contemporary Islamic discourses, *da'wa* and "market Islam"

In the introduction chapter, I discussed contemporary perspectives on "globalized Islam", the fragmentation of authority and the emergence of a global market for a certain kind of Islamic literature. While these perspectives may contribute to explaining why there appears to be a certain market for Yahya's works, I have argued that the discourse of Harun Yahya must be understood primarily in terms of the Turkish context in which it emerged and its quest for popular appeal. The Harun Yahya enterprise shares the market-orientation and celebration of wealth and entrepreneurial success that characterizes what Patrick Haenni calls "market Islam". However, in other respects, the discourse of the Harun Yahya enterprise differs from that of many new global Muslim preachers. First of all, while there is emphasis on a de-cultured universal religiosity in Yahya's global works, the discourse of Harun Yahya also has a distinctly local flavor. In coherence with the ideology of the Turkish-Islamic synthesis, it emphasizes Ottoman history and the notion that the meeting of Islam and Turkish culture created a particularly valuable and meritorious blend.

Much of contemporary *da'wa* discourse is influenced by currents that are sometimes referred to as neo-Salafi or neo-fundamentalist. Such currents often have a puritan interpretation of Islamic tenets and emphasize orthopraxy, Islamic law, and a return to the "true faith" of the early Muslims. They place importance on Islamic concepts of modesty and often propose strict regulations of gender relations. The discourse of the Harun Yahya enterprise stands in sharp contrast to such neo-Salafi discourses of authenticity and purity. Rather than calling for a return to the Islam of the first Muslims, Yahya upholds the Ottoman Empire as the height of Islamic civilization. As we have seen, this notion of the importance of Turks for the success of Islam is also sustained in Yahya's works for the global market, through the notion of an Islamic union led by Turkey.

Yahya is arguably less concerned with the restoration of an idealized Islamic past and more focused on the restoration of justice that he claims will take place in the near future. Moreover, Yahya places little emphasis on orthopraxy and Islamic law in his *da'wa* efforts. The focus of Yahya's *da'wa* effort lies in persuading the audience to accept "the existence of Allah", using all resources at his disposition and whatever strategies he deems to be the most effective. In an interview in 2011, Adnan Oktar explains his strategy:

> When I started my Islamic preaching effort at university, I aimed for the elite: People who were attractive, wealthy, educated and sophisticated and in a position of influence, because I had limited resources and little time. In order to have an impact in society as quickly as possible, I wanted to use an effective a power as possible (Zeki Ademoğlu 2011).[1]

When the interviewer asks him whether it would not be more conducive to his cause to include some people with a background in Islamic education on his team, Oktar replies "religion is not really that complicated. If you read the Qur'an from beginning to end, it is very obvious what is *halal* [permissible] and what is *haram* [forbidden]" (Zeki Ademoğlu 2011). He goes on to say that religious experts "complicate matters". Oktar's emphasis on preaching an "uncomplicated" and "accessible" form of Islam and his result-oriented approach is particularly manifested through his controversial talk shows.

## 2.4. Adnan Oktar's televangelism revisited

In the introduction chapter, I presented the latest platform for the outreach activity of the Harun Yahya enterprise, namely the TV channel A9 TV and its glitzy talk shows featuring Adnan Oktar and his entourage of big bosomed and scantily clad women in designer brand outfits. These shows have sparked both ridicule and indignation for portraying "a sexed-up Disney version of Islam" (Varisco 2013). While these shows may be viewed purely as a marketing ploy designed to attract attention, they may also be understood as the culmination of the trajectory of the Harun Yahya enterprise. As seen above, apocalyptic traditions and the figure of the Mahdi have given shape to the *da'wa* effort of the Harun Yahya enterprise from the outset. Yahya has with time recast the three tasks of the Mahdi as expounded by Said Nursi as the debunking of Darwinism and materialism; the freeing of Islam from the superstitions of the bigots; and the strengthening of Islam by creating unity. The efforts to debunk Darwinism

---

[1] Original: *İslami tebliğ başladığımda akademide, seçkincilikte dikkat ettim: Dış görünüm düzgün olması, zengin olmaları, çok kültürlü olmaları, etkileyici konumda olmaları; çünkü imkanım az, vaktim sınırlı. Çok çabuk topluma etkileyici olması için, olabilecek en yüksek gücü kullanmayı düşündüm.*

and the calling for a union of faiths under the umbrella of Turkish leadership continue to feature prominently in Oktar's televangelism. Moreover, an increasingly important aspect of the TV shows appears to be the promotion of an "ultramodern" interpretation of Islam. Already in *Mehdi ve Altın Çağ*, Yahya argues that the Mahdi will not just struggle against materialists, but also "bigots" and "extremists" who misrepresent Islam.

In a recent article published in the Huffington Post titled "Quality Is Very Important in Islam", Yahya expresses his chagrin over a "coarsening of the Islamic world":

> Now when we gaze upon the Islamic world, we see a degraded culture where shabby-looking men are held up as saints, where beautiful women are commanded by bigots to conceal their beauty, and where unkempt women are held up as paragons of virtue by the very nature of their appearance, as though having bad skin and uncombed hair somehow makes you pious (Yahya 2013).

He criticizes those Muslims who condemn women who show off their beauty or who claim that music is *bid'a* (innovation), and asks

> How is it that music, art and beauty is condemned, when music, art and beauty are gifts from God? Why are these gifts, which uplift and elevate the mind and soul, looked upon as curses from the devil himself? (Yahya 2013).

According to Oktar/Yahya, enjoying beauty – whether as attractive women or cute kittens[2] – is not merely acceptable but sanctioned by Islamic tradition. He seeks to justify his understanding of Islam and his preaching methods by referring to the Qur'an and the hadiths. Commenting on the fact that the women on the show are mostly blonde, Oktar claims

> Our Prophet (saas) told ladies to wear beautiful clothes and be well groomed. In the hadith, the companions ask our Prophet (saas) about black hair, red hair and blonde hair. And our Prophet (saas) says that he likes blonde hair the most. He says, "The most beautiful one is yellow" (Yahya 2012f).

Oktar frequently cites the Prophet Solomon as an exemplary model from tradition, as a man of "incomparable wealth", "superior wisdom" and "exemplary moral character" (Yahya 2005b). In an interview, Oktar draws parallels between the Prophet Solomon and himself, saying that Allah has blessed both the Prophet Solomon and Oktar with wealth (AdnanOktarRoportaj 2009). Oktar also appears to take Prophet Solomon as an illustrative model for his result-oriented approach

---

[2] A9 TV broadcasts a regular show titled "Sevimli Canlılar" (Cute Creatures), which features kittens, puppies and other cute animals <http://a9.com.tr/video/45/Sevimli-Canlilar> [Accessed 19.03.2013].

to *da'wa*. In one of his talk shows, Oktar relates a story about Prophet Solomon converting a woman to Islam by his "glorious pool":

> The woman tries to get into the pool but when she steps, it becomes obvious that it is made of glass. They laugh and Prophet Solomon (as) makes jokes. And the woman says, "Alhamdulillah" and she likes it. Prophet Solomon (as) gets into her heart through love. He first ensures that she feels attached to him by means of love, trust, quality, the understanding of arts, glory and his candid attitudes. Then he becomes instrumental in her having faith in Allah. And the lady converts to Islam and so does her community (Yahya 2011c).

These are but a few examples of how Oktar/Yahya employs themes from Islamic tradition to elucidate and justify aspects of the Harun Yahya enterprise as manifested through the talk shows, such as the group's promotion of a luxurious lifestyle, the emphasis on physical beauty and the flirtatious tone between Oktar and his female followers.

The Harun Yahya enterprise's apparent preoccupation with luxury, wealth, fashion, beauty, Western pop music and celebrities as manifested in Oktar's talkshow, and especially the prominence of the women featured in the show, may also be understood in terms of the way in which the enterprise targets an urban secular audience and position itself as a "modern" Islamic effort. As discussed above, dominant secularist discourse has tended to construe the alleged secularist-Islamist divide as concomitant with class and geography, portraying Islamists as rural and low-class. The so-called "White Turks" has sought to retain social status by highlighting the cultural and lifestyle differences and even physical appearance that differentiate them from Islamic actors (Demiralp 2012, p. 513). Seda Demiralp suggests that "the alienation of secularist groups from Islam should not be understood merely as an indication of their fear of an Islamist threat, as the dominant discourse suggests. It is also an outright manifestation of their status group (Demiralp 2012, p. 512). The Harun Yahya enterprise arguably seeks to appeal to this "alienated" segment by appropriating the urban elitist discourse and symbols of "the White Turks".

The Islamic movement in Turkey has challenged the Kemalist elite's claim to represent both "the real Turkey" as well as its notions of what it means to be "modern" through the development of "alternative modernities". As argued by Yael Navaro-Yashin, one of the ways through which both secularist and Islamic identities have been constructed, is through consumer culture. Both secularists and Islamists have sought to communicate consumer power, status and wealth through consumption, but through different sets of symbols. The interaction between Islam and consumerism can be witnessed in the proliferation of Islamic fashion, products and services geared towards an Islamic market. A shared feature of these products and spaces is that they perpetuate Islamic concepts of modesty, most visibly through the use of *tesettür* (modest dress for women, including but not limited to the headscarf). Thus, women's bodies have become a primary site of contestation. In the discourse of assertive secularists, the headscarf has become the principal symbol of the "Islamization" of Turkey. *Tesettür* has its symbolic opposite in *dekolte*, a word that means low-cut or cleavage, but that has assumed a broader meaning in Turkey as the opposite of being covered or veiled.

The Harun Yahya enterprise's attempt to distance itself from Islamism and emulate a "high-class" secularized Islam for "white Turks", thus finds its most symbolic expression in the unveiled women appearing on Oktar's talk shows.[3] They are not just casually *dekolte*: Their tight-fitting tops, high heels and heavy make-up are the antithesis to Islamic concepts of modesty. They embody a dramatized and sexualized version of *cumhuriyet kadını*: the ideal of the secular Turkish Republican woman.

Oktar's talk shows merge the preaching of a simplified version of Islam that make no demands for modesty, with popular culture idioms, entertainment and glamour. The message communicated through the Harun Yahya enterprise's televangelism, appears to be "you can have all this and still be a Muslim".

## 2.5. The global impact of the Harun Yahya enterprise today

The magnitude and span of the Harun Yahya enterprise operation suggests that this is an enterprise with very high ambitions in terms of having a major impact both in Turkey and globally. As indicated in the introduction chapter, the Harun Yahya enterprise does appear to have a considerable impact with regards to its promotion of creationism. As I have attempted to show, however, the purpose of the creationist activism of Harun Yahya is not only to convince the audience that the theory of evolution is wrong, but also to promote Adnan Oktar himself. This aspect of the Harun Yahya enterprise has, as we have seen, become more pronounced especially after 2009, with the publication of books that appear to be designed to create the impression that Adnan Oktar might be the Mahdi. One might speculate that the reason for this increasingly insistent and explicit approach is the recognition that Adnan Oktar, contrary to expectations, has not been widely recognized and affirmed as neither a Muslim authority, nor a Mahdi.[4]

The insistence upon emphasizing parallels between Adnan Oktar and the Mahdi as well as the increasingly more eccentric A9 TV talk shows have certainly given the Harun Yahya enterprise publicity and contributed to Oktar's fame both in Turkey and internationally. In terms of establishing Adnan Oktar as a Muslim authority, however, the recent trajectory of the Harun Yahya enter-

---

[3] It should be noted that not all of the women on the show are unveiled: Oktar's shows also features veiled women, albeit with heavy make-up.
[4] This view was put forward by former member "Mehmet" (personal interview 04.02.2012).

prise appears to have backfired. Various international Muslim internet debate forums feature heated discussions regarding Harun Yahya, where several discussants express disappointment that Harun Yahya, who in their eyes have "produced a great corpus of works in support of Islam", now appears to have "deviated from Islam" by claiming that he is the Mahdi and appearing in "sensationalist" TV shows.[5]

Although Yahya's influence may be limited in terms of persuading people that he is the Mahdi or even a particularly important Islamic figure, the works of Harun Yahya' still appear to have a considerable audience. Indeed, a significant factor in the impact of the Harun Yahya enterprise can be attributed to its having found a market niche in the global promotion of Islamic creationism, as I have alluded to above. Some might find Yahya's arguments regarding the theory of evolution and global Freemasonry truly compelling, others might be impressed by the sleek design and professional appearance of the publications and websites. However, the strongest card of the Harun Yahya enterprise in terms of reach and influence is arguably the aggressive manner in which the ideas of Harun Yahya are marketed globally, and the fact that the works of Harun Yahya are so widely available on the Internet and in Islamic bookstores worldwide. The Harun Yahya enterprise has virtually colonized the World Wide Web. If one browses the Internet looking for information on Islam, one is quite likely to stumble upon the works of Harun Yahya, due to the sheer intensity of the Harun Yahya enterprise's online presence. What Yahya lacks in terms of formal authority, then, he seeks to compensate by sheer market presence. The pervasiveness of the Harun Yahya enterprise contributes to the impression that the Harun Yahya enterprise seeks to convey, namely that Harun Yahya/Adnan Oktar is an important and influential "servant of Islam", and that his *da'wa* enterprise is successful.

---

[5] The author of the post "Harun Yahya has become harmful" writes: "I have been one of the biggest fans of his works, but now even I cannot deny any longer that Harun Yahya, Adnan Oktar, has either become bad or gone mad" (Abdul1234 2012).

IMAGE APPENDIX

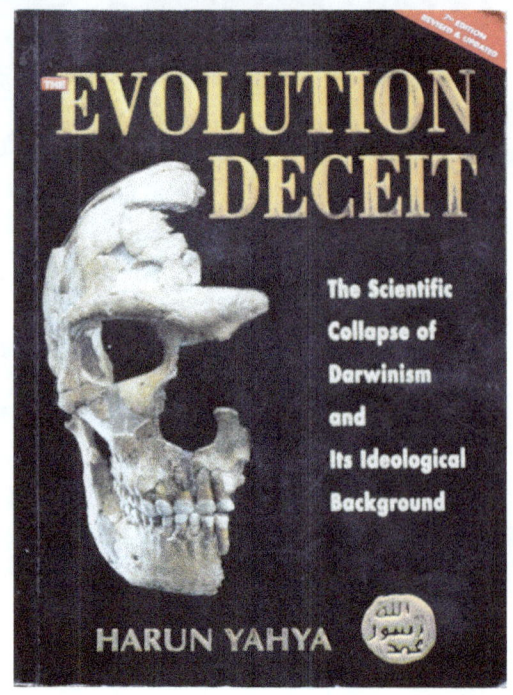

Opposite page

Top left: Yahya, H. (2007), *Atlas of Creation* vol. 1. Istanbul, Global Publishing

Top right: Yahya, H. (2002), *Evolution Deceit*. Istanbul, Araştırma Publishing.

Bottom left: Yahya, H (1995b), *Soykırım Yalanı*. Istanbul, Dergah Offset.

Bottom right: Yahya, H. (1989), *Mehdi ve Altın Çağ*. İstanbul, Nasajans.

This page

Top: The Harun Yahya enterprise's London bus campaign from 2011, which advertises the *Atlas of Creation* with the text "Modern Science Demonstrates that God Exists".

Bottom: Poster for Harun Yahya conference held in Malmö, Sweden in 2011.

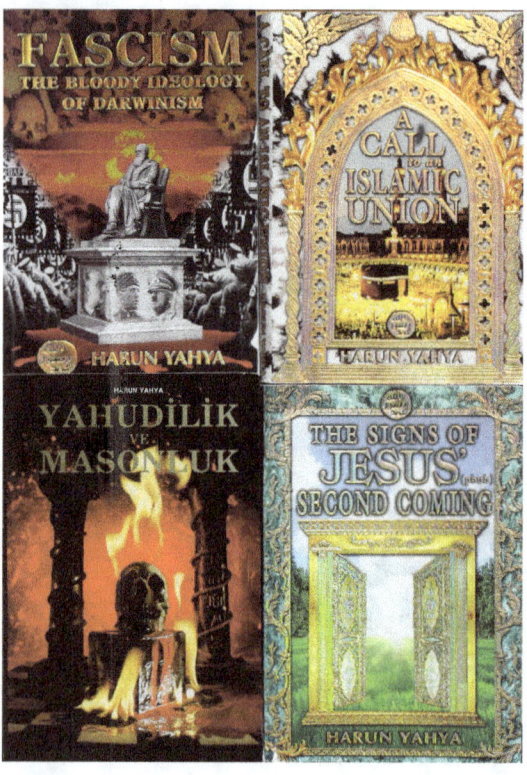

Top: 4 dvds

Bottom: 4 books

Yahya, H. (2002), *Fascism*, Istanbul, Arastirma Publishing.

Yahya, H. (2004), *A Call to an Islamic Union*. Istanbul, Global Publishing.

Yahya, H. (1987b), *Yahudilik ve Masonluk* İstanbul, Acar Reklam Yayınları.

Yahya, H (2004c), *The Signs of Jesus' Second Coming*. Istanbul, Global Publishing.

Top: "Adnan's angels" Gülşah Güçyetmez and Didem Ürer sporting Chanel and Armani.

"Adnan's angels": Five of Oktar's female associates who frequently appear on A9 TV's talk shows. From left: Ebru Altan, Damla Pamir, Ceylan Özbudak, Gülşah Güçyetmez and Aylin Kocaman.

Beyzah Bayraktar and Gülşah Güçyetmez in the A9 TV studios. The text on the screen in the background reads: "Islamic morality" (İslam ahlâki).

Photo of Gülşah Güçyetmez from www.ibelieveallah.com (26.04.13).

Middle: Adnan Oktar/Harun Yahya.

Bottom: Adnan Oktar in the A9 TV studios with a Jewish delegation from Israel.

**Opposite page**
Top: Screen-grab from www.awaitedmahdi.com (26.04.2013)
Middle: Screen-grab from www.byvirtueofharunyahya.com (26.04.2013)
Bottom: Screen-grab from www.endoftimes.net (26.04.2013)

**This page**
Top: Screen-grab from www.jesuswillreturn.com (26.04.2013)
Bottom: Screen-grab from www.mahidneversheldsblood.com (26.04.2013)

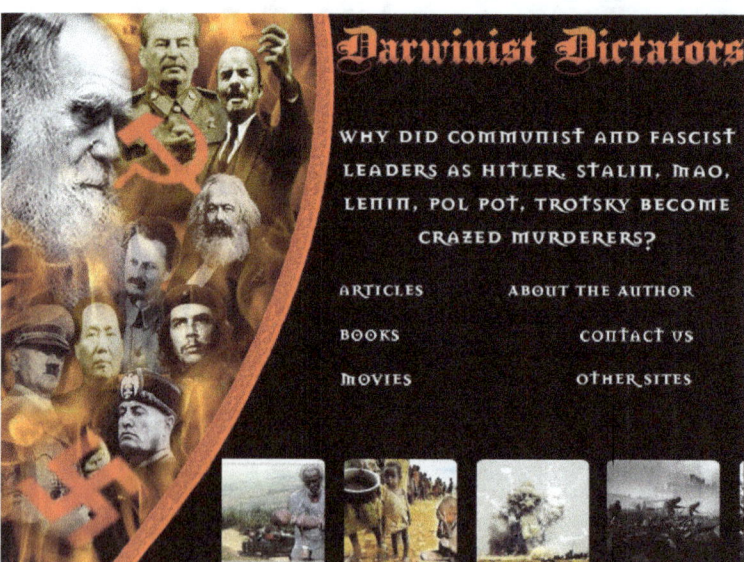

**This page**
Top: Screen-grab from www.darwinismisso19thcentury.com (26.04.2013)
Bottom: Screen-grab from www.darwinistdictators.com (26.04.2013)

**Opposite page**
Top: Screen-grab from www.darwinistsinapinch.com (26.04.2013)
Bottom: Screen-grab from www.miraclesofthequran.com (26.04.2013)

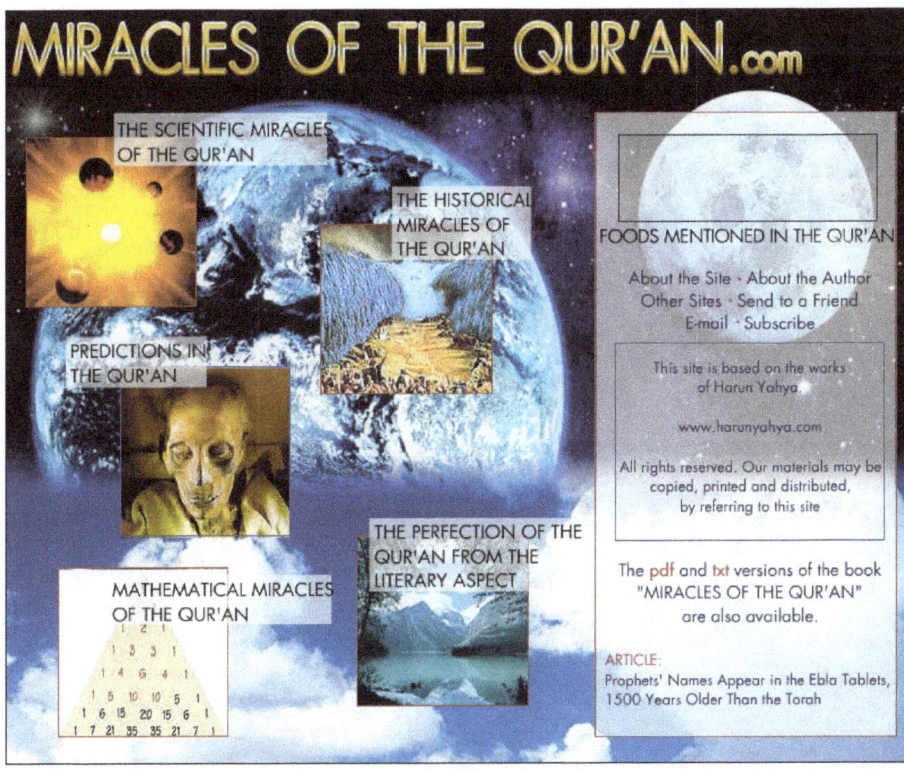

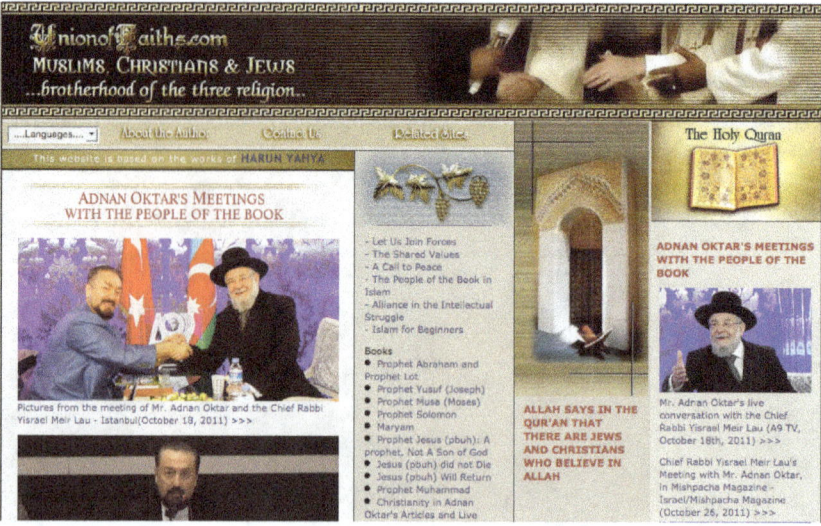

This page

Top: Screen-grab from www.turkishislamicunion.com (26.04.2013)

Bottom: Screen-grab from www.unionoffaiths.com (26.04.2013)

Opposite page

Top: Screen-grab from www.mahdi-antichrist-freemasonry.com (26.04.2013)

Bottom: Screen-grab from www.harunyahyaimpact.com (26.04.2013)

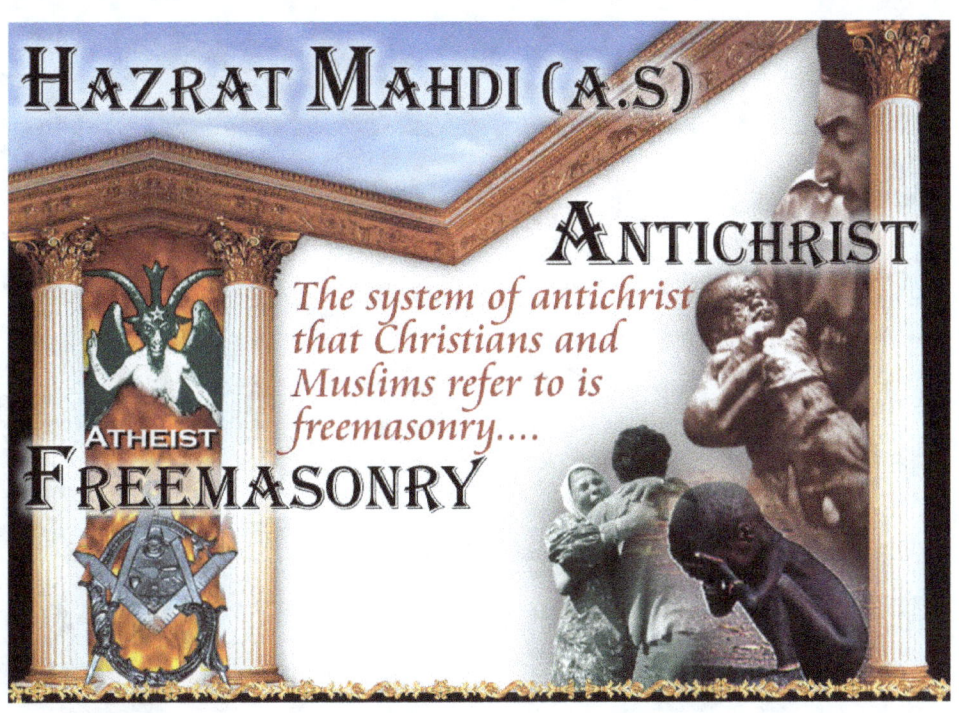

HAZRAT MAHDI (A.S)
ANTICHRIST
The system of antichrist that Christians and Muslims refer to is freemasonry....
ATHEIST
FREEMASONRY

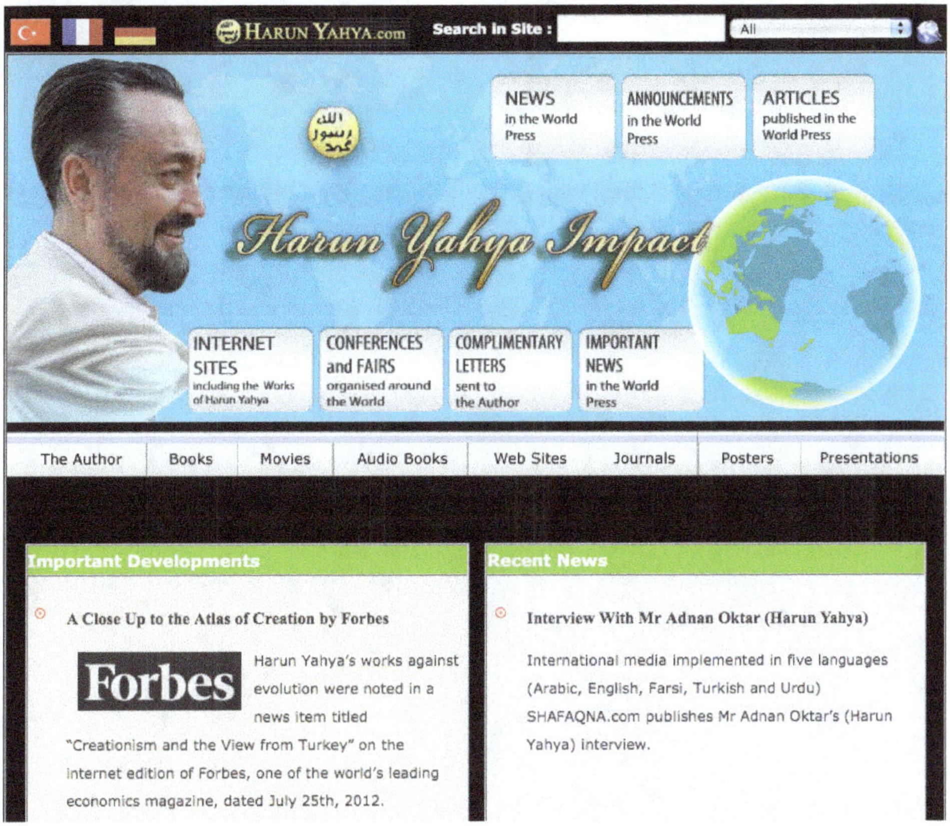

HARUN YAHYA.com
Search in Site :
All
NEWS in the World Press
ANNOUNCEMENTS in the World Press
ARTICLES published in the World Press
Harun Yahya Impact
INTERNET SITES including the Works of Harun Yahya
CONFERENCES and FAIRS organised around the World
COMPLIMENTARY LETTERS sent to the Author
IMPORTANT NEWS in the World Press
The Author
Books
Movies
Audio Books
Web Sites
Journals
Posters
Presentations
Important Developments
A Close Up to the Atlas of Creation by Forbes
Forbes
Harun Yahya's works against evolution were noted in a news item titled "Creationism and the View from Turkey" on the internet edition of Forbes, one of the world's leading economics magazine, dated July 25th, 2012.
Recent News
Interview With Mr Adnan Oktar (Harun Yahya)
International media implemented in five languages (Arabic, English, Farsi, Turkish and Urdu) SHAFAQNA.com publishes Mr Adnan Oktar's (Harun Yahya) interview.

Screen-grab from the main Harun Yahya online hub, www.harunyahya.com (26.04.2013)

# REFERENCES

"3 Rekat Namaz" (1999). *Hürriyet* [Online], 21 November. Available: http://arama.hurriyet.com.tr/arsivnews.aspx?id=-114594 [Accessed 19.03.0213].

13kahraman (2012a) "Başı Açık ve Abdestsiz Kuran Okunur Mu? (Adnan Oktar)" [Online video]. *YouTube*. Available: http://www.youtube.com/watch?v=KV97X1t35NA [Accessed 19.03.2013].

13kahraman (2012b) "Ben Hiç Kimsenin Tebliğ Yapamadığı Kesimlere Ulaşıyorum" [Online video]. *YouTube*. Available: http://www.youtube.com/watch?v=n6e95hj_FWE [Accessed 19.03.2013].

Abdul1234 (2012) "Harun Yahya Has Become Harmful" [Online]. *www.sunniforum.com*. Available: http://www.sunniforum.com/forum/showthread.php?88454-Harun-Yahya-Has-Become-Harmful [Accessed 19.03.2013].

Abel, Armand (2013). "Al-Dadjdjal". *Encyclopaedia of Islam, Second Edition*. Bearman, P., Bianquis, Th., Bosworth, C.E., Donzel, E. van & Heinrichs, W.P. (eds). Brill Online. Södertörn University College Library. Available: http://referenceworks.brillonline.com/entries/encyclopaedia-of-islam-2/al-dadjdjal-SIM_1654 [Accessed 10.03.2013].

Abu-Rabi, Ibrahim M. (2010) *Theodicy and Justice in Modern Islamic Thought: The Case of Said Nursi*. Farnham: Ashgate.

Abu-Rabi, Ibrahim M. (2008) *Spiritual Dimensions of Bediuzzaman Said Nursi's Risale-i Nur*. Albany: State University of New York Press.

Açıkgenç, Alparslan (2008) "Said Nursi". *Türkiye Diyanet Vakfı İslam Ansiklopedisi*, vol. 35. Ankara: Türkiye Diyanet Vakfı, 565–572.

"Adnan Hoca Artık Atatürkçü ve Vakıf Başkanı" (1990) *Cumhuriyet*. Istanbul. 27 March, p. 7.

"Adnan Hoca Paranoyak" (1987) *Cumhuriyet*. Istanbul. 27 February, p. 12.

"Adnan Hoca, Apo Kadar Tehlikeli" (1999). *Sabah* [Online], 17 November. Available: http://arsiv.sabah.com.tr/1999/11/17/p06.html [Accessed 19.03.2013].

"Adnan Hocacı Erbakan!" (2001). *Milliyet* [Online], 13 January. Available: http://www.milliyet.com.tr/2001/01/13/siyaset/siy03.html [Accessed 04.02.2013].

"Adnan Hocacılar Grubu Davasında 5 Sanık Beraat Etti" (2007). *Hürriyet* [Online], Jan 22 Available: http://arama.hurriyet.com.tr/arsivnews.aspx?id=5821157 [Accessed 04.02.13].

"Adnan Oktar'a 3 Yıl Hapis" (2008). *Yeni Şafak* [Online], 10 May. Available: http://yenisafak.com.tr/Gundem/?t=10.05.2008&i=116264 [Accessed 19.03.2013].

"Adnan'in GSM Ajani" (1999). *Hürriyet* [Online], 17 November. Available: http://arama.hurriyet.com.tr/arsivnews.aspx?id=-113829 [Accessed 19.03.2013].

AdnanOktarMuzik (2012) "Adnan Oktar Gangnam Style ile Coştu" [Online video]. *YouTube*. Available: http://www.youtube.com/watch?v=DFshyFDB8cA [Accessed 19.03.2013].

AdnanOktarRoportaj (2009) "Adnan Oktar'ın Kon TV (Konya) Röportajı - 1 - (29 Ocak 2008)" [Online video]. *www.youtube.com*. Available:

http://www.youtube.com/watch?v=ln09pxId0fQ&list=UU8MlFeE5rpsr9HyrfwA7v
WQ&index=1 [Accessed 19.03.2013].

Agai, Bekim (2005). "Discursive and Organizational Strategies of the Gülen Movement". Paper presented at *Islam in the Contemporary World: The Fethullah Gülen Movement in Thought and Practice,* Rice University, Houston TX, November 12–13, 2005. Available: http://www.fethullahgulen.org/conference-papers/the-fethullah-gulen-movement-i/2132-discursive-and-organizational-strategies-of-the-gulen-movement.html [Accessed 19.03.2013].

Agai, Bekim (2007) "Islam and Education in Secular Turkey: State Policies and the Emergence of the Fethullah Gülen Group". In: Hefner, Robert W. & Zaman, Muhammad Qasim (eds.) *Schooling Islam: The Culture and Politics of Modern Muslim Education.* Princeton, N.J.: Princeton University Press, 149–71.

Ahmad, Attiya (2010) "Explanation is Not the Point: Domestic Work, Islamic Dawa and Becoming Muslim in Kuwait". *The Asia Pacific Journal of Anthropology,* 11 (3-4), 293–310.

Akbulut, Şemseddin (1985) *Darwin ve Evrim Teorisi.* Istanbul: Yeni Asya.

Akçam, Taner (2004) *From Empire to Republic: Turkish Nationalism and the Armenian Genocide.* New York: Zed Books.

Akkaya, Fatih (2013) "Adnan Oktar'a Dair Herşey 2". *Habervaktim.com* [Online], March 8. Available: http://www.habervaktim.com/haber/316401/adnan-oktara-dair-hersey-2.html [Accessed 19.03.2013].

Akman, Nuriye (2004) "A Real Muslim Cannot Be a Terrorist" *fgulen.com* [Online], 20 December. Available: http://en.fgulen.com/press-room/nuriye-akmans-interview/1727-a-real-muslim-cannot-be-a-terrorist [Accessed 19.03.2013].

Akyol, Mustafa (2007) "What Made the Gülen Movement Possible?". In: Yılmaz, İhsan (ed.) *Muslim World in Transition: Contributions of the Gülen Movement.* London: Leeds Metropolitan University Press, 22–32.

Akyol, Mustafa (2011) "In Memoriam: Necmettin Erbakan". *Hurriyet Daily News* [Online], 28 February. Available: http://www.hurriyetdailynews.com/default.aspx?pageid=438&n=in-memoriam-necmettin-erbakan-2011-02-28 [Accessed 04.02.2013].

Akyol, Taha (2012) "Cemaat ve AKP". *Hürriyet* [Online], 9 April. Available: http://www.hurriyet.com.tr/yazarlar/20303198.asp [Accessed 03.03.2013].

Allah Sevgisi (2011) "The State Some Nur Students Are in as a Result of Refraining From the System of the Mahdi" [Online video]. *YouTube.* Available: http://www.youtube.com/watch?v=T5NbmSuVKmA [Accessed 19.03.2013].

Amanat, Abbas (2009) *Apocalyptic Islam and Iranian Shi'ism.* London: I. B. Tauris.

Anderson, Benedict (2006) *Imagined Communities: Reflections on the Origin and Spread of Nationalism.* London: Verso.

Anderson, Jon W. (2003) "The Internet and Islam's New Interpreters". In: Anderson, Jon W. & Eickelman, Dale F. (eds.) *New Media in the Muslim World : The Emerging Public Sphere.* Bloomington: Indiana University Press, 45–60.

Aras, Bülent (2004) "The Failure of Political Islam in Turkey". *Turkish Policy Quarterly,* 3 (1), 87–95.

Aras, Bülent & Çaha, Ömer (2000) "Fethullah Gülen and His Liberal 'Turkish Islam' Movement". *Middle East Review of International Affairs,* 4 (4), 30–42.

Araştırma Grubu (1986) *Yahudilik Ve Masonluk.* Cağaloğlu, Istanbul: Araştırma Yayınları.

Arda, Haluk (2009) "Sex, Flies and Videotape: The Bizarre Story of Creationist Cult Leader Adnan Oktar". *New Humanist,* 124 (5), 16–21.

Asad, Talal (1986) *The Idea of an Anthropology of Islam*. Washington, D.C.: Center for Contemporary Arab Studies, Georgetown University.

Aslaneli, Hakan (1999) "The Babuna Riddle". *Hürriyet*[Online], 10 March. Available: http://www.hurriyetdailynews.com/default.aspx?pageid=438&n=the-babuna-riddle-1999-10-03 [Accessed 19.03.2013].

Atik, Özlem (2012) "Adnan Hoca'ya Zorla Getirme Kararı!". *Haberturk* [Online], 18 December. Available: http://www.haberturk.com/gundem/haber/804597-adnan-hocaya-zorla-getirme-karari [Accessed 19.03.2013].

"Ayın Notları" (1990) *Altınoluk* [Online], 58 (42). Available: http://dergi.altinoluk.com/index.php?sayfa=yillar&MakaleNo=d058s042m1 [Accessed 01.03.2013].

"The Babuna Chaos" (1999). *Hürriyet Daily News* [Online], 7 November. Available: http://www.hurriyetdailynews.com/default.aspx?pageid=438&n=the-babuna-chaos-1999-07-11 [Accessed 19.03.2013].

Bali, Rıfat (1999) "The Image of the Jew in the Rhetoric of Political Islam in Turkey". *Cahiers d'Etudes sur la Méditerranée Orientale et le monde Turco-Iranien* [Online], vol. 28. Available: http://cemoti.revues.org/590 [Accessed 19.03.2013].

Bali, Rıfat (2005) "What Is Efendi Telling Us?". *Kabbalah: Journal for the Study of Jewish Mystical Texts,* 13, 119–127.

Barkun, Michael (2006) *A Culture of Conspiracy: Apocalyptic Visions in Contemporary America*. Berkeley, California: University of California Press.

Bartholomew, Richard (2005) "Hal Lindsey Puffs Kahanists at WND". *Bartholomew's Notes on Religion* [Blog]. 20 February. Available: http://barthsnotes.com/2005/02/20/hal-lindsey-puffs-kahanists-at-wnd [Accessed 19.03.2013].

Bartholomew, Richard (2009a) "'Holocaust Deception': Further Explanation". *Bartholomew's Notes on Religion* [Blog]. 18 July. Available: http://barthsnotes.com/2009/07/18/holocaust-deception-further-explanation [Accessed 31.01.2013].

Bartholomew, Richard (2009b) "Sanhedrin Makes Link with Turkish Author to Oppose 'the Unbelievers'". *Bartholomew's Notes on Religion* [Blog]. 12 July Available: http://barthsnotes.com/2009/07/12/sanhedrin-makes-link-with-turkish-author-to-oppose-the-unbelievers [Accessed 31.01.2013].

Bartholomew, Richard (2009c) "Who Wrote 'the Holocaust Deception'?". *Bartholomew's Notes on Religion* [Blog]. 17 July. Available: http://barthsnotes.com/2009/07/17/who-wrote-the-holocaust-deception [Accessed 31.01.2013].

Bauckhage, Christian (2011) "Insights into Internet Memes". *Proceedings of the 5th International Conference on Weblogs and Social Media*. Menlo Park, CA: The AAAI Press, 42–49.

Bayat, Asef (2007) *Making Islam Democratic: Social Movements and the Post-Islamist Turn*. Stanford, Calif.: Stanford University Press.

Bell, James (2012) *The World's Muslims: Unity and Diversity*. Pew Research Center Survey. Washington: Pew Research Center. Available: http://www.pewforum.org/Muslim/the-worlds-muslims-unity-and-diversity.aspx [Accessed 19.03.2013].

Benford, Robert D. & Snow, David A. (2000) "Framing Processes and Social Movements: An Overview and Assessment". *Annual Review of Sociology,* 26, 611–639.

Berger, Peter L. (1990) *The Sacred Canopy: Elements of a Sociological Theory of Religion*. New York: Anchor Books.

Bewley, Abdalhaqq & Bewley, Aisha Abdurrahman (1999) *The Noble Quran: A New Rendering of Its Meaning in English*. Norwich, England: Bookwork.

Beyaz, Zekeriya (1978) *Darwinizm'in Yıkılışı*. Istanbul: Sağduyu Yayınları.

Bierman, Til (2013) "Wenn Blondinen mit Dirndl-Figur den Koran Zitieren". *Die Welt* [Online], 4 February. Available: http://www.welt.de/kultur/article113359419/Wenn-Blondinen-mit-Dirndl-Figur-den-Koran-zitieren.html [Accessed 19.03.2013].

Bigliardi, Stefano (forthcoming 2013) "Who's Afraid of Theoscientography? Interpretive Hypothesis on Harun Yahya".

Bilgin, Tunca (2000) "Şantaj Holding A.Ş.!". *Milliyet* [Online], 31 January. Available: http://www.milliyet.com.tr/2000/01/31/haber/hab00.html [Accessed 19.03.2013].

Bilici, Mucahit (2006) "The Fethullah Gülen Movement and Its Politics of Representation in Turkey". *Muslim World*, 96 (1), 1–20.

Bilim Araştırma Grubu (1986) *Canlılar Ve Evrim*. Istanbul: Bedir Yayıncılık.

Bilim Araştırma Grubu (1993) *Yeni Dünya Düzeni'nin Gerçek Mimarları: Yehova'nın Oğulları ve Masonlar*. Istanbul: Araştırma Yayıncılık.

Bilim Araştırma Vakfı (2003) *Bilim Araştırma Vakfı Dış Politika Konferansları*. Istanbul: Bilim Araştırma Vakfı: Melisa Matbacılık.

Bilim Araştırma Vakfı (2007) "Sayın Adnan Oktar'ın Al Jazeera Televizyonuna Verdiğini Röportajın Tamamını Buradan İzleyebilirsiniz. 6 Ağustos 2007" [Online video]. *www.bilimarastirmavakfi.org*. Available: http://www.bilimarastirmavakfi.org/aljazeeraroportaj_070806.html [Accessed 19.03.2013].

Bilim Araştırma Vakfı (2013) "17. Hizmet Yılında Bilim Araştırma Vakfı" [Online]. *Bilimarastirmavakfi.org*. Available: http://www.bilimarastirmavakfi.org/html/vakif_hakkinda.html [Accessed 31.01.2013].

Bora, Tanıl (1994) "Komplo Zihniyetinin Örnek Ülkesi Türkiye". *Birikim* (90), 42–44.

Bora, Tanıl (2003) "Nationalist Discourses in Turkey". *The South Atlantic Quarterly*, 102 (2/3), 433–451.

Bora, Tanıl (2010) "Nationalist Discourses in Turkey". In: Kadıoğlu, Ayşe & Keyman, Fuat E. (eds.) *Symbiotic Antagonisms: Competing Nationalisms in Turkey*. Salt Lake City: The University of Utah Press, 57–81.

Bozarslan, Hamit (2000) "La Mahdisme En Turquie: L'Incident de Menemen' En 1930". *Revue des Mondes Musulmans et de la Méditerranée*, vol. 91–94 (July), 297–320.

Brasseur, Anne (2007) *The Dangers of Creationism in Education*. Luxembourg: Committee on Culture, Science and Education. Available: http://assembly.coe.int/ASP/Doc/XrefViewHTML.asp?FileId=11751&Language=EN [Accessed 19.03.2013].

Brekke, Torkel (2012) *Fundamentalism: Prophecy and Protest in an Age of Globalization*. Cambridge: Cambridge University Press.

Bruinessen, Martin van (2007) *Sufism and the 'Modern' in Islam*. London: IB Tauris.

"Bu Değirmenin Suyu Nereden" (1999). *Hurriyet* [Online], 13 November. Available: http://webarsiv.hurriyet.com.tr/1999/11/13/156599.asp [Accessed 19.03.2013].

Bucaille, Maurice (2003) *The Bible, the Qur'an, and Science: The Holy Scriptures Examined in the Light of Modern Knowledge*. Elmhurst, New York: Tahrike Tarsile Qur'an.

Bulaç, Ali (1983) *Kur'an-ı Kerim ve Meali*. Istanbul: Pınar Yayınları.

Burr, Vivien (2003) *Social Constructionism*. London: Routledge.

Çakır, Ruşen (1985) "Adnan Hoca'nin Kolejli Müritleri". *Nokta*.
Çakır, Ruşen (1990) *Ayet ve Slogan: Türkiye'nin İslami Oluşumlar*. Istanbul: Metis Yayınları.
Çakır, Ruşen (2005) "Yahudi Düşmanlığına Karşı Erdoğan Duruşu". *Vatan Gazetesi* [Online], 5 May. Available: http://haber.gazetevatan.com/0/52714/4/Haber [Accessed 04.02.2013].
Carvalho, Jean-Paul (2009) "A Theory of Islamic Revival". *Discussion Paper Series*, vol. 424. Department of Economics, University of Oxford.
Case, Holly (2013) "Two Rights and a Wrong: On Taner Akçam". *The Nation* [Online], April 1. Available: http://www.thenation.com/article/173325/two-rights-and-wrong-taner-akcam?page=0%2C0# [Accessed 19.03.2013]
Çengel, Yunus (2008). "Beyond the Body: Towards Understanding the True Nature of Man". Paper presented at *Conference on God, Man and Mortality from the Perspective of Said Nursi*. University of Durham, UK, 20–21 October 2008. Available: http://www.nursistudies.com/teblig.php?tno=492#_ftn1 [Accessed 30.01.2013].
Cetin, Muhammed (2010) *The Gülen Movement: Civic Service without Borders*. New York, NY: Blue Dome Press.
Chapman, Roger (2010) *Culture Wars: An Encyclopedia of Issues, Viewpoints, and Voices*. Armonk, N.Y.: M.E. Sharpe.
Cohen, Mark R. (2010) "Modern Myths of Muslim Anti-Semitism". In: Ma'oz, Moshe (ed.) *Muslim Attitudes to Jews and Israel: The Ambivalences of Rejection, Antagonism, Tolerance, and Cooperation*. Brighton: Sussex Academic, 31–47.
Cook, David (2005) *Contemporary Muslim Apocalyptic Literature*. Syracuse, N.Y.: Syracuse University Press.
"Cübbeli Ve Adnan Hoca Davalık Oldu!" (2011). *Radikal* [Online], 5 September Available: http://www.radikal.com.tr/Radikal.aspx?aType=RadikalDetayV3&ArticleID=1062350&CategoryID=77 [Accessed 19.03.2013].
Dağı, Ihsan D. (2005) "Transformation of Islamic Political Identity in Turkey: Rethinking the West and Westernization". *Turkish Studies*, 6 (1), 21–37.
Darwin, Charles (1859) *The Origin of Species by Means of Natural Selection, or, the Preservation of Favored Races in the Struggle for Life*. London: Murray
Demir, Ahmet (2005) *Hz. Mehdi'nin Çıkış Alametleri ve Özellikleri*. Istanbul: Güneş Yayıncılık.
Demiralp, Seda (2012) "White Turks, Black Turks? Faultlines beyond Islamism versus Secularism". *Third World Quarterly*, 33:3, 511–524.
Diyanet İşleri Başkanlığı (1964) *Nurculuk Hakkında*. Ankara: Resimli Posta Matbaası.
Dobzhansky, Thomas (1973) "Nothing in Biology Makes Sense except in the Light of Evolution". *The American Biology Teacher*, 35 (March), 125–129.
Dowsett, Gary Wayne (2009) "The 'Gay Plague' Revisited: Aids and Its Enduring Moral Panic". In: Herdt, Gilbert H. (ed.) *Moral Panics, Sex Panics: Fear and the Fight over Sexual Rights*. New York: New York University Press, 130–156.
Ebaugh, Helen Rose Fuchs (2009) *The Gülen Movement: A Sociological Analysis of a Civic Movement Rooted in Moderate Islam*. Dordrecht: Springer Netherland.
Edis, Taner (1999) "Cloning Creationism in Turkey". *Reports of the National Center for Science Education*, 19 (6), 30–35.
Edis, Taner (2007) *An Illusion of Harmony: Science and Religion in Islam*. Amherst, N.Y.: Prometheus Books.

Eickelman, Dale F. & Anderson, Jon W. (1997) "Print, Islam, and the Prospects for Civic Pluralism: New Religious Writings and Their Audiences". *Journal of Islamic Studies*, 8 (1), 43–62.

Eickelman, Dale F. & Anderson, Jon W. (2003) *New Media in the Muslim World: The Emerging Public Sphere*. Bloomington, Ind.: Indiana University Press.

Eickelman, Dale F. & Piscatori, James P. (2004) *Muslim Politics*. Princeton, N.J. : Princeton University Press.

Eldridge, Bruce (2007) "The Place of the Gülen Movement in the Intellectual History of Islam". In: Yılmaz, İhsan (ed.) *Muslim World in Transition: Contributions of the Gülen Movement*. London: Leeds Metropolitan University Press, 526–538.

Eligür, Banu (2010) *The Mobilization of Political Islam in Turkey*. New York: Cambridge University Press.

Eraydin, Osman (2012) "Sabahattin Önkibar ve Adnan Oktar" [Online]. *www.necmettinerbakan.net*. Available: http://www.necmettinerbakan.net/page.php?act=yaziGoster&yaziID=297&name=sabahattin-onkibar-ve-adnan-oktar [Accessed 04.02.2103].

Erdal, Büşra (2010) "Yargıtay, Adnan Oktar Hakkındaki Mahkumiyet Kararını Bozdu". *Zaman* [Online], 5 February Available: http://www.zaman.com.tr/gundem_yargitay-adnan-oktar-hakkindaki-mahk-miyet-kararini-bozdu_948301.html [Accessed 19.03.2013].

"Ergenekon'da Mason Şühpesi" (2008). *Yeni Şafak* [Online], 7 May. Available: http://yenisafak.com.tr/Gundem/Default.aspx?i=115776 [Accessed 19.03.2013].

Esposito, John L. (2003) *The Oxford Dictionary of Islam*. Oxford: Oxford University Press.

Esposito, John L. & Yilmaz, Ihsan (2010) *Islam and Peacebuilding: Gülen Movement Initiatives*. New York: Blue Dome.

European Forum on Antisemitism (2012) "Working Defintion of Antisemitism" [Online]. *European Forum on Antisemitism*. Available: http://www.european-forum-on-antisemitism.org/working-definition-of-antisemitism/english/ [Accessed 19.03.2013].

European Stability Initiative (2005) "Islamic Calvinists: Change and Conservatism and Central Anatolia" [Online]. *www.esi.org*. Available: http://www.esiweb.org/index.php?lang=en&id=156&document_ID=69 [Accessed 03.03.2013].

Fairclough (2005) "Critical Discourse Analysis". *Marges Linguistiques*, (9), 75–94.

Fairclough, Norman (2003*) Analysing Discourse: Textual Analysis for Social Research*. London; New York: Routledge.

"Fazilet Partisi Adnan Hocacıların Koruyucusu" (2000) *Cumhuriyet*. Istanbul. 5 February, p. 19.

Findley, Carter V. (2010) *Turkey, Islam, Nationalism, and Modernity*. New Haven: Yale University Press.

Futuyma, Douglas J. (1986) *Evolutionary Biology*. Sunderland, Mass.: Sinauer.

Gallup.com (2012) "Evolution, Creationism, Intelligent Design" [Online]. *Gallup, Inc*. Available: http://www.gallup.com/poll/21814/evolution-creationism-intelligent-design.aspx [Accessed 19.03.2013].

Gardet, L. (2013). " Al-Asma al-Husna". *Encyclopaedia of Islam, Second Edition*. Bearman, P., Bianquis, Th., Bosworth, C.E., Donzel, E. van & Heinrichs, W.P. (eds). Brill Online. Södertörn University College Library. Available:

http://referenceworks.brillonline.com/entries/encyclopaedia-of-islam-2/al-asma-al-husna-COM_0070 [Accessed 15.01.13].

Gerholm, Thomas (1997) "The Islamization of Contemporary Egypt". In: Evers Rosander, Eva & Westerlund, David (eds.) *African Islam and Islam in Africa: Encounters between Sufis and Islamists*. London: Hurst & Company, 127-158.

Giray, Saziya Burcu (2010) "Turkish Policy Towards the Israel-Palestinian Conflict". In: Ma'oz, Moshe (ed.) *Muslim Attitudes to Jews and Israel: The Ambivalences of Rejection, Antagonism, Tolerance, and Cooperation*. Brighton: Sussex Academic, 69–85.

Goffman, Erving (1974) *Frame Analysis: An Essay on the Organization of Experience*. New York: Harper & Row.

Göle, Nilufer (2001) "Authoritarian Secularism and Islamist Politics". In: Norton, Augustus R. (ed.) *Civil Society in the Middle East 2*. Leiden: Brill, 17–43.

Goodstein, Laurie (2005) "Judge Bars 'Intelligent Design' from PA Classes". *The New York Times* [Online], 20 December. Available: http://www.nytimes.com/2005/12/20/science/sciencespecial2/20cnd-evolution.html?_r=0 [Accessed 22.01.2013].

Gray, Matthew (2008) "Explaining Conspiracy Theories in Modern Arab Middle Eastern Political Discourse: Some Problems and Limitations of the Literature". *Critique: Critical Middle Eastern Studies* 17 (2), 155–174.

Gray, Matthew (2010) *Conspiracy Theories in the Arab World: Sources and Politics*. London: Routledge.

Griffel, Frank (2012) *Al-Ghazali's Philosophical Theology*. New York: Oxford University Press.

Grove, Thomas (2008) "Turkish Islamic Author Given 3-Year Jail Sentence". *Reuters* [Online]. Available: http://www.reuters.com/article/2008/05/09/arts-turkey-religion-sentence-dc-idUSL0992091620080509?sp=true [Accessed 19.03.2013].

Güner, Atilla (1986) "Adnan Hoca Bu Kez Tutuklandı". *Milliyet*. 4 July, p. 14.

Güven, Turan et al. (1986) *Biyoloji: Lise 1 Devlet Kitapları* Ankara: Milli Eğitim Bakanlığı.

Güzel, Cemal (2007) "Türkiye'de Maddecilik ile Maddecilik Karşıtı Görüşler". In: Gültekingil, Murat (ed.) *Modern Türkiye'de Siyasi Düşünce Cilt 8: Sol*. Istanbul: Iletişim Yayınlar, 49–66.

Haddad, Yvonne Yazbeck & Smith, Jane I. (1993) *Mission to America: Five Islamic Sectarian Communities in North America*. Gainesville: University Press of Florida.

Haddad, Yvonne Yazbeck & Smith, Jane I. (2010) "The Anti-Christ and the End of Time in Christian and Muslim Eschatological Literature". *Muslim World*, 100 (4), 505–529.

Haenni, Patrick (2005*) L'islam De Marché: L'autre Révolution Conservatrice*. Paris: Seuil

Hagemeister, Michael (2005) "The 'Protocols of the Elders of Zion' and the Myth of a Jewish Conspiracy in Post Soviet Russia". In: Brinks, Jan Herman, Rock, Stella & Timms, Edward (eds.) *Nationalist Myths and Modern Media Contested Identities in the Age of Globalisation*. London: I.B. Tauris & Co, 243–255.

Hameed, Salman (2008) "Bracing for Islamic Creationism". *Science*, 322 (5908), 1637–1638.

Hanioğlu, M. Şükrü (2012) "The Historical Roots of Kemalism". In: Kuru, Ahmet T. & Stepan, Alfred C. (eds.) *Democracy, Islam, and Secularism in Turkey*. New York: Columbia University Press, 32–60.

Haqqani, Shehnaz (2011) "Muslim Televangelists and the Construction of Religious Authority in the Modern World: The Case of Zakir Naik". Honors Thesis, Emory University, Atlanta.

"Harun Yahya Oymuş" (2000). *Hürriyet* [Online], 1 January. Available: http://webarsiv.hurriyet.com.tr/2000/01/03/168838.asp [Accessed 04.02.2013].

"'Harun Yahya' Erbakan Mi?" (2001). *Milliyet* [Online], 7 February. Available: http://www.milliyet.com.tr/2001/02/07/siyaset/siy06.html [Accessed 19.03.2013].

HarunYahyaEnglish (2011a) "Mr. Adnan Oktar: Ms. Kim Kardashian Is a Very Good-Natured and Kind Person " [Online video]. *YouTube*. Available: https://www.youtube.com/watch?v=cH8Q5cYC2EQ [Accessed 19.03.2013].

HarunYahyaEnglish (2011b) "The Solution to the PKK is the Foundation of Turkish-Islamic Union without Delay " [Online video]. *YouTube*. Available: http://www.youtube.com/watch?v=Hb7ovuhiW-k [Accessed 19.03.2013].

Helvacı, Pelin (2010) "A Critical Approach: Political Thoughts of Young Ottomans". *European Journal of Social Sciences,* 16 (3), 449–457.

Heneghan, Tom (2008a) "Harun Yahya's Islamic Creationist Book Pops up in Scotland". *FaithWorld* [Blog]. 7 April. Available: http://blogs.reuters.com/faithworld/2008/04/07/harun-yahyas-islamic-creationist-book-pops-up-in-scotland [Accessed 19.03.2013].

Heneghan, Tom (2008b) "Muslim Creationist Preaches Islam and Awaits Christ". *Reuters UK edition* [Online], 19 June. Available: http://uk.reuters.com/article/2008/06/19/us-turkey-religion-harunyahya-idUKL2926092420080619 [Accessed 19.03.2013].

Hofstadter, Richard (1965) The Paranoid Style in American Politics and Other Essays. New York: Knopf.

Hopkins, Michael (2003) "Harun Yahya and Holocaust Revisionism". *The TalkOrigins Archive: Exploring the Creation/Evolution Controversy* [Blog]. 7 December. Available: http://www.talkorigins.org/faqs/organizations/harunyahya.html [Accessed 19.03.2013].

Hoyle, Fred & Wickramasinghe, Nalin Chandra (1986) *Archaeopteryx, the Primordial Bird: A Case of Fossil Forgery.* Swansea: Christopher Davies.

Illıcak, Nazlı (2000) "Bir Yanlış Düzeltiliyor". *Yeni Şafak* [Online]. 11 February. Available: http://yenisafak.com.tr/arsiv/2000/subat/11/nilicak.html.

Ilıcak, Nazlı (2012) *Her Taşın Altında 'the Cemaat' Mı Var?* Istanbul: Doğan Kıtap.

*Imam-Hatip Liseli Öğretim Programları* (1985). T.C. Milli Eğitim Gençlik ve Spor Bakanlığı, Dinöğretim Genel Müdürlüğü. Ankara: Milli Eğitim Basımevi.

Institute for Jewish Policy Research (1999) "Turkey" [Online]. *Antisemitism and Xenophobia Today.* Available: http://www.axt.org.uk/antisem/archive/archive2/turkey/turkey.htm [Accessed 19.03.2013].

Iqbal, Muzaffar (2007) *Science and Islam.* Westport, Conn.: Greenwood Press.

Iqbal, Muzaffar (2009) "Darwin's Shadow: Context and Reception in the Muslim World". *Islam & Science,* 7 (1), 9–53.

Isaak, Mark (2005) *The Counter-Creationism Handbook.* Westport, Connecticut: Greenwood Press.

Işık, İhsan (1990) *Bediüzzaman Said Nursi ve Nurculuk.* Istanbul: Ünlem Yayınları.

"Islama Sosyetik Yorum" (1990) *Cumhuriyet.* Istanbul. 23 January, p. 19.

Ismailbakiofficial (2012) "Kedi Canını 4. Bölüm Part 1 (Ismail Baki Tv)" [Online video]. *YouTube.* Available: http://www.youtube.com/watch?v=HclV6ixjt1U [Accessed 19.03.2013].

Izlevideoo2 (2013) "Rasim Ozan Kütahyalı Adnan Oktar Kavgası" [Online video]. *YouTube.com*. Available: http://www.youtube.com/watch?v=ps362dC4wSE [Accessed 19.03.2013].

Janson, Torsten (2002) *Invitation to Islam: A History of Da'wa*. Uppsala: Swedish Science Press.

Jenkins, Gareth (2011) "Ergenekon, Sledgehammer, and the Politics of Turkish Justice: Conspiracies and Coincindences". *Meria,* 15 (2). Available: http://www.gloria-center.org/2011/08/ergenekon-sledgehammer-and-the-politics-of-turkish-justice-conspiracies-and-coincidences [19.03.2013].

"Joint Press Conference of Mr Adnan Oktar with Israeli Delegation" (2011) [Online video]. *harunyahya.com*. Available: http://harunyahya.com/en/Adnan-Oktarin-Sohbet-programlari/42045/Joint-press-conference-of-Mr-Adnan-Oktar-with-Israeli-Delegation-%28May-12-2011%29 [Accessed 25.02.2013].

Jonker, Gerdien (2005) "The Transformation of a Sufi Order into a Lay Community: The Süleymancı Movement in Germany and Beyond". In: Cesari, Jocelyne & McLoughlin, Sean (eds.) *European Muslims and the Secular State*. Aldershot: Ashgate, 169–182.

Kadıoğlu, Ayşe (1996) "The Paradox of Turkish Nationalism and the Construction of Official Identity". *Middle Eastern Studies,* 32 (2), 177–193.

Kalın, Ibrahim (2002) "Three Views of Science in the Islamic World". In: Peters, Ted, Iqbal, Muzaffar & Haq, Syed Nomanul (eds.) *God, Life, and the Cosmos: Christian and Islamic Perspectives*. Aldershot, Burlington: Ashgate, 43–75.

Kanra, Bora (2009*) Islam, Democracy, and Dialogue in Turkey: Deliberating in Divided Societies*. Farnham, Surrey; Burlington, VT: Ashgate Pub.

Karpat, Kemal H. (2000) *Ottoman Past and Today's Turkey*. Leiden: Brill.

Kazdağlı, Güneş (2001) *Atatürk ve Bilim*. Ankara: TÜBİTAK Yayınları.

Khaldun, Ibn (1967) *The Muqaddimah: An Introduction to History,* vol. 1. London: Routledge.

Kitiarsa, Pattana (2010) "Toward a Sociology of Religious Commodification". In: Turner, Bryan S. (ed.) *The New Blackwell Companion to the Sociology of Religion*. Chisester, West Sussex: Wile-Blackwell, 563–583.

Knight, Chris & Lomas, Robert (1997) *The Hiram Key: Pharaohs, Freemasons and the Discovery of the Secret Scrolls of Jesus*. London: Arrow.

Koenig, Robert (2001) "Creationism Takes Root Where Europe, Asia Meet". *Science,* 292 (5530), 1286–1287.

"Komünistlerle Mason Locaları Komplo Kurdu" (2000) *Cumhuriyet*. Istanbul. 8 April, p. 7.

Kotan, Betül (2006) "Bakan Çelik: Yaratılış Aynen Kalacak". *Radikal* [Online], 5 March. Available: http://www.radikal.com.tr/haber.php?haberno=180408 [Accessed 19.03.2013].

Kuru, Ahmet T. (2007) "Changing Perspectives on Islamism and Secularism in Turkey: The Gülen Movement and the AK Party". In: Yılmaz, İhsan (ed.) *Muslim World in Transition: Contributions of the Gülen Movement*. London: Leeds Metropolitan University Press, 140–151.

Kuypers, Jim A. (2009) *Rhetorical Criticism: Perspectives in Action*. Lanham, MD: Lexington Books.

Kuypers, Jim A. (2010) "Framing Analysis from a Rhetorical Perspective". In: D'angelo, Paul & Kuypers, Jim A. (eds.) *Doing News Framing Analysis*. New York: Routledge.

Laçiner, Sedat (2009) "Turgut Özal Period in Turkish Foreign Policy: Özalism". *USAK Yearbook of International Politics and Law,* 2, 153–205.

Lamarck, Jean Baptiste (1809) *Philosophie Zoologique*. Oxford.
Landes, Richard Allen (2000) *Encyclopedia of Millennialism and Millennial Movements*. New York: Routledge.
Lapidus, Ira M. (2002) *A History of Islamic Societies*. Cambridge: Cambridge University Press.
Lauria, Joe (2010) "Reclusive Turkish Imam Criticizes Flotilla". *Wall Street Journal* [Online], 4 June. Available: http://online.wsj.com/article/SB10001424052748704025304575284721280274694.html [Accessed 03.03.2013].
Lazarus-Yafeh, Hava (2013). "Tahrif". *Encyclopaedia of Islam, Second Edition*. Bearman, P., Bianquis, Th., Bosworth, C.E. & Heinrichs, W.P. (eds). Brill Online. Södertörn University College Library. Available: http://referenceworks.brillonline.com/entries/encyclopaedia-of-islam-2/tahrif-SIM_7317 [Accessed 30.01.2013].
Levitt, Peggy, Bender, Courtney, Smilde, David & Cadge, Wendy (2010) "Toward a New Sociology of Religion". *The Immanent Frame: Secularism, religion and the public sphere* [Blog]. 15 February. Available: http://blogs.ssrc.org/tif/2010/02/15/new-sociology-of-religion/ [Accessed 19.03.2013
Lewis, Bernard (1961) *The Emergence of Modern Turkey*. London: Oxford University Press.
Lewis, Bernard (1998) "Muslim Anti-Semitism". *The Middle East Quarterly*, 5 (2), 43–49.
Lewis, James R. (ed.) (2004) *The Oxford Handbook of New Religious Movements*, New York: Oxford University Press.
Lewis, James R. & Hammer, Olav (2011) *Handbook of Religion and the Authority of Science*. Leiden: Brill.
Lumbard, Joseph & Nayed, Aref Ali (eds.) (2010) *The 500 Most Influential Muslims 2010*. Amman: The Royal Islamic Strategic Studies Centre.
Ma'oz, Moshe (2010) *Muslim Attitudes to Jews and Israel: The Ambivalences of Rejection, Antagonism, Tolerance and Cooperation*. Brighton: Sussex Academic.
Madelung, Wilfred (2010). "Al-Mahdi". *Encyclopaedia of Islam, Second Edition*. Bearman, P., Bianquis, Th., Bosworth, C.E., Donzel, E. van & Heinrichs, W.P. (eds). Brill Online. Södertörn University College Library. Available: http://www.brillonline.nl/subscriber/entry?entry=islam_COM-0618 [Accessed 19.11.2012].
Madelung, Wilfred (2013). "Al-Sufyani". *Encyclopaedia of Islam, Second Edition*. Bearman, P., Bianquis, Th., Bosworth, C.E., Donzel, E. van & Heinrichs, W.P. (eds). Brill Online. Södertörn University College Library. Available: http://referenceworks.brillonline.com/entries/encyclopaedia-of-islam-2/al-sufyani-SIM_8902 [Accessed 19.03.2013].
Mandaville, Peter G. (2001) *Transnational Muslim Politics: Reimagining the Umma*. London: Routledge.
Mandaville, Peter G. (2007) *Global Political Islam*. New York, N.Y.: Routledge.
Mandel, Jonah (2011) "Interfaith Delegation Travels to Istanbul". *Jerusalem Post* [Online], 5 April. Available: http://www.jpost.com/JewishWorld/JewishNews/Article.aspx?id=219092 [Accessed 01.03.13].
Mardin, Serif (1989) *Religion and Social Change in Modern Turkey: The Case of Bediüzzaman Said Nursi*. Albany: State University of New York Press.
Mardin, Serif (2005) "Turkish Islamic Exceptionalism Yesterday and Today: Continuity, Rupture and Reconstruction in Operational Codes". *Turkish Studies*, 6 (2), 145–165.

Marty, Martin E. & Appleby, R. Scott (1991) *The Fundamentalism Project*. Chicago: University of Chicago Press.

"The Masons' Single Eye Is the Symbol of the Antichrist" [Online] (2009). *Freemasonsandtheirerrors.blog.com*. Available: http://freemasonsandtheirerrors.blog.com/2010/05/01/the-masons-single-eye-symbol-is-the-symbol-of-the-antichrist [Accessed 19.03.2013].

Mayr, Ernst (1997) *This Is Biology: The Science of the Living World*. Cambridge, MA: The Belknap Press of Harvard University Press.

Mayr, Ernst (2001) *What Evolution Is*. New York: Basic Books.

McCalla, Arthur (2007) "Creationism". *Religion Compass*, 1 (5), 547–560.

McCutcheon, Russell T. (2003) *The Discipline of Religion: Structure, Meaning, Rhetoric*. London: Taylor & Francis Ltd.

Meeker, Michael E. (1994) "The New Muslim Intellectuals in the Republic of Turkey". In: Tapper, Richard (ed.) *Islam in Modern Turkey: Religion, Politics, and Literature in a Secular State*. London: I.B. Taurus, 189–219.

Mermer, Yamine & Ameur, Redha (2004) "Beyond the 'Modern': Said al-Nursi's View of Science". *Islam & Science*, 2 (2), 119–160.

Meyer, David S. (2003) "Political Opportunity and Nested Institutions". *Social Movement Studies*, 2 (1), 17–35.

Miller, Jon D., Scott, Eugenie C. & Okamoto, Shinji (2006) "Public Acceptance of Evolution". *Science*, 313 (765), 765–766.

Miller, Kenneth R. (2008) *Only a Theory: Evolution and the Battle for America's Soul*. New York: Viking Penguin.

"Milyonlarca Yıllık Fosiller Yaratılış Müzesinde" (2006). *Milli Gazete* [Online], March 12. Available: http://www.milligazete.com.tr/haber/Milyonlarca_yillik_fosiller_yaratilis_muzesinde/18657#.UPm7G-h_Sb0 [Accessed 23.01.2013].

Moaddel, Mansoor (2005) *Islamic Modernism, Nationalism, and Fundamentalism: Episode and Discourse*. Chicago: University of Chicago Press.

Moran, Laurence (1993) "Evolution Is a Fact and a Theory". *The TalkOrigins Archive* [Blog]. 22 January. Available: http://www.talkorigins.org/faqs/evolution-fact.html [Accessed 19.03.2013].

Morris, Henry M. (1974) *Scientific Creationism*. San Diego, Calif.: Creation-Life Publishers.

Mullenweg, Matt (2007) "Why We're Blocked in Turkey: Adnan Oktar". *WordPress.com* [Blog]. 19 August. Available: http://en.blog.wordpress.com/2007/08/19/why-were-blocked-in-turkey [Accessed 19.03.2013].

Navaro-Yashin, Yael (2002) *Faces of the State: Secularism and Public Life in Turkey*. Princeton: Princeton University Press.

Nefes, Türkay S. (2012) "The History of the Social Constructions of Dönmes (Converts)". *Journal of Historical Sociology*, 25 (3), 413–439.

"Nihayet" (1999). *Hürriyet* [Online], 13 November Available: http://webarsiv.hurriyet.com.tr/1999/11/13/156483.asp [Accessed 19.03.2013].

Numbers, Ronald L. (1999) "Creating Creatonism: Meaning and Uses since the Age of Agassiz". In: Livingstone, David N. (ed.) *Evangelicals and Science in Historical Perspective*. New York: Oxford University Press, 234–243.

Numbers, Ronald L. (2006) *The Creationists: From Scientific Creationism to Intelligent Design*. Cambridge, Mass.: Harvard University Press.

Nursi, Said (2004a) *Emirdağ Lahikası*. Istanbul: Söz Basim Yayin.
Nursi, Said (2004b) *Kastamonu Lahikası*. Istanbul: Söz Basim Yayin.
Nursi, Said (1996) *The Damascus Sermon*. Istanbul: Sözler Neşriyat.
Nursi, Said (1998) *The Rays Collection*. Cağaloğlu, Istanbul: Sözler Nesriyat.
O'Leary, Stephen D. (1994) *Arguing the Apocalypse: A Theory of Millennial Rhetoric*. New York: Oxford University Press.
Oktar, Adnan (2011) *How Did the Dajjal Die?* Istanbul: Global Publishing.
Olsson, Susanne (2013) Preaching Islamic Revival: 'Amr Khaled, Mass Media and Social Change in Egypt. London: IB Tauris.
Öncü, Ayşe (2012) "Television and Media". In: Heper, Metin & Sayarı, Sabri (eds.) *The Routledge Handbook of Modern Turkey*. London: Routledge, 125–135.
Ortega, Tony (2005) "Your Official Program to the Scopes II Kansas Monkey Trial". Pitch News [Online], 5 May. Available: http://www.pitch.com/kansascity/your-official-program-to-the-scopes-ii-kansas-monkey-trial/Content?oid=2177607 [Accessed 19.03.2013].
Özdalga, Elisabeth (1998) The Veiling Issue: Official Secularism and Popular Islam in Modern Turkey. Richmond: Curzon.
Özdalga, Elisabeth (2000) "Worldly Asceticism in Islamic Casting: Fethullah Gülen's Inspired Piety and Activism". *Critique: Critical Middle Eastern Studies*, 9 (17), 83–104.
Özervarli, M. Sait (2003) "Said Nursi's Project of Revitalizing Muslim Thought". In: Abu-Rabi', Ibrahim M. (ed.) *Islam at the Crossroads: On the Life and Thought of Bediuzzaman Said Nursi*. Albany: State University of New York Press, 317–334.
Özgürel, Avni (1998) "Mürteci Mi, Çağdaş Müslüman Mı?". *Radikal* [Online], 21 June. Available: http://www.radikal.com.tr/1998/06/21/turkiye/murteci.html [Accessed 03.03.2013].
Özkan, Tuncay (2000) "Adnan Hoca ve Sessizler". *Radikal* [Online], 14 January. Available: http://www.radikal.com.tr/2000/01/14/t/yorum/adn.shtml [Accessed 19.03.2013].
Özkırımlı, Umut & Sofos, Spyros A. (2008) *Tormented by History: Nationalism in Greece and Turkey*. New York: Columbia University Press.
PACE (2007) "Resolution 1580" [Online]. *Council of Europe*. Available: http://assembly.coe.int/main.asp?link=/documents/adoptedtext/ta07/eres1580.htm [Accessed 19.03.2013].
Pandya, Sophia (2012) "Mahdi of Sudan (1844–1885)". In: Juergensmeyer, Mark & Roof, Wade C. (eds.), *Encyclopedia of Global Religion*. Thousand Oaks, CA: SAGE Publications, 739–740.
Pandya, Sophia & Gallagher, Nancy Elizabeth (2012) *The Gülen Hizmet Movement and Its Transnational Activities: Case Studies of Altruistic Activism in Contemporary Islam*. Boca Raton: BrownWalker Press.
Pipes, Daniel (1996) The *Hidden Hand: Middle East Fears of Conspiracy*. Basingstoke: Macmillan.
Poulton, Hugh (1997) *Top Hat, Grey Wolf and Crescent: Turkish Nationalism and the Turkish Republic*. London: Hurst.
Poyraz, Ergün (2007) *Musa'nin Çocukları* Istanbul: Togan Yayıncılık.
Riexinger, Martin (2002) "The Islamic Creationism of Harun Yahya". *ISIM Newsletter*, 11, p. 5.
Riexinger, Martin (2008) "Propagating Islamic Creationism on the Internet". *Masaryk University Journal of Law and Technology*, 2 (2), 99–112.

Riexinger, Martin (2009) "Die verinnerlichte Schöpfungsordnung: Weltbild und normative Konzepte in den Werken Said Nursis (Gest. 1960) und der Nur Cemaati". Habilitationsschrift, Georg-August Universität Göttingen, Göttingen.

Riexinger, Martin (2011) "Islamic Opposition to the Darwinian Theory of Evolution". In: Lewis, James R & Hammer, Olav (eds.) *Handbook of Religion and the Authority of Science*. Leiden: Brill, 483–510.

Riexinger, Martin (forthcoming) "Why in Turkey? The Emergence of Islamic Creationism".

Ritzer, George & Goodman, Douglas J. (2004) *Modern Sociological Theory*. Boston: McGraw-Hill.

Roy, Olivier (2004) *Globalised Islam: The Search for a New Ummah*. London: Hurst.

Roy, Olivier (2006) "Islam in Europe: Clash of Religions or Convergence of Religiosities?". In: Krzysztof, Michalski (ed.) *Religion in the New Europe*. Budapest: Central European University Press, 131–144.

Ruse, Michael (2007) "Creationism". *The Stanford Encyclopedia of Philosophy*. [Online] Metaphysics Research Lab, Stanford University. Available: http://plato.stanford.edu/entries/creationism [Accessed 19.03.2013].

Salman, Umay Aktaş & Saymaz, Ismail (2006) "Yaratılış Müzesi Skandalı". *Radikal* [Online], March 11. Available: http://www.radikal.com.tr/haber.php?haberno=181049 [Accessed 22.01.2013].

Salt, Jeremy (1995) "Nationalism and the Rise of Muslim Sentiment in Turkey". *Middle Eastern Studies*, 31 (1), 13–27.

Samuel, Geoffrey & Rozario, Santi (2010) "Contesting Science for Islam: The Media as a Source of Revisionist Knowledge in the Lives of Young Bangladeshis". *Contemporary South Asia*, 18 (4), 427–441.

Sarıkaya, Ercan (2006) "Adnan Hoca'cı Evlat Rezilliği". *Haberturk* [Online], 1 November. Available: http://www.haberturk.com/gundem/haber/4446-adnan-hocaci-evlat-rezilligi [Accessed 19.03.2013].

Saritoprak, Zeki (1997) "The Mahdi Question According to Bediuzzaman Said Nursi". Paper presented at *Third International Symposium on Beduizzaman Said Nursi: The Reconstruction of Islamic Thought in the Twentieth Century and Beddiuzaman Said Nursi*, 24–26 September 1995, Istanbul. Available: http://www.nursistudies.com/teblig.php?tno=324 [Accessed 19.03.2013].

Saritoprak, Zeki (2011) "Nursi on Theodicy and the Problem of Evil" [Online]. *Nursi Studies*. Available: www.nursistudies.com/teblig.php?tno=491 [Accessed 19.03.2013].

Sayin, Ümit & Kence, Aykut (1999) "Islamic Scientific Creationism: A New Challenge in Turkey". *Report of the National Center for Science Education*, 19 (6), 18–20, 25–29.

Schönig, Hannelore (1990) "Aids Als Das Tier (Dabba) Der Islamischen Eschatologie: Zur Argumentation Einer Türkischen Schrift". *Die Welt des Islams*, 30 (1/4), 211–218.

Schrode, Paula (2008) "The Dynamics of Orthodoxy and Heterodoxy in Uyghur Religious Practice". *Die Welt des Islams*, 48 (3-4), 394–433.

Scott, Eugenie C. & Branch, Glenn (2003) "Evolution: What's Wrong with 'Teaching the Controversy'". *Trends in Ecology & Evolution*, 18 (10), 499–502.

Scott, Eugenie Carol & Eldredge, Niles (2009) *Evolution Vs. Creationism: An Introduction*. Westport, Connecticut; London: Greenwood Press.

Siddique, Haroon (2013) "Hugo Chávez Will 'Return on Resurrection Day', Says Ahmadinejad". *The Guardian* [Online], 6 March. Available:

http://www.guardian.co.uk/world/2013/mar/06/hugo-chavez-return-resurrection-ahmadinejad [Accessed 10.03.2013].

Sisler, Vit (2007) "The Internet and the Construction of Islamic Knowledge in Europe". *Masaryk University Journal of Law and Technology,* 1 (2), 205–217.

Snow, David A. & Benford, Robert D. (1988) "Ideology, Frame Resonance, and Participant Mobilization". In: Klandermans, Bert, Kriesi, Hanspeter & Tarrow, Sidney G. (eds.) *From Structure to Action: Comparing Social Movement Research across Cultures.* Greenwich: CT: JAI Press, 197–217.

Snow, David A., Soule, Sarah Anne & Kriesi, Hanspeter (2004) *The Blackwell Companion to Social Movements.* Malden, MA: Blackwell Publications.

Solberg, Anne Ross (2007) "The Role of Turkish Islamic Networks in the Western Balkans". *Südost Europa,* 55 (4), 429–462.

Spetner, Lee M. (1998) Not by Chance!: Shattering the Modern Theory of Evolution. New York: Judaica Press.

Stack, George J. (1998) "Materialism". *Routledge Encyclopedia of Philosophy,* vol. 6. New York: Routledge, pp. 170–173.

Stenberg, Leif (1996) *The Islamization of Science: Four Muslim Positions Developing an Islamic Modernity.* Stockholm: Almqvist & Wiksell International.

Stowasser, Barbara Freyer (2003) "The Apocalypse in the Teachings of Bediuzzaman Said Nursi". In: Abu-Rabi', Ibrahim M. (ed.) *Islam at the Crossroads: On the Life and Thought of Bediuzzaman Said Nursi.* Albany: State University of New York Press, 229–235.

Sutton, Philip W. & Vertigans, Stephen (2005) *Resurgent Islam: A Sociological Approach.* Cambridge: Polity.

"Taktik Atatürkçülük" (1999). *Hürriyet* [Online], 25 November. Available: http://hurarsiv.hurriyet.com.tr/goster/ShowNew.aspx?id=-115370.

Tapper, Richard (1994) Islam in Modern Turkey: Religion, Politics, and Literature in a Secular State. London: I.B. Tauris

Tatari, Eren (2007) "Review Essay: Islamic Social and Political Movements in Turkey". *American Journal of Islamic Social Sciences,* 24 (2), 94–106.

Theunissen, Lionel (1997) "Patterson Misquoted: A Tale of Two Cities" [Online]. *The TalkOrigins Archive.* Available: http://www.talkorigins.org/faqs/patterson.html [Accessed 19.03.2013].

Turam, Berna (2007) *Between Islam and the State: The Politics of Engagement.* Stanford, Calif.: Stanford University Press.

Turner, Bryan S. (2007) "Religious Authority and the New Media". *Theory, Culture & Society,* 24, 117–134.

Uçar, Orkun & Turna, Burak (2004) *Metal Fırtına.* Istanbul: Timaş Yayınları.

Uğur, Etga (2004) "Intellectual Roots of 'Turkish Islam,' and Approaches to the 'Turkish Model'". *Journal of Muslim Minority Affairs,* 24 (2), 327–345.

Uzer, Umut (2010) "The Geneology of Turkish Nationalism". In: Kadıoğlu, Ayşe & Keyman, Fuat E. (eds.) *Symbiotic Antagonisms: Competing Nationalisms in Turkey.* Salt Lake City: The University of Utah Press.

Vahide, Sükran (2005*) Islam in Modern Turkey: An Intellectual Biography of Bedüizzaman Said Nursi.* Albany: State University of New York Press.

Vahiterek (2010) "Adnan Oktar Gerçeği - Tuncay Güney Anlatıyor" [Online video]. YouTube. Available: http://www.youtube.com/watch?v=ZMgkhd4yq1w [Accessed 19.03.2013].

*Valley of the Wolves: Iraq* (2006) [Motion picture]. Directed by Akar, Serdar. Turkey: Arsenal Pictures.

van Donzel, Emeri & Ott, Claudia (2013). "Yadjudj Wa-Madjudj". *Encyclopaedia of Islam, Second Edition.* Bearman, P., Bianquis, Th., Bosworth, C.E., Donzel, E. van & Heinrichs, W.P. (eds). Brill Online. Södertörn University College Library. Available: http://referenceworks.brillonline.com/entries/encyclopaedia-of-islam-2/yadjudj-wa-madjudj-COM_1353 [Accessed 19.03.2013].

Van Huyssteen, J. Wentzel (ed.) (2003) *Encyclopedia of Science and Religion.* New York: Macmillan Reference.

Varisco, Daniel M. (2012) "Harun Yahya: Abusing Islam to Spread Creationism". *Mideast Posts* [Online], 13 June. Available: http://mideastposts.com/middle-east-society/harun-yahya-abusing-islam-to-spread-creationist-myth [Accessed 19.03.2013].

Varisco, Daniel M. (2013) "Harun's Houris". *Tabsir.net* [Blog]. 27 May. Available: http://tabsir.net/?p=2076 [Accessed 19.03.20132013].

voithandwabco (2011) "Adnan Oktar Very Big Cat" [Online video]. *YouTube.* Available: http://www.youtube.com/watch?v=fO7cMvdZBAw [Accessed 19.03.2013].

Webb, Edward (2007) "Civilizing Religion: Jacobin Projects of Secularization in Turkey, France, Tunisia, and Syria". PhD dissertation, University of Pennsylvania, Philadelphia.

Whitcomb, John Clement & Morris, Henry M. (1961) *The Genesis Flood: The Biblical Record and Its Scientific Implications.* Philadelphia: P & R Publishing Co.

White, Jenny B. (2005) "The End of Islamism? Turkey's Muslimhood Model". In: Hefner, Robert W. (ed.) *Remaking Muslim Politics: Pluralism, Contestation, Democratization.* Princeton, N.J.: Princeton University Press.

White, Jenny B. (2012) "Adnan Oktar's Anti-Evolution Showgirls". *Kamil Pasha* [Blog]. 22 November. Available: http://kamilpasha.com/?p=6386 [Accessed 19.032013].

Wigen, Einar (2011) "Tyrkisk Utenrikspolitikk i Populærkulturen [Turkish Foreign Policy in Popular Culture]". *Babylon – Nordic Journal of Middle Eastern Studies,* 9 (1), 70–81.

Wiktorowicz, Quintan (2004) *Islamic Activism: A Social Movement Theory Approach.* Bloomington, Indiana Indiana University Press.

Yahya, Harun (1987a) *Aids Kuran'da Bahsi Geçen Dabbet-ul-Arz Mı?* Istanbul: Fersat Yayınevi.

Yahya, Harun (1987b) *Yahudilik Ve Masonluk.* Istanbul: Acar Reklam Yayınları.

Yahya, Harun (1989) *Mehdi ve Altın Çag: İslam'in Dünya Hakimiyeti.* Cağaloğlu, Istanbul: Nasajans.

Yahya, Harun (1995a) *Soykırım Yalanı: Siyonist-Nazi Işbirliğinin Gizli Tarihi ve "Yahudi Soykırımı" Yalanının Içyüzü.* Istanbul: Alem.

Yahya, Harun (1995b) *Soykırım Yalanı: Siyonist-Nazi Işbirliğinin Gizli Tarihi ve "Yahudi Soykırımı" Yalanının Içyüzü.* Istanbul: Dergah Offset.

Yahya, Harun (1996a) *Türkiye İçin Milli Strateji: Türk Dış Politikasına Osmanlı Vizyonu ile Yeni Bir Bakiş.* Cağaloğlu, Istanbul: Vural Yayıncılık.

Yahya, Harun (1996b) *Yeni Masonik Düzen: Dünyanın 500 Yıllık Gerçek Tarihi ve Dünya Düzeninin Gizli Yöneticileri.* 1st ed. Kültür Yayıncılık.

Yahya, Harun (1997a) *Evrim Aldatmacası: Evrim Teorisinin Bilimsel Çöküşü ve Teorinin Ideolojik Arka Planı*. Istanbul: Vural Yayıncılık.
Yahya, Harun (1997b) *Israil'in Kürt Karti: Israil'in Ortadoğu Stratejisi ve "Kürt Devleti" Senaryolari*. Cağaloğlu, Istanbul: Vural Yayıncılık.
Yahya, Harun (1999a) *Evolution Deceit: The Scientific Collapse of Darwinism and Its Ideological Background*. London: Ta-Ha Publishers Ltd.
Yahya, Harun (1999b) *Hazret İsa Gelecek*. Istanbul: Vural Yayıncılık.
Yahya, Harun (2000a) *Devlet'e Bağlılığın Önemi*. Istanbul Araştırma Yayıncılık.
Yahya, Harun (2000b) *Milli Birliğin Önemi*. Istanbul: Vural Yayıncılık.
Yahya, Harun (2000c) *The Miracle in the Ant*. New Delhi: GoodWord Books.
Yahya, Harun (2000d) *Ölüm, Kıyamet, Cehennem*. Istanbul: Vural Publishing.
Yahya, Harun (2001a) *Ahir Zaman Ve Dabbetü'l-Arz*. Istanbul Araştırma Yayıncılık.
Yahya, Harun (2001b) *Altınçağ*. Istanbul: Araştırma Yayınlar.
Yahya, Harun (2001c) *The Evolution Deceit: The Scientific Collapse of Darwinism and Its Ideological Background*. London: Ta-Ha Publishers Ltd.
Yahya, Harun (2001d) *Gerçek Atatürkçülük*. Istanbul: Araştırma Yayıncılık.
Yahya, Harun (2001e) *İslam Terörü Lanetler*. Istanbul: Kültür Yayıncılık.
Yahya, Harun (2001f) *İslam'in Kışı ve Beklenen Bahari*. Istanbul: Kültür Yayıncılık.
Yahya, Harun (2001g) *Jesus Will Return*. 1st ed. London: Ta-Ha Publishers Ltd.
Yahya, Harun (2001h) *Kehf Suresi'nden Ahir Zamana İşaretler*. Istanbul: Kültür Yayincilik.
Yahya, Harun (2001i) *Miracle in the Atom*. London: Ta-Ha Publishers Ltd.
Yahya, Harun (2001j) *Miracles of the Qur'an*. Toronto: Al-Attique Publishers Inc.
Yahya, Harun (2001k) *Türk'ün Yüksek Seciyesi*. Istanbul: Araştırma Yayıncılık.
Yahya, Harun (2002a) *Asker Atatürk*. Istanbul: Araştırma Yayıncılık.
Yahya, Harun (2002b) *Atatürk Ansiklopedisi* vol. 1. Istanbul: Araştırma Yayıncılık.
Yahya, Harun (2002c) *Atatürk ve Gençlik*. Istanbul: Araştırma Yayıncılık.
Yahya, Harun (2002d) *Atatürk'ü İyi Anlamak*. Istanbul: Araştırma Yayıncılık.
Yahya, Harun (2002e) *Atatürk'ün Vatan ve Millet Sevgisi*. Istanbul: Araştırma Yayıncılık.
Yahya, Harun (2002f) *Death, Resurrection, Hell*. New Dehli: Goodword Books.
Yahya, Harun (2002g) *The Evolution Deceit: The Scientific Collapse of Darwinism and Its Ideological Background*. Istanbul: Araştırma Publishing
Yahya, Harun (2002h) *Fascism: The Bloody Ideology of Darwinism*. Turkey: Araştırma Yayınları.
Yahya, Harun (2002i) *Global Impact of the Works of Harun Yahya* vol. 1. Istanbul: Araştırma Publishing.
Yahya, Harun (2002j) *Global Masonluk*. 1st ed. Istanbul: Araştırma Yayıncılık.
Yahya, Harun (2002k) *Islam Denounces Terrorism*. Istanbul: Araştırma Publishing.
Yahya, Harun (2002l) *Kıyamet Alametleri*. Istanbul: Araştırma Yayıncılık.
Yahya, Harun (2002m) *Matter: The Other Name for Illusion*. Istanbul: Kultur Publishers.
Yahya, Harun (2002n) *Samimi Bir Dindar Atatürk*. Istanbul: Araştırma Yayıncılık.
Yahya, Harun (2002o) *Siyonizm Felsefesi*. Istanbul: Kültür Yayincilik.
Yahya, Harun (2002p) *Soykırım Vahşeti*. Istanbul: Vural Yayıncılık.
Yahya, Harun (2002q) *Tapınak Şövalyerleri*. 1st ed. Istanbul: Araştırma Yayıncılık.
Yahya, Harun (2002r) *Türk'ün Şanlı Tarihi*. Istanbul: Kültür Yayıncılık.
Yahya, Harun (2002s) *Yeni Masonik Düzen: Dünyanın 500 Yıllık Gerçek Tarihi ve Dünya Düzeninin Gizli Yöneticileri*. 4th ed. Istanbul: Kültür Yayincilik.
Yahya, Harun (2003a) *Atatürk Ansiklopedisi* vol. 2. Istanbul: Araştırma Yayıncılık.

Yahya, Harun (2003b) *The Dark Clan*. Delhi: M.Wajihuddin.
Yahya, Harun (2003c) *The Day of Judgment*. Istanbul: Global Publishing.
Yahya, Harun (2003d) *A Definitive Reply to Evolutionist Propaganda*. Global Publishing.
Yahya, Harun (2003e) *The End Times and the Mahdi*. Clarksville, Maryland: Khatoons Inc.
Yahya, Harun (2003f) *Gelin Birlik Olalim*. Istanbul: Araştırma Yayıncılık.
Yahya, Harun (2003g) *The Golden Age*. Kuala Lumpur: A.S. Nordeen.
Yahya, Harun (2003h) *Hz. İsa (as)'in Geliş Alametleri*. Istanbul: Araştırma Yayıncılık.
Yahya, Harun (2003i) Idealism, the Philosophy of the Matrix and the True Nature of Matter. Istanbul: Global Publishing.
Yahya, Harun (2003j) *İsrail'in Dünya Egemenliği Politikası*. Istanbul: Araştırma Yayıncılık.
Yahya, Harun (2003k) *İsrail'in Kürt Kartı: İsrail'in Ortadoğu Stratejisi ve "Kürt Devleti" Senaryolari*. 3rd ed. Istanbul: Vural Yayıncılık.
Yahya, Harun (2003l) *Jesus Will Return*. London: Ta-Ha Publishers.
Yahya, Harun (2003m) *Kıyamet Günü*. Istanbul: Araştırma Yayıncılık.
Yahya, Harun (2003n) *Mesih Müjdesi*. Istanbul: Araştırma Yayıncılık.
Yahya, Harun (2003o) *The Religion of Darwinism: A Pagan Doctrine from Ancient Times Prevalent until Today*. Jeddah, Saudi Arabia: Abul-Qasim Publishing House.
Yahya, Harun (2003p) *Signs of the End Times in Surat Al-Kahf*. New Dehli: Goodword Books.
Yahya, Harun (2003q) *Signs of the Last Day*. Istanbul: Global Publishing.
Yahya, Harun (2003r) *Türk-İslam Birliğine Çağrı*. Istanbul: Araştırma Yayıncılık.
Yahya, Harun (2003s) *Türkiye'nin Geleceğinde Osmanlı Vizyonu*. Istanbul: Nesil Matbaacılık.
Yahya, Harun (2004a) *A Call to an Islamic Union*. Istanbul: Global Publishing.
Yahya, Harun (2004b) *The Glad Tidings of the Messiah*. Istanbul: Global Publishing.
Yahya, Harun (2004c) *The Signs of Jesus' Second Coming*. Istanbul: Global Publishing.
Yahya, Harun (2005a) *Soykırım Vahşeti*. Istanbul: Araştırma Yayıncılık.
Yahya, Harun (2005b) *Prophet Solomon*. Istanbul: Global Publishing
Yahya, Harun (2006a) *The Holocaust Violence*. Istanbul: Global Publishing.
Yahya, Harun (2006b) *Tapınakçılar ve Masonlar*. 2nd ed. Istanbul: Araştırma Yayıncılık.
Yahya, Harun (2006c) *Miracle in the Eye*. Istanbul: Global Publishing
Yahya, Harun (2007a) *Atlas of Creation* vol. 1. Istanbul: Global Publishing.
Yahya, Harun (2007b) *The Global Impact of the Works of Harun Yahya* vol. 2. Istanbul: Global Publishing.
Yahya, Harun (2007c) *The Importance of Alh Al-Sunna*. Istanbul: Global Publishing.
Yahya, Harun (2007d) "'Intelligent Design' Distraction" [Online]. *harunyahya.com*. Available: http://harunyahya.com/en/works/4311/intelligent-design-distraction [Accessed 19.03.2013].
Yahya, Harun (2007e) *Kabala ve Masonluk*. Istanbul: Araştırma Yayıncılık.
Yahya, Harun (2007f) "Life and Works of Adnan Oktar" [Online]. *Harunyahya.com*. Available: http://harunyahya.com/bilgi/yazarHakkinda [Accessed 19.03.2013].
Yahya, Harun (2007g) *Portents and Features of the Mahdi's Coming*. Istanbul Global Publishing.
Yahya, Harun (2008a) "Adnan Oktar Replies to Foreign Press Questions at Ciragan Palace (18 September 2008)" [Online video]. *Harunyahya.com*. Available: http://harunyahya.com/en/Harun-Yahyas-Interviews-and-Conversations/40601/adnan-oktar-replies-to-foreign [Accessed 19.03.2013].
Yahya, Harun (2008b) *Global Masonluk*. 4th ed. Istanbul: Araştırma Yayıncılık.

Yahya, Harun (2008c) *The Intellectual Struggle against Darwinism*. Istanbul: Global Publishing.

Yahya, Harun (2008d) "Intelligent Design: A New Age Theory" [Online]. *harunyahya.com*. Available: http://harunyahya.com/en/works/8382/intelligent-design-a-new-age [Accessed 19.03.2013].

Yahya, Harun (2008e) "Psikolojik Savaş" [Online]. *Psikolojiksavas.net*. Available: http://www.psikolojiksavas.net/ [Accessed 19.03.2013].

Yahya, Harun (2008f) "Sayın Adnan Oktar'ın Darwinizm'le İlmi Mücadeleyi Teşvik Eden Açıklamalarının Etkisi" [Online]. *harunhaya.com*. Available: http://harunyahya.org/tr/Harun-Yahya-Etkiler/9159/Sayin-Adnan--Oktarin-Darwinizmle-ilmi-mucadeleyi-tesvik-eden-aciklamalarinin-etkisi [Accessed 19.03.2013].

Yahya, Harun (2008g) *Tevrat'tan Hikmetler Ve Güzel Öğütler*. Istanbul: Global Publishing.

Yahya, Harun (2009a) "Adnan Oktar'ın ABC Televizyonu (Avustralya) Röportajı (10 Kasım 2009)" [Online]. *harunyahya.org*. Available: http://harunyahya.org/tr/Makaleler/18951/adnan-oktarin-abc-televizyonu-%28avustralya%29 [Accessed 19.03.2013].

Yahya, Harun (2009b) "Answers to the Claims against Mr. Adnan Oktar Which Appeared in the New Humanist Magazine and Internet" [Online]. *harunyahya.com*. Available: http://harunyahya.com/en/Articles/18958/answers-to-the-claims-against [Accessed 19.03.2013].

Yahya, Harun (2009c) *Ateist Siyonizm Felsefesi*. Istanbul: Araştırma Yayıncılık.

Yahya, Harun (2009d) "Atheistic Freemasonry, the System of the Antichrist (Dajjal), Deceives People by Pretending to Be Devout" [Online]. *harunyahya.com*. Available: http://harunyahya.com/en/Makaleler/15546/Atheistic_freemasonry_the_system_of _the_antichrist_(dajjal)_deceives_people_by_pretending_to_be_devout. [Accessed 19.03.2013].

Yahya, Harun (2009e) "The Enormous Global Impact of the Works of Adnan Oktar Is Today Reflected in the World Press" [Online]. *harunyahya.com*. Available: http://harunyahya.com/en/Articles/18869/the-enormous-global-impact-of [Accessed 02.04.2013].

Yahya, Harun (2009f) *Hz. Mehdi (as) Hz. İbrahim Neslindendir*. Istanbul: Araştırma Yayınları.

Yahya, Harun (2009g) *Hz. İsa (as) Ve Hz. Mehdi (as) Bu Yüzyılda Gelecek*. Istanbul: Araştırma Yayınları.

Yahya, Harun (2009h) "An Interview with Mr. Adnan Oktar by the Wall Street Journal (March 6, 2009)" [Online]. *harunyahya.net*. Available: http://onceki.harunyahya.net/V2/Lang/sa/Pg/WorkDetail/Number/12960 [Accessed 19.03.2013].

Yahya, Harun (2009i) "Sayings from Bediuzzaman Said Nursi Referring to the Dajjal's Deception of the World through Darwinism" [Online]. *harunyahya.com*. Available: http://harunyahya.com/en/Articles/16192/sayings-from-bediuzzaman-said-nursi [Accessed 19.03.2013].

Yahya, Harun (2009j) *Yeni Masonik Düzen: Dünyanın 500 Yıllık Gerçek Tarihi Ve Dünya Düzeninin Gizli Yöneticileri*. 8th ed. Istanbul: Araştırma Yayıncılık.

Yahya, Harun (2009k) "Hazrat Mahdi (as) Will Accept No Claims Regarding His Being the Mahdi" [Online]. *harunyahya.com*. Available: http://harunyahya.com/en/New-Information/13256/hazrat-mahdi-(as)-will-accept [Accessed 19.03.2013].

Yahya, Harun (2010a) *A Call for a Turkish-Islamic Union*. 2nd ed. Istanbul: Global Publishing.

Yahya, Harun (2010b) *Communist China's Policy of Oppression in East Turkestan*. Istanbul: Global Publishing.

Yahya, Harun (2010c) *Deccal Nasıl Öldü?* Istanbul: Araştırma Yayıncılık

Yahya, Harun (2010d) *Global Freemasonry: The Masonic Philosophy Unveiled and Refuted*. Istanbul: Global Publishing.

Yahya, Harun (2010e) *Hazrat Mahdi (Pbuh) Is a Descendant of the Prophet Abraham (Pbuh)*. Istanbul: Global Publishing.

Yahya, Harun (2010f) *İncil'den Güzel Sözler*. Istanbul: Araştırma Yayınlar.

Yahya, Harun (2010g) *The Prophet Jesus (as) and Hazrat Mahdi (as) Will Come This Century*. Istanbul: Global Publishing.

Yahya, Harun (2010h) "Sayın Adnan Oktar'a Karşı Yürütülen Psikolojik Savaş " [Online]. *harunyahya.org*. Available: http://harunyahya.org/tr/Kisa-filmler---Mutlaka-izleyin/22590/SAYIN-ADNAN-OKTARA-KARSI-YURUTULEN-PSIKOLOJIK-SAVAS [Accessed 19.03.2013].

Yahya, Harun (2010i) "The Turkish Islamic Union Is the Only Solution" [Online]. *Harunyahya.com*. Available: http://harunyahya.com/en/Articles/25385/the-turkish-islamic-union-is [Accessed 19.03.2013].

Yahya, Harun (2011a) "Highlights from Mr. Adnan Oktar's Interview on 28 August 2011" [Online]. *A9.com.tr*. Available: http://en.a9.com.tr/read/47782/Highlights-from-Adnan-Oktars-talk-programs/Highlights-from-Mr-Adnan-Oktars-interview-on-28-August-2011 [Accessed 19.03.2013].

Yahya, Harun (2011b) "The Sources of Some Hadiths About Hazrat Mahdi (as)" [Online]. *harunyahya.com*. Available: http://harunyahya.com/en/New-Information/40377/the-sources-of-some-hadiths [Accessed 19.03.2013].

Yahya, Harun (2011c) "Highlights from Mr. Adnan Oktar's Interviews on 1 September 2011". *Harunyahya.com.tr*. Available: http://m.harunyahya.com/tr/Highlights-from-Adnan-Oktars-talk-programs/95531/Highlights-from-Mr-Adnan-Oktars-interviews-on-1-September-2011 [Accessed 19.03.2013].

Yahya, Harun (2012a) "Highlights from Mr. Adnan Oktar's Interview on 17 July 2012" [Online]. *Harunyahya.com*. Available: http://harunyahya.com/en/Highlights-from-Adnan-Oktars-talk-programs/151200/highlights-from-mr-adnan-oktars [Accessed 19.03.2013].

Yahya, Harun (2012b) "Highlights from Mr. Adnan Oktar's Interview on 25 February 2012 " [Online]. *Harunyahya.com*. Available: http://harunyahya.com/en/Highlights-from-Adnan-Oktars-talk-programs/107745/highlights-from-mr-adnan-oktars [Accessed 19.03.2013].

Yahya, Harun (2012c) *The Prophet Jesus (as), Hazrat Mahdi (as) and the Islamic Union*. Istanbul: Global Publishing.

Yahya, Harun (2012d) "Tebliğde İlk Önce Kişinin İmanı Derinleştirmek Gerekir" [Online video]. *Harunyahya.tv*. Available: http://harunyahya.tv/tr/watch/152686/Tebligde-ilk-once-kisinin-imanini-derinlestirmek-gerekir [Accessed 19.03.2013].

Yahya, Harun (2012e) *İsa Mesih (as), Hz. Mehdi (as) ve İttihad-i İslam*. Istanbul: Araştırma Yayıncılık.

Yahya, Harun (2012f) "Highlights from Mr. Adnan Oktar's Interview on 17 July 2012" [Online]. *Harunyahya.net*. Available: http://en.harunyahya.net/highlights-from-mr-adnan-oktars-interview-on-17-14 [Accessed 19.03.2013].

Yahya, Harun (2013) "Quality is Very Important in Islam". *Huffington Post* [Online], 9 January. Available: http://www.huffingtonpost.com/harun-yahya/quality-is-very-important-in-islam_b_2429189.html [Accessed 19.03.2013].

Yalçın, Soner (2004) *Efendi: Beyaz Türklerin Büyük Sırrı*. Istanbul: Doğan Kitap.

Yaratilistr (2011) "Adnan Oktar Tekrardan Sordu: Beni Seviyor Musun? " [Online video]. Available: http://www.youtube.com/watch?v=zBpwfkOeP8Q [Accessed 19.03.2013].

Yaratilistr (2012a) " Adnan Oktar Erkek Talebeleriyle Sohbet Etti " *Youtube* [Online video]. *YouTube*. Available: https://www.youtube.com/watch?v=w8jSIe4G8jI [Accessed 19.03.2013].

Yaratilistr (2012b) "Adnan Oktar İsmai Baki Tuncer'in Son Taklidini Çok Beğendi " [Online video]. *YouTube*. Available: http://www.youtube.com/watch?v=LF_8G7ic5Qg [Accessed 19.03.2013].

Yaratilistr (2012c) "Çok Harika Bir Erkeksiniz" [Online video]. *YouTube*. Available: https://www.youtube.com/watch?v=-33f82meFPk [Accessed 04.04.2013].

Yaratilistr (2012d) "Adnan Oktar Mehmet Ali Kaya'ya Cevap Verdi 1" [Online video]. *YouTube*. Available: http://www.youtube.com/watch?v=RnA9spr_3hc [Accessed 19.03.2013].

"Yargıtay: Adnan Hocacılar Örgüt" (2007). *Milliyet* [Online], May 19. Available: http://www.milliyet.com.tr/2007/05/19/guncel/gun03.html [Accessed 19.03.2013].

Yavuz, M. Hakan (2003) *Islamic Political Identity in Turkey*. New York: Oxford University Press.

Yavuz, M. Hakan (2013) *Toward an Islamic Enlightenment: The Gülen Movement*. New York: Oxford University Press.

Yavuz, M. Hakan & Esposito, John L. (2003) *Turkish Islam and the Secular State: The Gülen Movement*. Syracuse, NY: Syracuse University Press.

Yildiz, Ahmet (2006) "Transformation of Islamic Thought in Turkey since the 1950s". In: Abu-Rabi', Ibrahim M. (ed.) *The Blackwell Companion to Contemporary Islamic Thought*. Oxford: Blackwell, 39–54.

Yılmaz, İhsan (2003) "Ijtihad and Tajdid by Conduct". In: Yavuz, M. Hakan & Esposito, John L. (eds.) *Turkish Islam and the Secular State: The Gülen Movement*. Syracuse, NY: Syracuse University Press, 208–237.

Yüksek, Fatma Sibel (2003) "AKP'nin Yeni Zarfı". *Radikal* [Online], 26 December Available: http://www.radikal.com.tr/haber.php?haberno=100157 [Accessed 03.03.2013].

Yüksel, Edip (2008) "Edip Yüksel Is Arrested in Turkey Upon the Complaint of a Sunni Cult Leader" [Online]. *IkhwanWeb*. Available: http://www.ikhwanweb.com/article.php?id=18526 [Accessed 19.03.2013].

Zaman, Muhammad Quasim (2006) "The Ulama and Contestations on Religious Authority". In: Salvatore, Armando and Eickelman, Dale F. (ed.) *Public Islam and the Common Good*. Leiden: Brill, 206–235.

Zeki Ademoğlu (2011) "Adnan Oktar, Nagehan Alçı Medcezir Programı Beyaz Tv" *Youtube* [Online video]. Available: http://www.youtube.com/watch?v=La4RDw-LhmQ [Accessed 19.03.2013].

Zürcher, Eric (1992) "The Ottoman Legacy and the Turkish Republic: An Attempt at a New Periodization". *Nation and Charisma*, 32 (2), 237–253.

SÖDERTÖRN DOCTORAL DISSERTATIONS

1. Jolanta Aidukaite, *The Emergence of the Post-Socialist Welfare State: The case of the Baltic States: Estonia, Latvia and Lithuania*, 2004
2. Xavier Fraudet, *Politique étrangère française en mer Baltique (1871–1914): de l'exclusion à l'affirmation*, 2005
3. Piotr Wawrzeniuk, *Confessional Civilising in Ukraine: The Bishop Iosyf Shumliansky and the Introduction of Reforms in the Diocese of Lviv 1668–1708*, 2005
4. Andrej Kotljarchuk, *In the Shadows of Poland and Russia: The Grand Duchy of Lithuania and Sweden in the European Crisis of the mid-17th Century*, 2006
5. Håkan Blomqvist, *Nation, ras och civilisation i svensk arbetarrörelse före nazismen*, 2006
6. Karin S Lindelöf, *Om vi nu ska bli som Europa: Könsskapande och normalitet bland unga kvinnor i transitionens Polen*, 2006
7. Andrew Stickley. *On Interpersonal Violence in Russia in the Present and the Past: A Sociological Study*, 2006
8. Arne Ek, *Att konstruera en uppslutning kring den enda vägen: Om folkrörelsers modernisering i skuggan av det Östeuropeiska systemskiftet*, 2006
9. Agnes Ers, *I mänsklighetens namn: En etnologisk studie av ett svenskt biståndsprojekt i Rumänien*, 2006
10. Johnny Rodin, *Rethinking Russian Federalism: The Politics of Intergovernmental Relations and Federal Reforms at the Turn of the Millennium*, 2006
11. Kristian Petrov, *Tillbaka till framtiden: Modernitet, postmodernitet och generationsidentitet i Gorbačevs glasnost´ och perestrojka*, 2006
12. Sophie Söderholm Werkö, *Patient patients?: Achieving Patient Empowerment through Active Participation, Increased Knowledge and Organisation*, 2008
13. Peter Bötker, *Leviatan i arkipelagen: Staten, förvaltningen och samhället. Fallet Estland*, 2007
14. Matilda Dahl, *States under scrutiny: International organizations, transformation and the construction of progress*, 2007
15. Margrethe B. Søvik, *Support, resistance and pragmatism: An examination of motivation in language policy in Kharkiv, Ukraine*, 2007
16. Yulia Gradskova, *Soviet People with female Bodies: Performing beauty and maternity in Soviet Russia in the mid 1930–1960s*, 2007
17. Renata Ingbrant, *From Her Point of View: Woman's Anti-World in the Poetry of Anna Świrszczyńska*, 2007

18. Johan Eellend, *Cultivating the Rural Citizen: Modernity, Agrarianism and Citizenship in Late Tsarist Estonia*, 2007
19. Petra Garberding, *Musik och politik i skuggan av nazismen: Kurt Atterberg och de svensk-tyska musikrelationerna*, 2007
20. Aleksei Semenenko, *Hamlet the Sign: Russian Translations of Hamlet and Literary Canon Formation*, 2007
21. Vytautas Petronis, *Constructing Lithuania: Ethnic Mapping in the Tsarist Russia, ca. 1800–1914*, 2007
22. Akvile Motiejunaite, *Female employment, gender roles, and attitudes: the Baltic countries in a broader context*, 2008
23. Tove Lindén, *Explaining Civil Society Core Activism in Post-Soviet Latvia*, 2008
24. Pelle Åberg, *Translating Popular Education: Civil Society Cooperation between Sweden and Estonia*, 2008
25. Anders Nordström, *The Interactive Dynamics of Regulation: Exploring the Council of Europe's monitoring of Ukraine*, 2008
26. Fredrik Doeser, *In Search of Security After the Collapse of the Soviet Union: Foreign Policy Change in Denmark, Finland and Sweden, 1988–1993*, 2008
27. Zhanna Kravchenko. *Family (versus) Policy: Combining Work and Care in Russia and Sweden*, 2008
28. Rein Jüriado, *Learning within and between public-private partnerships*, 2008
29. Elin Boalt, *Ecology and evolution of tolerance in two cruciferous species*, 2008
30. Lars Forsberg, *Genetic Aspects of Sexual Selection and Mate Choice in Salmonids*, 2008
31. Eglė Rindzevičiūtė, *Constructing Soviet Cultural Policy: Cybernetics and Governance in Lithuania after World War II*, 2008
32. Joakim Philipson, *The Purpose of Evolution: 'struggle for existence' in the Russian-Jewish press 1860–1900*, 2008
33. Sofie Bedford, *Islamic activism in Azerbaijan: Repression and mobilization in a post-Soviet context*, 2009
34. Tommy Larsson Segerlind, *Team Entrepreneurship: A process analysis of the venture team and the venture team roles in relation to the innovation process*, 2009
35. Jenny Svensson, *The Regulation of Rule-Following: Imitation and Soft Regulation in the European Union*, 2009
36. Stefan Hallgren, *Brain Aromatase in the guppy, Poecilia reticulate: Distribution, control and role in behavior*, 2009
37. Karin Ellencrona, *Functional characterization of interactions between the flavivirus NS5 protein and PDZ proteins of the mammalian host*, 2009
38. Makiko Kanematsu, *Saga och verklighet: Barnboksproduktion i det postsovjetiska Lettland*, 2009

39. Daniel Lindvall, *The Limits of the European Vision in Bosnia and Herzegovina: An Analysis of the Police Reform Negotiations*, 2009

40. Charlotta Hillerdal, *People in Between – Ethnicity and Material Identity: A New Approach to Deconstructed Concepts*, 2009

41. Jonna Bornemark, *Kunskapens gräns – gränsens vetande*, 2009

42. Adolphine G. Kateka, *Co-Management Challenges in the Lake Victoria Fisheries: A Context Approach*, 2010

43. René León Rosales, *Vid framtidens hitersta gräns: Om pojkar och elevpositioner i en multietnisk skola*, 2010

44. Simon Larsson, *Intelligensaristokrater och arkivmartyrer: Normerna för vetenskaplig skicklighet i svensk historieforskning 1900–1945*, 2010

45. Håkan Lättman, *Studies on spatial and temporal distributions of epiphytic lichens*, 2010

46. Alia Jaensson, *Pheromonal mediated behaviour and endocrine response in salmonids: The impact of cypermethrin, copper, and glyphosate*, 2010

47. Michael Wigerius, *Roles of mammalian Scribble in polarity signaling, virus offense and cell-fate determination*, 2010

48. Anna Hedtjärn Wester, *Män i kostym: Prinsar, konstnärer och tegelbärare vid sekelskiftet 1900*, 2010

49. Magnus Linnarsson, *Postgång på växlande villkor: Det svenska postväsendets organisation under stormaktstiden*, 2010

50. Barbara Kunz, *Kind words, cruise missiles and everything in between: A neoclassical realist study of the use of power resources in U.S. policies towards Poland, Ukraine and Belarus 1989–2008*, 2010

51. Anders Bartonek, *Philosophie im Konjunktiv: Nichtidentität als Ort der Möglichkeit des Utopischen in der negativen Dialektik Theodor W. Adornos*, 2010

52. Carl Cederberg, *Resaying the Human: Levinas Beyond Humanism and Antihumanism*, 2010

53. Johanna Ringarp, *Professionens problematik: Lärarkårens kommunalisering och välfärdsstatens förvandling*, 2011

54. Sofi Gerber, *Öst är Väst men Väst är bäst: Östtysk identitetsformering i det förenade Tyskland*, 2011

55. Susanna Sjödin Lindenskoug, *Manlighetens bortre gräns: Tidelagsrättegångar i Livland åren 1685–1709*, 2011

56. Dominika Polanska, *The emergence of enclaves of wealth and poverty: A sociological study of residential differentiation in post-communist Poland*, 2011

57. Christina Douglas, *Kärlek per korrespondens: Två förlovade par under andra hälften av 1800-talet*, 2011

58. Fred Saunders, *The Politics of People – Not just Mangroves and Monkeys: A study of the theory and practice of community-based management of natural resources in Zanzibar*, 2011

59. Anna Rosengren, *Åldrandet och språket: En språkhistorisk analys av hög ålder och åldrande i Sverige cirka 1875–1975*, 2011

60. Emelie Lilliefeldt, *European Party Politics and Gender: Configuring Gender-Balanced Parliamentary Presence*, 2011

61. Ola Svenonius, *Sensitising Urban Transport Security: Surveillance and Policing in Berlin, Stockholm, and Warsaw*, 2011

62. Andreas Johansson, *Dissenting Democrats: Nation and Democracy in the Republic of Moldova*, 2011

63. Wessam Melik, *Molecular characterization of the Tick-borne encephalitis virus: Environments and replication*, 2012

64. Steffen Werther, *SS-Vision und Grenzland-Realität: Vom Umgang dänischer und „volksdeutscher" Nationalsozialisten in Sønderjylland mit der „großgermanischen" Ideologie der SS*, 2012

65. Peter Jakobsson, *Öppenhetsindustrin*, 2012

66. Kristin Ilves, *Seaward Landward: Investigations on the archaeological source value of the landing site category in the Baltic Sea region*, 2012

67. Anne Kaun, *Civic Experiences and Public Connection: Media and Young People in Estonia*, 2012

68. Anna Tessmann, *On the Good Faith: A Fourfold Discursive Construction of Zoroastrianism in Contemporary Russia*, 2012

69. Jonas Lindström, *Drömmen om den nya staden: stadsförnyelse i det postsovjetisk Riga*, 2012

70. Maria Wolrath Söderberg, *Topos som meningsskapare: retorikens topiska perspektiv på tänkande och lärande genom argumentation*, 2012

71. Linus Andersson, *Alternativ television: former av kritik i konstnärlig TV-produktion*, 2012

72. Håkan Lättman, *Studies on spatial and temporal distributions of epiphytic lichens*, 2012

73. Fredrik Stiernstedt, *Mediearbete i mediehuset: produktion i förändring på MTG-radio*, 2013

74. Jessica Moberg, *Piety, Intimacy and Mobility: A Case Study of Charismatic Christianity in Present-day Stockholm*, 2013

75. Elisabeth Hemby, *Historiemåleri och bilder av vardag: Tatjana Nazarenkos konstnärskap i 1970-talets Sovjet*, 2013

76. Tanya Jukkala, *Suicide in Russia: A macro-sociological study*, 2013

77. Maria Nyman, *Resandets gränser: svenska resenärers skildringar av Ryssland under 1700-talet*, 2013

78. Beate Feldmann Eellend, *Visionära planer och vardagliga praktiker: postmilitära landskap i Östersjöområdet*, 2013

79. Emma Lind, *Genetic response to pollution in sticklebacks: natural selection in the wild*, 2013

80. Anne Ross Solberg, *The Mahdi wears Armani: An analysis of the Harun Yahya enterprise*, 2013

81. Nikolay Zakharov, *Attaining Whiteness: A Sociological Study of Race and Racialization in Russia*, 2013

GÖTEBORGS UNIVERSITET
LITTERATUR, IDÉHISTORIA OCH RELIGION

**Dissertations published by the Department of Literature, History of Ideas, and Religion, University of Gothenburg**

1. Susanne Dodillet: *Är sex arbete? Svensk och tysk prostitutionspolitik sedan 1970-talet.* (Disp. 21/2 2009).
2. Rangnar Nilsson: *God vetenskap – hur forskares vetenskapsuppfattningar uttryckta i sakkunnigutlåtanden förändras i tre skilda discipliner.* (Disp. 6/3 2009).
3. Tobias Hägerland: *Jesus and the Forgiveness of Sins. An Aspect of His Prophetic Mission.* (Disp. 20/3 2009).
4. Per Widén: *Från kungligt galleri till nationellt museum. Aktörer, praktik och argument i svensk konstmuseal diskurs ca 1814–1845.* (Disp. 28/3 2009).
5. Christian Mehrstam: *Textteori för läsforskare.* (Disp. 29/5 2009).
6. Christian Lenemark: *Sanna lögner. Carina Rydberg, Stig Larsson och författarens medialisering.* (Disp. 9/10 2009).
7. Cecilia Pettersson: *Märkt av det förflutna? Minnesproblematik och minnesestetik i den svenska 1990-talsromanen.* (Disp. 27/11 2009).
8. Ferdinando Sardella: *Bkaktisiddhanta Sarasvati. The Context and Significance of a Modern Hindu Personalist.* (Disp. 6/2 2010).
9. Kristina Hermansson: *Ett rum för sig. Subjektsframställning vid 1900-talets slut: Ninni Holmqvist, Hanne Ørstavik, Jon Fosse, Magnus Dahlström och Kirsten Hammann.* (Disp. 20/5 2010).
10. Gunnar Samuelsson: *Crucifixion in Antiquity. An Inquiry into the Background of the New Testament Terminology of Crucifixion.* (Disp. 21/5 2010).
11. Johan Alfredsson: *"Tro mig på min ort" – oöversättligheten som tematiskt komplex i Bengt Emil Johnsons poesi 1973–1982.* (Disp. 28/5 2010).
12. Nils Olsson: *Konsten att sätta texter i verket. Gertrude Stein, Arne Sand och litteraturens (o)befintliga specificitet.* (Disp. 4/6 2010).
13. Erik Alvstad: *Reading the Dream Text. A Nexus between Dreams and Texts in the Rabbinic Literature of Late Antiquity.* (Disp. 5/6 2010).
14. Georg Walser: *Jeremiah: A Translation and Commentary on Jeremiah in Codex Vaticanus.* (Disp. 8/6 2010).
15. Marie Fahlén: *Jesusbilden i samtiden. Ungdomars receptioner av nio samtida Kristusbilder.* (Disp. 23/10 2010).

16. Viktor Aldrin: *Prayer in Peasant Communities. Ideals and Practices of Prayer in the Late Medieval Ecclesiastical Province of Uppsala, Sweden.* (Disp. 11/11 2010).
17. Stina Otterberg: *Klädd i sitt språk. Kritikern Olof Lagercrantz.* (Disp. 12/11 2010).
18. Daniel Enstedt: *Detta är min kropp. Kristen tro, sexualitet och samlevnad.* (Disp. 29/1 2011).
19. Michael Tengberg: *Samtalets möjligheter. Om litteratursamtal och litteraturreception i skolan.* (Disp. 11/3 2011).
20. Eva Wahlström: *Fria flickor före Pippi. Ester Blenda Nordström och Karin Michaëlis: Astrid Lindgrens föregångare.* (Disp. 27/5 2011).
21. Rikard Wingård: *Att sluta från början. Tidigmodern läsning och folkbokens receptionsestetik.* (Disp. 31/5 2011).
22. Andrej Slavik: *X. Tre etyder över ett tema av Iannis Xenakis. (1922–2011). (1) Avhandling. – (2) Exposition, noter, bibliografi.* (Disp. 14/10 2011).
23. Hans Leander: *Discourses of Empire: The Gospel of Mark from a Postcolonial Perspective.* (Disp. 9/12 2011).
24. Helena Dahlberg: *Vikten av kropp. Frågan om kött och människa i Maurice Merleau-Pontys Le visible et l'invisible.* (Disp. 16/12 2011).
25. Anna Tessmann: *On the Good Faith: A Fourfold Discursive Construction of Zoroastrianism in Contemporary Russia.* (Disp. 16/5 2012).
26. Rosmari Lillas: *Hendiadys in the Hebrew Bible. An Investigation of the Applications of the Term.* (Disp. 1/6 2012).
27. Mattias Bäckström: *Hjärtats härdar – folkliv, folkmuseer och minnesmärken i Skandinavien, 1808–1907.* (Disp. 2/6 2012).
28. Sigrid Schottenius Cullhed: *Proba the Prophet. Studies in the Christian Virgilian Cento of Faltonia Betitia Proba.* (Disp. 30/11 2012).
29. Wilhelm Kardemark: *När livet tar rätt form. Om människosyn i svenska hälsotidskrifter 1910–13 och 2009.* (Disp. 18/1 2013).
30. Jessica Moberg: *Piety, Intimacy and Mobility: A Case Study of Charismatic Christianity in Present-day Stockholm.* (15/2 2013).
31. 31. Julia Nordblad, *Jämlikhetens villkor: Demos, imperium och pedagogik i Bretagne, Tunisien, Tornedalen och Lappmarken, 1880–1925.* (Disp. 26/4 2013)
32. 32. Anne Ross Solberg, *The Mahdi Wears Armani: An Analysis of the Harun Yahya Enterprise,* (Disp. 13/6 2013)

www.ingramcontent.com/pod-product-compliance
Lightning Source LLC
Chambersburg PA
CBHW081329230426
43667CB00018B/2878